To

Cathie Robertson.

With all good wishes for

a merry Christmas and

a Happy New Year

Herman Bevees

12-4-80

Being Lucky

Being Lucky

REMINISCENCES AND REFLECTIONS

Herman B Wells

INDIANA UNIVERSITY PRESS

BLOOMINGTON

Library of Congress Cataloging in Publication Data

Wells, Herman B
  Being lucky.

  Includes index.
    1. Wells, Herman B. 2. Indiana. University—
Presidents—Biography. 3. College presidents—
Indiana—Biography. I. Title.
LD2516 1938.W44A33   378'.111 80–7493
ISBN 0–253–11556–6   1 2 3 4 5 84 83 82 81 80

To
my father and mother
and colleagues,
who made it all possible

Contents

[vii]

Beyond the Presidency

To Begin . . .

THESE REMEMBRANCES and reflections were undertaken not through any desire of mine to write about the past but largely as a result of the urgings of my friends and colleagues. They seemed to feel that there was some magic that I could disclose about the years of my administration or that I ought to record some of my experiences and yarns that might not otherwise be preserved. As for the magic, there was none. By a set of fortuitous circumstances, I came to the presidency of Indiana University. These included parents who saw to it that I had a happy and wholesome youth and adolescence, the friendship of many people along the way who had confidence in me, and the fact that I was in place, so to speak, at the time President William Lowe Bryan decided to retire. Now, seen in perspective, the period in which I occupied the presidency of the university, for all of its difficulties (and there were many: a war, a recession, old tensions, traditional underfinancing), will probably be depicted as a golden era in higher education nationally and here as well.

Another reason for my attempting this book was Thomas D. Clark's urging that I record my own perceptions of my administration. While writing the third volume of his history of the university, he reminded me from time to time that he was writing about the university's history, not about me. Many topics he did not write about at any length—for example, the Indiana University Foundation—and he felt it essential that my knowledge of the Foundation and of such a matter as the classic challenge to Alfred Kinsey's academic freedom be recorded. But my principal reason for writing is the hope that the book will furnish a bit of perspective for future historians on an efflorescent period in the life of the university. Dr. Clark also wished me to make a statement of the philosophy that had guided the administrative team that constituted the presidency during my years.

When I first received these requests, I mentioned that I had urged President Bryan to write his reminiscences but that he had resisted all pressures to do so. I now realize, after the traumatic effort involved in my reconstructing the past—the research into the voluminous records to make sure that the reconstruction was accurate—how very wise he was. But I finally yielded and over a period of time have jogged along on the project as best I could while making a conscientious effort to carry on a wide range of responsibilities assigned to me by the university during my years as chancellor and while yielding occasionally to attractive opportunities for public service.

After a period of dictating chapters in a chronological sequence, which went very slowly indeed and seemed doomed never to end, I was advised by Bernard Perry, former director of the Indiana University Press, and by other persons simply to dictate thoughts about the past as and whenever they came to my mind, regardless of the topic. I followed this suggestion with a rapid acceleration of output as a result. It meant that my dictation and writing were done for the most part in unconventional ways: in my car when I was on long drives; during long flights in airplanes in this country and overseas; in the loneliness of dreary hotel rooms or at the University Club of New York or of Chicago; in my bedroom at two or three A.M. when I awakened; in my living room during convalescence from illness in response to questions from my perceptive and knowledgeable colleague, Dorothy Collins, and from our research assistant, John Haste; and in long sessions with those who were in with me at the beginning of my administration, so to speak, such as Edward Edwards and Croan Greenough. As a result of the marvel of a small portable tape recorder, topics were dictated in London, Cairo, San Francisco, Hong Kong, at the Ocean Reef Club in the Florida Keys, and in many other places around the world. Then these disjointed dictations had to be researched for accuracy (dates, names, proper spelling of names, and so on) and finally rearranged and joined together in a coordinated narrative—a job that Mrs. Collins has done with superlative skill, really incredible skill.

As a result of this manner of writing, a distinct change occurs after the first third of the book: after the early chapters, which are chronological, all others are topical. However, many of the activities dealt with in the topical chapters were going on simultaneously with the performance of my presidential duties. For those interested in the exact sequence of my various assignments, when each began and ended, the information can be obtained from the chronology in the Appendix (A), included by request of the publisher. It should be apparent from the chronology that in these recollections I have pared the full story to the bone, in part because of a lack of time and energy to write about the manifold activities that have filled the days of my years.

Thus my various undertakings are represented here only by examples; there is much, much more that should have been recounted. In fact, what is not recounted is substantially larger than what has been; at the same time, some portions of the recollections have been set down simply for the record, in order to give my version of how it was, as Dr. Clark suggested.

I have attempted to write candidly and honestly of events and personalities, but I have not sought to spice the record with innuendo, gossip, and rumor. When most of one's life has been that of a public person, it is necessary to write in a public vein. A professional writer can indulge in subjective evaluations and comments on personalities for color and interest, but that is a tactic I would not use, even if circumstances had made it possible.

The director of the Indiana University Press, John Gallman, has generously taken time to advise me about my manuscript. Pointing out that most people do not like to read long books and that, in any case, paper stock and printing are very expensive, he suggested that the completed manuscript be shortened. As a consequence I had to sacrifice mention of many colleagues who played a vital role in advancing the work of the university during my presidency. Likewise, but of lesser importance, I had to delete a number of the unusual experiences and yarns that I have related through the years that my colleagues and friends had admonished me to write down. As much as I regret these omissions, they were necessary in order to achieve a shorter book. I recognize the wisdom of John's advice and I am grateful for it.

I particularly regret leaving out a description of much of what was accomplished by my colleagues. I would have preferred to write about their activities rather than my own, but I was reminded that it is my responsibility to record my own involvements, not those of others.

As is apparent from the above, profit was not my motive for writing this book. If any income should result from its publication, it will be paid to the Indiana University Foundation for the benefit of the Indiana University Library book fund.

Because it would have been awkward to match each masculine pronoun with a feminine one throughout, I have used the masculine almost exclusively in the sense of "person." I hope that this choice is understandable and tolerable to my many women colleagues, whom I had no intention of slighting.

The extensive period covered in this book, from my ancestors to the present day, stretched the bounds of what I could recall from experience and from versions of family lore. To my regret, I had kept no systematic record, but we unearthed some journals and diaries of special trips and missions as well as letters I had written home during those periods. University documents served to refresh or confirm my memory in many instances. But frequently I have sought the aid of relatives, friends, and colleagues to supplement or correct my recollection. They have been helpful and well-wishing under whatever circumstances I happened to turn to them: by phone, by letter, by interview, or in casual encounter. To each and everyone of them, named or unnamed, I hereby acknowledge my debt and express my appreciation.

During the years of Mother's failing eyesight and sharpened memories of earlier times, we often discussed family history. These sessions were the indispensable basis of the first section of this book. My cousins Esther and Helen Heady supplemented and corrected some of these recollections and contributed memorabilia that were often useful. Along with relatives, two associates in the start of my career—my roommate Sam Gabriel and my recently deceased houseman John Stewart—supplied colorful detail. The late Peter Costas and Louise Cauble were similarly helpful.

Conversations with Leo M. Gardner, Paul DeVault, Lyman D. Eaton, M.D., Charles M. Cooley, Jack New, and Edward Edwards and letters from Elizabeth Parrish and Evelyn Cummins were of substantial assistance in my writing of the pages on the reform of financial institutions in Indiana. In this instance, as in several others throughout the preparation of the manuscript, I submitted pertinent sections to knowledgeable colleagues of the period for their review and criticism. Their written comments were an invaluable aid.

In my account of my deanship I am particularly indebted for such comments. Assistance came from Edward Edwards, George W. Starr, Nathan L. Silverstein, Harry Sauvain, the late Stanley Pressler, John Mee, Arthur Weimer, the late Joseph A. Batchelor, John H. Porter, Bernita Gwaltney, and Croan Greenough.

For my section on finance, I was aided by two stalwarts of my administration (whose memories I relied on in other sections as well), Joseph A. Franklin, Sr., and Claude Rich, and by Ray Butler and Robert Burton.

Peter Topping went to great lengths to ensure that the section on the Greek mission was accurate. The research on this period brought a welcome letter from Alison Frantz.

A recent book by Henry Kellermann, along with correspondence from him, proved to be exceptionally useful in my recounting of my months with General Lucius Clay. Peter Fraenkel has been a sure source of detail about both the German period and the years following in the presidency. Interviews with Werner Philipp, Wolfgang Krieger, John Gimbel, and Jutta-B. Lange-Quassowski added to my interpretation.

I am indebted to Willis Porter, Walter Laves, Lynne Merritt, and Raziuddin Siddiqi for their discussions with me and for materials about our technical-assistance programs.

William Armstrong, James Elliott, and Virginia Barr of the Indiana University Foundation have supplied useful data and comments. Others who responded readily and helpfully to my requests were Tom Miller, Harold Jordan, Dwight Peterson, Leon Wallace, Frank Edmondson, Ed Cohen, and Major General Joseph Butcher.

I would have been severely handicapped had I not been able to call upon Mary Craig for information from her vast knowledge of the university and her access to archival material. Dolores Lahrman and the University Archives staff have been cooperative and industrious in locating data and documents for me.

The difficult task of hunting down elusive facts, searching the files for explanatory or authenticating documents, calling various sources to verify information, checking names, and the like have been performed by two researchers: first, John L. Haste and, more recently, David Warriner.

My secretaries through the years have been valuable resources for historical details about my schedule, travels, staff, and miscellaneous events. Catherine Royer, my longtime secretary, in particular has been helpful as have been Mary Ellen Woods, who was in the president's office when I succeeded William Lowe Bryan, and my current secretary, Charlotte Pitcher. Every secretary on my staff has had a share in typing dictation for the book, but responsibility for the finished manuscript has fallen in turn to Bridget Tolpa, Darlene Heck, and Sharon Teulle, all of whom have been patient, painstaking, and hardworking.

I would be remiss if I failed to acknowledge my debt to Thomas D. Clark, with whom I discussed my administration and my problems in the unaccustomed activity of writing my recollections. Tom was helpful in his counsel, interested and interesting, perceptive and gracious in his comments. Inevitably, his three-volume history of Indiana University has had some effect in the shaping of this book.

The informal sponsorship of my work by the Distinguished Alumni Service Award Club and its continued interest have served to goad, encourage, and inspire me.

For the past thirty-eight years Dorothy Collins has been associated with the university and has firsthand knowledge of all that has happened during this era. Not only is she an expert editor, but, because of her extensive background of information about the university (some of it myth!), she also has been able to jog my memory and to suggest topics to be included and others to be deleted. In addition, she was both a stern taskmistress and a constant source of inspiration, keeping me at the job when the temptation to chuck the whole thing was great. Without her sacrificial help and guidance there would have been no book.

I wish to record as well my profound gratitude to the president, administrative officers, and trustees of the university for their helpfulness in furnishing the physical and human resources essential to the writing of this volume. I thank the officers of the university and of the Indiana University Foundation for their understanding sufferance, allowing me to take the time required for producing a manuscript, time that otherwise might have been utilized directly in the furtherance of their goals.

Being Lucky

Preparation for the
Presidency

○　　○　　◯　　○　　○

[1]

○ ○ ○

Growing Up in Jamestown and the County Seat

I'M A fifth-generation Hoosier, a native of a small town. Jamestown, founded in 1832, was and still is a typical agricultural trading center located in Boone County about halfway between Indianapolis and Crawfordsville. Indiana at the time of my birth was mainly an agricultural state with Indianapolis its governmental, commercial, and financial hub.

Within two decades, however, Indianapolis became the national center of the automotive industry, its lead closely followed by the development of component-parts manufacturing plants in the whole of the central part of the state—in Kokomo, Anderson, Marion, Richmond, and elsewhere. Thus central Indiana grew highly industrialized and dependent upon the motor industry, symbolically celebrated in the gala week of the Indianapolis 500.

It was the thrust of the steel and refining industries that turned the northern part of the state into a great industrial complex in the first quarter of the century, while in southern Indiana, along the Ohio River, agriculture remained a major economic and social factor even though furniture manufacturing and shipbuilding brought national awareness of that part of the state.

In my little town a flour mill, a tile factory, and a grain elevator were the sole industries, and the important business establishments were blacksmiths' shops, general stores, wagon repair shops, and hardware stores. Roads were so poor that a country hotel, the Phoenix, still flourished. The community had to be largely self-sustaining and also had to satisfy the needs of farmers living within horseback and wagon distance.

The time, between the Civil War and World War I, was one of

[3]

relative stability and calm, giving no inkling of the great wars yet to come in this century. People still believed in the inevitability of progress and firmly upheld the Puritan ethic of hard work and thrift. It was prior to the rapid rise of the evangelical sects so visible now, and church life in Jamestown still centered in two denominational groups, the Methodists and the Campbellites. Between the two there was considerable debate as to which offered the better and surer route to heaven. My dear grandmother, who believed devoutly in the Methodist route, beginning with baptism by sprinkling rather than immersion, had grave doubts about the inevitability of salvation for the Campbellites.

Both the Methodists and the Campbellites regularly sponsored series of meetings under evangelistic leadership at which the town drunkards and other malefactors, real or fancied, were received at the altar to repent their sins in public, much to everyone's righteous satisfaction. Supplementing the churches in their role as social and ritual centers were the lodges. The Oddfellows, the Knights of Pythias, the Modern Woodmen, the Red Men, and Masons, the Eastern Star, the Rebeccas were all very active and absorbed a not inconsiderable amount of the time, effort, and thought of good, responsible citizens. In fact, these fraternal groups wielded political as well as social influence in the community.

Despite the primitive roads, Jamestown was not isolated. Both passenger and freight trains of the Peoria division of the Big Four made a station stop there and helped make the town a good trading center. Telephones were not as yet common enough to provide a communications network, but there was a weekly newspaper of fifty years' standing that was a reliable source of local information and of little else. Mail came by train and news traveled by telegraph line, courtesy of the telegrapher posted at each station.

Residents of Jamestown were dependent upon the professional services of men and women based in the town. There were six doctors, several lawyers, and a dentist or two. Along with these esteemed citizens, the oldest descendants of the town's settlers were also held in special respect, as were the Civil War pensioners.

In this rather complacent community with its bustling weekday activity and important social and church life there lived two people of central importance to my story.

Following a brief courtship, Joseph Granville Wells and Anna Bernice Harting were married on June 26, 1901, in a very simple ceremony conducted by the Methodist minister in the parsonage at Jamestown. They chose not to invite any guests and departed immediately by train for Buffalo and Niagara Falls on their honeymoon. Such an extensive honeymoon, although popular in that day, I am sure must have been the idea of my father, the groom, who always believed in doing things properly. My guess is that Mother considered it extravagant.

Niagara Falls was an especially strong magnet for honeymooners in 1901 because of the Pan-American Exposition in Buffalo. The feature of the exposition was millions of small, twinkling electric light bulbs illuminating the fairgrounds. Most of the visitors had not seen electric lights before, nor would they soon again see them used on such a scale. The memory of that occasion remained vivid in the minds of my parents throughout their lives. In her later years, when we would drive through the countryside at night and could see the electric floodlights in the barnyards of brightly lighted houses in between the glare of passing automobiles, my mother would frequently remark on how much lighter the world was then than it had been when she was young. In her youth the country roads had been pitch-black at night, the darkness broken only by an occasional feeble glow from a farmhouse or by the light of a swaying lantern on a buggy.

My father was the eldest son of Isaac Wells and Jane Emmert Wells, of whom I shall say more later. The Wells line migrated from the southeastern United States—the Carolinas and Georgia—into Tennessee and Kentucky before the Civil War, settling a while in each of these areas. The family's original emigration from Europe is thought to have taken place in the eighteenth century. The trek to Indiana was in keeping with the tradition of westward migration: families moving, settling, again moving and settling until a permanent location was found—in their case, Indiana.

My mother's mother was an Endicott,[1] a direct descendant of Governor John Endecott, who in 1628 emigrated to the United States, sailing on the *Abigail* from Weymouth, Dorset, England. He became the first governor of the Massachusetts Bay Company's plantation in New England and a member of the first Board of Overseers of Harvard.[2]

1. Spelled "Endecott" until the third generation.
2. His name appeared on the list at the first Commencement, although he is not listed among the original Board of Overseers.

Most of my ancestors had emigrated to the United States prior to the nineteenth century, according to our best information, and all had entered the state of Indiana by the middle of the last century. The last arrival was my great-grandfather Harting, my mother's grandfather, who emigrated as a lad of sixteen from a little farming village south of Bremen, Germany, called Klein Bokern, a typical peasant village consisting then, as now, of only a few houses with surrounding fields. I visited it just a year after the centennial of my great-grandfather's departure. He came as a bound boy in 1846, a time of political unrest in Germany and of heavy emigration to the United States. Prior to his departure he had bound himself to work for a farmer south of Richmond, Indiana, for five years in return for having his passage paid to America. All his worldly possessions he brought with him in a small box. When at the end of five years he had gained his freedom, he possessed a horse, a new suit of clothes, and twenty-five dollars. With these modest assets he married Willa Jane Small, of old New England stock, and came to Boone County, where in time he became a highly successful farmer.

Our family had its share of vivid and interesting personalities. One of the most intrepid and imaginative was my great-great-grandmother Fanny, about whom I learned a great deal from my father. Her maiden name was New, and she was reputed to have been a *Mayflower* descendant. Fanny lived throughout most of the last century. She was brought to Indiana by her parents as a baby in 1808. She married William Emmert in 1832 and the two moved to Boone County, where they purchased government land. From that date until her middle life they accumulated a substantial amount of land, and then her husband died, leaving her with six children. Deciding that the land in Boone County would not be enough for all the children, she gave that land to the older children and set out again in a covered wagon, this time for Iowa to homestead more land so that the boys whom she had taken with her would have some property with which to build their security and, perhaps, prosperity. In her later years she made the trip back to Boone County occasionally and remained for extended visits.

Fanny was the one who encouraged my father to study and protected him against interruptions and the taunts of the other, more carefree children; she procured books for him and kept them safe from loss in her room. Remarkably, although her travel up until the time she settled in Iowa had been by horseback, covered wagon, and riverboat, she lived long enough to retrace part of that trek, this time in a Pullman and dressed, not in calico, but in black silk.

My maternal grandfather Harting started his career as a school-teacher. Then, upon inheriting a sizable farm from his father, he became a rather progressive farmer, interested in innovations, new kinds of crops, and experimental methods of operating. He was an avid student of agriculture and read agricultural publications and magazines, newspapers, and literature of a general nature. Unfortunately, he developed hypertension early, retired, and died not long afterward.

My grandmother Harting, Ida Belle Endicott Harting, was the mother of nine children, the first of whom died young. The other eight lived to adulthood, and my mother, Anna Bernice, was the oldest of the surviving children, all bearing middle names beginning with B. This tradition, though somewhat diminished by my parents' inability to agree on a name, resulted in the *B* that is the whole of my middle name. Grandmother was the matriarch of the clan, vigorous, industrious, and strong, and our family gatherings in my early years were always at her farm. There I enjoyed the lively companionship of my Jamestown cousins, Helen and Esther Heady, and of my mother's youngest brother and sister, Earl and Aletha.[3] Grandmother Harting lived into her mid-eighties. It was she who insisted upon our attendance at family reunions and traditional festivals, especially Christmas.

When I was a child Christmas was celebrated at Grandfather and Grandmother Harting's farm with all their sons and daughters and their families. Somehow or other everyone was accommodated in a not overlarge farmhouse, filling it from kitchen to attic. Many of the children had to sleep on the floor. In the living room there was always a tall Christmas tree standing beside the massive fire-place full of huge, brightly burning logs. The tree was decked out with homemade decorations and popcorn strung into garlands. Gifts were inexpensive, simple, and often handmade, but the Christmas dinner was altogether lavish. Even for the "second table," which accommodated the smaller children after the "first table" had finished, it was a feast. Grandmother so strongly implanted this Christ-

---

3. A cousin on the Wells side of the family, Gene Revercomb from Cincinnati, spent his summers in Jamestown. I looked forward then, as I do now, to the keen enjoyment of his visits. I have had many delightful visits, too, from another cousin, Wayne Gill.

mas-gathering tradition into our lives that it continues to this day, and only once, when I was unavoidably abroad, did I miss the family get-together at Christmastime. Even then I shared a bit of it through a long-distance call to my parents on Christmas day.

Because she died while I was still young, I have little memory of my grandmother Jane Emmert Wells except to be conscious of the fact that she was a dutiful and hardworking wife who baked biscuits every morning of the year and made light bread regularly in order that my grandfather never need suffer the indignity of eating "store-bought" bread, which he called "punk."

My grandfather Isaac Wells was a bit of a character—a vigorous farmer but fun-loving and a great storyteller. He retired early from farming allegedly to have more time for fishing and even in his late years he went fishing nearly every day year-round. I do not recall seeing any evidence of large catches, but the stories about the fish he caught were prodigious. An upstanding, forthright individualist, he liked to take a swig of alcohol from time to time and to smoke big, black cigars. As his years stretched into the mid-eighties, he took mischievous pleasure in planning a last word to spite the pronouncements of some meddlesome, small-town ladies belonging to such organizations as the Women's Christian Temperance Union: "When I die," he would say, "I hope that the Jamestown *Press* will say that Ike Wells died early from the lifelong use of alcohol and tobacco."

I enjoyed traveling with Grandfather Wells, and on two occasions I had what was to me the rare privilege of driving with him to Barbourville, Kentucky, in the Cumberland Mountain region to visit his distant relatives—those who had remained there when others in his branch of the family migrated to Indiana. They lived in an area so isolated that they still spoke with the English accent of their forebears, and a few Elizabethan phrases colored their speech. Each time they welcomed Grandfather and me royally within the limits of the resources available on their mountain farm.

Our headquarters on the first trip was the Faulkner Hotel, a family establishment with austere bedrooms but bountiful board. The guests were all fed around a long table laden with huge platters of ham, beef, chicken, and vegetables galore. Since my secondhand Packard Phaeton—silver with maroon fenders—was too low-slung for the mountain roads, we had to be driven to the Owens' home. Aunt Polly, an angelic-looking, white-haired mountaineer, was sitting on the front porch of her unpainted farm house in a colorful apron and gingham sunbonnet. After only a moment's hesitation, having not seen Grandfather for forty years, she said, "Ike, is that you?"

In some magic way word of our visit spread, and friends and relatives began gathering from all around to join in welcoming us. The younger women set about preparing a huge dinner, huge by their standards, and as a mark of special attention they used some of their precious white flour to bake a small cake. Normally they used only cornmeal for baking. Dinner consisted of home-cured pork, beef, chicken, and a variety of garden vegetables. Grandfather and Aunt Polly visited the whole day until it was time for us to bid a reluctant goodbye, warmed by having shared this simple way of life for a day, yet relieved that we were spared its hardships.

As I look back, it seems to me that I was born in the best of all times and under the best of all possible circumstances. With no shadow of a major war, past or on the horizon, and with opportunities all around, the new century began in an atmosphere of calm, stability, and confidence. I was also extremely fortunate to have been born in a little country town that afforded me as a youngster growing up a wonderful chance to explore nature and to know people. My best fortune of all was to have had for parents an ambitious young couple who were wise, encouraging, and loving.

My father was a studious young man and, as there was no high school in his community, he continued his schooling after the eighth grade at Central Normal College, located in Danville, about nineteen miles away from his farm home. The college program was comparable to present-day high school training but in addition prepared him to teach the first eight grades. He was taken there by his father in a horse and buggy, so he once related to me and went on to tell how, homesick for a weekend at home, he walked the whole distance back to the farm. Central Normal College was a noted school of that era and many of its alumni had become quite successful, particularly in the teaching profession. It continued in existence until some twenty years ago.

My father attended school there for a few terms, then transferred to the State Normal College at Terre Haute. Although he spoke of his teachers at Central Normal now and then, it was the teachers at State Normal who made the greater impression on him. Some of them were master teachers, and he continued to pay tribute to their influence on him throughout his life, quoting them frequently.

He was very fond of English and American literature, particularly the Victorian and New England poets, and he read widely and deeply. Mathematics, history, and psychology were also favorite subjects. The psychology of learning, new in this part of the world at the time, seemed to fascinate him, and I well recall his discussions with me about it in his later life. He was also very interested in geography and knew a great deal about various parts of the world, including exotic areas, gleaned in part from avidly read issues of the *National Geographic* or a kindred magazine. Perhaps the filtering down of this interest was the source of my wanderlust.

The rhythm of his life then was to teach in the wintertime and attend normal school in the spring and summer. As the school year in the township was rather short, he actually spent more of the year as a student than as a teacher. And he made high grades. When I was honored in 1964 with the first LL.D. degree ever given by Indiana State University, President Raleigh W. Holmstedt mentioned in his citation my father's brilliant record there in an earlier day.

My father was eighteen and teaching in the Hostetter School when my mother started attending school there at age ten. She walked the mile and a half to school and back each day, often freezing her feet and ears in the wintertime, with painful lingerings that troubled her for years, but she never missed a day. My father was from the beginning an exceptional teacher and Mother remembered that he greatly enriched the subject matter by drawing on his store of reading in a variety of fields—poetry, history, literature, and geography in particular. He was her teacher for four or five years before he was transferred to the Jamestown school.

At Jamestown Father began by teaching the eighth grade but later became principal. The story is told that there were two women teachers at Jamestown who could not control the students. Rather promptly after his arrival, my father gave the two ringleaders a sound thrashing, and from that time on he was in complete control. Occasionally he resorted to a mighty thump with his middle finger and thumb or directed a well-aimed piece of chalk at a sleepy or whispering student. There was no question about his authority. His victory over this unruly group was the talk of the community. Long years afterward girls who had been in his class, recalling the thump, told my mother that it felt like a blow from a thimble-capped finger.

In the absence of a high school it was the custom of many older boys and girls to continue in school, taking additional work after they had graduated from common school. Serving as assistants to the teacher, they would also teach the younger students. Mother, in line with this pattern, taught for a couple of years after graduation from the eighth grade. Armed with the additional work and her experience as an assistant teacher, she took an examination when she was seventeen or eighteen and won a license to teach. Her first position, at eighteen, was as the first-grade teacher in Jamestown, in the same school with the popular Granville Wells. By June his savings had reached about one thousand dollars, sufficient to ask young Miss Harting to become his wife.

To supplement his school salary my father had worked for several summers in a hardware store and he continued to do so after their marriage. In fact, he had been out setting up a self-binder the night before I was born. On June 7, 1902, a young doctor, Fred Austin, delivered me with the help of a neighbor, Aunt Nan Camplin, who served as midwife and, later, as my babysitter while I was growing up.

But to return to the newlyweds: They had leased a modest little cottage from the Camplins, who had built it, just to rent, on the same lot as their larger house. Out of their savings, supplemented by gifts, my future parents had furnished the house with two bedroom suites, a cookstove, a heating stove, a dining table, living room chairs, a bookcase with a folding desk top (which I still have), a rocker or two, and rugs. Mother had made some of her bedcovers, feather mattresses, pillows, and linens before her marriage, and some were given to the young couple by their parents.

There was no electricity; the few street lights were tended by a lamplighter. The rented cottage had a living room, kitchen, two bedrooms, and a dining porch. (Serving meals on a porch is a custom our family still favors today.) There was no bathroom. The bath water for the bowl was heated in the cookstove. The house was warmed by a stove—at first by a Florence hot-blast stove, later by a base burner presented to my father as a bonus for his good work at the hardware store. I still remember the cheerful light of the base burner and the warmth it spread in the wintertime. But at night my father preferred to have the windows open, even in the coldest weather, a preference that I came to share.

I was the only child in our block. On the other side of our house lived the Summervilles, elderly people, or so they seemed to me then, as did the Camplins. Aunt Drew Summerville was a good friend to Mother and Father and acted as an occasional babysitter and auxiliary nurse. I grew very attached to her and spent many happy hours in her house. The Summervilles seemed to have plenty of time to entertain me. They had no visible source of income; people in those days needed so little that they might appear to live on nothing, my mother once explained.

A block away was a family by the name of Hiller with many children. One of the sons later acquired the Jamestown *Press* and his son now publishes it. The Hiller children seemed a happy lot. As an only child, I found the attraction of the big family quite irresistible and ran away regularly to play at the Hiller house. Mother punished me to no avail. Then one day Mrs. Hiller, who had come to the Camplins to buy some of the milk brought in from their farm, stopped to speak with Mother at the front porch. A couple of older Hiller boys were with their mother and I asked to go back with them to their home. Mother promptly offered to get my clothes and send me there to live because, as she said, Mrs. Hiller did not have enough children and needed more. The Hiller boys took up the spoof and offered to get their wagon to haul my clothes to their house. My embarrassment cured me of my errant ways.

In our village there was neither great wealth nor extreme poverty. If there was much poverty at all, I was unaware of it. People were self-reliant and prudent. Nothing was wasted. The laundry was all done at home and most of the clothes were made there as well. My parents had a small garden at their first house. The produce from it was supplemented by the loads of foodstuffs brought by Mother from my grandparents' farms from time to time after she helped her mother-in-law and her mother can peaches and beans, make apple butter, and otherwise stock the larder.

Band concerts, church affairs, visiting relatives or friends, Sunday afternoon walks, reading good literature in the evening and on Sunday—this was the social life of Jamestown. Reminiscing, Mother once said, "Life was simple, but we were happy—we had all the better things of life. We were happy and very content. We thought it a good life."

For diversion there was also the Chautauqua, which found its way to Jamestown even though the town was small. Its tent was pitched in a pasture at the edge of town; the program was put on for several days or a week, both afternoons and evenings. It consisted of speakers, musical troupes, and all manner of presentations thought to be culturally uplifting and constructive. My parents supported such events as a matter of course. Father could not attend the matinees but attended the evening sessions; Mother and I attended both. There was great activity in our house to get the work done beforehand—the house clean, the garden in good shape, plenty of food prepared in the kitchen (ham, beans, pies, and cakes) so that we would all be free to attend the Chautauqua regularly and attentively.

It was a great thrill to have this contact with the outside world of ideas and music, and I did not mind that the programs were sometimes more visually pleasing than artistically noteworthy. Perhaps I first gained my taste for theater from the Chautauqua. During my high school years, my parents indulged me in this interest by permitting me to go alone by the electric railway line, the Interurban, to Indianapolis to the English Theatre and the Murat Theatre, where the dramatic fare was of the best. Nearly all the famous plays and great actors went on tour in those days and regularly visited Indianapolis.

Another aspect of our cultural life in Jamestown was the band. When I was about nine years old, the Jamestown Boys' Band was organized as a communitywide enterprise. I signed up to take lessons on the alto, the simplest of all the wind instruments. Later I advanced to the French horn, and in succession the baritone, the cello, and, after I was in college, the harp. The band boys were instructed by George Darnell, a newspaper publisher, and by George Piersol, an officer of the bank and a blithe spirit in the town. For such a small town, it was a rather large band—twenty-eight to thirty boys. We played once a week in the summer at the Saturday night concert, which was designed to bring the people to town for weekly trading at the local stores. The farm ladies brought eggs, chickens, and butter to trade for staples at the groceries. The men would visit the hardware store. The eligible girls paraded up one side of the street and down the other while young men strolled around looking them over. The older folks chatted about crops and family affairs, engaged in trading, and treated themselves to ice cream at the parlor with the marble-top tables and bentwood chairs. The music was only incidental, but the fact that Jamestown had a band playing on Saturday night meant that shoppers went there instead of to quieter surrounding towns.

Sometimes in addition to the band's lure there was an ice cream supper sponsored by one of the churches, which enhanced the excitement of the evening. Quite a bit of money would be made for some good cause in this way, because the ladies donated the cakes and often would get one of the stores to donate the ice cream.

The Jamestown Boys' Band became rather well known and on the strength of its reputation was offered contracts to play weeknights at other towns—ten, fifteen, or twenty miles away—and for special events such as street fairs and horse shows. These civic bands were the forerunners of the high school bands that play such an important part in local communities today.

When I was nine we moved to the north side of town, where we had bought nearly ten acres and had built a larger house and barn. We had electricity in our new house and a bathroom, but water had to be carried to it. Also, we had a basement and, by the second year, a furnace. Much of the work on the finishing of the house, such as laying the walks and doing the exterior and interior painting, was done by my parents.

We had a cow, pigs, and chickens, and we had one field to cultivate. There I learned to shuck corn, take care of livestock, milk the cow, and do various additional chores ever present on a farm. It was during this period that Mother had an attack of tuberculosis, from which she recovered with medical care and good luck, but my father and mother each lost a brother and sister to tuberculosis, the dread disease of the time.

At our new place I became the envied possessor of a pony and cart in which I could take Mother the ten or twelve blocks into town for shopping. Soon thereafter, however, my father bought one of the early Fords as a surprise for my mother. Since it cost between $350 and $400 her enjoyment of its convenience was tempered by the thought that its purchase had been a little extravagant. In wintertime the Ford was placed in hibernation, jacked up to save the tires, its motor drained and other precautions taken to prevent damage. For financial reasons we had to acquire gradually such things as were then thought to be luxuries. By careful management my parents had paid for the house before it became necessary for them to sell it when we moved to Lebanon during my sophomore year in high school. The acreage, the house, the barn and outbuilding brought $4,500.

But I am ahead of my story. About the time of our move to our new house in Jamestown, my father had begun working at the bank in the evening and on Saturdays in addition to his teaching. He had long before given up thought of completing his degree at the State Normal College in Terre Haute. Even though my mother had encouraged him to finish, believing that teaching would be his life's work, he had felt that, with a family, he could not afford the year's residency in Terre Haute required to qualify for a degree. The move into banking was a fateful decision, for before long he gave up teaching to devote full time to his work at the bank. Like so many young men of the period, teaching served for him as a stepping stone into business, where he could earn more money to provide for his family. Whether or not he would have been happier to remain a teacher, had economic considerations not been a deciding factor, it is certain that his skill as a teacher was exceptional and that he took great joy in his teaching. People who had been his students frequently remarked on his dedication long afterward. After his death Mother received many, many letters from his former pupils testifying to his influence on them.

Mother and Father shared a great love for learning. Even before I was born they were determined that I should go to college—an unusual ambition for that period and in that particular rural village, where college experience was a rarity, especially for people in such modest circumstances as my parents'. They knew it was going to be a real financial tussle to see me through college and wanted to be sure that their child could have as good an education as desired. Had I been blessed with brothers and sisters, it might have been at the expense of a college education.

My parents had bought a toy bank right after my birth. The odd change around the house went into this bank for my college fund. I was able to add to the fund myself from time to time as a youngster, first from my earnings as a carrier for the Indianapolis *Times* when it began publication. My mother enjoyed telling the story of my salesmanship for the *Times*. My prospective customers were all subscribers to the Indianapolis *News*, but I touted my newspapers so enthusiastically that I sold a lot of new subscriptions and had the satisfaction of watching my pile of papers grow steadily larger week by week while the stack delivered to the boy who carried the long-established *News* route noticeably declined.

When I was about thirteen I began to work in the Jamestown Bank during the vacation periods and learned to operate the first Burroughs posting machine in the county. It was a stand-up installation, as they all were in those days, and since I was too short to reach the keyboard a box had to be made on which I could stand to do the posting. Later, after our move to Lebanon, the Boone County State Bank bought posting machines and turned to me, though still in high school, to teach the bookkeepers how to operate them.

Our move to Lebanon, the county seat, in 1917 had been occasioned by my father's appointment as deputy county treasurer by an old friend there, John Thomas. The difficulties of changing schools and friends at that age were intensified for me by two illnesses: my mother and I both had the mumps during our first year in Lebanon, and my father and I contracted smallpox the following year.

Lebanon was quite a metropolis compared to Jamestown. In fact, I suppose the population of Jamestown was about 600, whereas Lebanon was a small city of about 6,000. It was a pleasant place with tree-shaded streets, a handsome county courthouse that is still in use today, a thriving business center with many good stores, a number of hotels, four banks, three railroads and an Interurban, and several small but successful factories. It had seven or eight well-established churches, one of which was the Centenary Methodist, now in a new location and still one of the outstanding churches in Indiana Methodism. Late in her life Mother and I gave the church a bell tower and a carillon in memory of my father, who had taught the adult Sunday School class there for many, many years.

There was more observable social stratification in Lebanon than in Jamestown; that is, there were greater differences among families in their share of worldly goods. But there were only one or two families of any major wealth and a very small number of people really in destitute circumstances, so far as I can recall. Many of the residents were successful, retired farmers who had moved to town after having sold or rented their farms and subsequently lived off the income.

When we moved to Lebanon we first had to rent a house while we searched for a permanent home. After a year or so Mother and

Father found a commodious and comfortable house on North Meridian Street in what was at that time, I suppose, the preferred residential section of the city. It was a typical turn-of-the-century house with a nice front porch where one could sit and exchange pleasantries with the people who were walking to and from town, about four blocks away. The house had eight rooms: living room, library, dining room, bedroom, bath, and big kitchen downstairs; and three bedrooms and a bath upstairs, with front and back stairways. It is now owned and maintained as a branch of the Indiana Methodist Children's Home.

Like many other young people at the time, I grew a victory garden soon after we moved to Lebanon. One fruit of it remained with us for years: a prize in the form of an atrocious still life of a watermelon slice and other fruit that Mother loyally hung in the dining room.

Lebanon was small enough to be a friendly town, and many of my good friends date from that period although I spent only three of my high school years there and just two years after college. My parents, on the other hand, lived for thirty-five years in Lebanon and formed many of their closest friendships there.

One of Lebanon's principal attractions for us was its school system, considered among the best in the state with a high school that was outstanding in every respect, from its basketball teams to its Latin classes. Another asset of the town was its Carnegie Library. Whereas the high school had a reasonably good library, the public library was outstanding. It became a favorite haunt of mine for study and reading and the selection of books to enjoy at home. Its general collection covered a whole variety of fields beyond the usual popular fiction that public libraries have to buy. I shall always be grateful for the opportunity that the library furnished me, greatly expanding the reading resources that the high school and our own home library together afforded. The librarians were invariably interested and willing to help students with reference material for a paper or with suggestions for general reading.

It was my good fortune that Lebanon High School, from which I was graduated in 1920, maintained a strong college preparatory program. I had an excellent Latin teacher, as well as superior English, history, and math teachers. Many of the students had college expectations, and the academic competition was keen. In addition, I had an opportunity to participate in extracurricular activities, mostly in managerial positions such as business manager of the *Cedars*, our senior yearbook. I was also an active member of a committee that sought to make money to finance class activities and the Boosters Club. Our projects varied: at a sectional basketball tournament we sold apples that we bought by the bushel for five or ten cents apiece (a large markup); we organized pitch-in rabbit suppers; we ran sandwich-and-Coke concession stands at the games. It was a very busy time in my life since I worked after school. With my studies, extracurricular activities, and several hours of outside work, I had little time for dating, dances, or social functions other than those held at school.

Lest I give the impression that my high school years were all work and no play, I should mention that there were two movie houses in town, one of which obtained first-run pictures. All the great movies of that era were shown in Lebanon, and it would have been unthinkable for me to have missed a top movie. Nor did I miss a home basketball game of Lebanon High, often going with my father to see the championship-calibre teams that Lebanon produced in those days.

Another exception to the all-work image was a high school club, or fraternity, that some of us organized and named the Dilbo Club. We did not give it a Greek-letter name because high school fraternities were frowned upon then, but it was in all respects a high school fraternity. I think our membership perhaps was about fifteen or eighteen, maybe more, and it included Willett Parr, still one of my good friends, an Indiana University alumnus, and a prominent attorney; Gene Higgins, later to be the leading banker in town; and Raymond Blackwell, who became the national executive secretary of Phi Delta Theta. We rented a club room in the upstairs over a downtown store and furnished it with odds and ends of furniture that we could scrounge. We had regular meetings and a series of social events, including a party for our fathers to allay the misgivings and apprehensions of our parents concerning our organization. Even with my outside work and diversions, I graduated in the top ten percent of my class and was elected to the honor society. I believe I might have been admitted to almost any university, but I chose to enter the University of Illinois.

I had a variety of jobs during my high school years in Lebanon, including work in a clothing store on Saturdays and other days when additional clerks were needed. Sometimes I would go via the interurban line to neighboring towns to pass out advertising bills for the store. However, most of the time I worked in the Lebanon bank after school and on Saturdays as one of the two bookkeepers. The double bookkeeping was a checking device by which we could catch each other's mistakes.

Another source of income for me was the Lebanon band, led by Walter Huckstep. Nearly every summer evening he conducted a band concert at some place within driving distance of Lebanon. We played in the park in Lebanon on Sunday afternoons and received some subsidy from either the Lebanon Chamber of Commerce or the Park Board, I forget which. Mr. Huckstep had a policy of carrying his first-chair men with him when he conducted other local bands, and it was my good fortune to hold one of those chairs. We were paid rather well for the performances, and for a couple of summers, at least, we played every night except Monday as well as on Sunday afternoons. I made as much money from those concerts as I did working all week in the bank during the daytime.

My father, after two years as deputy county treasurer, during which time he actually ran the office since Mr. Thomas had no training in fiscal matters, ran for county treasurer and won. My mother became his main deputy for his two-year term. He then joined the First National Bank of Lebanon as cashier, where he served for about four years before running successfully again for county treasurer. His victory in a second race for treasurer was unprecedented in the county. Mother again served as his deputy during his second term.

A year and a half after my father left the treasurer's office, Miss Merle Harvey, the county auditor and first elected woman officer of Boone County, was suddenly in need of an assistant and prevailed upon Mother to help her until she could find a deputy. The "temporary" assignment lasted six and one-half years, during the remainder of Miss Harvey's first term and through her second term. Mother subsequently assisted two other county treasurers until they learned the duties of the office. She was able to undertake these several positions because her mother, who lived with us much of the time, could help with the running of the house.

Meanwhile Father, in addition to his other duties, managed my grandmother Harting's farm while she stayed with us, but he did it partly as an avocation, for he enjoyed farm management. In the late 1920s the First National Bank, with which Father was associated after leaving the treasurer's office, was reorganized. As he did not particularly like the new organization and had been urged to return to the Jamestown bank, he left the First National and became vice president of the Citizens State Bank of Jamestown, where he devoted himself principally to fiduciary and trust matters. Since my mother and father continued living in Lebanon, Father had to drive to Jamestown each day. On the way back and forth he often stopped at the farm, and there he found relaxation from the worries and pressures of his work. In time he was elected president of the bank. He had previously been admitted to the practice of law in Boone County Circuit Court. Not only had he had a great deal of practical experience at the bank in trust and estate work, but also he had specialized in tax matters and had done quite a bit of tax work as bank attorney at Jamestown, accumulating in the process a sizable law library.

My father was always interested in constructive developments in the community. For every good cause he was available to serve on a committee, to help raise the money, or to do whatever else was necessary. He believed in adequate expenditures for good schools, in the fostering of good churches, and in the support of civic and community enterprises. He was one of the moving spirits in getting the road from Advance to Jamestown designated a state road and then in getting it blacktopped. He was also one of the prime movers in obtaining a very early stretch of brick road through Jamestown to a mile or so beyond the western part of town.

My father had a very keen sense of fiduciary responsibility. At the time of the bank crisis in 1933 he worked ceaselessly to get the Jamestown bank reopened quickly so customers would not suffer. Enroute to Chicago to arrange for reopening with the Federal Reserve authorities, he told me that he and Mother had decided that the bank should reopen and the depositors be protected even though it took every dollar they had in their lifelong savings. He felt a sense of personal responsibility to the depositors. He removed some of the notes that had gone bad and paid them off to the bank with his own funds. He felt that, since he had been the lending officer in each case and the people had failed to pay, he should make these loans good. He did so at great personal sacrifice and by Mother's continuing to work to help with the family income.

Nevertheless, with Mother's help my father managed to have a comfortable estate by county-seat standards at the time of his death. How he did it is beyond my comprehension. He was generous in civic causes and he persisted in the habit of personally picking up notes at the bank that were defaulted by persons to whom he had authorized loans. I am sure that under happier economic circumstances he would have had even greater financial success and certainly less strain in his business life.

Perhaps it is apparent from what I have written that my parents entertained great hopes for me and were willing to make great sacrifices to realize those hopes. As I look back on my life, I am sure that they were more responsible for the kind of career I have had than was any other influence.

A Tribute to My Parents

As a young man my father had been reasonably slender and only later on did he become heavy. However, as he was of better than average height, he carried his weight well and could have been thought handsome. He had a spontaneous friendliness and a ready smile that was engulfing in its warmth. He was cordial and courteous to every person with whom he came into contact, and yet there was about him a reticence and reserve that appeared a part of his general seriousness. People tended to be in awe of him, and the expression of their affection was restrained by deep respect. Although he surely had a few enemies, I never heard anyone speak ill of him. He concentrated on what seemed to him matters of importance, his responsibilities: his business, his family, and the community. He was one of the most industrious men I have ever known; in fact, he was a man of nearly sacrificial industry. As a consequence, he belonged to very few organizations, developed no hobbies, did not play golf, hunt, or play cards. His principal recreation, when he took time for it, was reading and, after the advent of the radio, listening to the news and some of the better programs.

In his prime Father was a man of remarkable intellectual capacity. I recall how impressed I was by his ability to remember what he read. He could remember his college courses with great clarity and could quote his professors. He was essentially a man of intellectual tastes and interests. He was also a religious man, although he did not join the church until after he was married, but, once having joined the church, he served it loyally and adhered to the religious ethic. He taught a Sunday School class in Lebanon for,

I think, more than twenty-five years. It was the adult class and he made careful preparation for it by reading the Bible and finding illustrations from literature. The class was a very popular one and, just as in the case of his school teaching, people universally admired his teaching and spoke of it with appreciation.

He was a virtuous man. He must have had some weak spots in his religious and personal code but, if so, they were not apparent. I do not recall his ever telling a dirty joke, swearing, or indulging in malicious gossip. He was rarely, if ever, angry. The only displays of anger I remember were quite brief and never personal but about issues or the frailties of colleagues. He did not drink alcohol and gave up cigars in middle life. Although his income was modest, he never failed to respond generously to every appeal for a worthy cause, often giving beyond his means without thought of return but simply from a sense of duty.

Yet there was another aspect to Father's nature. He was introspective much of the time and worried with the problems that faced him. His standards for himself were so high that he worked on a matter unceasingly until he thought he had done his very best. When he was unable to achieve perfection, he would sometimes become depressed—and small wonder because those were difficult times even for someone less self-demanding. After the hard struggle to get his education and become established without help, he had to take the blows of the Great Depression and of his mother's suicide. He had adored her, and her death weighed heavily upon him. Most of the time she had been a very warm, stable, and wonderful human being.

His integrity was unassailable, as some Klansmen were to learn. When he was an officer of the First National Bank of Lebanon and president of the school board, a committee from the Ku Klux Klan waited upon him one day to serve notice that he must dismiss the social science teacher. My father asked why and was told, "Because he's talking about internationalism and the League of Nations and other subversive topics of that sort." My father asked, "Is he a good teacher?" Well, they didn't know but they just didn't like such Communistic matters mentioned in the classroom. My father firmly responded that so long as he was on the school board and the man was a competent teacher, he would not be dismissed. The Klan representatives countered with "Oh yes you will dismiss him because we'll make you. We know the condition of your bank. Your head bookkeeper is a member of the Klan. We know the bank's frozen and if you don't dismiss ———— we will start a rumor that the bank is frozen and can't pay depositors. You know what will happen—a run on the bank and that will close it." My father, without a moment's hesitation, said, "Do as you wish. Start the rumor, and if the bank closes it will have to close. Remember, though, your money is in the bank too. No matter what you do, that teacher, so long as he does his duty, will not be fired." The bank was indeed frozen and this response had taken extraordinary courage and integrity. During that period all country banks were frozen as a result of farm loans that could not be liquidated because of the fall in the price of farmland and farm products following World War I. It was a period in which many country banks were being closed by rumors and by rumors of rumors and a time of great strain for country bankers. Nevertheless, my father did not think of yielding to that kind of immoral pressure. Although a peaceful man by nature, he did not hesitate to fight.

Compassionate, considerate, and responsive to a person's problems, Father would drive endless hours through the countryside doing errands for shut-ins and for old men and women who could no longer look after their own affairs. He would perform this function for them most of the time outside his regular working hours and almost always without any compensation.

My father had the faculty of relating one-to-one with every type of individual. Anyone seeking his aid or advice would get his undivided attention, freely given and conveying a sense of his genuine interest. An important element of this relationship was the absence of either criticism or the least condescension on my father's part. He simply accepted people on their own merits and listened openly to what they had to say. Another of his traits that was remarkable was his instinctive flair for easing situations of potential conflict or similar difficulty. He seemed often to know how to bring people together, how to arrange matters to ease the tension between people of differing opinions or opposing stances.

Because of his feeling for others, he was very hospitable, welcoming people to his home. My cousin Helen Heady, who lived with Father and Mother for some years after I left home, relates that my father would urge her to have her friends come in when Mother was away visiting, and he would stock the kitchen with food so she could entertain. Eager for her to enjoy herself, he would withdraw after greeting her young guests. After Mother became employed, he would often help Grandmother and Mother in the kitchen, even doing part of the cooking on Sundays, particularly when they were entertaining guests at dinner. He was also a wonderful provider for the table: he loved to eat and he made certain that, although we lived simply, we lived well.

Much of the regular entertaining in our household was for family members from various parts of the state and country who seemed always to congregate there. Our house was more or less the headquarters for both sides of the family, since Grandmother Harting, my father's bachelor brother, and for a time Grandfather Wells lived with us. It seemed to me, growing up, as if family guests were always coming and going. Aunt Rosa, my mother's sister and mother of the Heady girls, was a favorite relative and, since she was particularly close to Mother, she was often at our house. Although Father would take part in the conversation during these gatherings, he had a habit of going to sleep in his chair after dinner in the midst of the buzz of family chatter, a habit that I have come to understand and follow.

Father was always kind and loving with Mother, rarely ever cross; I cannot recall a serious argument between them. He adored my grandmother Harting and she adored him. During the many years she lived with us, he looked after her as though she were his own mother, attending to her business affairs and concerning himself with everything about her welfare.

Father was inordinately proud of me. I doubt that there was ever a father who was prouder of a son than he was of me, and this was true, I think, from the time I was born. As he told me once, he considered it remarkably good fortune that he and Mother could have a son who was born strong and healthy, without defects. A perfectionist himself, he was a stickler for having everything done right. As a youngster growing up I would be corrected even for the smallest mistake. He would insist on repetition of a task until it was performed to perfection, whether it was some household chore or my lessons for school. Report cards came to him first always and it was his expectation that I would make A's in everything including deportment unless there was some very good reason for a lower grade. I knew this was the standard that I must meet. Later he took pride in what I was doing and what I was trying to achieve.

It was my custom after I left home to try to spend at least one

Sunday a month with my parents, arriving Saturday night and having Sunday dinner with them. Father was always quite interested in my work with the Indiana Bankers Association, of course, because banking was his daily work, but when I became a teacher, dean, and president of the university, he took an extra interest in all that I was doing. After Sunday dinner we spent long afternoons on the front porch or in the living room, talking of our respective activities.

All in all I have never known a better man, a man of more unswerving integrity, morality, and decency. I have never known anyone to work harder and to have higher goals for society. He was always concerned with improvement of the state and nation as well as of our community: improvement in human relations, improvement in government, improvement in human welfare. Although a banker he would now be considered for his day a liberal in politics, I suppose. He was a Democrat in a county that was at that time mostly Republican. He was a firm supporter of Franklin D. Roosevelt's New Deal, which was in line with his sense of responsibility for the social welfare. In fact, although they were different in many ways, the only other man that I have ever known who I thought equalled my father in all-around civic and personal standards was William Lowe Bryan, and they admired each other tremendously. Father was a passionate believer in education and he supported it steadfastly at all levels. He believed it was essential, not only for the maintenance of our society, but also for the improvement of individuals and society as a whole. Education and the church were the two institutional pillars of his life. Even in retrospect, he seems a most unusual man and I still miss him keenly.

I wrote a tribute to my mother at sea off the coast of Spain on October 3, 1973, the ninety-first anniversary of her birth and almost six months after her death. As an expression of what she had meant to our family and what she would come to mean to me, it has a place here.

Mother made a great contribution to our physical and psychological well-being. Although my father was always a gracious host and enjoyed entertaining, he was a serious-minded man and a bit introverted. Mother on the other hand was more extroverted and outgoing. She was essentially an optimist who saw the bright side of life.

She was also an industrious and thrifty housewife who could stretch the family income. Though it was always modest, she was able to help ensure for us a comfortable, middle-class standard of living. Even though carrying a full-time job, she continued to do much of the cooking and housework for the family. She was aided by my grandmother, who lived with us, and she, my father, and I all did some portion of the work. She fully shared my father's ambition that I should have a good college education and willingly sacrificed toward that end. She was in a sense a liberated woman before the phrase took on its present meaning.

After my father's death, when she came to live with me in Bloomington, Mother's contribution to my career was unique. At the age of sixty-five she quickly learned and began to discharge the role of official hostess. This role was entirely foreign to her background and experience but she moved into it with vigor and enthusiasm. Because of Mrs. Bryan's frail health through many of the later years of President Bryan's administration, the Bryans had done little entertaining. I had disliked formal, official functions such as dinners and avoided them myself. The Indiana University community, therefore, was ready and eager for an official hostess. Mother not only fitted into the role but, in the course of it, began to draw me into more and more social affairs until in time I came to enjoy them, sharing the pleasure of many an occasion with her. The personal popularity that I seemed to acquire dated from this period and was altogether due to her guidance in involving me in the life of the university community. This involvement also helped to cure me of the periods of acute loneliness I had suffered periodically before, almost to the point of depression.

In addition, Mother kept a schedule of her own: she entertained frequently, participated in an amazing number of events—many for wives of young faculty members and students—and engaged in the club and organized social life of the campus community. The wives of my colleagues saw aspects of my mother that were not always apparent to me, as I realize now as they talk to me about her. They speak of her gregariousness and her fun-loving spirit, her sense of social responsibility and leadership as "First Lady," her indirect guidance, her fairness and impartial treatment, her softly guised firmness, and her deep personal interest in each friend. They recall her mothering of many a foreign student and her extraordinary memory, which enabled her to keep track of student and faculty families. To her friends in the women's clubs she seemed a person of strong character and beliefs, yet gentle and even tender in her many acts of kindness. It has been a source of recurring pleasure to me when Mother's friends recount incidents about her that reveal facets in her personality I had not recognized before.

Mother traveled extensively with me until a year or so before her death. She attended the meetings of the International Association of Universities, on whose governing board I served, at Istanbul in 1955, at Mexico City in 1960, and at Tokyo in 1965. She also attended several annual meetings of the board held in Europe during this period. Because of her graciousness and enthusiasm she became a well-known figure in international educational circles—so much so that, when the board met in London in conjunction with the fiftieth anniversary meeting of the Association of Universities of the British Empire, she was singled out for presentation to the Queen, to the Queen Mother (a favorite of hers) twice, to other members of the Royal Family, and to political and educational dignitaries. She attended every Grand Chapter of my fraternity during the years I was on the High Council and was the center of attention and affection at the Grand Chapter in Toronto when I presided as regent. She was then almost eighty-eight years old. Earlier she had accompanied me on visits to alumni meetings in innumerable places at home and abroad, including Manila, Bangkok, Hong Kong, and Tokyo. In Tokyo we were personally received by the Emperor and Empress as members of the International Association of Universities meeting there. In Bangkok she was received by the Queen Mother; Prince Dhani and Prince Wan entertained us and then honored us by attending the farewell party we gave there for our Thai friends.

In view of her rather sheltered life as a small-town housewife and clerical worker, Mother's achievements during the last twenty-five years of her life were a little short of incredible. Her formal education had ended with the eighth grade, though she had two or three years of posting, or advance courses, in grade school; yet she learned to walk with the great and near-great throughout the world and in doing so touched their lives and captured their hearts to a remarkable degree. Her contribution to my professional career was incalculable.

I received about fifteen hundred letters at the time of her death, nearly all of them relating some personal way in which she had affected a life, often unbeknown to me. For her invaluable role in humanizing my own life and helping me to overcome my public shyness and for her contacts essentially on my behalf, I shall ever be grateful. In retrospect, I am filled with awe.

{2}

○ ○ ○

Widening Horizons

ONE OF my high school teachers had sold me on the idea of going to a business school. Business schools were in their first flush of popularity then; they were new. As the University of Illinois had the outstanding one in the Midwest at that time, I chose to go to Champaign. Other considerations such as fees and transportation did not loom large. Out-of-state fees were low enough to be of little comparative consequence in those days, and I could go by train to Champaign from either Crawfordsville or Jamestown.

The summer before I left for college I had traveled to Whites-town daily to run a little country bank that had been organized there in opposition to the established bank. My income was rather good for a teenager, and in four months I had saved quite a bit of money for college. Later, at the end of my sophomore year in college, the bank offered me a permanent job at two-hundred dollars a month, which to me seemed like so much money that I tried to persuade my father to let me leave college to accept the job. In those days even college graduates were not being paid as much as that on their first jobs. My father was unyielding.

A friend from Lebanon, Paul Fletcher, went to Illinois with me. We found a room with a family named Keller. There were few if any dormitories then, and people with large houses and a spare room or two customarily rented their extra space to students. The Kellers had a daughter and two sons, one of whom later became a prominent judge, following in his father's footsteps, but when we lived with them Mr. Keller was a court reporter. The Kellers treated Paul and me and another freshman roomer, from Illinois, like members of their family. Even so, I was wretchedly homesick.

The campus was large, impersonal, and a little stifling to me. Social life was dominated by the Chicago crowd. Paul and I knew no one at Illinois when we went there, we ate in student hangouts and restaurants bordering the campus, and the friendships we made were with students in our classes, as lost as we were.

My circle of acquaintances was somewhat enlarged by two activities I entered: I tried out successfully for the concert band, and I served on the staff of the *Daily Illini*, in time being placed in charge of its advertising copy desk. The director of the band, A. A. Harding, had already won recognition for his masterly direction and later he became famous. I valued my work with him and maintained contact with him for many years afterward. In midyear I was invited to join a fraternity, but by that time I had determined to leave Illinois and I thought it inappropriate to pledge there.

Paul and I rather regularly attended programs and meetings at the Wesley Foundation. It was the leading campus religious group at Illinois and was the most successful of the Wesley Foundations nationally. The Foundation and the Methodist church are located right on the campus. It was very much a university church, a beautiful structure, and later attracted the fine young minister, Benjamin Garrison, to it from the Methodist church here in Bloomington.

Athletics were an important part of campus life—football games attracted huge crowds—but my participation was limited to the band. I had come to Illinois with keen awareness of the longtime effort my parents had made to enable me to have a college education and of the high expectations my father held for my success. The desire not to disappoint him and to prove worthy of their struggle for me, intensified by freshman qualms, probably made me a more serious student than some who came to the university with the idea that football was inseparable from collegiate life.

I was extraordinarily lucky to have, as a mere freshman, four professors who were among the most noted Illinois had in its commerce college. Charles Thompson, the dean, was a dynamic, driving individual who brought the college along rapidly and demonstrated his business skills by amassing large landholdings on the side. Ernest L. Bogart, a Princeton man who had taught at Indiana University at the turn of the century, was my teacher in beginning economics. He was distinguished in appearance, sported a goatee, and dressed rather formally in the manner of professors of an earlier time. His lectures were well prepared and well delivered. My accounting teacher, Hiram Scovill, headed his department, and my other teacher was Simon Litman, son of a Lithuanian emigré.

All my courses were in the commerce college, of which economics was an integral part. The college offered a four-year program and admitted freshmen directly into the program. That arrangement was one of the reasons that I was attracted to Illinois. But psychologically I was never quite at home there. The place had the atmosphere of a mass operation—as many as five hundred students were enrolled in some of my lecture sections—and it lacked color and excitement.

Although I did well in my studies and enjoyed myself probably as much as the average freshman at Illinois, I decided to transfer to Indiana University. Its business school was beginning to move forward and, since I expected to spend my life in Indiana, I thought that my Indiana University associations would be useful in the future. Also, many of my friends were in Bloomington. Father objected to this move; he thought that, as the business school of Illinois was better established, I should stay there. But I finally won him over and came to Indiana University for my sophomore year.

From the very beginning I fell in love with Indiana University (and the romance has continued to this day). It was a simple place in those days, with not yet three thousand students, but it had great charm and appeal for me. The campus was, as it is today, wooded and delightfully informal. All the buildings except the gymnasium were contained in the crescent extending from the old library— now the Student Services Building—to what is now Swain East. Within this arc was the beautiful wooded area that we now refer to as the Old Campus. The paths, where they existed, were of brick or boards, and an unpaved roadway entered the campus at Kirkwood and Indiana streets, passing in front of the old College Row buildings where now there is a wide walk. William Lowe Bryan, then president, used to come by horse and buggy from his home on North College Avenue and tie his horse outside Maxwell Hall, where the president's office was located. The university had no dormitories then, and the only group housing available was in fraternities and sororities or in privately maintained rooming and boarding houses. Many of the rooming houses became somewhat legendary because of the people who lived there or because of the particular accommodations furnished by the owners. The fraternities and sororities housed a fairly small proportion of the student body. At that time only two houses had been built to be fraternity houses, those of Phi Gamma Delta and Phi Kappa Psi, and even they would be considered seriously inadequate by present standards. The other Greek-letter houses had all been large, private residences that were converted to fraternity use, and most of them had become ramshackle places.

The student body was a mixture of youngsters just out of high school and veterans returning from World War I, and yet they had enough in common to be congenial. The whole air of the place was friendly and relaxed, and for some reason that I cannot explain it nurtured individuality and creativity.

One event that contributed to the unique atmosphere on the Bloomington campus was the freshman induction ceremony at the beginning of the academic year. It was held in front of the Student Building at 7:30 on the Monday morning of the first classes in September. The band played prior to the beginning of the ceremony in order to attract to the affair as many students and other members of the university family as possible. Since all Greek-letter freshmen were required to attend, a considerable crowd was always assembled. The participants in the ceremony gathered in the main room under the clock tower of the Student Building, donned academic regalia, and were put in order by the redoubtable George Schlafer, who considered the running of this annual ceremony one of his most important extracurricular activities. The officers of the university and such faculty members as would turn out were lined up in two rows inside the building, and as the clock struck 7:30 they marched out of the front doors and to each side of the south steps of the Student Building under the clock tower. The last person to emerge from the building was a highly regarded coed draped in classical white folds to represent the Spirit of Indiana. She opened the program with lines written by Professor Lee Norvelle, and then the president stepped to the microphone and administered the induction oath to the incoming students. The brief rite ended with the singing of the Alma Mater, accompanied by the band.

When as a student I first witnessed this ceremony, the colorful regalia, the beautiful ritual, the excitement of starting another school year combined to make the moment memorable. I always enjoyed participating in the annual event as a faculty member and later as president. I regret that it has been dropped from university tradition. Because the ritual impressed me, I have included in the Appendix (B) the message of the Spirit of Indiana and the oath administered by the president.

A wonderfully stimulating, exciting spirit pervaded the campus during the 1920s, and everywhere there was great interest in and beyond the issues of the day. Here and elsewhere students were so actively concerned by what they perceived as the special problems that had grown acute in their time that, I believe, the campus became one of the spawning grounds of the Roosevelt New Deal. At the emergence of the New Deal, it was from the Indiana campus and others that young men and women were drawn to forge the greatest of all governmental social efforts for reform and progress that I have known in my lifetime.

Yet campus life was so informal and unstructured that students fashioned their own fun for the most part and turned their ideas into enterprises. In this simple, unsophisticated, tolerant climate were bred the talents of a singular number of students who later won fame and fortune on the national scene. A flourishing literary magazine called the *Vagabond* was developed by the students themselves under the vigorous leadership of Philip Rice, later a distinguished professor of philosophy at Kenyon College. Hoagy Carmichael, Wad Allen, Bill Wright, and other talented students who before many more years became luminaries in the musical and theatrical worlds enlivened the local scene. Men such as Charles Halleck, Al Cast, and Dick Heller rose to leadership in student politics, later becoming prominent political figures. An editor of the *Daily Student*, Nelson Poynter, in time came to be one of the nation's most respected publishers, as well as a generous university benefactor.

Since there was not yet a union building or its equivalent, extracurricular activities centered in a campus hangout known as the Book Nook, later called the Gables. In my day it was the hub of all student activity; here student political action was plotted, organizations were formed, ideas and theories were exchanged among students from various disciplines and from different sections of the campus. For most of this period the Book Nook was presided over by something of a genius, Peter Costas, a young Greek immigrant who transformed a campus hangout into a remarkably fertile cultural and political breeding place in the manner of the famous English coffee houses. All in all it was a lively, exhilarating place.

Again, I was fortunate in many of my teachers. I had the great good fortune to have such teachers as J. E. Moffat and Lionel D. Edie in economics, U. G. Weatherly in sociology, William A. Rawles in corporation finance, William E. Jenkins in English, John L. "Jack"

Geiger in music appreciation, and many others who stimulated me. Moreover, the atmosphere of the Indiana University campus in those days seemed to nurture creativity—a heady atmosphere for one of college age. I found an opportunity for development in extracurricular activities such as the YMCA, *Red Book, Daily Student,* Union Board, and the University Band. I was able to qualify for the concert band as a baritone player, but Archie Warner, the conductor, named me manager of the University Band in my junior year, and thereafter I devoted most of my time to that function rather than to playing the baritone.

My principal job was to try to finagle enough money by one means or another to get us to an out-of-town football game or so, which I did by various economies and money-raising schemes. For instance, when the game was at Purdue and we were going there by the Monon train, we would stuff as many people as we could between the seats by turning the seats back to back, making a place underneath for a person. The train conductor, wise but sympathetic, ignored the teeming spaces beneath the arches of the back-to-back seats. In that way we were able to pay fewer fares and could cut down on the expense.

I achieved a couple of firsts in that job. I was able to negotiate with Walter "Pop" Myers, the longtime manager of the Indianapolis 500, a contract for the band to play for the race. When I went back the second year to negotiate a return engagement, he expressed satisfaction with our performance the previous year and we readily reached an agreement. As I rose to leave he said with a twinkle in his eye, "This year don't try to bootleg all your fraternity brothers and friends into the race." My other first was to get our band's first contract to play for the Kentucky Derby in Louisville. These were desirable and delightful outings for the band members and made the arduous work of playing for Reserve Officer Training Corps (ROTC) drills and parades and for other university functions more palatable.

In my senior year I played once with the band in a formal concert in old Assembly Hall. It was in the springtime toward the end of the academic year. I put my baritone back in the wings after the concert, then told a freshman brother in the Sigma Nu house to see that it was put in my room at the house and promptly forgot all about it. When I next needed the horn it could not be located and the loss ended my active musical career.

My college fraternity at Indiana University afforded me many opportunities. I suppose I had a natural affinity for fraternity life, and my experience in Sigma Nu was a very happy one. As an only child I found the fellowship of the fraternity family an especially pleasing and satisfying experience. From the very beginning I devoted myself to fraternity activities, running the whole gamut of typical fraternity committee responsibilities until, at the end of my junior year, although having been pledged as a sophomore and although having been a member for only two years, I was elected Eminent Commander for my senior year. This position proved to be not only a challenging experience but also one of great value to me in later life. It was an excellent training course in leadership and the acceptance of responsibility. I think that the office taught me more than any course in the university could have about those qualities, and throughout my life I have been grateful for that lesson. It presented the problems and potentialities in microcosm that I later faced in full scale as dean and as president.

The Sigma Nu House was located on the southwest corner of Kirkwood and Grant streets in an old stone building that is now used for offices. It had one great feature—a large front porch on which we could sit and watch the girls go by between town and campus. Most of the fraternities and a few of the sororities at that time were located in the blocks between town and campus. But our house was woefully small and crowded. The veterans from World War I were returning and we were figuratively bursting at the seams, very much in need of an addition. Our alumni were poorly organized and opposed to a building program, so the active chapter took the matter into its own hands. Under my direction we laid out a plan for an addition and took it to Ward Biddle, who was then our faculty advisor. He reluctantly assented but warned that it was up to us to raise the money. In the summer between my junior and senior years I traveled throughout the state, raising money from our Sigma Nu alumni to help pay for the addition to the chapter house; subsequently I was active in arranging for the loan to finance the unmet remainder. This effort gave me my first introduction to the highways and byways of the state, which I later came to know even more intimately in other capacities. My fraternity brothers, during the years I lived in the house as an undergraduate and later when I was back for my master's degree and lived nearby, were for the most part the closest friends I had in my youth.

Even though I grew up in a small town, I had a remarkable opportunity to experience the best in the legitimate theater during my days in high school and college. In those days Indianapolis had two theaters that regularly presented the very best of stage fare: both straight drama and musical comedy and revues, in which America excelled in the 1920s. When I look over the list of plays and the actors that appeared during those years I am astonished by the richness of the fare. At that period the top actors and actresses toured regularly and typically played Indianapolis. It was one of the standard stops on a national tour. They would play a split week or a full week depending upon the popularity of the offering. The legitimate plays usually were at the English Theatre on Monument Circle whereas the larger musicals played at the Murat Theatre, which had more seats. The Ziegfeld Follies came regularly with such stars as Leon Errol, Bert Williams, and Ed Wynn. Other perennials such as George White's Scandals, George M. Cohan's revues, and Earl Carroll's Vanities played each year. Among the renowned I saw were William Faversham, Maxine Elliott, Sarah Bernhardt, Mrs. Patrick Campbell in her great role in *Pygmalion*, Margaret Anglin in *Lady Windemere's Fan*, George Arliss in the Forsyte plays, David Warfield, John Drew, Jane Cowl, William Gillette, Helen Hayes, May Robson, Marie Dressler, Ina Claire, Ethel Waters, the Barrymores—Lionel, Ethel, and John—Otis Skinner and his daughter, Cornelia Otis Skinner, and a host of others.

In addition to the English Theatre, there were B. F. Keith's, the Lyric, and the Lyceum with excellent vaudeville. Also in the summer a good resident company performed important plays. Shakespeare was not neglected. During that time famous actors such as Robert Mantell, noted for their Shakespearean roles, performed. All the great romantic musicals of the period—for instance, Sigmund Romberg's *Student Prince, Blossom Time, Desert Song*, and *The New Moon*—visited Indianapolis. The Duncan sisters came in *Topsy and Eva*. The Music Box Review made regular stands with stars such as Fannie Brice, Bea Lillie, Bobby Clark, and Charlotte Greenwood. All in all it was a great period of the American theater in musical comedy, musical revue, operetta, and legitimate theater, and I had an opportunity to benefit from it all.

Indianapolis had less to offer in the way of music. Not yet having a symphony orchestra of its own, the city had to rely on occasional, single-performance visits by the major symphony orchestras of other cities. Soloists—Madame Schumann-Heink, Fritz Kreisler, José Iturbi—made guest appearances with the orchestras or performed alone, and the San Carlos Opera Company provided us with live opera in the traditional vein.

Following my graduation from Indiana University in 1924, I returned to Lebanon and to a position as assistant cashier in the First National Bank. I had always thought I should like to be associated with my father in the bank and make small-town banking my career. I learned a great deal from this experience, but it lacked the challenge and opportunity that I had anticipated. At the end of two years my proposal to return to school for further academic work met with my parents' approval. I should mention, however, that from my banking experience I had become acutely aware of the agricultural depression and the resulting widespread failure of country banks. Country bank failures, their causes and methods of prevention, were to become an important part of my graduate study.

When I returned to Indiana University in 1926 for graduate work, I enrolled in the Department of Economics, even though my father had wanted me to go to law school. It was Christmastime before he discovered that I was working on a master's degree in economics, a fact he accepted gracefully since law was his interest rather than mine. I had close contact with Moffat, Weatherly, and Edie, all outstanding scholars and teachers. I made a study of country bank earnings under the direction of Edie. The essence of my thesis was published in the magazine *Hoosier Banker*, was favorably received by the banks, and undoubtedly led the Indiana Bankers Association (I B A) to offer me the position of field secretary a few years later.

When I finished my master's degree, Weatherly and Moffat suggested that I apply for an assistantship at Cornell, at Wisconsin, and at Illinois. Each school responded with an offer, but I early decided to accept the one from William H. Kiekhofer, chairman of the Department of Economics at the University of Wisconsin. He offered me two sections in money and banking and one in general economics in return for a salary of $750 and the remission of out-of-state fees. At that time Wisconsin had remarkable faculties of economics and sociology. It was world famous. Richard Ely had just left but his influence was still there. Besides Kiekhofer, there were William A. Scott, John R. Commons, E. A. Ross, and Selig Perlman, the greatest labor scholar in the country. Weatherly and Moffat both encouraged me to accept the Wisconsin bid.

Not long before I went to Wisconsin to work on my doctorate, so my mother often recounted, a conversation took place on our front porch in Lebanon. I have no recollection of my reported comment then: that I thought I should like to be president of a small college and have plenty of time to read and write and do as I please. My parents were rather amused at the idea of my being president of any college, and I am amused now that I had such a distorted view of the life of a president. The remark must have been a passing thought because I am sure I did not hold such an ambition consciously or unconsciously for long. Later, when the Indiana University presidency was offered to me, I felt no desire or eagerness for it, nor had I planned for or thought of the possibility in advance.

Wisconsin had distinguished men in my field of study, I knew, but in addition the atmosphere of the place was exciting. Like Indiana, it was one of the seminal spots—the departments of Economics, Sociology, Philosophy, and Political Science and the Law School—producing men and women who later were to staff the New Deal.

Wisconsin was a much larger school than Indiana was in those days, and about a third of the undergraduate student body was from out of state. Its graduate school, of course, was cosmopolitan, as graduate schools typically are. With its scholarly reputation, its strong research programs, and its steady production of Ph.D.'s, Wisconsin had become the preferred school for a certain class of Chicagoans and Easterners to attend. Sophisticated and from families of social position and wealth, these young men lent an air to student life that was almost Princetonian, and at the same time the campus had a strong La Follette-Progressive political cast. The interaction of these forces, egalitarianism and liberalism on the one hand and elegance and affluence on the other, curiously enough was salutary. Living side by side, tolerating each other, students with these divergent views somehow thrived on the mixture.

I lived at the University Club, an agreeable residential arrangement, built like a large city club with bedrooms, dining rooms, library, recreational facilities, and similar conveniences. Many of the bedrooms were rented to teaching assistants and some to bachelor professors. Three or four of us from the economics department had quarters there. It was quite a gathering place. Occasionally I joined the Sigma Nus for dinner at their house. The chapter had been a leading one on campus, with many boys from Philadelphia, Chicago, St. Louis, and Milwaukee, and with a house near the lake. Fraternities generally, and the Sigma Nu chapter in particular, were in a decline, though, by the time I went to Wisconsin.

Economics was a topflight department. Scott was the head of its money and banking division. He was a conservative, oldtime money man, the great apostle of the gold standard. I was taught by him to believe that the economy of the world would be destroyed if the gold standard were ever tinkered with in any way. Scott was a dynamic lecturer. His classes were large, and I was assigned as a teaching assistant (T A) to two of his quiz sections, made up of juniors and seniors. Their age presented something of a problem, for I was not much older than they, but I solved it in a way that would be no solution today—by growing a mustache.

Another section to which I was assigned as a T A was general economics, taught by Kiekhofer. He was one of the great showmen in the field of economics and so popular that hundreds of students took the course as an elective simply to hear him. He had 1,800 in his lecture sections. A meticulous teacher, he was equally meticulous with his T A's, whom he drilled before each session. Because of this careful training for which Kiekhofer was noted, he came to be known as the father of college economics teachers. Scott, on the other hand, gave little guidance to his assistants, a lack that handicapped me less than it did my fellow T As because of my banking experience. Kiekhofer not only was author of one of the very popular textbooks in the field but also was in great public demand as a lecturer. He went all over the country giving popular lectures in economics and using a variety of devices for audience appeal that stood me, in turn, in good stead later when I lectured to students.

John R. Commons was the opposite of Kiekhofer. Since Commons' lectures were unplanned, his teaching had the air of spontaneity. I was in his advanced seminar both semesters and had the rare opportunity of seeing a great mind evolve a whole new theory of value. The value theory is central in economics. Lost in the process of working out the facets of his theory, a highly creative act, Commons would wander into the seminar of forty doctoral students and simply begin thinking aloud about the subject that had been occupying him in his study moments before. When he left us he was preoccupied, as if continuing his line of thought but in silence. For those classroom hours we were audience to a creative mind at work.

Students often complain about teachers whose lectures are unstructured as Commons' invariably were, but I found them exciting and I regarded him with admiration and awe. He was unquestionably one of the great figures of American economic thought. Later, after his retirement, he would stop by in Bloomington to see me on his way to Florida each year.

Among my close associates at Wisconsin were William Neiswanger, who subsequently made a name for himself at the University of Illinois; Guy Morrison, who taught at Indiana University and then became an insurance executive in Indianapolis; Walter Morton, successor to Scott at Wisconsin; and Jacob Perlman, Professor Selig Perlman's brother.

Mother and Father drove up to Madison to visit me while I was a T A there. They were very proud of the new Chevrolet that they had bought not long before and proud, too, that their son was starting on a doctorate. They also enjoyed the drive around the beautiful city of Madison and the university, which was more beautiful then than it is now. I did not have a car at the time; in fact, I did not have a car until I became field secretary for the I B A, when a car became a necessity to do my work. Contrary to the vivid recollections of fellow alumni, who have a great propensity for remembering things that were not so, I had neither a Stutz Bearcat nor a coonskin coat in my undergraduate days. I had not learned to drive an automobile as yet, much less own one, and a coonskin coat or anything approaching it was a luxury beyond my means. Corduroy suits were then in vogue and I did have a corduroy suit.

After a year at Wisconsin, the I B A persuaded me to accept, for what I thought would be an assignment of only a year or so, the job of field secretary. I have the lingering memory that my father was rather reluctant for me to leave my graduate work at Wisconsin to take the position although he was pleased and proud for me to have this promising recognition so young in life. However, he was fearful that I would not return to complete the degree. His fear turned out to be well founded.

{3}

○ ○ ○

What It Was Really Like

WHAT WAS INDIANA UNIVERSITY like in my college years? Through the mist of more than fifty years it is difficult for me to recall precisely the features of my own life as a student here. But of one thing I am certain: my collegiate experience profoundly changed my life.

The Bloomington campus in the 1920s had a colorful student body. Many highly individualistic characters were drawn to the university from other, less hospitable places and they contributed an effervescent quality to the student life. With companions like these life was never humdrum. Although the university had conventional rules and a strong tradition of in loco parentis, tolerant officers and faculty, if they chanced upon infractions, for the most part looked the other way.

We shared unquestioning pride in our university and a firm faith in its future. Student publications reflected this loyal stance, praising student activities when possible and, when not, revealing improvements in the offing. Unfortunate circumstances were the culprit when our teams lost, circumstances that were certain not to reoccur and hamper the teams next year. Such is my rosy recollection.

At night with studies completed, "boress" sessions, the rap sessions of today, formed around the den fireplace at the fraternity house, at the Book Nook, or elsewhere, frequently running until the small hours of the morning. On the spur of the moment a safari was launched: a trip to Indianapolis, to a home-brew speakeasy cabin on the banks of White River beyond Bedford, or even to Chicago for a weekend to listen to great jazz in the South Side night spots. Football weekends were regularly observed, ostensibly to back the team whether the game was played at home or away, and the score little altered the ritual of the occasion.

It was an era of elaborate formal dances, junior proms, formal Greek-letter State Day dinners at the Lincoln or the Claypool hotel in Indianapolis, and a variety of other regularly observed social occasions. For me at least it was a time of nearly unlimited physical vitality and exuberance. Little sleep was required. There was not much of the expensive decadence of the Ivy League collegiate life during that era, yet F. Scott Fitzgerald's *This Side of Paradise* served to picture much the same world as ours and was avidly read even by students largely unread.

The nightly boresses went on endlessly, solving the world's problems, sometimes stimulated by horrible home brew or white-lightning moonshine from nearby Jasper, the mere memory of which makes me shudder. In these sessions and in many other forums, I found a glittering, swirling atmosphere of ideas, fed by regular reading of the *Nation*, the *New Republic*, or our own magazine, the *Vagabond*, and, if I or my friends became a trifle complacent, H. L. Mencken would prick our egos in a new number of the *American Mercury*. Then Carl Van Vechten, Edith Wharton, Willa Cather, Zona Gale, Sherwood Anderson, and other contemporary novelists opened new vistas of the human condition and revealed Huneker's "pathos of distance."

For me it was an efflorescent period when my mind was open to receive a myriad of new ideas. It was also a time when my senses were so keen that they eagerly absorbed the beauty of the changing seasons in southern Indiana, the delicate pastel colors of spring, the drowsy lushness of summer, the brilliance of the fall foliage, and the still but invigorating atmosphere of winter. Music, literature, and art—my whole being responded to the stimuli of collegiate life, in and out of the classroom. It was for me a time of response, growth, transformation, and inspiration. Finally, toward the end of my college days, I discovered the excitement and the responsibility of leadership. Those years revealed a hitherto unimagined world to a small-town boy.

For all of us it was a time of dreams of future usefulness and achievement.

My own dreams were realized far beyond all of my expectations. When the incredible opportunity came for me to serve Indiana University, my personal ambitions became ambitions for the university's greatness, for the realization of the university's full potential, including the wish that every student, undergraduate and graduate, could enjoy as exciting and stimulating an experience as I had had.

[4]

○ ○ ○

Country Bank Failures

THE OFFICES OF the Indiana Bankers Association (IBA) were located in Indianapolis, and during my two years with the association I lived in Indianapolis although much of my time was of necessity spent in traveling throughout the state. I attended county and regional meetings of the members of the association and called on both members and nonmembers to stimulate their interest in the program of the association.[1]

I had left the University of Wisconsin with the understanding that I would return after one or two years with the IBA. Dr. Kiekhofer agreed with me that the experience in the IBA would give me an excellent opportunity to gather material for my dissertation, which was to be concerned with country bank management and prevention of bank failure. It was appropriate, therefore, that I keep him advised of my activities in Indianapolis.

On March 13, 1929, I wrote in a letter to him:

> My work has been very absorbing. Our Association has undertaken a campaign of self-improvement for the banks in the state of Indiana that is unique in the history of cooperative bank endeavor. Our Better-Banking Practices platform includes fifteen planks such as universal service charges, establishment of a credit bureau for the dissemination of credit information on duplicate borrowers in every county, secondary reserves, limitation of amount of money to be loaned to any one borrower, etc. It is being pushed by three key men in every county, with whom I attempt to keep in touch in order to keep them working and informed. I speak on different phases of this program of Better Banking as best suits the occasion, before county and group meetings of our membership frequently. At certain periods I speak several times per week.

1. My work was facilitated by efficient and skilled office colleagues: Forba McDaniel, Mae Dennis, and Zona Coiner.

Our work is carried on in nine divisions as follows: Better Banking Practices, Education, Banker-Farmer Cooperation, Protection, Taxation, Legislation, County Organization, Publications, Research, and Public Relations. The last two it may be seen are related to all of the others, so my work covers all of the fields.

In connection with Taxation I have had to cover in the past few months more material than I knew existed. We are not only involved in a tax fight ourselves but are attempting as well to give sympathetic support to various proposals now before the legislature to help clarify our antiquated present system of taxation on all forms of property. Those that have been advanced are a preferential rate on intangibles, a state income tax, and a tax on luxuries. I have spent the last six weeks at our present session of the Indiana legislature, pleading with legislators, drafting amendments and otherwise working for some progressive bank legislation. As a consequence, I am somewhat cynical about the fate of any meritorious measures. I do not mean to imply that we have lost our fight yet, but the path of the "righteous" is indeed thorny when there is a lobby full of politicians present who individually are indebted to their banks in amounts in excess of those permitted in one of our bills. A great deal of fundamental study went into our pending bank bills on cash reserves, loaning policies, methods of examination and problems of chartering. It seemed more like an advanced course in Banking to me, however, rather than a task.

Recently our educational committee has started a survey of all texts and courses of study used in the schools of the state from Primary thru the Universities in order to ascertain just what our educational activity should be. Luckily I have been given the supervision of the survey.

During the months that have passed I have also had the opportunity of visiting hundreds of banks and bankers of all varieties. All of this has turned out to be just the sort of background that I had hoped the job would afford. I have not had quite the time allowed me for thesis work that I had expected but I made some progress nevertheless. I spend every weekend in Bloomington and occasionally stay all week.

Fortunately for me the Indianapolis Chapter of the American Institute of Banking was short of teachers this fall and asked me to teach their class in Banking Fundamentals and their class in Advanced or Standard Banking. I meet each class ninety minutes each week. The students are all bank clerks or junior bank officers.

Interesting and satisfying tho my work is, it has not diminished my ambition to teach. I think with great regularity of the pleasant days of last winter. Never a Thursday noon goes by but that I am reminded of the Ia staff conference and wish that I could be with the group to receive its counsel and fellowship. I certainly am looking forward to the day when I can come back if you will let me.

In the spring of 1930, my second year with the IBA, I was invited by U. G. Weatherly, then head of Indiana University's Department of Economics and Sociology, to come to Bloomington for Sunday noon dinner. It was customary in those days to use the Sunday noon dinner for entertaining. I remember the visit vividly. J. E. Moffat and his wife also were guests, Dr. Moffat then being the senior professor in the department next to Dr. Weatherly. The Moffats were good friends of mine, with whom I had often shared social occasions during both my undergraduate and my graduate days.

Mrs. Weatherly had an excellent dinner, a fine roast, and it was all beautifully served in the dining room with the best linen and china by help who had been brought in for that occasion. After dinner Dr. Weatherly asked the ladies if we might be excused, and Dr. Weatherly, Dr. Moffat, and I went into Dr. Weatherly's study, where he began the laborious task of filling his pipe, a task that went on sporadically during the whole of any conference with him. He cleared his throat a time or two and then said that he and Dr. Moffat had been discussing their staff situation for the next fall and they had determined that there would probably be an instructorship open. He asked if I would be interested in accepting the position if the opening occurred. I was surprised, but after swallowing a couple of times I replied that I would be honored to accept. I did point out that I was engaged in some interesting research with the IBA at that particular time, and I raised the question of my possibly continuing some research for the association in addition to my teaching duties, thus maintaining a practical connection with the financial field. (This later proved to require my driving back and forth to Indianapolis two or three times a week.) They expressed approval of the idea and then said we would consider the matter settled and I would in due course receive a formal letter. There was no discussion of salary. In fact, I did not find out what my salary was to be until I received either the formal letter some weeks later or my first salary check, I do not recall which. I drove back to Indianapolis and then on Monday, enroute to Lafayette on my regular rounds, stopped to see Father and Mother to discuss the matter with them. Afterward I wrote Dr. Weatherly: "Monday I discussed with my Mother and Father the matter of accepting the position in your department in case the opening occurs as expected. They were enthusiastic over the idea. Consequently I now confirm the favorable decision I gave you Sunday." I was greatly flattered by the offer and really tremendously excited by it. I realized from Dr. Weatherly's reaction when I told him my present salary that I would be receiving a salary perhaps less than half my current rate, but, so long as I had enough money to live on, that salary reduction seemed a small matter compared to the prospect of being a member of the faculty and having the opportunity to teach full time. The very thought of being on the faculty was exhilarating to me.

When fall came I plunged into my teaching with great enthusiasm. I taught four sections, which kept me busy with class preparations and paper grading in addition to meeting the classes. Dr. Weatherly had undergone surgery in August at Johns Hopkins Hospital and was on leave during my first semester. After his surgery he spent time recuperating in Washington, D.C., and Atlantic City. In a letter dated October 15, 1930, I wrote to him expressing how happy I was and how much fun it was to be teaching:

> I am delighted with my work. I do not believe that I have ever been happier in my life, and am looking forward to the day when increasing general culture and mastery of my own field will make it possible for me to make my class appearances as satisfactory as I wish them to be. When that day arrives I can think of no happier work in the world than teaching. . . .
>
> I have so many reactions that I might write you that I hardly know where to begin. One of the things that has been keeping me busy has been trying to convince charming and solicitous faculty wives that I do not really play bridge. I suppose that they never will believe me and will always think that I am just trying to avoid their parties. For a few days I even contemplated learning to play, but since cards bore me terribly I know that I never shall. The round of faculty smokers, teas, and receptions, etc., that seem to accompany the opening of school, was another drain on my time that I did not anticipate. I suppose faculty members who have their lectures all prepared and rarely change them find all that sort of thing necessary to fill their days; not so with a young struggling instructor like myself.

On a more serious side, I wrote:

> I had one severe jolt, however, a few days ago. I suggested to my classes in Political Economy that the work of the course should cause some change in their thinking. That is, if they began the course with strong socialistic or extremely liberal views, by the end of the two semesters they should be able to at least comprehend some of the conservative viewpoint; and, if they began the course with decidedly

conservative and reactionary viewpoints, they should by the end of the course be able to appreciate some of the merit of the liberal point of view. I suggested that it seemed to me that in this course the reading of the liberal magazines of opinion would be proper and helpful in influencing this change. I suggested that they read, if they had time, such magazines as the *New Republic*, the *Nation*, the *Outlook* and *Independent*, *Mercury*, etc. Quite naively I suggested that all of these magazines would be available at the Varsity Pharmacy bookstand or at any other bookstand catering to an intelligent class of people. The same evening I walked by the Varsity newsstand to buy for myself a copy of the *New Republic* and was amazed to learn that they had to discontinue carrying it because they never sold any of the copies up until the past few months persistently carried. They informed me, however, that they quite regularly sold fifty copies of the *American*, enormous copies of *Liberty*, *True Romances*, etc. The thing so aroused me that I resolved that I would require every member of my classes to subscribe to the *New Republic* and in that method distribute two hundred copies over the Campus. Fortunately, I had a pleasant night's rest and got up the next morning realizing that after all I was at Indiana and so they did not have to subscribe.

On the whole I had a happy first year in teaching. My major effort, of course, was directed to collecting and organizing the material for my classes and carrying out my duties such as counseling students and participating in committee work, but I did make regular trips to Indianapolis and continued to carry on certain work for the I B A, including statistical studies, which were needed. This served as well to satisfy the research and public service contribution expected of every member of the faculty.

The unsettled banking conditions of the period made my I B A work increasingly important and justified the request I had made of Dr. Weatherly and Dr. Moffat that I be allowed to keep close personal contact with the I B A and the banking field. When I made the request, little did I realize that events would lead to far greater research responsibilities than I had ever imagined. In fact, the responsibilities became so heavy and important that they occupied as much as or more of my time than teaching did. To understand how this came about, it is necessary to know what was happening to the economic life of the state in general and to banking in particular.

In the popular mind the stock-market crash of 1929 and the Bank Holiday declared by President Roosevelt on March 5, 1933, were the focal points of the Great Depression. For the country banker in Indiana, however, the Great Depression had begun early in the decade of the 1920s. The cause was to be found in the prices of agricultural products during World War I and immediately following.

A worldwide shortage of food caused a great inflation of the prices of farm products in the United States. There was a shortage of manpower also. Many of the young men were away in the army, yet factories needed more workers. Even prior to the war, Indiana was in the throes of rapid industrialization that in itself drained men from the farms. As a result there was pressure to mechanize farming, and the expense of the machinery increased the need for farm credit. Mechanization in turn called for larger farm units, that is, for consolidation of farms, a phenomenon that has been progressing ever since. Between 1916 and 1920 the average price of farmland rose 50 percent. The result was a heavy demand on our Indiana banks, especially the country banks, for loans to finance the purchase of farmland and to pay for the new machinery and equipment. It was a boom period in Indiana and many new banks were chartered, sometimes without sufficient investigation of their financial strength and of the communities' need for the institutions. (It is doubtful, for example, that two banks were needed in towns with a population of five hundred or less such as Whitestown.)

At the end of the war farm prices collapsed, and many farmers found themselves loaded with an impossible debt. By May, 1920, wheat had risen to $2.16 a bushel from a prewar price of 90¢, and corn from about 65¢ to $1.52. The next year corn dropped to 52¢ a bushel, and wheat to $1.03. Naturally, land prices began to drift downward, returning in 1924 to their 1916 level. But the drift continued until 1934–35, when the index for farmland prices reached a low of 50 percent of the 1916 level.

Few rural banks were untouched by the value erosion and, starting with the recession of 1921 and continuing through the decade, the typical country bank in Indiana was highly vulnerable to a run engendered by loss of public confidence. This situation existed prior to the great nationwide collapse of the financial system and to Roosevelt's famous declaration of the Bank Holiday. Contrary to popular belief, between 1921 and 1929 more banks failed or folded (5,712) than in the three climactic years following (5,096).

The savings and loan associations in rural states suffered a similar erosion of their assets. They were not, however, as vulnerable to runs because legally they did not accept demand deposits. Instead they sold shares without guaranteeing immediate pay out on demand (although they sometimes pretended otherwise). As a result shareholders in these associations frequently found themselves unable to draw out their money and had to await their turn until cash became available. That process did not, of course, allow runs that could close the institutions, but it was no less calamitous for the individual.

It is now difficult to recapture the economic distress of this era in Indiana. From 1925 to June 30, 1932, 429 state-chartered and supervised banks out of an average of 760 in operation closed. Of these, 182 were sold, merged, or reopened after reorganization and the infusion of new capital. The remaining 247 had to be liquidated, and they held 25.2 percent of the average resources of all state-supervised banks during the period. Frequently these institutions could pay only a small percentage on the dollar to their depositors. Moreover, in those days shareholders were subject to double liability. Thus shareholders invariably both lost their investment in the bank and became legally liable for an amount equal to the par value of their stock. Double liability for shareholders was once thought to be an essential safeguard for depositors, but in practice it proved to be inadequate, and it typically helped to bankrupt, hence to destroy, the influence and service of the financial leadership of the community.

Out of the chaos arose a public demand for better and more objective criteria in the chartering of financial institutions and for close supervision and regulation of their operation as a protection for depositors and shareholders. The IBA and the Indiana Savings and Loan League, each with different motives, took the initiative of asking the 1931 General Assembly to pass a concurrent resolution that called for the creation of the Study Commission for Indiana Financial Institutions.

The resolution was passed, and in the spring of 1931 I was asked by Governor Harry Leslie to become secretary and research director of the Study Commission. The commission was to study bank and building and loan failures in Indiana and make recommendations for remedial legislation. The large number of failures then occurring made the subject one of urgent public concern. The mandate of the General Assembly authorized the Study Commission to investigate the organization, operation, activities, and control of financial institutions in Indiana, and also to look into the laws of other states and countries concerning similar corporations to ascertain how well their laws operated. This was to be done with a view to standardizing and improving the body of Indiana laws governing financial functions within the state.

Governor Leslie appointed the members of the Study Commission. The effectiveness of the commission depended upon the quality of its members, and fortunately the governor selected a distinguished group of citizens who had a statewide reputation for integrity and competence and who had served in many civic leadership posts. The commission was chaired by Walter S. Greenough of Indianapolis, banker and former newspaperman. A very talented man with a keen sense of civic responsibility, Greenough was the catalyst and entrepreneur for the study, and without his initiative and leadership I doubt that such a thorough and far-reaching effort would have been made. The vice chairman was Willis S. Ellis of Anderson, a savings and loan executive. The treasurer, Curtis H. Rottger, was then a retired head of Indiana Bell Telephone Company. Other members were Paul N. Bogart, a banker of Terre Haute; Franklin M. Boone, savings and loan executive of South Bend; Myron H. Gray of Muncie, an attorney specializing in bank matters; Charles Kettleborough, the director of the Indiana Legislative Reference Bureau; William G. Irwin, industrialist and banker of Columbus; Hugo Melchior, banker of Jasper; William F. Morris, banker of Pendleton; and George Weymouth, an editor of the *Indiana Farmers Guide*, one of the leading farm journals of the day, published in Huntington.

As I have stated previously, during the course of my work as field secretary with the I B A, I had visited each of the nearly 1,100 banks in the state, both state-chartered and federally-chartered banks being members of the I B A. Therefore, I had a speaking acquaintance with all the bankers in the state, had frequently also met with the boards of directors, and had some understanding of the strength of the leadership of these institutions and their role in the community. Moreover, in doing the work for my master's degree, I had studied country bank earnings and had published some articles, which had received favorable attention, suggesting certain steps to increase bank earnings—a move I held to be essential if the banks were to remain solvent and able to serve their communities. The bankers, apparently thinking my background appropriate, sponsored my appointment as secretary and research director of the commission.

The I B A and the Indiana Savings and Loan League, despite the fact that they were hard-pressed then, financed the Study Commission. Indiana University agreed to provide working space in the basement of its library, and the research was performed by my small staff under the direction of the Study Commission and with the participation of some of its members. In 1931 our enterprise was unusual enough to attract considerable campus attention. In an earlier day Carl H. Eigenmann and David Starr Jordan had been able to secure some outside support for their work in biology, and Lionel D. Edie was well known as an economic and financial consultant, but on a private basis. So far as I can discover, our little research unit in the basement of the old library building was perhaps one of the earliest, if not the earliest, example of sponsored or contract research at Indiana University in the social science field. Today, sponsored and contract research projects are commonplace, and a substantial portion of the university's resources and manpower is devoted to that type of research activity.

Our staff, which conducted all the research into the history of the development of financial institutions in the state, their numbers, their regulation, their causes of failure, and possible remedies, consisted, besides myself, of three part-time students and a couple of part-time secretaries. I was fortunate indeed in the choice of the three young men who carried the principal load of the research: Paul DeVault, Lyman D. Eaton, and Charles M. Cooley.

DeVault was at that time a law student and member of Phi Beta Kappa engaged in completing his A.B. and J.D. degrees. He made a comparative study of the banking statutes of the other states and showed a remarkable aptitude for that kind of work. Lyman Eaton was an accounting and statistics major, working toward a master's degree. He was an industrious and productive member of the staff. Charles Cooley was a candidate for a master's degree in economics. He had a skeptical, analytical mind that caused him to ask the right questions to save us from falling into obvious traps. Our secretaries were Elizabeth Chapman (Parrish), an undergraduate student, and

Evelyn McFadden (Cummins), who had just completed her A.B. degree and who was working in the history department's placement office. They were highly competent, both as secretaries and as researchers.

We made the required investigation and, based on our findings, we developed reform proposals for consideration by the members of the Study Commission. The commission met frequently, sometimes accepting and occasionally modifying our recommendations. The chairman and several members of the commission were helpful participants in our work, assisting with criticisms and suggestions. Throughout we had the wise counsel of Donald S. Morris, Indianapolis banker and lawyer. That small, part-time staff in the course of an eighteen-month period turned out a 174-page report of closely printed text and tables. Now, when I read it, I am awed that so much could have been done with so small a staff and I am astonished by the quality of it. Providence and Walter Greenough had certainly taken us by the hand.

In addition to our general historical and comparative studies, we made a detailed study of the causes of failures in the closed banks and savings and loan associations. Taking into consideration the impact of the desperate rural economic conditions, the members of the research staff and the members of the Study Commission nevertheless came to the unanimous conclusion that these failures could in large measure be eliminated by a more adequate system of state supervision and control. (For the reader who may become entangled in the titles of entities proposed by the Study Commission, I should explain that the old state banking department that had supervised banks and similar institutions in Indiana from 1920 on was to be reorganized as the Indiana Department of Financial Institutions and was to have a lay governing body entitled the Commission for Financial Institutions.) We believed that such a system could be achieved by removing chartering powers and state supervision from partisan political control; giving the chief executive of the supervisory division and the personnel of a proposed department of financial institutions greater job security in order to attract capable persons to the field; enlarging the authority of that department of financial institutions in the examination and guidance of financial institutions and in the granting of new charters; placing responsibility for liquidation of failed financial institutions in the hands of the supervisory department instead of court-appointed receivers; and making the banking industry aware of the need for it to police itself, subject to the direction of the state.

We recommended that the two principal trade associations, representing banks and building and loans, should submit to the governor a list of persons for appointment to a commission for financial institutions, thereby assuming some responsibility for adequate operation of the new department of financial institutions. Another factor involved was the limited number of examiners in the 1920s; a state statute passed in 1919 had fixed the number of bank examiners at ten and the number of building and loan examiners at three. Although the number of state-chartered banks had grown rapidly during the years following, and, although there were more than four hundred building and loan associations by 1930, the number of examiners for each type of institution had remained the same. The Savings and Loan League had protested this situation for years because of its patent inadequacy.

At the time of our study 350 institutions were under the jurisdiction of the small-loan division of the old banking department, and that division was limited to one examiner with the entire state to cover. For the most part it was impossible for him to do more than simply look at whatever reports were submitted. Salaries were hopelessly inadequate, having been fixed long before by statute. As a workable corrective we recommended that banks and other financial institutions pay for the whole cost of supervision, thereby making the revenues susceptible to the changing needs of the new department of financial institutions.

We found no evidence to indicate that branching beyond county limits would in itself prevent bank failures; hence an extension was not necessary for future stability. Our report therefore recommended the continuation of the statute passed two years before by the General Assembly permitting countywide branch banking and suggested that, if this provision were continued for the time being, it would allow banks to gain the experience necessary to manage a more extended branch-banking structure later. We did not deal with the need for wider-spread systems to serve the economic needs of the state. In fact, neither statewide branch banking nor even regional branch banking was then considered necessary for the economic development of the state.

Now, more than forty years later, the situation has changed

radically. As the economy has grown, the need for larger banking units to serve the state is apparent. In my judgment it would be desirable now to allow branch banking beyond county lines, either regionally or statewide. It is unfortunate that the provisions of the reform statute of 1933 should have achieved such an acceptance that our findings are now quoted as gospel long after the conditions we were correcting have changed.

Although insurance of deposits was then a very lively issue, we recommended against a state system of deposit insurance because of the dismal record that had been made in state or smaller-scale trials elsewhere. We did not address ourselves to a national insurance-of-deposits system, except to note that such a system without strict supervision could stimulate poor practices. Little did we foresee the great success of the Federal Deposit Insurance Corporation (FDIC); however, it succeeded only because it met the problems we had anticipated. Fortunately, we did recommend giving to the proposed state department of financial institutions the authority to allow banks under its jurisdiction to participate in any future national plan that the federal government might launch if the department felt that participation served the best interests of the public and the institutions.

With the study largely completed, a mountain of policy decisions by the Study Commission had been amassed and numerous parameters developed for a new financial institutions code. The Study Commission chairman and I early had agreed that the commission's recommendations must be put into legislative form for introduction as a bill in the 1933 General Assembly or the work would perish. We assembled a drafting team of three: two members of the commission, Myron Gray, the commission's lawyer, and Charles Kettleborough, widely recognized as a master draftsman; and Leo M. Gardner, a brilliant young lawyer recently graduated from the University of Illinois Law School.

The drafting team had individual assignments: Kettleborough's was the structure of the proposed department of financial institutions in consonance with existing state statutes; Gardner's was the sections governing banks; and Gray's was the sections for building and loans. All other parts of the bill as ultimately presented to the governor and to the leaders of the 1933 General Assembly were essentially the work of these draftsmen as a team. All draftsmen and I worked on the language vesting in the new department the power to examine, supervise, and discipline financial institutions within departmental jurisdiction. I also had the responsibility for monitoring all the provisions to see that they were in accordance with the recommendations of the Study Commission.

During the fall Walter Greenough led a campaign to present our recommendations to the public in the hope that the General Assembly in its next session might be persuaded to enact the financial-institutions code. I was active with Greenough in making presentations, not only to financial and legislative leaders, but also to the officers of the Farm Bureau, the Indiana Manufacturers Association, the State Chamber of Commerce, labor organizations, and representatives of the entire economic spectrum of Hoosier life. Walter Greenough was a genius at that type of interpretation, and I learned from him a great deal about the techniques of presenting complicated material to a wide audience and the necessity of preparing thoroughly, maintaining complete integrity, and touching all bases. Although we won many converts in other fields, quite a few members of the banking and building and loan industry were skeptical or opposed. I have no doubt that there were those who felt that the members of the Study Commission and I had betrayed them.

One of the most important of our specific reforms called for the transfer of the duties of the old banking department to the new department of financial institutions with flexible rule-making powers for the examination and control of banks, trust companies, savings and loan associations, small loan companies, and other related financial entities chartered by the state. We also recommended a much more conservative policy for chartering banks, departmental control of all liquidations, general strengthening of the supervisory statutes, readily understandable published statements of financial conditions, more adequate requirements for invested capital and surplus, and many other, similar steps designed to protect depositors, shareholders, and the public. In general the same kinds of recommendations were made concerning savings and loan associations.

That was a large order for the financial institutions to accept, and we had not won their universal support before the opening of the General Assembly in January, 1933. However, we were helped by an unexpected and very dramatic national development, namely, the acceleration of the runs on financial institutions by depositors during January and February, prior to President Roosevelt's order declaring a Bank Holiday as of March 6, 1933. From the day of the opening session onward, public pressure mounted steadily for the General Assembly to take action.

The code we were sponsoring made provision for the governance of the new department of financial institutions by a bipartisan commission that would have flexible rule-making power having the force and effect of law. This was the period when it began to be popular to give governmental agencies such power. Faced with the unexpected and complicated problems of reopening the banks, which could not be handled under existing statutes, state leaders, too, concluded that it would be necessary to have flexible rule-making authority in the state machinery dealing with banks. Fortunately, we had exactly what was needed.

Paul V. McNutt had been elected governor of Indiana in the Roosevelt landslide of November, 1932, and he had carried with him heavy majorities in both houses of the General Assembly. Because he had an effective organization he was able to get almost anything passed that he wished. His legislative team, having found in the rule-making power of the proposed commission a solution to the state's emergency needs, adopted our code as its own. Leo Gardner was elected a member of the Indiana House of Representatives in 1932, and, with approval of the governor, was appointed chairman of the House Banking Committee by Speaker Crawford, hence was in a strategic position to push the passage of the bill.

But even with the strength of the governor's office behind it, there were difficulties. I was helping Walter Greenough and the Study Commission members on an informal basis at that time—going up to the State House each day after I had met my classes in Bloomington. We had some dramatic moments in the Assembly. I remember one in particular involving a private banker from northern Indiana who was a man of great political power and skill in legislative maneuvering. He sent word to us that he would use his influence to kill the bill containing the new code unless the provision limiting loans to 10 percent of the capital and surplus to a single borrower were eliminated. This provision was a key reform and we could not yield. His opposition aroused our suspicion that he might have a personal conflict of interest, and indeed there was a rumor that he had made a very large loan on certain farmland to some members of his family. To check the rumor I telephoned a friend of mine, the publisher of the local newspaper in that county, and asked him to go to the courthouse to find out the nature and size of the recorded mortgages held by the banker's own bank. He called back the next day with the news that the bank had loaned $800,000 on a large acreage to a member of the banker's family. Since the bank had assets of only about $1,000,000, this loan so froze the condition of the bank that it would have been unable to pay its depositors upon demand. Armed with this information, we sent word to the gentleman that we had learned from courthouse records of a certain family loan and knew it to be the reason for his lobbying against the bill. He realized that a leak of this story to the newspapers would undoubtedly result in a run on his bank, soon closing it. Not surprisingly, he decided to drop his opposition to the bill, which was reported to the floor and overwhelmingly passed. This was only one of several dramatic incidents that occurred in the bill's course, and it gave me some insight into the extent of effort that sometimes has to be made to secure passage of important reform legislation.

When the bill passed and was signed by the governor, my relief was immense, as I wrote to my parents:

> Feb. 25, 1933
> 6:30 P.M.
>
> Dear Folks:
> The Gov. signed the bill yesterday morning in the presence of Mr. Gardner, Mr. Greenough and myself. We had been up all the night before checking the enrolled bill to see that it was right. I came to the room here last night to work before dinner and dropped down on the bed for a little rest. It was midnight when I roused and then I slipped out of my clothes and went back to bed and did not awaken until 10:30 this morning.
> You can't realize how I feel. I feel like a boy again with all of the responsibility and strain of the last two years over. I will go to Bloomington with nothing in the world to do but teach school except a few odds and ends such as correspondence, etc., which seem like nothing compared with what I have been accustomed to and I would come out home for the weekend so that we might celebrate together if it were not for the fact that I wish to get even the odds and ends over before Monday so that I may start the week right.
>
> Lots of Love,
> Herman

With the bill passed and signed, and with an outstanding Commission for Financial Institutions[1] appointed to chart the course of the new Department of Financial Institutions, my thoughts turned back to Indiana University. At that time in my life, I was eager to visit Europe, not only to see other cultures, but also to gain background for my teaching. One of my teaching subjects was the economic history of Europe, and I felt that a trip to Europe would provide me with visual images and perspectives that would help me teach the subject more effectively. During the previous semesters I had had a teaching load averaging nine hours a semester. My basic preparation for teaching had been scanty at best, and the pressure of deadlines and the volume of work involved in the Study Commission were such that they left me dissatisfied with the amount of my preparation for class and with the material I was able to present to the students. Moreover, I had been looking forward to the time when the Study Commission's work was over so that I could concentrate on my teaching duties. My father had had the reputation of being an excellent teacher, and I hoped to discover whether I had the ability to follow in his footsteps.

The new Financial Institutions Act creating the Commission for Financial Institutions did not become effective until July 1, 1933, but all during the troubled months from the bank closings on, the old banking department had been swamped with work. A longtime friend of mine, Richard McKinley, a country banker from Jeffersonville, had been made the state bank commissioner with the understanding that he would become director of the new department when it came into being. He had the difficult task of administering the department under the old statute in the interim until the new act fully took effect. Consequently, McKinley frequently called on me for interpretations of the new statutes, and then, as the problems of reopening the banks increased, he requested that I come to Indianapolis as many afternoons each week as I could to advise and help him. Since hundreds of banks were still closed and had to be reopened on a selective basis, the old banking department staff was simply not large enough to handle the work. Moreover, all of the troubled banks had to be assisted in selling preferred stock or notes

1. Members were Robert Batton, lawyer of Marion, chairman; Harvey B. Hartsock, Indianapolis lawyer; Myron Gray of Muncie; Oscar P. Welborn, financier of Indianapolis; and C. M. Setser, Columbus banker.

to the Reconstruction Finance Corporation and in qualifying themselves for membership in the FDIC.

It had been agreed previously that when the new Commission for Financial Institutions assumed office I would become its secretary. This was to be a part-time job in which I would function only at the times of the meetings of the commission. The commissioners were all busy men of affairs who accepted this assignment in addition to carrying on their own professions. A preliminary meeting of the commission took place on May 25 in preparation for the official takeover in July. At the meeting I was elected secretary of the commission. On June 1, at a follow-up meeting it was agreed that I would be made the part-time supervisor of the newly created Division of Research and Statistics in the new Department of Financial Institutions. The expectation was that the division's work would be done on the Indiana University campus, the staff functioning more or less as had the Study Commission staff, and that we would continue working on some items that time had prevented us from finishing before. Aware of my intention to leave for Europe, McKinley had begun pressuring me instead to spend the summer working full time with him. I felt some sense of obligation to our recommendations and knew that knowledgeable administration was required to make them work. I changed my plans and spent the summer of 1933 in the Indiana State House.

Those were hectic days. There was not even adequate space in which to work, and in the beginning I found myself for the most part working on a window ledge as I dealt with problems of reopening the banks, classifying their assets—millions of dollars' worth of assets—and making decisions that were of vital importance, not only to the owners of the institutions, but also to the economic welfare of the communities they served.

Then by midsummer, because McKinley and the Commission for Financial Institutions had decided that my interim assistance needed to be retained full time after September 1, it was proposed that I serve in three capacities: as Secretary, Commission for Financial Institutions, and as both Bank Supervisor and Supervisor of the Division of Research and Statistics, Department of Financial Institutions. The proposal was acted upon in a meeting of August 3, 1933, and Governor McNutt, who had been a friend of mine on the faculty of Indiana University, later accepted the commissioners' recommendation. Control of the Research Division was crucial because it provided the machinery to continue our studies of needed additional regulatory procedures. Thus my new triple role was especially attractive: it gave me great authority and power in the Department of Financial Institutions as well as a substantial salary.

I had to request and was granted leave from my university duties. Too, I had had to forego my trip to Europe, and I did not get a chance to see Europe until after the destruction caused by World War II.

[5]

○ ○ ○

Reopening, Reconstruction, and Reform

TWO VERY BUSY YEARS followed my appointment in 1933 as secretary of the Commission for Financial Institutions and head of two divisions in the Department of Financial Institutions. The pace was terrific, from about nine o'clock in the morning frequently to about midnight, seven days a week, with most meals taken at the desk or conference table. In our dealings with bank officers and directors, my staff and I were guided by the conviction that, with the return of prosperity, assets that appeared to be worthless would again be valuable. Time proved this assumption to be correct as we lessened the economic impact of the bank and building and loan closings in many Indiana communities, and I made a host of lasting friends.

The case of each closed institution had to be studied. Its assets and liabilities, the strength of its leadership, the need for it in the community, and its prospects for success if reopened—all had to be analyzed. Since depositors' funds were frozen, rapid decisions were desirable, but the labor involved was enormous. We worked under intense pressure. Believing that reform could come after recovery with less social cost, we took the position that our mission was to help speed recovery rather than to achieve immediate reform by liquidation of marginal units. In some departments in other states and among some federal bureaucrats, the attitude was almost the reverse. Reflecting the national anger against the banks and disillusion with all financial institutions, they took a punitive point of view and were eager to find ways to liquidate rather than to reopen banks.

In that period it was difficult to be optimistic about the future.

In order for banks to reopen, additional capital was usually needed to offset the apparent losses. As much of this capital as possible had to be raised locally and, when the local source was exhausted, the rest typically had to be obtained from federal agencies. Board directors were often so depressed and discouraged that they had little will to attempt to raise the funds required for reopening. In some cases it became clear that the banks could not be reopened, but in most cases, with sacrifice and effort on the part of the owners and management, reopening was possible.

When we talked with the boards and officers, while making firm conditions for reopening, we encouraged them to do better rather than criticized them for past mistakes, and we tried to create a sympathetic climate for innovative solutions to their problems. We stressed the point that their assets were far more valuable in operation than in liquidation. Once the package for reopening a closed bank was determined—the value of its assets, the amount of new local funds it could raise, and the amount to be sought elsewhere —the next steps involved seeking a loan from the Reconstruction Finance Corporation or refinancing frozen loans with the Federal Land Bank, the Farm Credit Administration, or other agencies. The final step was to win approval of the refinancing plan from the Federal Deposit Insurance Corporation (F D I C) in order for the deposits of the reopened bank to be insured. A similar procedure had to be followed in many instances for banks that had already reopened following the Bank Holiday, in order for them to be qualified for membership in the F D I C.

This was a heady experience for me. I was only thirty-one when I became bank supervisor and, due to the particular circumstances of that era, of course, the bank supervisor had greater authority and weight and had to make more important decisions than ever before or ever since. I traveled regularly to Washington, D.C., taking with me individual cases to be presented to Jesse Jones, the chairman of the Reconstruction Finance Corporation, and to Leo Crowley, the chairman of the F D I C, and hoping for the approval of our proposals. I likewise journeyed regularly to New York, where were tied up some important assets that meant the life or death of certain Indiana banks. I spent a great many nights on Pullman sleeping cars, going east one night and coming back the next.

I had been lucky enough to persuade Edward "Eddie" Edwards to join the Department of Financial Institutions and to take charge of the Division of Research and Statistics. He had met some of my classes in Bloomington for me the previous year and I had come to have a very high regard for his analytical ability. During the years 1933–35 he and his staff were busy studying the problems that had arisen out of the administration of the financial institutions code, seeking ways to correct errors and overcome inadequacies. They also did much of the analysis of the assets of frozen banks.

One of our first tasks in which Eddie had a very important part was to draft a qualifying test for all bank examiners. The Study Commission had included among its recommendations the upgrading of the examining staff in the Department of Financial Institutions by selection on a merit, rather than a political, basis. Before that time there had been many good examiners, but among their ranks had also been some political hacks who had little idea of the professional nature of their work. Numerous young college graduates took our first and subsequent examinations and passed them with flying colors. It was a time of few job opportunities for college graduates, and some took the examination no doubt simply to qualify for a job. Others, however, were excited by the idealism of our enterprise, which by that time had received much favorable publicity. A talented group attempted the test. Several qualified for examining posts, where they gained their first experience either in our own department or in the field. Others used the results of the examination to secure positions in the banking or the savings and loan field, where they invariably became successful.

Eddie Edwards made a brilliant record as the operating head of the Division of Research and Statistics. Probably its most important recommendations resulted from its study of the small-loan field, the operations of consumer credit agencies not under the supervision of the Department of Financial Institutions, the dealings of pawnbrokers, and the retail installment selling area. The Study Commission did not have enough time, sufficient staff, or available records to make a full report. The 1933 General Assembly, however, passed an amendment to the Indiana Small Loan Law that provided for a small initial cut in the maximum interest rate and that granted to the new Commission for Financial Institutions the power to set maximum rates and to require necessary financial data on which such maximum rates could be set. This action opened the opportunity to study the field, and Eddie and his colleagues gave priority to this study.

They made some amazing discoveries of practices that were reprehensible and that violated all canons of public interest. A number of small-loan companies were abusing the high rates they were permitted to charge on small loans by allowing the loans to stand year after year without reduction in principal. The worst case uncovered was of a farmer who had borrowed three hundred dollars in 1920 or 1921 and still owed that amount in 1933 although he had paid well over one thousand dollars in interest. We called these loan companies "country clubs" because it seemed to us that the borrowers were just paying dues and getting nothing much from them. Based on the results of these studies, regulations were promulgated to lower the maximum rate of interest and to place a limit on the amount of interest a lender could collect in excess of the Indiana usury law.

Another group of lenders, some of whom were regulated because they held small-loan licenses, were the pawnbrokers. A model pawnbroking act that had been drafted years earlier proved readily adaptable to the Indiana situation, and there was no particular trouble getting the Pawnbroking Bill through the 1935 legislature.

The largest and most interesting of these investigations was in the field of retail installment selling, which was widely rumored to have many, many undesirable practices. Not only were finance charges often excessive, but there were other serious abuses: sellers sometimes failed to give buyers written contracts or to state the finance charge when they did give contracts; particularly in the automobile business, sellers would neglect to furnish an insurance policy or certificate of insurance to the customer, even though an insurance charge was included, or to disclose the amount of the insurance premium, usually buried in the finance charge. To control these and other abuses the Division of Research and Statistics proposed a comprehensive package of new legislation. A very important feature of the entire proposal was that installment sellers would have to give a buyer a copy of a written contract signed by the buyer and that the contract would have to include the cash price of the merchandise, the finance charge (if any), the amount of any insurance included in the package, the amount of the down payment, the amount of the unpaid balance for which the purchaser was liable, and the size and number of the monthly or periodic payments. Equally important were the provisions for licensing and subsequent periodic examination of sales finance companies; for authorizing the Department of Financial Institutions to set maximum finance charges (and minimum rebates in case of prepayment) for various types of contracts; and especially for requiring that dealers who plan to sell their contracts limit the finance charge to the amount being charged to the bank or to the finance company, thus eliminating the "bonus" or "pack" that had come to be a serious abuse. Most important of all, perhaps, was the definition of the cash price as the difference between the time price and the finance charge rather than as the price the dealer would sell for cash. This definition made it possible for the courts to hold that there was no fixing of prices of merchandise, but only of finance charges, thus overcoming constitutional difficulties that had long kept the business from being regulated.

When it came time to put the proposed legislation into bill form, again the brilliant Leo Gardner was the draftsman, and he performed the difficult task with such remarkable skill that it stood court tests in those days when lower tribunals were unfriendly to regulations. This bill, when it finally was enacted by the 1935 General Assembly, was an entirely new approach to the regulation of consumer credit and to the control of finance charges in retail installment contracts. It was a pioneering achievement of national significance. The bill withstood legal attacks by those affected and became the basis for legislation in all other states and, finally, in the federal government. Indeed, the Indiana Retail Installment Sales Act of 1935 was the first comprehensive legislative regulation of time-sales financing in the nation, and it resulted entirely from the work of our Division of Research and Statistics.

But I have jumped ahead of my story. Knowing that consumer credit was a hot issue and that Governor McNutt controlled the 1935 legislature, I went alone to see him. As I remember the conversation, I said, "Governor, I've read in the newspapers that you are ambitious to be president of the United States. I don't ask you to comment, but I think I should tell you that we have developed in our Research Division a piece of legislation that is explosive and I want to tell you about it." Then I described it to him in some detail, starting with our findings that had served as a basis for the proposed legislation. I then said, "I know that the automobile industry, the appliance industry, and the big financial concerns like General Motors Acceptance Corporation, CIT, and Associates Investment, which buy finance contracts on appliances and autos, will be bitterly opposed to it. I'm also realistic enough to know that if you want to run for president you probably are going to have to look to these interests for campaign funds. I thought you should hear this story and I want to know whether you can support this legislation. If we have the bill introduced and you oppose it, we are going to get whipped and there's no point in going through such an exercise. You and I are alone and if you wish me to scuttle it, I will do so and keep the reason confidential." He asked many probing, substantive questions, for he was a man of quick intelligence. Finally he said, "Is this right? Is it in the public interest?" And I replied, "Yes, it certainly is." After a moment or so he said, "Very well, I'll tell the boys to put it through." In due course he instructed his legislative leaders and other members of his legislative floor team to support and, if possible, to pass the bill.

Indeed, Governor McNutt went further than that. During the weeks preceding the fall election in 1934, he made a number of speeches throughout the state, promising the electorate that he would recommend to the 1935 General Assembly corrective legislation regarding finance companies, including control of finance charges. His statements, of course, were widely publicized and were influential in the final successful battle fought in the 1935 General Assembly. Even with the governor's influence, securing passage of the bill was not easy because of the forces lined up against it. But it did pass, and with that action the second peak of this four-year period of financial reform, 1931–35, was reached.

The creation of an effective, modern system of supervision and control for financial institutions in Indiana was not the only important result of those years. One of the happy by-products of the Study Commission's work and of the two years invested in the reorganization of the old banking department and the rehabilitation of the financial institutions in the state was the opportunity that they provided for a group of very capable young men to get started in the field of financial institutions and later to achieve considerable success in it.

Of the three students who first worked with me in the basement of the old Indiana University library on the research for our recommendations to the Study Commission, two followed careers in which that preparation proved useful. Paul DeVault entered an Indianapolis law firm that specialized in the financial area. In time he became one of the preeminent figures in financial legal work. He has been the general counsel of the Federal Home Loan Bank of Indianapolis for many years and, since I served on its board for thirty-five years and as its chairman for thirty of those years, I had the pleasant privilege of continuing my relationship with him through a significant part of our productive lifetimes.

Lyman Eaton taught and practiced accounting briefly before yielding to a desire to become a physician. He has long been a highly successful practitioner in Indianapolis with the additional distinction of serving for an extensive period as chief medical counsel for the Indiana Farm Bureau Insurance Company.

Charles Cooley found his career first in the armed forces and then, for twenty years, as a teacher in the California school system.

Many of my young colleagues in the Department of Financial Institutions also turned to careers associated with the financial field. For example, Edward Edwards returned to Indiana University after his stint in the State House and played an important role in the life of the university as a distinguished professor of finance. He became widely recognized as an inspiring, imaginative thinker whose innovative ideas, though sometimes ridiculed at first, were later embraced by the financial fraternity. Through his presence on numerous key boards, commissions, and committees, he has rendered service to the nation as well as to the university. In addition and parenthetically, I would mention that, by his straightforward evaluations of my programs and policies, he gave me invaluable aid as assistant to the president in the early years of my presidency.

Another colleague, Edward Schrader, recently deceased, retired a few years ago as a senior partner in Goldman Sachs, America's largest investment corporation. Croan Greenough, who spent two summers in the Division of Research and Statistics, has just retired from the position of chairman and chief executive officer of TIAA-CREF. Leo Gardner carried on a very successful practice until his recent retirement, continuing to represent various segments of the financial community as a recognized authority in the field. Edward DeHority came into the Department of Financial Institutions as special representative in the liquidation division but later became bank supervisor and, following that assignment, had a long career as chief of the examinations division for the FDIC in Washington, D.C.

Among the young men who became examiners after passing the qualification test, Blaine Wiseman entered his family's bank at

Corydon and proved so able that he was elected to the presidency of the Indiana Bankers Association not many years ago. Floyd Call distinguished himself as the exceptionally competent secretary of the State Bankers Association in Florida. Hal Kitchen had a highly successful savings and loan career. Milton Martin qualified as a bank examiner but then was transferred to the building and loan division and later became president and board chairman of the Union Federal Savings and Loan Association in Indianapolis, one of the largest.

In retrospect it appears that the work of the Study Commission, including the struggle to establish a new, regulatory department for financial institutions, not only achieved most of its objectives for the state of Indiana but also perhaps made a modest contribution to the science and art of the social control of financial institutions. In part this is true because of the timing of our enterprise. Ours was the first independent, comprehensive study of state regulatory machinery to be completed and to have its recommendations adopted in the post–Bank Holiday period. In our new code we tried to incorporate all that was best of what was then known about safe bank operation. Hence it was a statement of proper bank practice.

It was inevitable, therefore, that in much of the reform legislation throughout the United States that rapidly followed the Bank Holiday at both the state and federal levels, many provisions similar to ours were to be found. Whether they were borrowed from our statute, as was frequently asserted in meetings around the country or resulted from similar conclusions from other sources is difficult to determine. In any event, our Indiana enterprise received widespread and favorable attention for its progressive features and was often cited as a source of important information for those working in the field.

Certainly our study and statute must have reinforced those preaching the importance of need as a prerequisite for granting new charters, capital adequacy, stricter supervision by well-trained professional examiners, flexible rule-making power to meet unanticipated emergencies, closing and liquidation controlled by the supervisory departments rather than by receivership proceedings through the courts, and, finally, fairness in lending to consumers and in financing retail installment sales. The consumer-credit studies and statutes were truly a pioneer breakthrough, for those in this business had been able to convince both state and federal legislative bodies up to then that regulation of this kind would be held unconstitutional because neither the business of finance companies nor the time-price of goods sold was subject to constitutional regulation and control.

In the spring of 1935, after I had been on leave from Indiana University for two years, some of my friends from Bloomington called on me to see whether I was willing to be considered as a successor to William A. Rawles, dean of the School of Business Administration, who was retiring at the end of the academic year. We talked for an hour or more in the library lounge of the Athletic Club in Indianapolis, where I was then living. It seemed to me a fanciful idea. I finally concluded that, if it were the wish of the faculty, the president, and the trustees, I would assume the post— foolhardy as that decision now might seem. (I also remember a conversation with Professor Clare Barker, then one of the senior members of the business faculty, who was active in supporting me for the deanship.)

President Bryan privately offered me the position. I then called on Governor McNutt to tell him of this offer and of my intention to accept it, which would necessitate my resignation from my position in the State House. He tried to discourage me, saying that I was needed in the State House and that the business school was in a moribund state, as he saw it, and would be difficult to revive. These reasons, of course, were a part of the challenge that had attracted me to the deanship and, having failed to persuade me, he finally gave the move his blessing.

I became dean of the Indiana University School of Business Administration on July 1, 1935.

After I assumed the deanship I remained secretary of the Commission for Financial Institutions for an additional year, and Edward Edwards was nominally director of the Bureau of Research and Statistics although he took a leave in order to head the National Youth Administration of the state. Thus we were able to continue a close contact with the commission. It enabled us to arrange for a grant from the commission to the business school to provide for an analysis of the bond and security portfolios of the state banks, a task beyond the time and competence of the Department of Financial Institutions.

At about this time, too, I was appointed a member of the executive council of the American Bankers Association (ABA), with

membership on its research and economic analysis committee. I
continued to be reappointed for approximately a quarter of a century. The A B A executive council was made up of three or four
hundred bankers in the commercial banking field, financial writers,
a few scholars, the executives of the state bankers associations, the
supervisors of the state banks and of the federal banks. They met
each spring at the Greenbriar Hotel in West Virginia. Leading
figures in the commercial banking field, the controllers of the currency, officers of the F D I C, and members of the Federal Reserve
Board regularly attended the meetings. The assemblage attempted
to adopt a set of policies and positions to guide the commercial
banking industry for the year ahead.

This was a very useful association for me. It enabled me to keep
in contact with the state and federal supervisory personnel, including those of the F D I C, with the top officers of the American Bankers
Association, and with leading bankers, many of whom were also
trustees of universities. Since I was the only active university president who attended the annual meetings regularly, they frequently
sought me out to discuss university policies. Because of this relationship, when I needed to know something about other institutions, I could telephone a banker friend and get a first-hand, confidential appraisal.

I kept in contact with the Savings and Loan Association through
my long membership on the board of the Federal Home Loan Bank
of Indianapolis. It gave me topside contact with that industry, particularly in Washington, D.C. and throughout the states of Indiana
and Michigan.

⟦6⟧

○ ○ ○

Apprenticeship
in Academic Administration

I WAS appointed dean of the Indiana University School of Business Administration in a meeting of the Board of Trustees on May 18, 1935. Previously, Assistant Dean James R. Hawkinson of Northwestern's business school had been offered the position at $5,250. Although there is no record of his response, he apparently refused the offer. I was appointed at a salary of $5,000, a rather handsome figure compared to the offer made to him as he had greater experience and standing in the field. I like to think that the amount of my offer reflected a rather favorable opinion of me by the president and the Board of Trustees, which was responsible for the cooperation I subsequently received from them during my term as dean.

My predecessor, William A. Rawles, class of 1884 and a member of the university faculty for forty-one years, was a remarkable man with a traditional and austere training in history and economics. Had his graduate work been in applied fields, say, at Wharton, he would have been less effective in defending Indiana University's School of Commerce and Finance—as the business school was originally named—against the attacks of those members of the university faculty who thought that vocational or applied courses did not belong in a university. The orthodoxy of his background and the breadth of his previous experience in a variety of administrative and organizational capacities in the university made him the ideal man to serve as the first dean of the School of Commerce and Finance. I had studied corporation finance with him. He was an excellent teacher, sound, thorough, and demanding.

A reading of the minutes of the business school faculty meetings from 1925 to 1935 reveals a graphic picture of the evolution of the business school from its earliest days to the time when I became its dean. Although the enrollment had grown, the faculty remained quite small, necessitating for all a heavy load of teaching and committee work. Meeting after meeting, report after report, this dedicated band painstakingly and thoughtfully tackled the everyday problems of their developing school. Carefully they considered problems of curriculum, of student personnel, of admission standards, and of relationships to the other divisions of the university. But overshadowing all these was the ever-present shortage of financial support. This problem was so grave that they finally found it necessary to recommend a mandatory professional fee of $7.50 per semester for each student in the business school. From the funds yielded by this fee in the fall semester of 1926, such purchases were made as a Monroe calculator, three Burroughs calculators, three Burroughs portable adding machines, five Underwood typewriters, pencil sharpeners, bookcases, and a phonograph for the typewriting department. In addition, a sum of $219 was distributed among individual faculty members for clerical assistance, having papers graded, and miscellaneous other needs. The allotments ranged from 50¢ for Fred Chew and $6.40 for Tom Luck to a high of $35.25 for Jesse McAtee. Dean Rawles received $33. These figures graphically illustrate how poorly the school was financed. One gets the impression of a mighty effort made by a valiant few to develop the School of Commerce and Finance during that ten-year period.

In the year 1932–33 the faculty successfully proposed a significant reorganization of the school, important changes were made in the curriculum, and, as if to mark a new era, the School of Commerce and Finance was renamed the School of Business Administration. (In 1938 the name was shortened to the School of Business, which I use hereafter.) Of the curricular changes the most revolutionary was the elimination of foreign languages as a prerequisite for graduation, but in addition the science requirement was moved to the freshman year and students were permitted to take more courses in the social sciences.

From all appearances the alterations were well received by the students. In my judgment the elimination of the foreign-language requirement increased the drawing power of the business school. The educational wisdom of such a step is debatable, but it is a fact that many students headed for careers in business hated the foreign-language requirement of the College of Arts and Sciences and jumped at the chance to avoid it by enrolling in the School of Business. There were other reasons for the increase in enrollment that were perhaps even more important. The country was beginning to emerge from the Great Depression, and it was apparent both that our economic system would survive and that the business field would offer an excellent opportunity for graduates. Moreover, the Indiana University School of Business, along with other pioneering business schools such as Wharton and Illinois, began to win from businessmen a growing appreciation of the value of specialized training for those who were to make their careers in business. There may have been other reasons, but at least these influences had an important bearing on the surge of enrollment. As I shall relate, during my administration we made additional innovations that also proved to be popular with the students.

Prior to 1933 the business school had admitted only juniors and seniors, but, beginning with the fall term of 1933, it also accepted freshmen and sophomores. For the next two years pre-business students, formerly counted in the enrollment of the College of Arts and Sciences, were included in the enrollment of the School of Business even though they were still taking Arts and Sciences courses. The change made a significant difference in the business school's enrollment figures but did not increase its teaching load proportionately. To illustrate, the enrollment for 1932–33 was 267; after the change in admission policy, the enrollment jumped to 583 in 1933–34 and to 723 in 1934–35. By the first year of my deanship, 1935–36, when the four-year curriculum had its real start, the student count in the business school was 879; the figures mounted to 1,304 and 1,595 in the two succeeding years. Of course, the increases from the year 1935 on were in students to be taught wholly within the business school and did constitute a huge additional teaching load for the business faculty.

I wish I could recall precisely the events of my first few days in the office of the dean, but, unfortunately, without a diary or a journal it is impossible to do so. Colleagues from that period confirm what seems to me to be apparent, that the first few days and weeks were devoted to doing what anyone would do in a similar situation, namely, consulting with colleagues on the business school faculty, discussing with them their views of the school's strengths and weaknesses and what was most needed for further advance, and generally trying to arrive at a consensus on what to do next. We also began a comparison of our offerings, degree programs, and enrollment with those of the other leading schools of business. As a result of these early discussions, at the first formal meeting of the faculty of the business school I asked each of the members to submit a plan for the next five years. These plans were then to be integrated into a master plan for the future.

For many years, the number of faculty had remained at ten with the occasional addition of a part-time member, a very small faculty indeed to cover the specialties that were required for the degree. It was apparent to me that we had to break through the barrier of a fixed number and increase the faculty size to prepare for anticipated enlarging enrollments. We had some success in doing so. During my period as dean, the number of faculty grew to twenty-eight full-time and five part-time members. An expansion of this size was possible only because of the backing of the university president and trustees.

The faculty of the School of Business when I became dean was dedicated, effective, and energetic. We functioned from the very beginning as a cooperative team, and faculty meetings were organized to assure the participation of every member. Ten standing committees were appointed and charged with responsibility for each of the important areas of the work of the business school: curriculum, library, laboratories and mechanical equipment, faculty promotions, graduate study, a proposed Purdue-Indiana cooperative course in agriculture and business, contacts with the business community, contacts with alumni, contacts with commercial teachers for the expansion of the summer-school program, and personnel and placement (with the Department of Economics).

Throughout those beginning days and months Clare Barker, a senior member of the faculty, was especially helpful. He had been among those who had strongly urged my appointment as dean. Then he became my mentor, friend, and active collaborator in all the early adjustments. Because of his own fine training, his popularity with students, his prestige among the other members of the faculty, and the quality of his ideas for improvement and modernization of the business school, his tutelage was extremely valuable.

During the first year the faculty met more than once a month on an average. The committees also met regularly to formulate their recommendations for each faculty meeting. By early January, 1936, the curriculum committee had proposed a revision of the curriculum and the addition of new professional courses leading to several new degree specialties. These recommendations were adopted in time to offer some of the new courses for the spring semester and, as was the case with the changes in 1931–33, they received favorable reaction from students. Moreover, the business community also reacted favorably.

During 1935–36 members of the faculty made long trips, visiting high schools throughout the state to counsel with high school seniors interested in entering business and to explain the Indiana University offerings. I soon discovered that the university offices in the spring and summer were always closed on Saturday afternoons and sometimes all day Saturday. Many parents of prospective students visited the university on weekends, only to find all the offices closed and no source of official information on hand. In those days there was no summer program for orientation of new students such as the university now has. To fill the need for a source of reliable information on the weekends, I adopted the custom of keeping my own office open on Saturday afternoon and nearly all day Sunday —at least from after church through the afternoon. An astonishing number of prospective students and their parents would somehow find the open door to my office and come in for a chat. Naturally, many of these youngsters in the course of the conversation became interested in the School of Business and decided to enter it at the beginning of the next term.[1]

1. After instituting the new policy, I received the following letter:

May 11, 1937

Dean Herman B Wells
School of Business Administration
Indiana University

Dear Hermie:

Mr. Elliott has forwarded to me your letter in regard to high school students' wandering over the campus.

I am the "official shepherd" for those groups which ask for conducted tours, and with members of the Indiana Union Board acting as guides we have been able to have approximately thirty tours in the past few weeks. However, there are many high school groups which come to the campus under the leadership of one of our own graduates. These groups do not ask for guides. Probably the alumnus feels that he knows the campus as well as the next fellow.

In the past we have thought that the faculty did not wish to be disturbed by visitors at all hours. However, in the future I will have the guides inquire at your office as to whether it will be convenient for you to meet the groups. I am sure that they will enjoy being received in your office, and I want to thank you for your

Another matter to which we addressed ourselves that year was the form of recognition we should plan for Dean Rawles' long service. Since we were eager to strengthen the business library, it occurred to us to launch a fund drive for expanding the library collection, which we would then house in a special room to be named for him. With the sudden death of William Rawles in the spring, the recognition became a memorial that eventually took the form of the beautiful Rawles Room adjacent to the library of the Business and Economics Building, renamed Woodburn Hall, which now houses the Department of Political Science.

It was logical that we should give the matter of building the book collection of the School of Business an urgent priority. The collection of specialized material that was then available was quite meager, and during my first year as dean the library appropriation was quickly exhausted. We made a special appeal to President Bryan, who promised to try to put into the next budget a sufficient allocation to enable us to acquire long-needed books and others required by the new curriculum. I urged that, since this was to be a special appropriation and not a recurring item, and in view of President Bryan's great interest in our need, we should be bold in forming the list of essential books that would constitute the basis of our urgent request for library funds. Thus encouraged, the members of the business faculty built a strong case for the request. They also took note of a number of deficiencies in library operations. One can sense how pressing the library problem was from the fact that the faculty urged the library committee to visit the librarian and to ask for something to be done to shorten the length of time that library materials were kept in the bindery because of the great need for every single available copy.

During the first year we also increased our summer offerings. This move enabled us not only to make employment more attractive to the faculty, but also, and of greater consequence, to interest high school teachers of business subjects in taking courses. The attraction of those teachers helped to accelerate the growth of our graduate program and ensured that we had recruiters in Indiana high schools

---

offer to instill a little more personal contact with the actual University into their tour of its buildings. I only wish it were possible for them to see more of our men. Yours for better "shepherding."

Sincerely,
Charles E. Harrell
Assistant to the Registrar

for the business school. In this effort we had the active cooperation of Dean H. L. Smith, who was director of the university summer session and who was ambitious to build its program.[2] The members of the business faculty readily accepted this opportunity and, in order to provide the maximum number of courses with limited funds, cooperated by agreeing to have the equivalent of four full-time salaries divided among a number of them, each teaching part-time.

All in all the first year was a happy and productive one. On September 29, 1936, at the business school's opening faculty meeting for the second year, I spoke briefly of the past year and asked Professor Alvin Prickett as senior member of the faculty in point of service to bring greetings to the new faculty members from their incumbent colleagues. He reviewed the different stages in the development of the school: its establishment as a separate school on the campus in 1921, at which time the business program consisted of a two-year course in the school superimposed upon two underclass years in the College of Arts and Sciences; the reorganization of the business school in 1933 on a four-year basis; and the expansion made in 1935–36 when a number of concentration groups of study were added and definite plans were formulated to develop courses for graduate study. Pointing out that the freshman and sophomore enrollment had grown by 50 percent over the preceding year and that the faculty had increased by more than 60 percent, Professor Prickett welcomed the new members to the growing and dynamic School of Business at Indiana University.

This preoccupation with enlarging the enrollment was not motivated by desire to achieve size per se. At about this time the university budgets began to be influenced by enrollment. Additional enrollment meant the likelihood of additional support. With increased funds we were able to add faculty members, each with a specialty not previously represented in the business school. Happily, at about the time we were enabled to increase the faculty, a new and large crop of Ph.D.'s and comparable degree holders became available as a result of greatly increased graduate enrollments

2. A longhand memorandum from Dean Smith in the university files is explicit: "When Dr. Wells became Dean of the School of Business I suggested to him that if he were interested in building up business school courses in the Summer Session I felt there would be a good demand for such. I suggested that to try the experiment out I would subsidize from the Summer School budget courses that he might suggest. I did this over a period of two years and the demand for Business School courses grew rapidly."

in business schools. They brought with them the backgrounds and abilities needed to develop and maturate the school's specialized fields. Furthermore, the business school's position within the university was strengthened by the increased enrollment. Historically each of the professional schools, with the exception of law, medicine, and dentistry, was spun off from the College of Arts and Sciences. As is the case in families, the youngsters were not taken seriously until they had achieved considerable size and strength, and indeed the courses in the School of Commerce and Finance in the beginning were few, and their content thin. Later, even though the curriculum had become more academically respectable, the rapid increase in enrollment brought some quality-control problems. A great amount of time and thought was devoted to setting standards to be followed in the elimination of students who failed to make satisfactory progress from one semester to another. Every effort to have the faculty participate fully in the decision-making process resulted in the release of the creative energies of these excellent men with a beneficial effect on the morale of the business school. Ours was a happy working relationship, soon bringing about a sense of forward movement and cooperative achievement.

There was a remarkable esprit de corps among our students as well, engendered no doubt by the feeling that they were in a developing and growing field, and in part, too, by the maintenance of a close faculty-student relationship and the high priority the faculty gave to good teaching. Good teaching is not only the best builder of internal morale in an institution, but also the most effective public-relations medium. I assured the freshmen in my welcome to them in September, 1935: "My door will always be open to you for the discussion of any of your problems. I am sure that I may say the same for each of the other members of our faculty. Come to us frequently. We wish to know each of you personally, and to share with you your experiences and problems." I could make that offer because the members of the faculty were truly dedicated teachers. I should like to think that the Junior Chamber of Commerce, later named the Collegiate Chamber of Commerce, was also effective in enlisting the students' cooperation and drawing from them helpful suggestions and discussions. To this day when I meet alumni of that era they invariably express their enthusiasm for their experience and frequently quote something they heard in a class of mine or of some other member of the business faculty.

The desperate financial condition of the business school forced us from the very beginning to think about ways to increase our support. The entire business faculty began to consider how we might better present our need to the university administration and to the state. Previously I had been—on either an informal or a formal basis, I do not know which—associated with the prestigious Committee for the Promotion of University Interests, which made an extensive and persuasive presentation to the citizens of Indiana in support of the university budget request. Dr. Burton D. Myers, the committee chairman, sought ideas wherever he could find them and apparently found me responsive to some of his questions. The university was seeking restoration from the depression-induced cuts of 1932–33 as well as increases needed for future progress. Its financial problems were nearly overwhelming during the dreadful years of the Great Depression, and because of my Myers Committee experience I was able to help the members of the business school faculty realize that we must aid the university effort to secure money by making our case as graphic as possible. To that end we attempted to stimulate our relationship with the business community. We instituted a number of research projects to obtain useful data for them, and we invited business leaders to speak to our classes and to participate in an advisory way in our discussions of curriculum and services needed by the state.

Another way in which we attempted to relate the school to the business community was through the establishment of the Investment Research Bureau to offer to the Indiana Department of Financial Institutions a mechanism for analysis of the bond portfolios of the state-chartered banks. Even with all the corrective measures that had been taken at the time of the bank reopenings, many of the bond portfolios remained in a distressed and chaotic state. The plain fact of the matter was that there was insufficient expertise in the typical bank to handle the bond account, even though at that time the bond investments constituted a substantial portion of the bank's investments. A brilliant young D.C.S. by the name of Harry Sauvain, who had studied finance at New York University and in close contact with Wall Street, was recruited to be the director of the bureau. He was joined by a bright Ph.D. recruit from Wisconsin, Nathan Silverstein, and by Dwight Cragun, who had had considerable practical experience in the New York investment community.

The staff also included Leo Dowling, later to be an Indiana University administrator, as a part-time executive secretary.

The typical bank examiner, although competent in the mechanism of examination, had little specialized expertise to enable him to make professional comments on bond portfolios. Therefore, the Investment Research Bureau filled a great need. As banks were examined their bond portfolios were forwarded to the bureau. Our staff analyzed and evaluated the list of securities in each case, adding constructive comments about the policy that should govern the portfolio of the bank. These reports were sent to the Department of Financial Institutions and through the department to the banks. Naturally a close working relationship developed between the state-chartered banks and the finance department of the School of Business; soon it was thought desirable by the Indiana State Bankers Association to hold annual conferences or short courses for the bank staffs on our campus, and the practice continued for many years. Thus the Investment Research Bureau performed a remarkable professional and public service.

Much of my time had to be spent in a persistent search for promising young men for the business faculty, with the advice and cooperation of the existing faculty. We were unable to offer high enough salaries to attract established scholars, but we believed that we could find talented young men who had the potential both to be excellent teachers and to be productive in research and writing. The search for talent I considered my most important job, to be undertaken with as much skill and as extensively as could be managed. I requested senior colleagues in other schools of business to nominate promising candidates for our positions. Our own faculty's contacts in other graduate schools were fully utilized. Once we had in hand the vitae of candidates, the members of the faculty and I tried to select those whose records were the most promising and I undertook to visit them on their own campuses. I was sometimes accompanied by faculty colleagues and, on occasion, a colleague who had business on a prospect's campus would undertake the first interview. But for the most part I dedicated the time and energy necessary to make a personal visit to the candidates. This seemed to me then, as it does now, one of the best ways to interview potential faculty members. By seeing something of the institution in which a candidate had worked, I could gain some knowledge of the standards and styles of which that person had been a part and could evaluate better the candidate's statement of his ambitions. Too, it was possible to judge him comparatively in relation to his colleagues. Frequently on such visits other good candidates came to my attention and so enlarged my list.

An important byproduct of those visits was that I became acquainted with more persons in the field and learned more about the institutions with which we were in competition. Whenever I began to feel self-satisfied either as dean or later as president with what we were accomplishing at Indiana University, all I needed to do was visit some other first-rate institution. Such visits never failed to suggest to me many things that were being done better elsewhere and to stimulate new ideas, new initiatives, new thoughts as to what we should be doing.

Our expectations in assembling a strong young faculty were handsomely realized in the years 1935–37 as we were able to recruit an extraordinarily promising group of young men. With the passage of time a few left the university, but most of them made their careers here, becoming leaders in building the great national distinction of the Indiana University School of Business. It was during these years that Lyle Dieterle, Harry Sauvain, Nathan Silverstein, Stanley Pressler, and Edward Edwards joined the faculty; Arthur Weimer, Robert Walden, and John Mee came soon after. These new men began immediately to make a major contribution to teaching and to research. Looking back on that period, I am still astonished by the cooperative and generous way in which they were received by the older members of the faculty and were initiated into the work of the business school.

In addition to the other innovations, we began a persistent effort to join with other schools of business in support of federal legislation for funding bureaus of business research that would offer research and service support to owners of small businesses, just as the federally funded agricultural experiment stations provided research and service support to farmers.

At the faculty meeting of February 8, 1937, I reported thus on certain legislative matters:

> 1. Good progress is being made on the project to secure federal aid for bureaus of business research in state universities. Senator Sheppard of Texas has introduced a bill in the U.S. Senate. At the request of Dean R. A. Stevenson of the Michigan School of

Business Administration, arrangements have been made for former Governor McNutt, President Lindley of the University of Kansas, and Dean Stevenson to have a conference with President Roosevelt whose interest, it is thought, has been engaged. Several state delegations have been approached. While the bill may not be passed during the present session of Congress, much has been accomplished toward arousing an interest in such a bill. The bill makes provision for bureaus of business research in state universities to have the same contact with the U.S. Department of Commerce as the university agricultural experiment stations have now with the U.S. Department of Agriculture.

2. Another interesting development is the proposed bill to create in Indiana a division of government research in the Legislative Bureau. The bill is drawn up so that, in the main, investigations will be carried on by the departments of social sciences of the state schools. This proposal is to be presented in the near future to Governor Townsend.

3. The George-Deen bill is another legislative matter which is of special interest to the School of Business. Professor Lewis of the School of Education, Professor Barker, and I have given considerable time to seeing that Indiana University offers its services and that its services are used in the working out of this vocational act. Conferences have been held with the Governor of Indiana and with experts in Indiana and in Washington, D.C. From the present prospect our facilities and resources will be used in carrying out the provisions of this act.

I was a member of the national committee of the Deans of the Schools of Business supporting this legislation (items 1 and 2, above) and afterward, as president of Indiana University, continued my interest in the effort. Arthur Weimer, after his appointment as dean of the business school, also devoted much time and energy for several years to the promotion of this legislation. The schools of agriculture and the agricultural experiment stations of the land-grant colleges fought the measure vigorously in an effort to maintain their exclusive role as the channel through which federal funds for higher education flowed. Unfortunately we failed in our efforts; thus the land-grant colleges won the first battle. In the long run they lost the war since federal funds are now appropriated for many purposes through many channels. However, a special relationship for bureaus of business research with a federal agency has never been established. Had we won that first battle, it not only would have strengthened our business school but also would have greatly aided in the development of business research and business in the state of Indiana.

A matter that occupied a great deal of our time arose from the recurring ambition of Purdue University in the field of education for business. We early believed that the needs of Hoosier students could best be met through coordination and cooperation of the two schools, thus avoiding costly duplication of effort. Our difficulties in persuading Purdue officials to this view were chronicled in the minutes of our faculty meetings, of which the following excerpts tell much of the story:

December 9, 1935: Dean Wells reported for the Purdue-Indiana proposed cooperative course in Agriculture and Business. His report was in the nature of a letter that had been received from Purdue University indicating that that school was contemplating the establishment of a Business course, rather than the cooperative course that was thought to be in process of being formed by Indiana University and Purdue University. The comments which followed indicated that the Indiana University School of Business Administration should be responsible for administering business education to the students of the state of Indiana.

February 8, 1937: Dean Wells told of a joint Purdue-Indiana committee meeting which he attended in Indianapolis on January 23. Besides President Bryan and President Elliott, five other representatives from each school were at this meeting. Various administrative problems which have arisen between the two schools were discussed. It was agreed that the two schools should work in closer harmony, and that the mere circumstance of having the higher educational work of the state divided and given in two places one hundred miles apart should not be allowed to impair the efficiency or the prestige of either school. President Elliott has already cautioned the editors of the student paper of Purdue University against publishing disparaging remarks about Indiana University. He suggested at the meeting that something might be done to end the alumni feud or bitterness. All this indicates that there is a real and thoughtful attempt toward greater harmony and cooperation. The group of persons who attended the Indianapolis meeting was made a standing committee to meet from time to time, and sub-committees are to be appointed to consider points of difference and to report back to the larger committee. The members of the sub-committee which concerns the School of Business Administration the most are Dean Potter of the Schools of Engineering, Dean Freeman of the School of Agriculture, and Dean Wells. Deans Potter and Freeman are to visit Indiana University soon to confer with various faculty members. Dean Wells is to spend a day at Purdue University in the near future.

After these preliminary steps are made, details will be worked out. At the present time there is a hopeful outlook.

March 9, 1937: The dean reported that he spent two very interesting days at Purdue University recently. Members of the Purdue faculty with whom Dean Wells met in conference were Dean Potter and Professor Knapp of the Schools of Engineering, Dean Matthews of the School of Home Economics, Dean Enders of the School of Science, Acting Dean Freeman of the School of Agriculture, and Professor Estey, head of the Department of History and Economics. Combinations of courses between the two universities were discussed. The combination most favored by the Purdue men was one in which the student might spend three years in the engineering school and one year in the business school for the Bachelor's degree, or two years in the business school for the Master's degree. There was some disposition on the part of the men in the School of Science for a four-year course (two years at Purdue and two years at Indiana) planned to get a combined curriculum in engineering or agriculture and in business. The men from the School of Agriculture were the most inflexible in the group. An interest was manifested by the Purdue group in the development of our graduate work, the feeling being that there would be a considerable number of the Purdue students interested if they could come to the School of Business Administration on a graduate level. The dean mentioned the money which Purdue is getting from industry to carry out projects, and made the suggestion that the School of Business should give some thought to research projects which might enable us to interest industry in this way. Mr. Wells left the Purdue campus with the understanding that each school would have a committee work on possible course combinations. He asked the Curriculum Committee to give this matter consideration.

Unfortunately the dream of a joint program was never realized but did represent one phase in the long effort to bring about voluntary coordination and cooperation between the two universities. During my presidency of Indiana University, the most successful step in this never-ending effort occurred when Indiana, Purdue, Ball State, and Indiana State universities agreed upon a formula for a joint budget request to the legislature (see chapter 10).

I was active in teaching during the two years of my deanship and did my share of the supervision of graduate students. At different times I taught courses in introduction to business, bank portfolios and management, business policy, and regulation of financial institutions. The introduction to business course, an innovation, provided an orientation for the students both to the university and to the business school. The business policy course served as a vehicle for bringing business leaders to the campus so that students could learn current business practice from them and the leaders could become familiar with the school.

My schedule of speaking engagements, which seemed heavy at the time, now appears a warm-up for what was to come. Naturally numerous requests resulted from my work with the Indiana Department of Financial Institutions and reflected my professional interest. The geographical scope and specific nature of these speeches can be gathered from the following list:

Atlanta, National Association of Supervisors of State Banks, "Standardization of Reports"

New Orleans, State Bank Division, American Bankers Association, "Management and the New Supervision"

Indianapolis, National Association of Cost Accountants, "Federal Financial Developments"

Cleveland, City Club of Cleveland (one of the oldest and most prestigious of the city-wide discussion clubs), "Sound Public Policy in Bank Supervision"

Chicago, Midwest Conference on Banking Service, "Sound Public Policy in Chartering Banks"

Indianapolis, Indianapolis Bankers, "Banking Frontiers"

Chicago, Investment Analysts Club, "Governmental Regulation of Bank Investments"

Indianapolis, Indiana Bankers Association, "Report of the Research Committee"

Indianapolis, Indiana Academy of Social Sciences, "The Federal Deposit Insurance Corporation"

In other addresses my emphasis or focus was on education. To the Indiana State Teachers Association I spoke on the contribution to the public welfare of good education in business. A similar theme was the subject of a panel discussion, with professors Clare Barker and George Starr, before the Indianapolis Marketing Research Club. My welcome to the freshmen in the School of Business both in 1935 and in 1936 attempted to set out a philosophy of education for business that would assist in guiding them. I am amazed that freshmen tolerated such long speeches. I gave longer speeches in those days before learning the wisdom of the old maxim that no souls are saved after twenty minutes.

One of our coups during this period was securing the selection of a scholar in the field of business to launch the Patten Foundation Lectures. The Patten stipend, in combination with money we had in our budget for a junior faculty member specializing in insurance, enabled us to bring Alfred Manes, the famous German scholar in the field of international reinsurance, to the campus as visiting professor for a full year. He brought an international dimension and distinction to our faculty that otherwise would have been unaffordable. His lectures were important because they not only inaugurated, but also set the tone for, future series.

I well recall the first Patten Lecture. It was scheduled for the afternoon of February 28, 1937. At four o'clock a large, curious, and expectant audience had assembled in Alumni Hall. I was waiting for Alfred Manes at the nearby elevator stop in the original Union Building tower in order to accompany him to the platform and introduce him. When the elevator door opened and he stepped out, I was startled to see that he was in full dress—white tie, tails, white vest—and that his chest was emblazoned with his many decorations and medals. In that era in Europe such dress was proper on an occasion of this type and in fact was expected of a distinguished scholar. I had an uncomfortable feeling, however, that few in our audience would understand his ceremonial dress and that he might even be greeted with some laughter, producing an unfortunate though unforgettable beginning for the Patten Lectures. Moreover, I felt his style of dress would prejudice the faculty at large against him, and we in the business school had already decided that we wished to recommend him for a permanent appointment. Since Manes was a sensitive and nervous man, I hesitated for a moment before taking him into a corner, quietly explaining the American custom, and asking if he would be willing to change into an ordinary business suit. Much to my relief he understood, even though he was surprised and disappointed, and returned to his room. In less than ten minutes he was back, dressed immaculately in a conservative business suit—sans decorations. His lecture was impressive and well received, but I remember more vividly those moments preceding it.

Another innovation was the occasional joint meetings between the faculties of the School of Business and the Department of Economics because of the interests they had in common. The student body of the two faculties was largely one and the same. This co-operative move was possible because of the good relationship that existed between the economics chairman, J. E. Moffat, and me in contrast to the strained relationship that had existed between our predecessors, Professor Weatherly and Dean Rawles.

With the rapid increase of students we soon began to run out of space and had to use rooms in other buildings. Many suggestions were forthcoming about ways to use existing space more effectively, including those made in the faculty meeting of February 8, 1937, that classes start at 7:00 or 7:30 A.M., that the noon hour be scheduled for classes, that more use be made of the late afternoon hours, and that classes be held on Saturdays. Prior to that time the university had had enough space for most classes to be held from 8:00 to 12:00 in the morning, leaving the afternoons largely devoted to laboratory sections, group examinations, athletics, and other extracurricular activities. There were no Saturday classes. This was, of course, a pleasant and efficient way to operate insofar as academic work was concerned, but it was not an efficient utilization of building space. The move to expand the hours of classroom use, which began in 1937 and which was rapidly accelerated by necessity in the 1960s, has now resulted in a wholly different way of campus life. Classes and laboratories are occupied steadily from 7:30 A.M. throughout the afternoon and well into the evening hours. Stemming from the shortage of space suffered by the university continuously since 1937, such a schedule inevitably produces innumerable conflicts with group activities.

In the end the School of Business chose to move various segments of our work to several other buildings rather than to attempt to push the history, government, sociology, and economics departments out of the Business Building, since we hoped to maintain their goodwill. We felt that in the long run our strategy would dramatize the need for much more space than would be available even if we had the exclusive use of the Business Building. These needs were met eventually with the construction of a new building on Seventh Street, which provided not only adequate space but also the specialized features required for proper teaching of professional courses in business.

Unbeknown to me, the meeting of the School of Business faculty on June 9, 1937, was to be the last one over which I would preside.

It addressed itself to the routine business attendant upon the conclusion of an academic year such as the certification of degrees and the recommendation of honors for the graduates with laudable records. In addition, the faculty dealt with two very important matters designed to insure the quality of instruction in the business school. The Committee on Admissions, Scholarships, and Student Relations recommended in its report that there be a requirement of remedial work for students deficient in the use of the English language. A motion to that effect carried readily.

Another very important recommendation involved an innovative set of requirements for admission to the junior year in the School of Business. It was thought that the faculty could observe the students in their freshman and sophomore years and in the course of that time determine which students would be successful in their junior and senior years. Dean S. E. Stout of the College of Arts and Sciences and C. E. Emondson, Dean of Men, had given this recommendation of the committee hearty support, and Dean Stout went so far as to say that in taking such a step the School of Business would be setting a good example for the other schools on the campus. After general discussion and thus encouraged, the faculty voted to institute a rule governing selective admission to the junior year. There was no hint, of course, of my leaving as I myself had no inkling of it. The final entry in the minutes for that day recorded my taking note of the fact that this was the last meeting of the faculty for the school year 1936–37 and accordingly wishing everyone a pleasant summer.

Customarily, then as now, the Indiana University Board of Trustees met prior to Commencement for its most important meeting of the year. In March, 1937, President Bryan had informed the trustees that he wished to be relieved of the duties of the presidency at the early convenience of the board. They had assumed that they would have considerable time to seek a replacement since they expected him to serve at least until the first of January. But at their meeting on June 10, 1937, President Bryan informed the board that he would serve only to June 30, and some provision would have to be made for a successor by then. After their initial shock, the trustees went into a long executive session. None of this, of course, was known beyond the board room at that time.

In those years I lived during the summertime in Nashville in

Brown County and drove back and forth to Bloomington each day. I had driven home on the Thursday before Commencement and had gone to bed before ten o'clock. In Brown County the electricity was turned off at ten. The telephone switchboard closed at nine o'clock and, generally, the place folded. At around midnight the telephone rang, and my first thought was "Who's dead?" because Marie, who ran the switchboard, would accept a call after nine o'clock only for a very great emergency. I stumbled in the dark through a couple of rooms to the telephone, hitting my shins on furniture all along the way. The voice was that of Judge Ora Wildermuth, who was chairing the Board of Trustees meeting in the absence of the board president, George Ball. The Judge said, "The board has been in executive session all afternoon and evening. Dr. Bryan dropped a bombshell. He informed us that he was stepping down on July 1. We've been trying to decide what to do." I thought it curious that he was seeking my advice, but then he said, "We finally decided we wish to make you acting president."

I stuttered, "Why Judge, that's, that—that's a very strange, that's a preposterous idea, it seems to me, because I am just a young dean and a new one at that. I think I might make a pretty good dean of the School of Business eventually, but I don't think I know enough to be president. Far be it from me to tell you what to do, but you should take one of the other men." I added, "The other deans have much more training and are much more experienced than I, and one of them could be tried out for the job."

"Well," he said, "to be perfectly frank with you, the reason we don't want to take one of the other men is that we might want him for the president. We know we won't be considering you. We can make you acting president without prejudicing the choice of any of the others."

It was some moments before I could say, "Under those circumstances, if you will promise me that during this period you won't consider me for the Presidency—I don't want to get involved with that—I'll do it. I'll try to be a good soldier and do it, if you will get me back to my dean's job as soon as possible." He made those promises and then after some months broke them.

In retrospect, this move had a felicitous by-product as it eventually cleared the office of dean for Arthur Weimer, under whose inspired leadership the business school was able to bloom and develop into a truly golden era.

Woodburn House

As I have just mentioned, I lived in Nashville in the summertime and drove back and forth to Bloomington each working day, even though I had a year-round apartment in Bloomington consisting of the upper floor of Woodburn House, 519 North College Avenue. It is one of the oldest houses in Bloomington, the earliest part dating from about 1829. The Woodburn family occupied it from about 1855 until 1924 when James Woodburn, who had had a long and distinguished career in the Indiana University history department, retired and moved to Ann Arbor, his wife's former home. Through the years the structure had been enlarged, and, when I leased it from the Woodburns in 1932, it was a sizable house. Faced with the new responsibility the Board of Trustees had given me, I decided that I needed to make adequate arrangements to discharge the duty of entertaining that is a part of the president's job. At that time the Union Building's facilities for private entertaining were quite limited. When I had first leased Woodburn House, I had sublet the lower floor to persons who took care of my apartment on the upper floor. My longtime friend, Sam Gabriel, shared the apartment with me, and for a time Dan Stiver, a medical student, also lived with us. Although the upper floor was commodious, consisting, as we arranged it, of a sitting room, study, three bedrooms, and two baths, it had no facilities for dining and our sitting room was inadequate for entertaining. I decided that I must undertake to operate the entire house, and during the summer, with the help of a good decorator from Indianapolis, Dorothy Helmer, the house was put in order. At the same time I was fortunate enough to secure Lorene Shields as a housekeeper and cook and John Stewart, a student friend of mine, as houseman and butler.

John Stewart had come to the university at the behest of the Indianapolis Press Club, where he had been a waiter while attending Butler University. Many of the members of the Press Club were Indiana University alumni and they persuaded John to transfer. They had then given me the responsibility of helping him find work sufficient to pay his way through school. He was a fine young man, only six years younger than I, with a wealth of experience in catering and already far advanced in his educational program. He readily assumed responsibility and soon became invaluable. He was an expert in his position as houseman and butler, and in fact performed an enormous range of duties. Yet he still found time to be a leader of the Black students and was, therefore, able to advise me as to their special problems and needs. In many ways he was like a brother with whom I could discuss my problems and, indeed, often share a confidential matter. He later had a distinguished career in education, culminating in the posts of dean of students and professor of biology for many years at North Carolina College in Durham. Until his death in March, 1980, we exchanged visits whenever possible, and I counted him one of my most valued friends.

Mrs. Shields was an expert cook and housekeeper, and soon Woodburn House began to function quite well for me, not only as a place in which to live, but also as a suitable accommodation for entertaining official guests of the university. It happened also to be the perfect setting for the antiques that I had been collecting for some years. Guests often commented on how beautiful and pleasant the interior was.

There were several reasons why I had to set up my own establishment. Of course, as merely acting president it would have been inappropriate for me to occupy the President's House (later also called Bryan House) on campus. Moreover, the Board of Trustees had told Dr. Bryan that he could remain in the house if he wished.

After I became president, Dr. Bryan considered leaving the President's House for another residence on the campus. However, I was very comfortable in Woodburn House, which seemed to be adequate for my purposes, and he and Mrs. Bryan were comfortable and at home in the President's House. I urged him to avail himself of the trustees' offer that he occupy the house as long as he and Mrs. Bryan lived. He continued to live there until his death in 1957, preceded by his wife's, and I occupied the President's House for not quite five years before I left the presidency.

The Woodburns had been very pleased with the treatment I had given Woodburn House and with its use. Partly as a consequence they later gave the house to Indiana University with the understanding that the university could use it for any purpose other than a multifamily residence. In the years since I left it, first Mr. and Mrs. Joseph A. Franklin, Sr., and then Mr. and Mrs. Thomas Cosgrove lived in Woodburn House and were hosts to various university groups each year before the Alumni Association began to maintain the house as a university hospitality center, for which it is very well suited.

The house is typical of many houses of the mid-nineteenth century, having had originally two open side galleries, or porches, which had served as the means of connecting the various rooms that had been built one after another without an inside hallway to connect them. As our entertaining needs grew and after the house became the property of the university, we fitted the two side galleries with sliding windows and thereby made two additional rooms for year-round use.

Following my father's death my mother came to live with me at Woodburn House, and at that time we enclosed both the front and back yards with redwood fences, therewith gaining two small, private, landscaped gardens that gave us a place for dining and entertaining out-of-doors, a consideration of some importance in those days before air conditioning. We also added onto the rear, in a style so similar to the house that no one realized that it was an addition, a wing that provided space for our staff or for any students we might have living with us. The new addition consisted of a sitting room, a bedroom, and a bath. The last of our alterations was to convert the old summer kitchen, which earlier had been made into a garage, into an excellent service room to hold laundry facilities and the large refrigerators and to store the extra chairs needed for big parties.

Much of my official and unofficial entertaining was done at Woodburn House rather than in other university or local facilities. Perhaps the most notable of these affairs were on the occasions when the Metropolitan Opera made its annual visit to Bloomington to perform for three nights in the Indiana University Auditorium. Following the performances we entertained members of the cast and out-of-town guests at supper in our two gardens with tents over them, which in the springtime beautifully served such a purpose.

⟦7⟧

○ ○ ○

The Fate of a Noncandidate

T HOMAS D. CLARK, in the second volume of his history, *Indiana University: Midwestern Pioneer*, states that whereas I may have borne the title "acting president" I never really cast myself in that role. He went on to say, "Clearly, he acted like a president from the start." While Dr. Clark was writing this volume he made similar remarks to me. At the time they seemed farfetched, almost preposterous. I remembered little of what took place from July 1, 1937, to June 30, 1938. Throughout my life I have tended to think infrequently about the past, concentrating rather on the future. I have that habit even now. The story of an incident that occurred long ago might illustrate the point.

At the death of Val Nolan, a trustee of the university, it was of course the sad duty of the trustees and officers of the university to attend the funeral. The transportation from Bloomington to Evansville was organized by Ward Biddle, the university comptroller. President Emeritus Bryan was to take his Buick, driven by his old chauffeur, Rocky, and Mr. Biddle assigned Trustee Paul Feltus and me to go with him. Feltus approached Ward Biddle privately, I heard later, and objected to his assignment, saying, "Can't you put me in another car? I don't want to ride 120 miles to Evansville and 120 miles back with two men who don't smoke and don't even know they live in the present. Bryan talks only about the past and Wells is somewhere off in the future."

What little memory I have of that period centers on the incident, of which I have already written, when I told Judge Wildermuth that I would undertake the acting presidency if he would promise not to consider me for the position of president. I also recall a great sense of inadequacy in undertaking the office. In other words, I was just plain frightened at the prospect of stepping into the po-

[94]

sition that William Lowe Bryan had held with great distinction for thirty-five years. Thus I discounted Dr. Clark's comments almost wholly. Much to my surprise, however, when I began to read the minutes of the Board of Trustees' meetings for the fall of 1937 and the spring of 1938, reviewed my correspondence files for that period, and read some of the contemporary accounts of the events of the year in Alumni Association publications and in newspapers, I came to understand the basis for Dr. Clark's conclusion. From the record, one can easily gather the impression that he had.

My interpretation of that record is something like this: When I began as acting president I had been a dean for two years, had had many contacts with President Bryan, and had been active in university-wide administrative affairs. I was already familiar with the university's current problems and opportunities. It seemed to me that in the final years of his presidency Dr. Bryan had grown even more vigorous and had accelerated the pace of his leadership. Several new members had joined the Board of Trustees in the previous two or three years. They were youthful, vigorous, ambitious for the progress of the university, and quite imaginative and courageous in their outlook. In the period just prior to 1937 a building program had become possible because of the availability of federal Works Progress Administration (W P A) and Public Works Administration (P W A) grants, which encouraged the state either to appropriate matching funds or to provide them by a general-purpose bond issue. These federal funds had been appropriated to help states alleviate their unemployment. The state legislature wished to get its share of these funds to stimulate the economy of Indiana, which was still sluggish after the Great Depression. Further, the General Assembly in the spring of 1937 had authorized and funded a pension system for the faculty in the state universities. This provision had been long sought because a large number of our faculty had grown old in the service of the university without any state provision having been made for pensions and thereby for a dignified retirement. The only choice faculty members had under such circumstances, if they were not independently wealthy, was to teach as long as they lived, even though their health might be failing or they might have grown weary after so many years of worthy service. In other words, a fluid and dynamic period had arrived in the life of Indiana University; much work was to be done, and the record seems to indicate that the university community, faculty, trustees, and administrators were eager for action even though they had an acting president. I was caught up in the mood.

Immediately in July, 1937, we began to address problems that needed answers and to take actions upon which there seemed to be a general consensus already. Also, we began rather promptly to discuss the possibility of creating a mechanism to study the more profound problems that needed research and analysis. These problems were soon delegated for consideration to the Self-Survey Committee created for this purpose. I had first discussed the creation of such a committee with the Board of Trustees and gained their consent to proceed with securing a pledge that all records and reports of actions would be made available to the survey team. The proposal for a self-study committee was then discussed with the deans of the professional schools and the College of Arts and Sciences, who gave it their enthusiastic backing. Next, approval was sought and received from the general faculty. Of course, these steps brought forth many suggestions about needed areas of study, which were later made available to the members of the committee when work began. The faculty was then canvassed for opinions as to the makeup of the committee. Armed with suggestions from these various parties, I recommended and on January 15, 1938, the trustees appointed three men who agreed to undertake this arduous task: Herman T. Briscoe, Professor of Chemistry; Wendell W. Wright, Professor of Education; and Fowler Harper, Professor of Law. These men had differing viewpoints and to a remarkable degree had had the type of experience that enabled them to interpret fully the ideas of the various constituencies of the university. Wright possessed a comprehensive knowledge of the public school system and an awareness of the attitudes of the state's teachers, as well as a sense of the university's responsibility to offer whenever possible, calling upon our expert faculty, practical assistance to the school system and to the state in general. He was a man of courage and strong opinions. Briscoe was a trusted, major figure of the liberal arts college and of course knew the world of science both as a teacher and as a scholar. He had been a high school teacher of Latin so he had a feeling for the humanities as well. Briscoe was a man of wisdom, tact, and patience, with an understanding of the importance of good teaching alongside good scholarship. For chairman of the committee I picked Harper, one of the university's brilliant young law professors, who not only was a representative of the older professional schools of the university but also was familiar with academic thinking in the leading schools of the country at that time. In their points of view, Wright was conservative, Briscoe was moderate, and Harper was liberal. Therefore they provided a good balance with which to look at our problems.

The committee sought the views of students, faculty, alumni, the general public, and educators beyond our campus. They involved many members of the faculty in service on subcommittees and in active deliberation. Before they finished they brought forth on March 21, 1939, a report that presented a searching analysis and a large number of recommendations for the restructuring of the university. Reflected in the report were the votes of faculty members on each relevant recommendation. Unlike many surveys, which are filed away to gather dust and be forgotten, this one led to effective action. In the course of the succeeding years all major recommendations were implemented, except in those few instances where passage of time brought new circumstances that made them unnecessary or inapplicable, and they had a far-reaching influence upon the direction of the university. It was a highly successful venture. Although Harper left the university after a few years, Briscoe and Wright spent all of their professional careers here and became in due course stalwarts of the administration, Briscoe as vice president and dean of the faculties and Wright first as director of the Junior Division, then later as vice president.

Whereas the most optimistic long-term dreams for the study were realized over a period of time, the appointment of the Self-Survey Committee and the beginning of its work also served an immediate purpose. As I have mentioned, the faculty, the student body, and even alumni were teeming with ideas for change and were in no mood to have a long period of stagnation while an acting president sat on his hands in the chair. Yet many of the kinds of changes being suggested were not of the type that should be taken during an interim administration. The existence of the committee, however, gave the members of the faculty an opportunity to air their views and to have them seriously considered. This outlet relieved the pressure for immediate action, enabling us to take care of problems that were appropriate to be solved during and just after the interim period. I shall always be profoundly grateful for the superb work of the survey team and to all of those who helped them. Their efforts and their report represented a very important milestone in the development of Indiana University.

Throughout the year Ward Biddle, the members of the Self-Survey Committee, the deans, and I also spent considerable time trying to devise ways and means of improving our long-term financial situation. We came to the conclusion that the university must reach for money from private donors or from government agencies other than the state much more vigorously than we had in the past. To work on this rather long-range project, two new committees of the faculty were formed. One committee, comprised of the academic deans, was charged with compiling a list of every need the university had, together with its cost. The list was then to be published and could be used in approaching private donors for gifts, ranging from a few hundred dollars for certain items to several hundred thousand dollars for others. A second committee, the Faculty Committee on Grants-in-Aid, was appointed to explore new sources of income. Since we had great need for money to support the scientific work of individual faculty members, large foundations seemed to offer one of the best sources as this period was prior to the federal government's immense activity in research and education. The grants-in-aid committee was charged with the task of studying the functioning of the great foundations to determine the fields in which they were interested and the principles that guided and directed their grants. This committee was asked also to make a study of projects then in progress at the university or about to be launched, or which could be started if funds were available. In other words, it was to determine what the foundations could offer us and what we had to offer the foundations in the way of manpower, skill, and equipment.

Those two committees began to lay the foundation for a vigorous search for outside funding, a search that has gone on from that time to this and that has yielded many, many millions of dollars in support of the university's scientific and professional activities. In fact, outside funds through the last thirty-five years have made it possible for us to achieve peaks of excellence that otherwise would not have been possible. In chapter 11 I comment on the special role of the Indiana University Foundation in this effort during the days of my administration.

My first Board of Trustees meeting was held on July 12, 1937.

In that meeting and in two subsequent executive committee meetings of the board, held in July, we dealt with something over one hundred items. Some were routine administrative and housekeeping items, but a remarkable number of others were substantive matters such as the complaints of Butler University about our low fees for extension services in Indianapolis, an effort to secure new P W A grants for additional buildings, a proposed survey of the water system of the university, the appropriation of a special fund of $20,000 for additional library purchases, and the possibility of buying the Smithwood property on East Third Street, the tract of land on which now are located Read Hall, University Apartments, and Forest Quadrangle—in fact, the area extending east from Jordan Avenue to Rose Avenue and south from Seventh Street to Third Street, a major expansion.[1]

One interesting pattern began to develop. We made minor adjustments in salaries in the first board meeting as well as many others in the two July executive meetings. We also made small appropriations for needed research equipment and for the remodeling of various areas to enable faculty members to carry on special kinds of assignments. We had inherited a welcome unallocated reserve and early adopted the philosophy that money entrusted to us was to be spent wisely and economically but to be put to work, not hoarded merely for the sake of providing the administrative and financial officers comfortable reserves that would protect them against every contingency. Apparently there were believed to be certain salary inequities that had been discussed for some time until the need for adjustment had won consensus. So, in response, we moved rather actively to make individual salary adjustments and departmental budget adjustments within the limits of the funds available. I have long believed that the only way to make any kind of bureaucratic organization tolerable is to have at some point an administrative mechanism for making exceptions and to have administrators operating that mechanism willing to make the exceptions, even though such decisions may create the kinds of problems that result from an otherwise rigid adherence to a set of rules that cannot possibly meet all situations.

1. George Ball of Muncie, president of the Board of Trustees, counseled the board to acquire every piece of land adjacent to the campus whenever it became available. He thought that the university would have an ever-expanding need for real estate.

Another major move was the organization of a group to recommend priorities for a ten-year building program. There had been only one classroom building constructed on the Bloomington campus with state funds during the period from 1910 to 1930 when other state universities were actively developing their physical plants. The lag would have become even more exaggerated had we not started immediately to plan a building program. At the same time, we began an expanded residence-hall construction program that, once begun, never ceased during my administration. A miscellany of other physical plant items also required our action. We made several property purchases, looking toward enlargement of the campus. We launched a campaign for an armory. We gave some consideration to the landscaping of the Bloomington and Indianapolis campuses and sought an appropriate location for the Thomas Hart Benton murals, most of which were later placed in the lobby of the Indiana University Auditorium. And we spent an immoderate amount of time not only on change orders for the building to house the laboratory school of the School of Education, the Service and Stores Building, the Medical Building (now Myers Hall), and the Clinical Building in Indianapolis—all then under construction— but also on additions to the Indiana Memorial Union and on the correction of faults in the women's swimming pool in the Student Building.

Among other administrative matters that concerned us during that first year were the creation of the University News Bureau, the inauguration of a weekly luncheon of the academic deans as an administrative and communications mechanism, the exploration of the possibility of increasing train service to Bloomington, and a study of the university's police, water and light systems. Other, academic items ranged from exploring the possibility of closer relationships with the John Herron Art Institute in Indianapolis to launching a summer-session camp at McCormicks Creek State Park. Of more significance, perhaps, was the consideration of establishing a fine arts school and a library school, extending police training, and authorizing Alfred Kinsey to offer a course on marriage—the course that led indirectly to his famous research.

But throughout all this time, our major thrust was the search for new faculty. Dean Fernandus Payne helped search for men in science, and Dean Henry L. Smith for people in education and in other fields, but I carried much of the load myself, traveling an inordinate amount of time all over the country. It seems to me that during this period I must have spent about 40 percent of my nights in sleeping cars. I could not travel by air very much because in that day air service was slow and infrequent, and a limited number of cities were served by the airlines. My correspondence files indicate the itineraries that I followed, two of which will serve to illustrate our strenuous travel schedule.

One trip during that year began in Louisville, continued to Paducah, from there to Memphis, then to Little Rock, from Little Rock to New Orleans, from New Orleans to Atlanta, from Atlanta to Daytona Beach, from Daytona Beach to Orlando, Orlando back to Daytona Beach, Daytona Beach to Atlanta, Atlanta to Spartanburg, South Carolina, from Spartanburg to Chapel Hill, North Carolina, and from there to Washington, D.C., and then home. In the course of that trip I traveled by Illinois Central and Missouri Pacific railroads and by Eastern and National airlines. Another trip included the University of Illinois at Champaign-Urbana, Cornell College at Mount Vernon, Iowa, Kansas State University at Manhattan, another stop at the University of Illinois, the University of Iowa, the University of Nebraska at Lincoln, the University of Missouri, back to the University of Iowa, Iowa State Teachers College at Cedar Falls, Illinois-Wesleyan at Bloomington, Illinois, the University of Kansas, and MacMurray College at Jacksonville, Illinois. Looking back on such schedules, which had to be jammed in between all of the busy activity carried on at the university every day, I am grateful for the stamina and the recuperative powers of youth that blessed me then.

Those are only examples of the many trips that were taken during that first, exacting year. We were determined to make an exhaustive search for highly qualified, available faculty prospects and, whenever possible, to interview them first in their home situations. By doing so we expected to learn how they measured up in the institution where they had been and later to bring to Bloomington those who seemed worthy, to see how they would measure up when seen on our campus. This method of selection had proven effective when I was dean of the business school. I believed then as I believe now that the quality of the faculty is the most important ingredient in the success of the university. Many things can be done to help members of the faculty, but the greatest laboratories, the finest buildings, and the largest salaries will mean little without men of absolutely top quality to use them. And so the recruitment and retention of superior faculty members must be the first objective of any administration and must have top priority in the use of the administrator's energy, mind, and body. With the great help of Dean Payne, Dean Smith, and many others, this was our first priority during that hectic first year.

At the end of the year I could say in a general summary to the Board of Trustees that we were ready to make recommendations for many important appointments, and I related the following:

> These appointments came as a culmination of the past year's intensive search for new men, a search which involved 33,414 miles of travel and interviews with 190 persons suggested for the positions, besides numerous conferences with approximately 50 advisers. The search has been extensive and it has been difficult; yet I think we have every reason to believe that the results will justify the effort.
> . . . The principal discussions in the Board meetings concerning new men have centered on the persons recommended for the headships.[2] It is proper that this should be so; yet I want to call attention to the fact that, in my opinion, the majority of the persons appointed to secondary positions are men of exceptional background and promise. No person has been appointed to any position during the past few months who has not won the right to that appointment by the competitive process of selection.

Thirty-three thousand miles may not seem a great distance under today's conditions of four-lane highways and nonstop jets that move at great speed, not only about the continental United States, but also throughout the world; in 1937, however, that much of a trip represented real effort and a substantial coverage of territory. Searching, searching, searching for top men, wherever they might be found and, after finding them, using all the powers of persuasion we had to interest them in our positions. Sometimes we had persuasion as our only weapon because our resources frequently were not competitive. We early determined that when an exceptional man was available we would breach our scales and schedules in order to hire him, believing as we did that occasional breaches would in turn help raise the salary level as a whole and result eventually in a faculty of greater distinction.

Of course, at the very beginning of the year I had to discuss with the men who were then past retirement age whether they should

2. Department administrators were then called "heads."

continue or not. Since it was a high-priority matter, I interviewed every member of the faculty who was seventy or older during my first two weeks as acting president. In some instances it was determined by an advisory committee, wisely provided for me by the Board of Trustees, which of these men were to remain for a semester or year in an acting capacity and which were to have retirement at once. Such a procedure involved a great deal of individual discussion, as much tact as possible, and as much kindness and compassion as we could summon, since some of the men who had spent their lives building the university felt that they should be allowed to continue indefinitely. It was our job—the job of those in administration during that transitional period—to make retirement as palatable as possible for these great and good colleagues and to assist them in every way to move into a dignified and happy retirement. This effort took no small amount of time.

To me, the climax of the year came before its end, when in a special meeting on March 22, 1938, I was elected president of Indiana University.[3] The Board of Trustees had been in executive session, and at the conclusion of its meeting I was summoned to appear before it. The president of the board, Judge Wildermuth, made the following statement to me:

> The Trustees of Indiana University have come to a decision on the most momentous question that has come before the Board in thirty-five years. We have by unanimous ballot elected you President of Indiana University. In so doing we have brought very great honor to you. But, we have also given you equally great responsibilities.
>
> Your responsibilities are great because of the footprints that have been made by the giants whom you succeed. Remember that you follow in the steps of Dr. David Starr Jordan, Dr. Joseph Swain, and Dr. William Lowe Bryan, three of the greatest educational administrators of this country. They made Indiana University a great university, respected and revered by her sister schools and educators everywhere. These colossal figures who marched across this campus have cut a pattern that will not be easy to fill.
>
> No university in America ever had three succeeding presidents that stood higher in their fields than these three men. So your responsibility is great—greater, perhaps, than if you were to become the president of almost any other university. It seems to us that you

3. My formal inauguration took place on December 1, 1938. For the text of my address, see Thomas D. Clark, *Indiana University: Midwestern Pioneer*, vol. 4, *Historical Documents Since 1816* (Bloomington: Indiana University, 1977), pp. 376–84.

have the qualifications to carry on the important functions of this office. You have youth, ambition, courage, ability, and intelligence of a high order, and with these qualities you cannot fail. You must, you will succeed.

The members of the Board have interviewed in the last year the leading educators of the country, from Maine to California, in an effort to find the very best man possible to be found to assume the leadership of this great University. We have interviewed a great many men who have been recommended to us, some of them repeatedly. We have made a study of their fitness, character, ability and qualifications. This election of yours did not come by default, but came as the result of an extensive study. After having examined all of these men from everywhere in the country, and after comparing their qualifications with yours, we were satisfied with your superiority. We have picked one of our own sons, a native Hoosier, in whom we place our trust and hopes.

I am sure that you will have the cooperation of the Board. I know you will have mine to the fullest extent in carrying on these responsibilities and upholding the University, and keeping it in that high place which it achieved under these three great men, and making it still an even greater University.

We pledge to you our entire support, feeble though it may be. I stand ready to do everything I can to help you succeed in this important position.

According to the minutes, I then replied as follows:

Judge and Members of the Board:

I deeply appreciate the compliment you have paid me. I think I am more impressed, however, by a realization of the responsibility of the position than by any other feeling. In fact, to be altogether frank, I feel wholly inadequate to undertake this important task. I told Dr. Bryan as much when I talked with him in my office this morning. He assured me, however, that he was frightened by the responsibility when he was called upon thirty-five years ago to accept the office. I hope the decision made here today will prove in the years to come to be at least in a small part as wise as was the decision made by that earlier Board. There is a great opportunity here. To meet it, I shall need your cooperation very much. I shall do my best—I shall give all my thought and energy to this work. And I pray that that will be enough.

When these formalities were over the trustees issued a statement as follows:

Herman B Wells is this day elected President of Indiana University.

With great expectations, we invite him to great responsibilities. His observed experience, practical wisdom, admirable temperament, and high ideals give conspicuous assurance of enduring achievement. With trust in him, we have confidence in the future.

Throughout the year, whenever the board members had spoken to me about a permanent appointment I had urged them not to consider it since I wished to return to the business school. However, I was persuaded finally to accept because it seemed to me further delay would be detrimental to the university. Dr. Bryan's resignation had been long contemplated. Then there had been great excitement over the selection of a new president, and the board members had interviewed many candidates, had themselves traveled extensively talking to people, all of which had given rise to many rumors, often disturbing the university morale. When the board came to the end of their list of candidates, unable to agree upon anyone outside, and turned to me, I realized that if I declined the board would have to start the whole selection process over again, a process that would have taken an indefinite number of months. It seemed to me that the welfare of the university demanded that the matter be settled without further delay. Of course, my friends rejoiced over the decision. I received a shower of well-wishing in flowers, telegrams, and letters, and there was a considerable amount of hubbub and excitement. (I am well aware that there was also skepticism about my selection on the part of some faculty, alumni, and other citizens of the state.) However, the minutes of the meeting indicate that, after the trustees had taken their action and issued their rather dramatic statement, we immediately sat down and started transacting business. We approved the minutes of the last board meeting and then moved to considering a lounge addition to the Union Building and such earthshaking matters as key and locker deposits, and diploma and Alumni Association fees. We also considered in that meeting investment recommendations, the possibility of building a golf course, real estate matters, the settlement of will cases, and many other items requisite but routine. The board had met at ten o'clock in the morning and by noon had not only elected the president but also had transacted its usual quota of items of business.

One event in the early summer of 1938 offered a great opportunity, but it was not one that a beginning president would have sought so early in his career. A special session of the legislature was called by the governor to consider a number of problems dealing with the recession. This seemed to President Edward Elliott of Purdue University and to me an opportune time to make a joint request for auditoriums, and with the consent of our boards we made such a request to the special session. After long and strenuous discussion that lasted for more than a month, finally in the very closing hours of the session we were successful in getting an appropriation for Indiana and Purdue each to build a long-needed auditorium. In addition the bill authorized us to accept P W A money that was available for that purpose and issue fee bonds (paid off by funds from student fees) for the remainder. The present magnificent Indiana University Auditorium came from that legislative session of the first summer. It was paid for by a $300,000 cash appropriation from the state legislature, $450,000 from P W A, and $350,000 from the bond issue. The funding enabled us to build one of the outstanding auditoriums in the country, noted from coast to coast as the home of many superior cultural attractions, and to provide the Little Theatre and classrooms for our Department of Speech and Theatre. It likewise, as is still the case, provided a home for the University Band.

In planning the building we decided to locate it as near as possible to what we envisioned as the future center of the campus—the place where an auditorium should be. We reserved in our own minds a space for a library nearby, now occupying that space. As a consequence of that planning, the Auditorium and the Library both are near the center of the greater university campus of today. At the time the Auditorium was built it was at the outer edge of the campus. We also at that time began dreaming of a fine arts center, which has been realized with the Fine Arts Building, the Lilly Library, and the Radio and Television building, and the complex will continue to develop with the new art museum now under construction. (See Appendix [C] for an early interview on the arts.) These buildings, grouped around the beautiful Showalter Fountain, are truly the aesthetic as well as the physical center of the greater campus.

Ironically during this first year we seem to have dealt with several matters that continued to reappear throughout the twenty-five years of my presidency. For instance, there was the omnipresent problem of budget. In addition we were concerned with the many administrative decisions that had to be made to install our retirement system, to provide for security in retirement, and, through the years, to continue to improve the staff and faculty benefits. The whole matter of faculty replacements was never far from our minds. During that first year the Sheppard Bill (see chapter 6), continued to be an active issue, and I made trips to Washington on its behalf. Building programs, expansion of the extension division, the development of a university radio system and securing an outlet for it through W I R E, a Purdue-Indiana joint curriculum in engineering and business that we adopted in the first year, the stimulation of our research, the improvement of our legislative relations and our public image, and concern for the aesthetic and physical quality of the campus—all required our careful attention.

Understandably, traditional procedures and organizational patterns that had grown inadequate or outmoded came under scrutiny with the beginning of the new administration. One of these was the College of Arts and Sciences, whose departments up to this time had dealt directly with the president's office, leaving the dean of the college and his staff with few functions and little or no opportunity for leadership. By the end of the year this pattern was to be changed, and Dean Stout accepted an expanded role as a true dean of a discrete college, comparable to the School of Business, School of Education, School of Law, and School of Medicine in organization and relationship with central administration.

Our regular staff in the president's office during the initial year of the acting presidency and the first few months of the presidency was quite small. If my memory is correct, it consisted in the beginning of only Ruth McNutt, who had been both executive and social secretary to President Bryan, and Mary Ellen Cook (Woods), who had been his secretary. I brought from the business school Bernita Gwaltney as an additional secretary. As I have noted, the volume of work during this year was enormous. I am still amazed that these three could have handled it and handled it excellently. That they did so is a tremendous tribute to their skill, dedication, and efficiency.[4]

Several members of the faculty and administrative staff gave willingly of their time to assist in every way possible. One of these was Ward Biddle, who of course had heavy responsibilities of his own as the university comptroller but who, in the role of wise and

4. Ruth Correll, who had worked in the University Archives for almost a decade, gave invaluable aid in supplying records and documents for our use.

indispensable counselor, readily helped tackle many presidential problems. The service of Edward E. Edwards was invaluable during this period. Although he was only in the second year of his appointment in the business school, he spent time as my administrative assistant in addition to carrying out his other duties. He worked without title but with his usual effectiveness.

Throughout this first year the Advisory Committee, consisting of Ward Biddle, Dean Payne, Dean Smith, and W. A. Alexander, members of the Self-Survey Committee, and I spent a major part of our time exploring our immediate financial problems to determine the most acute needs, where if possible we might alleviate them, and what could be eliminated to save money and increase efficiency. Near the end of the year, on Founders Day, May 4, 1938, I spoke to the Indianapolis Alumni Club and characterized the period as one of intense activity at the university, a period of experimentation, exploration, and self-analysis in an attempt to discover the raw materials of a worthy future program. It had been an exciting, exhilarating year. I explained that the exploration and the self-analysis were in the main centered in three major problems, problems as old as the university itself, yet ever new in an institution that is eager to go forward, that is sensitive to the impact of a dynamic world in which change and the necessity of adaptation to change are constant factors of existence. The three problems are personnel, the budget, and the reorganization of an academic and pedagogical administration.

I ended my remarks to the alumni with the following words, words that attempted to express the special nature of the first year and the enthusiasm that was present with the beginning of dreams for the future:

> Our problems are many and great, it is true. But they need not overwhelm us, for our resources are likewise great: a forward-looking Board of Trustees; a large, enthusiastic, vigorous group of alumni; an excellent faculty—sincere, loyal, distinguished; a student body composed of healthy, wholesome American youth second to none in the country. With the cooperation of these four groups, anything can be accomplished.
>
> In his classes, Dr. Weatherly frequently spoke of the efflorescent period that men and institutions sometimes enjoy. An efflorescent period—a period of glorious blossoming as a tribute to the intelligent husbandry of the past. The roots are strong and deep. The plant is

a sturdy perennial, its strength preserved by the judicious pruning of unhealthy and unnecessary branches. Surely we may look forward to the blossoming period with confidence and expectation.

Vignette of William Lowe Bryan

My predecessor as president of Indiana University was William Lowe Bryan, a Monroe County native and member of the class of 1884. His father was an itinerant preacher, but, from all accounts, his mother was the driving force in the family. The family occupied a small farm about two and one-half miles from the courthouse square. The farm was operated for the subsistence of the family. Dr. Bryan never forgot his farm upbringing and always enjoyed the vegetable garden in the rear of the President's House. Each year he personally oversaw the crop of fruits and vegetables that were canned, dried, or otherwise preserved or frozen. Although he had an epicure's delight in food, he also enjoyed simple food, the food of his boyhood. He once said to me that, after a big noon meal, he enjoyed having only a very light evening meal—especially mush and milk or cornbread and milk, two staples of a pioneer farm family.

Dr. Bryan was president of the university when I was an undergraduate. I did not know him personally then, but, as was the case with most students, I admired him from afar. I listened to his inspirational speeches and read his delightful columns in the *Daily Student* in which he discussed whatever was on his mind for the benefit of the students, faculty, and other readers of the paper. He was a masterful speaker. His delivery was deliberate, forceful, and effective. His word choices were beautiful and appropriate. With his ability to hold an audience he could make even the commonplace seem profound. His decision to become a scholar-teacher-administrator deprived the stage of a man who would have been a remarkable interpreter of Shakespeare and other classical dramatists.

Dr. Bryan was a man of more than average height with a face whose expressive features one did not forget. His physique was trim like an athlete's, bringing to mind his baseball prowess and I-Man award. Mother often spoke of the time when she and my father brought my grandmother to Bloomington for my Commencement in 1924. On a stroll through the campus before the ceremony, I suddenly saw Dr. Bryan and proudly drew their attention to the awesome figure: "Look! There's Prexy!" My grandmother turned too quickly and twisted her ankle painfully, a misfortune that later turned Dr. Woodburn's almost two-hour-long Commencement address (his swan song) into an ordeal as the ankle swelled and throbbed, to Mother's great concern.

During Dr. Bryan's active years, an occasional person belittled him as provincial. Nothing could have been further from the truth. He was a well-educated man, a master of his own fields of scholarship—psychology and philosophy—and also well versed in poetry and the great works of literature. His training was enhanced by study abroad, principally in psychology, under the tutelage of faculties at Berlin, Würzburg, and Paris. He read constantly and continued to grow intellectually throughout his lifetime. Of his early work in philosophy and psychology, David Starr Jordan said it was "the best I have ever seen done anywhere" and added that Dr. Bryan was "one of the most gifted teachers in the state."[5]

Because he held to a rigid moral code and believed fervently in his ideals of personal conduct, he appeared intolerant to some. However, he was not intolerant of others, at least not that I was able to observe. His lifestyle and my lifestyle were poles apart, and yet he was a warm, understanding, and sympathetic administrator during the days when I reported on the School of Business Administration to him as president, and that relationship was unchanging through the years in which he lived on the campus after his retirement. We had frequent and sometimes daily discussions of the issues and problems of the university, during which he would freely draw upon his background to make clear the reasons for the adoption of certain established policies, a practice which was extremely useful to me. The historian Thomas D. Clark calls him a Puritan. Perhaps Dr. Bryan's code of personal conduct was Puritan in some respects, but he did not eschew gracious living. A skillful host, he—and Mrs. Bryan when her health permitted—delighted to entertain. He gave attention to the minutest details of his luncheon or dinner parties, hoping to have them as nearly perfect as possible for the pleasure of his guests. For example, although he did not serve wine (it would have been unusual for a president of Indiana University to have done so in his day), Poland Springs or other bottled spring water was always provided for guests. The menu was excellent and the

5. Burton Dorr Myers, *History of Indiana University, 1902–1937*, vol. 2 (Bloomington: Indiana University, 1952), p. 483n.

cooking superb. He loved good beef, particularly porterhouse steaks, and he had an arrangement by which Charlie's Steakhouse in Indianapolis would sell him a number of porterhouse steaks from their cooler—steaks of top quality.

He adored his wife, Charlotte Lowe Bryan. She collaborated with him on his first book, *Plato the Teacher*. As she was in frail health much of their life together, he could use this as an acceptable excuse for not attending many of the multitudinous evening functions that characterize a campus community. Instead, with the gain of these precious hours, he would stay at home and read.

President Bryan had an unusual style of administration but an efficient one. Before going to his office in the morning, he did his reading or his writing in his study. Then by ten o'clock he was in his office, devoting the first hour to correspondence, telephone calls, and the minutia of administration. For the next hour he had appointments with members of the faculty and staff and with his administrative associates. While a dean I discovered that his appointments rarely lasted more than ten minutes and I therefore went to them well prepared. Also, it was the custom in those days to come to him with two matters in mind, one of which was unimportant and the other important. Shrewd administrators attempted to explore his mood in the opening minute of the conversation and, on the basis of that, to decide which matter to bring forth, the unimportant or the important one. After the presentation, Dr. Bryan would ask such questions as he wished, and, by the end of the ten minutes, he had given his decision from which, as the university was then organized, there was no appeal. I must add that so far as I was concerned the decisions were on the whole fair, wise, and appropriate.

I have never known a more efficient administrator than President Bryan. I admire enormously the fact that he could take care of the routine of the day in two hours of a morning. After lunch he returned to his study, remaining until four o'clock, when he went back to the president's office to sign the mail and handle any pressing items that had arisen since noon.

There are those who allege that he was an ineffective leader. With them I disagree. Had he done nothing but secure the medical school for Indiana University, a step necessary to make the institution a true university, he would have achieved more than most university presidents do during their tenures. Moreover, he was the architect of an academic framework so broad, comprehensive, and wise that for the whole twenty-five years of my administration, with rare exceptions, we found it quite adequate as a blueprint for the university's development; in fact, it took the entire twenty-five years to complete the structure President Bryan had charted.

I consider him one of the three greatest presidents of the university along with Wylie and Jordan. He was a man of extraordinarily high ideals—the only man his equal that I know was my own father—and Dr. Bryan was in many ways like a father to me. And so he, too, may have felt when he addressed me at my inaugural:

> President Wells: Thirty-six years ago you and I were beginners. I was beginning what was thought to be a difficult and sometimes dangerous enterprise. You were beginning what is known to be a more difficult and more dangerous enterprise. I began with very little experience and very little idea of what I should have to live through. At the same date you had no experience and no idea of what you would have to live through. I took my risk and somehow lived through it. You took your risk and here you are at thirty-six, eleventh president of Indiana University, and more than that, my son, a man.

I shall ever be grateful to William Lowe Bryan for his friendship, his sponsorship, and his aid.

Looking at the birdie, 1903.

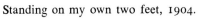

Standing on my own two feet, 1904.   Looking forward to my first day of school.

"Crawdad" hunting was great sport.

With Scottie, my first pet.

Summer companions at Grandfather Wells' farm—cousins Gene Revercomb and Wayne Gill.

The Jamestown Boys' Band. I'm third from the left in the middle row.

With Jamestown classmates in middies and suits. I'm
third from the right in the middle row.

Senior class picture at Lebanon High School.   My father, Granville Wells, about 1918.

Playing the baritone horn in the Indiana
University Band.

A trio of Sigma Nu bachelors.

As a graduate student at Indiana University,
1926–27.

With Sigma Nu brothers and our mascot, Thibideau.

With Father and Mother in front of our Lebanon house.

As field secretary of the Indiana Bankers
Association, 1929.

My old Packard Phaeton is the lead car in the Book Nook "Commencement"
procession in 1931, with Peter Costas (standing), Ward Biddle (holding
cigar), and Ray Thorpe.

In the dean's office, School of Business Administration, dictating to my secretary, Bernita Gwaltney.

The Presidency

⟦8⟧

○ ○ ○

A Few Observations on Collegial Administration

UNIVERSITIES tend to be structural enigmas to the general public and, surprisingly, to a not inconsiderable number of faculty members, students, and staff. Beyond the primary units of departments and schools, lines and areas of authority are familiar to junior and senior administrators, whose business it is to know them, but for others the locations of decision making are often unclear, and the organizational relationships among faculty, administration and governing board are obscure and without parallel in their experience. Since the nature of what is being administered is an essential background for understanding its administration, some comments on the anatomy of a university may be in order.

A university or college has a structural order all its own. That it is typically incorporated by legal charter in a given state does not mean that it has the structure of the typical business corporation. Quite the contrary is the case. A university is an association of professional scholars and learners; its organization and administration would be more nearly analogous to that of the professional association found in a large law firm or in a medical group practice than in the business corporation. For reasons founded in long experience and tradition, the right to hire and fire in a university is quite limited and circumscribed, subject to the direction of the professional staff and to the implementation, if approved, by the trustees. A university does not exist to make profit but rather to teach and to enhance scholarship and learning. A university, of course, is expected in this modern day to make the expertise of its faculty—when needed and when possible to do so—available to solve immediate, emerging problems of society, but problem solving for society is not the first priority of its existence. The university is therefore an organization designed to take the resources made available to it and, rather than hoard them, use them as effectively as possible for achieving its central purpose.

In a business corporation the administrator is almost solely responsible for the entrepreneurial function. That the academic administrator, whether he be head of a department, dean of a school, or president of a university, has some entrepreneurial responsibility none can deny; the welfare of a department or school in a university may be advanced by a carefully planned program of development utilizing the available resources of manpower and equipment. Planning and dreaming of future development are essential. However, in a university the entrepreneurial function is not exclusively the responsibility of the administrators. That responsibility is shared by each and every member of the staff, without exception; and since so many capable men and women must shoulder the load, the resultant program should be unusually effective.

An institution of the special nature or particularity of a university logically requires a type of administration adapted to its structure. In my experience—which incorporates experience as an administrator of business as well as of a university—the role of the university administrator bears no resemblance to that of a corporate head. Therefore a quite different set of general principles should guide the day-to-day function of the academic administrator and should create the state of mind with which he approaches his work. I would emphasize, however, that while the principles remain the same they must be interpreted in different eras through the personalities involved and the society in which the university functions. No two administrations can be alike because of these differing circumstances. I can illustrate this point with a bit of background information about President Bryan's administration, mine, and then the present one.

My predecessor spent his life as an administrator in a university that was growing, and growing rapidly, but that was still much smaller during most of his period than the university I inherited. In his case, as in every case, the administrative responsibilities were distributed, not so much according to some magic in an organizational chart, but according to the talents of the people who were part of the general administration. John W. Cravens, whose titles under President Bryan were secretary of the university, secretary of the trustees, and registrar, would have been labeled in a modern-day organizational chart an executive vice president. U. H. Smith, the bursar, was also charged with maintaining administrative liaison with the university units in Indianapolis and with the Indianapolis business community. Ruth McNutt, the president's executive secretary, performed many functions beyond those typically associated with that position simply because of her vast experience and great capacities. The librarian, William A. Alexander, possessed talents and interests that involved him in public relations and fund raising for much of this period. Frank Elliott, head of the News Bureau, performed many public-relations functions that would now be assigned to a public-relations vice president.

President Bryan had as a central objective the creation of a true university structure. That meant, in the first instance, making sure that Indiana University had the medical school and the other medical sciences in its orbit.[1] It meant also creating a number of professional schools such as Commerce and Finance, Education, and Music. Dr. Bryan felt that the university had been, prior to his inauguration, for the most part a large teacher's college with most of the emphasis and energies of the university directed toward the production of teachers, a worthwhile purpose but still a limited one and one that could not meet the needs of the burgeoning economic and industrial expansion of the state in the first third of the century. So he undertook to create the new professional schools that would provide the skeletal structure of a university.

When I came to the presidency I inherited that skeleton, a sound skeleton, and during most of my administration our central purpose was to grow in strength and depth rather than in breadth. We resisted the creation of any new professional schools that were foreign to our nature such as engineering and agriculture although we could have justified these additions. In fact, engineering schools are in all separated state universities in the United States other than ours,[2] but we thought that this was Purdue's field and that Purdue should develop it. The only professional additions during my period were

1. See Thomas D. Clark, *Indiana University: Midwestern Pioneer*, vol. 2, *In Mid-Passage* (Bloomington: Indiana University Press, 1973), chapter 4, for the crucial significance of gaining the medical school.

2. A separated state university is one that is separate from the land-grant institution in a state. The Morrill Act of 1862 made provision for federal subsidies to state universities offering programs in engineering and the mechanical arts. Purdue is Indiana's land-grant institution. In some states, such as Wisconsin and Minnesota, the two types of schools are combined into one.

the Optometry Division, which fitted in with the health-science rubric, and the School of Health, Physical Education, and Recreation, which had become so large an appendage to the School of Education that, for administrative reasons, it seemed wise to spin it off into a separate administrative unit. Persons interested in that profession and the School of Education faculty agreed to the change. We availed ourselves of the opportunity to take into the university family the Normal College of the American Gymnastic Union in Indianapolis, which had to find an accredited university affiliation in order to survive and to carry on its valuable work. One further change in our structure originated from the law school, our oldest professional school. A proprietary institution in Indianapolis, named the Indiana Law School, had violated American Bar Association (A B A) standards and was in danger of losing its approved status. Its graduates would then have been ineligible to take the state bar exams. Representatives of the A B A approached the dean of our law school, Bernard Gavit, about the possibility of having an evening law school in Indianapolis. By agreement of the parties concerned, we acquired the Indiana Law School and made of it an evening school of high quality, linked to the law school in Bloomington but geared to part-time students. Dean Gavit's sure and judicious leadership was a significant factor in bringing this about.

Another underlying condition that had an important effect upon my administration was the rapidly growing economy and the steadily advancing industrialization of the state. These lent urgency to the need for research. Thus when federal funds for research and graduate studies became available, we were in an advantageous position to make use of the funds because of the state's research needs and because of the university structure that we had inherited. Burgeoning university enrollments nationwide forced an increase in graduate studies as the demand for scholars grew. These two influences upon the graduate area—research, which required research assistants, and a greatly enlarged undergraduate population, which required teaching assistants—accelerated the development of Indiana University's graduate school.

The present administration has to work in an entirely different setting. In the first place, the university has grown enormously in size. The regional campuses have come of age and the university has become a multicampus institution in the truest sense, whereas during my time the regional centers were small, effective units within a community and, at their stage of development then, could be administered from the center. Now an entirely new kind of organization is necessary, one that President John Ryan has brilliantly achieved. Moreover, in recent years, the state's continued growth in population, industrialization, and political complexity has placed new demands upon the university. But the most overwhelming and the most striking of all of these changes with which the present administration must labor is the great proliferation of federal and state legislation affecting universities, which restricts the flexibility of administrators. The restrictions make it impossible for them to take initiatives and seize opportunities as we were able to do. Also, the horrendous growth of both state and federal regulations circumscribes nearly every activity of the university—certainly every activity having to do with personnel and financial administration. Now, with the creation of the Indiana Higher Education Commission, even the introduction of new courses in long-established fields or the dropping of old ones is controlled. Moreover, social forces have had profound influence on the curriculum. For example, the women's movement has led to a program in women's studies; the heightened sensitivity to the special needs of minorities has caused the introduction of Afro-American studies and Chicano-Riqueño studies; and the demand for better health care has placed enormous pressure upon the medical sciences to offer new specialities.

These random illustrations of the way in which administrations are subject to the conditions prevailing in their times are intended mainly as a caveat to precede my observations about administration generally: First, in a university organization the simpler the administrative structure the better. One might express this principle in Jeffersonian terms as the least administration is the best. I do not mean to imply, however, that the small, everyday housekeeping problems of operating an institution should not be well and efficiently discharged by administrative officers. Inability to take care of the details of the organization creates many irritations, and faculty and students have every right to be freed of those by the efficient working of the administrative staff.

Second, academic administrators need to try to cultivate the ability to lead rather than command. The house of intellect is by nature averse to orders. Besides, one cannot command spirit, cannot command learning, cannot command an atmosphere; but one can, with the proper leadership, contribute to the nurture of all of these. The corollary of this principle is a point that bears repetition: administration is not an end unto itself. Administrators should remind themselves that it takes no genius to increase overhead, and in general the simpler their machinery—the more informal, more decentralized it can be—the better.

The most important element in the effective operation of a university is the spirit present in the academic community. In this peculiar kind of organization, the spirit of a place becomes the principal motivator to effective action, and therefore administrators, it seems to me, need to pay greater attention to spirit than to statistics. With the right spirit, the right atmosphere, the right ambience, nearly all things become possible in the learning process, which is the central purpose of a university. The administration should be a source of information and expedition, not a bottleneck. One of the most important contributions administration can make to the spirit of an institution is to be receptive rather than negative toward suggestions and ideas, habitually to seek how something can be done when nobody else can see a way to do it.

A university president never has all the talents required to deal with his many and varied duties as the leader of an important university faculty. Therefore, he must seek to have around him administrative aides of the highest competence, all of whom, if possible, complement his qualities. In fact, I made it a rule throughout my tenure always to try to attract to the central administration of the university men who I felt had talents superior to mine. That seems to me to be almost a cardinal principle of a good administrator—to recruit people as strong or stronger than himself whenever possible. In any large university, the office of the president becomes in miniature something like the office of the president of the United States; that is, it is not a one-man office: it is two, three, four, or five men—depending on the presence of first-rate men, all of whom have certain responsibilities—working together to discharge the duties of the office.

To accomplish all that was necessary, we found personalities as time went on who could be a part of the presidential team, and their responsibilities were in large part determined by their own abilities. Although they did, generally speaking, carry the title of vice president, not always did the title correctly and fully describe each officer's functions. We simply tried a pragmatic type of organization, to put the people who could do the particular jobs that needed to be done in the places to do them. This proved to be successful for that period and enabled us to meet our central objective. An example may serve to illustrate, as follows.

One of our very important goals early in my tenure was to bring about a more adequate funding of the university. To do so, we needed to gain parity with Purdue and to arrive at a cooperative arrangement with Purdue and the other two state schools for the presentation of the budget to the Indiana General Assembly. The man who took a leading part in many of these negotiations was Vice President Wendell Wright, whose official responsibilities did not include anything remotely related to these budgetary problems, but it turned out that he had a great facility for working with those intermural negotiations. Joseph Franklin, assisted by his staff, was an indispensable counselor and aide in this effort also. The team that we assembled and their relationships with each other worked well for our time.

If one subscribes to this view of the presidency, that is, the presidency being a group responsibility of a number of compatible but complementary personalities, it follows logically that the president must have the right to select his own aides. If he is to be held responsible by the faculty, students, and trustees for the discharge of the work of the president's office, he must be allowed to surround himself with the kinds of people who can interact best with him and each other and who can form together the most effective and efficient team. In building such a staff the president, if he is worthy of the office, will take into account not only the personal qualities of the individuals but also their sensitivity to and their knowledge of the significant aspects of the life of the university. A similar principle applies to the dean of a large college or school who is selecting his aides. If he is to be held responsible for the duties assigned to him by the faculty and trustees, he should not be handed an excuse for poor performance by reason of having had to work with people whom he had no part in selecting.

Inevitably, an administrator who serves any length of time gains some wisdom about the ways and means of successful operation. Certain of these observations may seem obvious but others, perhaps, are less apparent. The timing in making administrative decisions is all-important; where the problems are difficult and the decisions are controversial, timing is incredibly important. A decision announced at the wrong time can create a disturbance that is unnecessary and that far exceeds in intensity the essence of the issue. On the other hand, the same decision, if reported at a different period, even though equally explosive or difficult in terms of consequences, would hardly cause a ripple. By timing I mean not only calendar but also the general state of mind in the academic community. It is a subtle, intangible kind of judgment that has to be made, but little else is quite so crucial as the timing of announcing controversial decisions. Moreover the terms in which the decisions are expressed are extremely important. The use of unnecessarily abrasive or inflammatory phrases or words can cause a great deal of trouble, generate a lot of heat and no light, and be a handicap to progress or to the solution of difficult problems. In fact, timing and the method, place, and manner of expression of a decision are all part of the same technique.

In my own experience I frequently tested an idea for reactions. When I discovered the reaction would be unfavorable, I dropped the proposal for the moment; yet, if I thought the proposal or idea was important, I simply put it "on the shelf" for the time being and waited for a propitious opportunity to present it. Over a period of weeks, months, or years those opportunities would arise, and when they arose the idea's time had come and instead of being resisted it was accepted graciously and enthusiastically. Had one pushed them originally by sheer strength or pressure, they might have been accepted, but there would always have been attached to them a certain stigma that would have handicapped their effectiveness. With a little patience and time, the idea could be brought forward without risking that handicap.

One of the best ways administrators can contribute to the atmosphere or the spirit of a university community is to dedicate themselves to the never-ending search for talented faculty members and to their retention. This means that the administrator must support the work of a talented man in both word and deed and, where necessary, with financing and equipment. He must, whenever possible, help a talented man achieve his academic goals insofar as administrative machinery can accomplish that. The university will be the better for having abetted the scholar's success.

A university can have no greater asset than talented persons who can find in the institution a congenial place in which to realize their own scholarly and personal goals. Even though there may be opportunities to carry on elsewhere—and in most instances there are several such opportunities—they resist them all and spend their lifetimes here. I like to believe that in most instances talented men who do this achieve more than it would be possible for them to do if they spent a good deal of their time and their energies moving around and restarting again and again. Also, I am certain that not only their own rich achievement, which reflects credit upon the university, but in addition their own continued residence here, which leads them to have an understanding of, a true comprehension of, the university's strengths and weaknesses and manner of functioning, makes them invaluable colleagues in interpreting those factors of the university to incoming faculty members. It also enables them to give students a better sense of the resources of the university and allows them to share their own devotion and understanding of the institution with students who become therefore much more loyal alumni once they go out from the university. Distinguished men who spend long years here become valuable sources of wisdom, counsel, and guidance also for the general administrative officers—for deans, for department heads, and for others who bear responsibility for making administrative decisions.

The administrator should ever be alert to recognize achievement on the part of his colleagues and to express appreciation to them personally and on behalf of the institution. When a good man is threatened by circumstances beyond his control, the administrator should go out of his way to help. I am reminded of an instance that took place many years ago when Herman Muller, the great geneticist and Nobel Laureate on the Indiana University faculty, was summoned by the House Un-American Activities Committee, a notorious, red-baiting congressional committee. Once upon a time Dr. Muller had headed a research team in a laboratory of the National Academy of Sciences of the U.S.S.R., but he left Russia because of the persecution of scientists and the distortion of genetics by the Soviet government. Although he thereby became an enemy of the Russians, he was nonetheless considered by some anti-Russians in America to be far-left-wing. Dr. Muller was less perturbed by the summons than was his family, whom it filled with fear. But when he came to my house to inform me, he seemed nervous and agitated, and I quickly assured him that he would have the full backing of the university. We asked the university's Washington lawyer, Douglas Whitlock, who had many congressional contacts, to make himself available to Dr. Muller before the questioning. There was, however, really insufficient time for Dr. Muller to seek much help if he had wished it because he had a speaking engagement in Boston just before the hearing—a speech about the suppression of science in Russia. However, Dr. Muller made a brilliant appearance before the committee and created such a favorable impression that they complimented him on his views. He returned home in triumph and, I am certain, grateful for the fact that he had carried with him to Washington the full backing of his university.

Instances of this sort, usually less major and dramatic, occur frequently in the day-by-day work of the university. In my judgment they present to the administrator an opportunity that should not be overlooked to demonstrate to the members of the faculty that the university administrative structure truly believes in the supreme importance of academic freedom and values top scholars over all else.

One of the great joys of life in a university community is the presence of many strong personalities, and these can be extraordinarily varied and can exhibit many eccentricities. An early university mentor of mine, U. G. Weatherly, always alleged that a university faculty needed to have a rich ingredient of faculty eccentricity—the more the better—as only thus did one have the color and excitement of really extreme points of view and attitudes. There are likely to be many people with unusual behavior in any large faculty—eccentric by ordinary standards—simply because the man who prepares for the life of scholarship and teaching is by the very nature of his vocation a person who likes independence of thought and action. He is the very antithesis of the organization man, the conventional man, the Madison Avenue type, the gray-flannel-suit kind of person, and he exhibits this difference frequently by his informal style of dress, his individuality, his behavior in many respects. I believe that an administrator should not only tolerate this idiosyncrasy but accept it and rejoice in it. He must never let a man's personal quirks obscure his true worth, scholarly distinction, or the contribution he may make to the collegial life of the academic community.

A great faculty is never homogenized nor does it have the characteristics of the organizational stamp. A faculty is an aggregation of individualists and should be accepted as such, and that individualism should be utilized to the nth degree insofar as it is possible for the administration to do so in achieving the university's ends.

The university as an institution should stand for and in support of all that is best about which men have written and thought and produced in times past in philosophy and literature, and in art, music, and science. The university should be an upholder of the best of its inheritance and in so doing should serve to inspire such standards of thought and conduct. But the past should not be used as an excuse to inhibit the development of new ideas, new ways of thinking, and new ways of expressing artistic and aesthetic values in current society. The members of the university community must exemplify these values. Therefore, the quality of their lifestyles, of their basic integrity, of their commitment to the truth even when it is unpopular and to ideals of scholarship is of paramount importance. They are ideally a community that is humane and is concerned with every segment of society, that believes in the dignity and the worth of every individual and is concerned with the quality of the community, its environment, its health, its hospitality to talent and its opportunity for aesthetic development. These ideals should not be espoused as dogma but rather in terms of the commitment and belief of the officers and particularly of the faculty who come in regular contact with students. History is filled with illustrations of how great teachers have touched the lives of talented students who in turn have made remarkable contributions to society through a new philosophy, a new insight, or enlightened standards.

Certain other things may be done to contribute to making the university community a good place in which to work, learn, and discover new truth. In a small community an effort needs to be made to provide those cultural facilities that would be automatically available in a large city, namely, first-class art exhibits, music, and theater, stimulating outside speakers, and similar cultural events. In a university that has a fine arts department, a theater department, and a music school, these can all, of course, be an extension and a part of the academic program. At Indiana University we have superb music, excellent theater, and an increasingly exciting program in the visual arts available for our people, so much so that we really need not go elsewhere to receive the aesthetic and intellectual stimulation that such art forms offer.

Of course, an excellent library is of preeminent importance for scholars in most fields, and the additional boon of a rare-books library can stimulate an intellectual excitement on the campus.

A pleasant and attractive campus providing physical beauty which soothes the spirit is desirable and, of course, good working facilities in offices and laboratories are an important requisite. In a rapidly growing institution it is nearly impossible to keep up with the demand for academic space but when the members of the faculty believe that an effort is being made to provide facilities as rapidly as possible, they are less frustrated by inconveniences and imperfections and less likely to let that factor harm the spirit of the institution.

All of these measures are helpful but, to repeat, it seems to me that the first task of the academic administrator is to try to attract and hold the most talented faculty members, encourage them, support them, and then get out of their way and let them go wherever their talent and energy lead them.

Whereas talented faculty members have a right to be relieved of routine problems of housekeeping, as I have mentioned, there must be at the same time an opportunity for them and their colleagues to have a voice in all major policy decisions. Such an input is requisite for the formulation of sound policy and is essential for the maintenance of the esprit de corps of the enterprise.

The spirit of community is further fostered by continued respect for and acknowledgment of the presence of the retired members of the faculty and the contributions it is possible for them to make, not only as functioning scholars, but also in the providing of experience and perspective based upon their lives at the university. It seems to me that an institution is penny wise and pound foolish to discard the rich resource that is the retired faculty. Every effort should be made to give retired faculty members the space in which to work so long as they wish it, to find some funds if needed to assist their research, and to continue to involve them in the university committees that should have the benefit of their backgrounds. In addition, other types of recognition should be given them—in general, efforts to mute the distinction between active and retired members other than the fact that the retiree is no longer engaged in formal teaching. Not all faculty members will wish to have full participation, but all those who do should have that opportunity, and they will, out of their sense of well-being and gratitude, radiate to the younger members of the faculty the assurance that their institution is one that puts the highest premium upon the faculty contribution and does not mean merely to use the man and woman and discard them when they are past some fixed retirement age.

A happy university faculty and a happy university community depend in no small measure upon the activities of the spouses of the members of the faculty. One of the joys of the university community is the social intercourse that is provided by informal dinner parties among members of the faculty. The dinners bring relief and relaxation from the tension of work and enable the members of the faculty to come to know each other in some depth, to learn in a relaxed setting more of each other's activities and departmental interests, and promote thereby a commonality of goals and ambitions for the total institution that is of utmost importance. An administrator needs to be mindful of the role that the faculty wives play in promoting the general spirit of the institution, to show an appreciation of their role, and, wherever possible, to provide facilities for their own group activities through which they may share especially their interests, problems, frustrations, and triumphs.

Campus spirit is, of course, dependent in no small measure upon the reaction of students to their environment including their teachers, their library, and the cultural and recreational opportunities available to them. Thus, by and large, a sufficiently strong and stimulating faculty can inspire even the most phlegmatic student. Since students learn from each other, I have always believed that group housing, whether it be a university dormitory or a student-organization house, can contribute to their learning. I must admit, however, that the potentialities of group living are seldom even barely realized, and there is a tendency on the part of the administrative hierarchy to think of the campus living units as mere feeding and sleeping stations. If this is all they are to be, the university should not be burdened with them; they should be eliminated and the students should be allowed to find their own group associations whenever and wherever they can. Every effort should be made to involve student living units in academic activities even to the extent of having classes held in those buildings.

It seems to me, moreover, that administrative leadership needs to address itself regularly, year after year, to pointing out to unsophisticated and inexperienced students that they have the richest possible opportunity to savor the academic life, more than they are ever likely to have again. Learning is a lifelong process, but on a campus they can concentrate on learning with unparalleled resources of library, faculty, interpreters, tutors, and associates of different backgrounds and experience, and with exceptional access to the arts. All these in the well-regulated and typical great university are more readily and easily available to the students than will ever again be true for them. And so their first and foremost effort should be to plunge into the life of the intellect and of the spirit, to take advantage of the many opportunities at hand. Administrative leadership, itself aware and appreciative of those opportunities, can help to make them clear to the students.

Students are human beings and they like to be recognized as human beings. Therefore it is highly desirable for the general administrative officers to make themselves available to students whenever and wherever possible, not simply as a ritual, but as a means to learn their concerns and ambitions, their views of the institution, and the character of the particular student generation. I do not except the student dissident or adversary. He is usually ill-informed; his challenge presents an opportunity to the administrator to educate him. I discuss student relationships at some length in a later section.

One of the rich opportunities available to students in an institution like Indiana University is the great diversity to be found in the student body: cultural diversity, diversity of economic backgrounds, religious diversity, and so on. Moreover, we have been fortunate through the years also to have on our campus the rich resource of many students from overseas representing the widest variety of religious, political, and geographical backgrounds; for the most part they have entered well into the life of the campus community. Thus any student in the university, regardless of how small or provincial the town from which the student came, can become acquainted with students from various places throughout the world, and through their eyes and through their minds come to gain a new appreciation and new understanding of the world in which we live.

In the first fifty years of this century the American university became tremendously involved in what is typically known as "in loco parentis"—that is, standing in the place of the parent—while the student is at the institution. I believe our institutions went too far in this respect. Perhaps the happiest relationship is the one that existed when I first came to Indiana University: a student signed up, with any luck, for the right courses and did his classwork; if he did not, he was out. In the best of all possible worlds student regulations would consist only of those that David Starr Jordan issued when he was president of Indiana University. He is alleged to have done away with all student rules except two: students were not permitted to shoot the faculty or to burn any buildings. Beyond that they were to find an outlet for their energies as best they could, but especially in the classroom and the laboratory, and to learn from experience about the hard realities of getting along with their colleagues.

Members of the nonacademic staff are important contributors or detractors, as the case may be, to the spirit of the community, and efforts should be made to attract and hold people who plan careers in which they can take pride as supporting staff members, including the secretaries, the laboratory assistants, and those who tend the grounds and the physical plant. One of the great figures at Indiana University for many years was William R. Ogg, who loved the flora and fauna of the campus and continually watched over their development. As a result he earned the respect of the entire community. His own children went on to distinction in academic fields: his daughter was a successful public schoolteacher, and his son became a nationally known scholar and professor of political science at the University of Wisconsin. But their father's contribution to the creation of a beautiful campus, and hence to an inspiring setting for scholarly work, was an achievement as worthy as their own. One could cite other illustrations of staff members who became nearly indispensable to the life of the university and its smooth functioning simply because they knew their jobs and were proud of them and thereby won for themselves positions of recognition, dignity, and appreciation. There should be an appropriate kind of respect between the academic and nonacademic members of the staff. The nonacademic members rely for a livelihood on an institution in which academic members are essential, and the academic members' work is dependent in no small measure upon the work of the supporting staff. Throughout the administration, throughout faculty ranks, throughout the staff, there should be proper concern for each other's welfare and for the total goals of the university.

Members of the nonacademic staff have a rich opportunity to influence and encourage students. A cheery greeting or helpful information given by the front office is a great booster to student morale. An encouraging word from a dormitory maid or cook has helped many a homesick freshman to overcome his depression. Recently I was on a cruise ship that had a courteous, skillful, and cheerful crew from the captain to the room stewards; it was a happy ship radiating a sense of well-being that enhanced the enjoyment of every passenger. A similar atmosphere is needed in a university. The junior administrative and secretarial staffs and receptionists can play an indispensable role in making the university operate as a happy ship radiating a sense of respect and belief in the academic enterprise.

The president must find some time to devote to alumni affairs. The alumni have a right to expect him to assist in their organizational activities and to report to them on the state of the university. In turn, through the alumni machinery or from individual alumni, he can receive valuable comment and criticism about the operation of the university. As a group, alumni are the people in the body politic of the state who would normally be expected to have the greatest interest, an informed interest, in the welfare of the university and be able to serve the university as good interpreters of the state's needs. They would have knowledge of the university's capabilities or lack of capabilities, so the university president must find some time for them. Because their achievements represent the fruits of the university's efforts in teaching and learning, the quality of their careers is of utmost importance to the university's standing and claim upon society for continued support.

The president must find some time also for the various publics that constitute the normal university constituency, such as the teaching profession, the legal profession, the medical profession, the organized business community as represented by the Chambers of Commerce and the Manufacturers Associations. He must find time for the farmers, as expressed through their organized farm organizations, and, in our industrial society, for the labor unions as they represent the aspirations and needs of the industrial worker. All these groups have legitimate claims on the president's attention and contribute to the exacting, demanding, and time-consuming nature of successful job performance on his part.

The preceding pages constitute a personal statement that represents my own view of what I have found by experience to be successful. Not always, perhaps, did I live up to these principles in their entirety but I can truthfully say that I fully believe they are essential for a happy and productive career as an academic administrator. I have tried to write about the role of administration as I interpreted it in my years in the presidency from 1937 to 1962. If I were to become president again, I would still try to adhere as closely as possible to these principles, priorities, and practices. So far as Indiana University is concerned, the role of administration has since then been greatly modified and complicated by the vast proliferation of government regulations, federal and state. These, of necessity, have increased the size of the administrative staff. In fact, they have made an extraordinary increase almost mandatory, and the cost of meeting all of these state and federal regulations is a considerable portion of the rapidly increasing costs of higher education.

Indiana University, now that it has become truly a multicampus institution, requires a whole variety of new administrative techniques and procedures. To cite a simple example, if the president wishes to speak to all of the university's faculty and students simultaneously, there is no way for him to do so except by television or radio. Another modifying factor in the practice of administration in this institution arises from the more frequent sessions of the legislature. The Indiana General Assembly now has an annual meeting, and at least every other one of these extends over a longer period than was the case in my day. As a result, the general administrative officers of the university have little time between sessions of the General Assembly to concentrate on academic matters. Instead, they must always be adapting to the changes made necessary by legislative action at the conclusion of one session while preparing their presentations to the next sessions. The situation is further complicated by the fact that we now have an Indiana Higher Education Commission, which is given great power and authority to coordinate the work of the state institutions. This development has meant in practice that budget presentations particularly have to be prepared far in advance and be given hearings in the Higher Education Commission and the Budget Committee of the General Assembly before the all-important hearing in the General Assembly.

I served as president of the university for a quarter of a century in part because I believed that frequent changes in the top leadership of an institution typically were disruptive and detrimental to the realization of long-range goals. I hope my judgment was correct at that time in the life of the institution. The history of American higher education will probably substantiate my opinion that the American system of extended tenure for the president and his colleagues is more appropriate to our nation's institutions than the European system of two- to four-year terms for top administrators would be.

Holding to this belief in the value of long-term tenures for top administrative officers, I have generally felt that a president is obligated to serve a substantial period of time even at the loss of what he might consider other, better personal opportunities. But I realize that there are circumstances in which a change of leadership, even after a short incumbency, would be beneficial, and so the time, the place, and the type of institution are the determining factors.

During my administration I refrained from accepting board directorships in reputable corporations that occupied a competitive position. I would have liked very much to have accepted some of the offers I received because I would have found the experience interesting. I refused such invitations for two reasons: one, a competitive company of any size would have Indiana University alumni in other companies competing with it, and it seemed unfair for me, in my position, to favor one over the other; two, I felt that the university was paying me adequately for my services and that therefore I owed the university all of my time with the exception of the time every citizen in academic work or any other owes to community services—those community tasks that have to be performed in the field of education in the local communities, in the state, and in the nation. These are typically volunteer, nonsalaried responsibilities. I did accept membership on one important board, however, that of the Indiana Bell Telephone Company. In the first place it was noncompetitive and in the second place in that position I would be representing one of Indiana Bell's largest customers. I consider this an enlightened kind of consumer policy established long before such policies were being advocated by organized consumer groups.

I tried to speak only where I thought it would be to the benefit of the university regardless of the size of the fee offered. It was my practice never to accept a fee for speaking to any organization in the state. In a few instances where other universities insisted that I accept a fee, I gave the fee back to them to use for scholarship purposes. I likewise made a practice of giving to the university any honorarium that I was paid for an out-of-state speaking engagement because I felt that I was using university time for the speech. Fellow university presidents for whom I have the highest regard followed different policies. For example, some of them accepted membership on boards of large, national corporations; they did so not only for their personal interest but possibly because they felt that the prestige of such a position would reflect favorably on their own institution. I have no doubt that in most instances they were correct in their judgments. I therefore feel that my policies were appropriate to Indiana University and to my own style of operation and do not necessarily represent guiding principles for others in other times, here or elsewhere.

Finally, after I had served for a good many years in the presidency and had gained a host of friends throughout the state, political leaders tried to interest me in running for high political office —for governor or senator. A particularly strong appeal was made to me at the time I stepped out of the presidency after twenty-five years during which, I suppose, my name had become something of a household word. I refused all such invitations because I thought it would be improper and unfair to the university constituency for me to use this widespread voter recognition for the benefit of either political party. Particularly I felt that it would inevitably, in this state, give a partisan political tinge to the university that would be detrimental to its welfare. I also felt that I would be using the prestige that the university had given me for my own career.

My attitude and policies are not universally applicable. I can think of many instances where the willingness of a university president to stand for high political office was good for the institution and for the country. Frank Graham served in the U.S. Senate and the United Nations brilliantly after he left the presidency of the University of North Carolina. William Fulbright was an excellent president of the University of Arkansas, but I think any observer would agree that his willingness to serve in the U.S. Senate was a great public service. No one would maintain that Princeton was injured by Woodrow Wilson's political activities, I believe, or that Columbia was made less by the successful candidacy of General Eisenhower or by his final great service to his country as president of the United States. So, here again, the type of institution, the period, and the special circumstances in each instance have to be the governing factors.

On Being Peripatetic and Present at the Same Time

Early in my career, in some mysterious fashion, I seemed to have a total vision of what I hoped the university could become in my time. With this to guide me, *all* my activities were undertaken with the thought and expectation that they would be of benefit to the institution as it moved toward what I believed to be its manifest goals.

My whole being was concentrated in this work; yet, like any great opportunity, it was so challenging that extraordinary effort was not only possible but exhilarating. The refreshment received in turning from project to project dispelled the tedium. For that reason I did not require the usual forms of regenerative recreation. I could devote myself completely to the effort because I had no family obligations to discharge. Moreover, I could carry on these many outside activities without impeding the day-by-day decision-making process for the university because I had remarkable backup from my central administrative colleagues. The support team operated without personal jealousy or jockeying for individual advantage. Our decisions were made collectively and their execution was assigned to one or another of the group. My colleagues knew what their individual responsibilities were. More important, they knew they would be supported in their decisions and therefore could function freely in my absence. The president's office in this way was never vacant; there were always people present to make necessary decisions. Even with the backup of my colleagues, I tried to keep in daily telephone contact with my office when I was away. Detailed itineraries and schedules for all my trips were also part of the machinery to maintain constant contact. If I had to change plans during the trip for any reason, I notified my staff immediately and indicated where I could be reached under the new arrangement. Then, upon my return, I shared with the group what I had learned that was of interest to the university. Some of my colleagues were also active in national and international affairs and brought back the fruit of their contacts to share with us. Naturally, from time to time I was privy to decisions of concern to us being made by associations or by government agencies in Washington and we were thus enabled to seize opportunities as they arose.

In addition to having a strong support team with authority to make decisions and an effective communications system when I was away, I was facilitated in carrying on a number of activities simultaneously by careful planning and budgeting of time. The result was a compact, multipurpose schedule. As many tasks as feasible were accomplished on each trip, thereby saving a substantial amount of time and energy. Usually I carried routine mail and other materials with me and attended to them in the course of travel. In like manner, I tried to see faculty members with whom I needed to make contact either at committee meetings or at social gatherings in order to save their time and mine. The piggybacking of tasks and contacts is a useful, efficient device. I also attempted to budget both short-range and long-range periods for specific important tasks and to deal with them if possible in the time span allotted. Of course, I was not always able to meet such deadlines, but setting them helped to impose a discipline on my use of time.

On Coordination and Cooperation

It is incumbent upon the university not only to husband its own resources, but also to participate in any plan which would husband the total resources for higher education in Indiana. State and regional coordination and cooperation of effort have been much discussed by educational leaders recently, both in this state and elsewhere. The opportunity for the successful development of a program of this nature is excellent here because there has long existed the friendliest spirit among all of our institutions, both public and private. Distances are not great, and communication and transportation facilities are unexcelled. It seems to me, therefore, that there is no reason why the institutions in this state might not assume a position of national leadership in developing cooperatively a plan for higher education which would ensure the elimination of unnecessary overlapping and duplication and allow each institution to draw upon the specialized facilities of the others. More important, the successful operation of the plan would mobilize the resources for higher education, and in so doing would provide the maximum benefit for our youth and for society. In the development of such a plan, Indiana University should be ready to make any necessary adjustments in its own program, deterred neither by tradition nor by institutional pride.

H. B Wells, Inaugural Address, December 1, 1938

Consistent with this statement of policy, throughout my years of responsibility for administration I have been motivated by a strong belief that the resources of higher education are so insufficient and the opportunities and responsibilities so vast, the only sensible course is to attempt in every way to avoid unnecessary duplication among or within institutions. Several examples of this practice, some also cited elsewhere, follow.

When I was dean of our business school, Dean A. A. Potter of Purdue and I tried to work out a coordination of curriculum in the offering of business and engineering between the School of Engineering at Purdue and the School of Business at Indiana. While the attempt was unsuccessful, it was nevertheless an early illustration of my belief.

The Indiana Conference on Higher Education, which Indiana University helped found in 1944, had for its first objective the utilization of all collegiate resources in the state to ensure that returning Hoosier veterans who qualified would have an opportunity to go to college at the conclusion of World War II. Through the years the conference has attempted to stimulate coordination and cooperation and avoid proliferation and duplication wherever possible.

The cooperative budget and allocation of areas of responsibility among the four state institutions (described in chapter 10) is another example. Of course, we at Indiana University had as a primary objective in this effort breaking the straitjacket of parity that had been so disastrous for our institution, but breaking parity was important also for the other state institutions if they were to follow their natural lines of development. The parity could not be arrived at in any sensible way without delineating individual areas of responsibility and respecting that delineation in the policies of the four state institutions. In my judgment this arrangement has served all four fairly well.

Further, in our regional campus policy through the years we sought to avoid a proliferation of new units, taking into account the offerings of the private colleges in the state and the branches of the other state institutions. Two ventures in coordination on the regional basis resulted in the Midwest Inter-Library Center (now the Center for Research Libraries) and the Committee on Institutional Cooperation.

Early in my administration, the Council of Ten, an organization of the Big Ten university presidents, began to consider the possibility of creating a midwest center for the storage of little-used materials from the libraries of the member institutions. The council thought that, by grouping a great amount of little-used material in one place, not only would space be freed in the badly crowded library stacks of the individual institutions, but in addition the library might attract scholars whose research would be expedited by this concentration. In time the concept was broadened to include subscriptions to certain rarely used documental series that would then be available to any member institution.

A practical scheme for library loans was developed so that it was possible for an institution to receive requested materials within two days, thereby reducing the inconvenience to campus scholars caused by the remote storage. When the program had been worked out in considerable detail, ground made available by the University of Chicago was agreed upon for the location of the library because of its geographical centrality among the Big Ten institutions. Outside funding of the construction and equipment had to be sought, as the individual institutions could not legally contribute from their own construction funds to build an out-of-state facility. On the other hand, the cost of operating the facility could be defrayed by the individual institutions from membership or user fees. To solicit funds for the buildings, we approached the Carnegie Foundation and Corporation, which were then interested in promoting coordination among institutions in the interest of reducing costs and increasing efficiency. The initial contact by letter resulted in an invitation to send representatives to the Carnegie office in New York to make a presentation of the project. Robert Hutchins, president of the University of Chicago, and I were selected for this mission. In due course we traveled to New York and made our presentation to the principal administrative officer of the corporation. At the conclusion of our conference we received verbal assurance of favorable action and Bob and I went on our way rejoicing. I remember riding up Fifth Avenue in a taxi with him as we congratulated each other on this interinstitutional effort. This was my first participation in making a request to a major foundation for private funding, an experience that I of course was to repeat many times in the years following.

Once in the early years of my presidency and of my service on the board of the Carnegie Foundation for the Advancement of Teaching, I was at the Carnegie office in New York speaking with James Perkins who was then vice president of the corporation. During the course of that conversation he remarked that whenever he read in the newspapers anything about the Council of Ten, it had to do with some athletic matter. He asked, "Don't you ever discuss education?" A bit stung, I quickly replied that we spent most of our regular meetings discussing mutual problems in education. However, the character and by-laws of the Western Intercollegiate Athletic Association, popularly called the Big Ten, relegated certain questions to the presidents for decision. These matters were first on our agenda and, having rather quickly disposed of them and released the result of our actions to the awaiting press, we then turned to our mutual academic problems. He kept pressing: "Well, then, why don't you have some publicity concerning your discussions? Your ten institutions carry a lot of weight, and any pronouncements of the presidents as a body on educational issues would be not only interesting but useful and important in promoting consideration of academic policies regionally and nationally."

My reply was that to give organization and coherence to our discussions we would need a secretariat—a secretariat that would arrange agendas, ask for position papers to be drafted, keep minutes, write reports, and prepare press releases. "Would the members be interested in an organized program of cooperative educational discussion?" he asked. I replied that I thought they would. I was then president of the Council of Ten, and it was my best judgment that they would be both willing and eager to undertake a program of this kind. In answer to his question about the cost of such an operation, I replied off the top of my head, after a moment's hesitation, "For a five-year program $250,000 or $50,000 per year for five years." As the council was to meet in a few months, he suggested, "Go back and sound them out. If they're interested, I'll recommend the project to our trustees."

I related my conversation to my fellow presidents at our meeting in the University Club in Chicago the following December. Their reaction was enthusiastic. As a consequence, during our April meeting at Ohio State University, we organized the Committee on Institutional Cooperation (CIC), composed of the chief academic officer of each of our institutions, and set up the machinery by which a formal proposal could be made to the Carnegie Corporation. The rest is history. The CIC has launched many programs such as the Traveling Scholar Program and the Far Eastern Language Institute. It is now nationally recognized as an important coordinating and cooperative device.

Another significant effort of coordination and cooperation arose from a request by the Ford Foundation, when Peter Fraenkel was its representative in Peru, for me to go there to bring the gospel of voluntary coordination and cooperation to the Peruvian University Rectors Association. The Peruvian universities were supported in large part by appropriations from the central government. Regional political influences were pressing for the establishment of several more universities, some of which seemed unnecessary and would have disastrously diluted the funds available for the established institutions. It was felt that if the rectors could agree among themselves upon an allocation of the appropriation that would be acceptable to the central government, that would in all probability be a sounder use of educational resources than an allocation distorted by political considerations. Happily, we were able to agree upon a report that did provide a formula for the voluntary allocation of appropriations and in addition recommended solutions of lesser problems to achieve greater cooperation and coordination among the Peruvian institutions.

{9}

○ ○ ○

How to Succeed
without Really Trying

DURING MY PERIOD in the university presidency, the National Association of State Universities (NASU) was a very active and useful organization. The members of the group had developed through the years a considerable camaraderie and a confidence in each other that enabled them to exchange important information freely and confidentially. So their meetings were held in high regard by the presidents. The final session of the spring meeting in New York City, the most important each year, was usually in a lighthearted vein and consisted of a dinner at the University Club followed by the valedictory of one of NASU's members. Since college presidents spend their lives making and listening to speeches, the task of speaking to such a jaded group under any circumstance is not easy. To speak to them after they have had cocktails and an excellent four- or five-course dinner with two wines is a challenge indeed.

Some time after I announced that I would be stepping out of the Indiana University presidency on July 1, I was asked by the president of the association, Ray Olpin, to be the speaker for the spring meeting on May 7, 1962. Knowing the hazards, I found it difficult to dream up a format, much less the content, for my talk, but, as I related in the speech, I eventually jotted down some notes that served for the occasion. The notes took the form of "Maxims for a Young College President, or How to Succeed without Really Trying," paraphrasing the title of a popular show on Broadway at that time, *How to Succeed in Business without Really Trying*. My remarks were recorded even though they had been conceived, not as a speech, but rather as a bit of entertainment to mark my last dinner with the group. However, the maxims were then published in the *Transactions and Proceedings* of N A S U, discovered by others, and republished from time to time, including a much more sedate version in the prestigious *Educational Record* of the American Council on Education. Since that time there have been many requests for copies of the transcription, and some of the maxims have been used by others with or without attribution. Because of this continuing interest, I looked at the text to judge whether or not the maxims still held in light of all that has happened since 1962. If so, they might bear repeating. The comments had represented a wholly personal point of view, intended only as a semiserious rule-of-thumb. Seen from my present vantage point, a few of the maxims seem to need additional comments. These follow the text of the transcript.

First let me identify the persons whose names are in the text. Ray Olpin was then president of the University of Utah in Salt Lake City and president of N A S U. The Charlie referred to was Charles McCurdy, the executive secretary. He was a valued friend and colleague of mine as well as a useful and adroit executive officer of the association.

Lightly Expurgated Transcript of Remarks
Made at the Annual Banquet Meeting of the
National Association of State Universities
by Dr. Herman B Wells, Indiana University

University Club, New York City, May 7, 1962

. . . .

When Ray Olpin asked me to speak, I thought the whole idea that I should be your speaker tonight was ridiculous. Of course, I know very well that no group ever wants a speech—they only want a speaker. Custom dictates that there must be a speaker at a dinner, but I thought it was strange to draft me.

I finally forgave Ray and Charlie because I sensed how desperate they were. Besides, I know how difficult it is to get a speaker when you don't pay anything!

Ray asked me to reminisce about my years in the presidency and to tell how to be a president. That's an absurd assignment, of course. Presidential experience isn't transferable, and we all carry on these jobs in terms of our own personalities and our own situations. Moreover, I don't like to look backward—only forward. It is more important for me to look forward now than it has been at any time in the past.

.   .   .   .

After an administration [President Bryan's] of thirty-five years' duration, naturally nearly all the members of the faculty had great ideas about the way the university should be reorganized. As an acting president, I wasn't responsible for reorganizing the university, so I used an old technique. In a great spirit of democracy I suggested a self-survey and that the survey committee hold hearings in which all members of the faculty would be asked to tell what they'd like to do to the university.

This went on for some months, all were heard, and each re-former gained the general impression that his ideas for reorganiza-tion of the university would be approved. Meanwhile, I had not had to make a decision, hence had made no one mad. When the trustees could not agree on anybody else, having become accus-tomed to me, they turned to me. And that is the way I came to be a university president.

Well, it's been great fun—whether successful or not, I don't know. This, time will tell!

A week or so ago I spent the night in Chicago in the other Uni-versity Club. The bed was hard, the switch engines noisy, and the room too hot to sleep, so I began to make some notes. I would make a note or two and then take an aspirin, make another note or two and take a Seconal. Four Seconals and four aspirins later, these notes were finished, and I went to sleep. You will probably be asleep sooner as I give you the results of that evening's effort.

I thought I might take for my title something from one of the volumes of a great specialized library at Indiana University, the Kinsey Library of Erotica. The title of a famous volume published in London in 1792 seemed a possibility: *Useful Hints to Single Gen-tlemen Respecting Marriage, Concubinage and Adultery, in Prose and Verse, with Notes Moral, Critical and Explanatory.*

That erotic theme, perhaps, is not entirely appropriate. In one respect it is: if you will develop a love affair with your university, her seduction will be easier and more satisfying.

But I have chosen a more conventional title for my remarks tonight: "Maxims for a Young College President, or How to Succeed without Really Trying."

And now, I give you these tongue-in-cheek rules for success, recognizing that many of you have others much better. These are not maxims in the sense of being any final word. I hope you will realize they are not presented in any such pompous frame of reference, but only as a way of saying a few things that may be of interest.

There is little consistency in my advice, and thus is illustrated the first principle of administration—consistency is a greatly overrated virtue.

Board and General Administrative Relationships

My first maxim is, Be lucky.

Remind yourself daily that general administration must always be the servant, never the master, of the academic community. It is not an end unto itself and exists only to further the academic enterprise. It follows, therefore, that generally the least administration possible is the best.

Inherit or recruit talented administrative colleagues who can excel you in performance, including your assistant and your vice presidents. Especially, find a financial vice president who believes it is his job to spend money wisely rather than to hoard it.

Find a public-relations counselor in whom you have confidence for your close associate who has the ability and courage to tell you when you are wrong—and that's difficult, as many of you know. It has been especially difficult in my case, because in my entire adult life I have had only one job lasting for two years that would be classified as routine work. I have been in administrative work all my life and, of course, I have great confidence in my own judgment. I fortunately was able to find a great public-relations counselor who told me frequently, nearly every day, how wrong I was.

The central administration should always be a source of inspiration and expedition, rather than a bottleneck practiced in the art of saying "No." The central administration should be a place to see how it can be done rather than why it cannot be done.

Another very important maxim for a young president is to pick a state with a good, rich economy, few schools, and relatively low taxes. I don't have to explain this rule.

Make board service an exciting intellectual experience for the board members and, above all else, a delightful social experience for their wives. The members deserve this and more for the essential service they perform.

Make sure you have board members who believe in quality and who are willing to pay for it. If you have board members who do not have this belief, you have failed in your first task as a teacher—the task of teaching your board members what they need to know.

Never let you or your trustees get into the stance of being employers. It not only destroys faculty morale but also allows the faculty to shift impossible responsibilities to the administration.

Student Relationships

Save time for student contacts of all types. You will learn more from them than they will from you. From these contacts your sense of mission will be repeatedly refreshed and renewed.

Honor the freshmen and sophomores no less than the graduate students. They pay the bills! They support the expensive academic tastes of the graduate faculty. I think of these lowly undergraduates in biblical terms: "Consider the lilies of the field, how they grow; they neither toil nor spin; yet, I tell you King Solomon in all his glory was not arrayed like one of these!" How on earth could we run a graduate school without the freshmen and sophomores?

In matters of student discipline, remember that the sap runs in the spring and be not filled with envy by recalling your own undergraduate days.

It is the ambition of each student editor to reform the university, so thank God that their terms are short and that when the next one comes he will have a different program.

General Policies, Internal and External

Avoid proliferation, either internal or external. In our sessions today we talked a good deal about this subject. It is the greatest curse of American higher education and an insurmountable barrier to the achievement of excellence unless resources are astronomical. On the other hand, lack of proliferation is not ipso facto a guarantee of public willingness to pay the price of greatness.

My predecessor had an effective way of dealing with this issue. Each time the legislature would create a new institution, he would call on the governor to ask for a veto. His standard argument was this (in those days we were an agricultural state): "What happens when you put too many grains of corn in a single hill?"

The governor would reply, "Why, of course, you get stunted, spindly stalks and a poor yield."

Dr. Bryan would reply, "That's precisely what happens when you plant too many institutions in the soil of the state—more than the state can afford." He was always successful in getting the bill vetoed.

All over America we are trying to correct the errors of over-proliferation of high schools no longer necessary because of improved transportation. It seems strange that we are about to repeat the same mistake in higher education and with less cause than was once true in the high schools.

Next to proliferation, uniformity is the greatest enemy of distinction—uniformity of treatment of departments, of individuals, and of subject matters. They are not all of equal quality, and to try to treat them all precisely alike is a great mistake.

Recruitment is the most important of all presidential responsibilities; only second- and third-rate men are expensive. Recruitment, promotion, and retention of top men should be the first objective of every president.

Be frank with the faculty on salaries and other financial matters. Without facts the faculty will accept rumors as truth.

Create a climate of competitive productivity in teaching and research in both quality and quantity; men need to be stimulated to produce as much as they are capable of and to carry their share of the load.

Roger Keyes' famous story about the Oxford don was called to my mind by some of the statements today that we are teaching less and less. Some of you have heard Roger tell the story of the old Oxford don, asked one night at high table about his teaching load.

He said, "Oh, yes, I am still teaching: I lecture once a year, some years!"

Provide for the esoteric, exotic, and impractical in the curriculum; the practical and pedestrian will take care of itself. If it does not, you have not lost much anyway; so I think the impractical things are the most practical and important in the long run.

Academic amenities are not a luxury but an essential part of the atmosphere that promotes morale, institutional pride, and loyalty.

Make no small plans for your institution; the small plans are very difficult to achieve.

When you build, build for a long time. Build for a thousand years—do not build structures that will be cast away by tomorrow's fashion. Tradition has a role to play in our institutions, and traditions grow in part around physical symbols.

Academic freedom is not only essential for morale, teaching, and research; it is a priceless public-relations asset. The Kinsey incident at Indiana, I suppose, is one of the most famous incidents in the history of American academic freedom. I think we gained far more in our public-relations stance by protecting Kinsey and his study than we lost by reason of the unusual nature of the material with which he was working.

. . . .

Another maxim that has nothing to do with erotica, but nevertheless is important: Help build the private institutions in your state; they, in turn, will help you to build. Anyway, as a state university, you can afford to be generous.

Don't let competitors make academic policy for your institution. Don't let worry about events on other campuses distract you from the policies on your own.

Rejoice in the other institution's success. Your turn will come next. The other fellow's victories help us all by establishing a higher general standard for university education.

The Personal Role of the President

The president needs to be motivated by three *D*'s—Dedication, Drive, and Determination.

Professional longevity is essential. You can't win any institutional battles out of office.

Be yourself while you are in office because, if you try to be anything else, you won't fool anybody but yourself.

It is not what you do that counts, it is what you help others to do that makes progress.

Don't resist your job. Go to meet it rather than stand aside from it. If you don't like to be president, resign; many others would like a crack at it.

Never be guilty of using eloquence to avoid the painstaking labor of the job. All of us have seen men who "got by" in that fashion. Instead, work like hell because the job deserves it, needs it, and is worth it. Universities have been injured more by lazy presidents than by incompetent or dictatorial ones.

Always be available to faculty and students for discussion of individual, personal problems because the deans, department heads, and others who are supposed to assume this responsibility rarely have time to do so.

Attend as many informal social gatherings as possible on your campus. They are a great place to interpret policy, gather information, and express interest in individual plans and aspirations. Moreover, if things get a little rough when you are trying to defend policy, you can always move on and meet the next guest, which you cannot do if you talk it out in your office.

If you read a little from time to time outside your professional field, it won't hurt you; you *may* get an idea, and the time you spend in reading will keep you from taking some action that would probably be unwise anyway.

Be a good educational citizen—locally, nationally, and internationally. Somebody has to do the group work. By doing your share you will gain inspiration and ideas for your local job. You will likewise gain because the campus will not be bored with having you around all the time.

Educate your board and your colleagues about your responsibilities for group work nationally and internationally. They understand if you give time to the local Community Chest drive, but they seem to forget that other chores—educational civic chores that are national and international—have just as great a call upon the time of the president as the chores in his local community or state.

Be born with the physical charm of a Greek athlete, the cunning of Machiavelli, the wisdom of Solomon, the courage of a lion, if possible; but in any case be born with the stomach of a goat.

Strive to avoid the deadly occupational disease of omniscience and omnipotence. Only the physician, surrounded by nurses and frightened families of ill patients, is as tempted as is a president to be omniscient and omnipotent.

On Legislative, Alumni, and Public Relations

The first rule of public relations is never get into a contest with a skunk! If you do, you will never smell the same again. Most academic people have a fanatical urge to try to convince the bigot and put the world right. As president you must restrain your natural desire to convince bigots, remembering it takes two to make an argument. You leave your adversary impotent if you won't give him an opponent.

Don't shirk your obligation to attend funerals. Your presence will be appreciated. Rarely do you have to make a speech. And in Indiana the "Establishment" transacts an enormous amount of business in connection with important funerals.

The faculty and students are the most effective public-relations representatives of a university. When they believe in their institution, they will tell the world of their enthusiasm. Elaborately contrived public-relations departments that do not command faculty respect are in the long run self-defeating. A university cannot be "sold" by the Madison Avenue techniques used to sell cosmetics or automobiles. Those who believe otherwise do not understand the nature of the academic community and its product.

Pick a top man for alumni secretary who commands the respect and loyalty of the alumni and make him one of your inner circle. Alumni are the great, unexplored resource of American higher education in general and in state universities especially. Only a few institutions have involved them in a meaningful way.

The Harvard alumni visiting committees are illustrations of alumni being seriously and honestly involved in institutional affairs. Only when we treat the alumni in this way can we expect them to behave responsibly and be interested in things other than athletics.

The importance of athletic success is a figment of the imagination of sports writers and sophomoric alumni. A member of the National Academy has more public-relations value than a championship team does, and, from a straight public-relations standpoint, I will trade two championships for a Nobel Laureate.

Pride and prestige are more powerful legislative arguments than poverty is in securing funds.

For the most part, legislators are dedicated public servants. As statesmen, of course, they like the role of founding fathers, so unfortunately they would rather found an institution than pay for its upkeep.

You must always remember that the ability of legislators to absorb entertainment is completely without limit. You can exhaust yourself on their behalf and they are still ready to go.

Don't be afraid of the future of your institution; don't be afraid of the future of higher education. If you need a little encouragement at any time, read the 1921 and 1922 proceedings of this association following World War I. You can read there that it will be impossible to accommodate the increasing numbers of students; that standards will be lowered by the rising tide of students; that universities are too large, et cetera. However, the bulge of the era was accommodated, standards are higher, and our institutions much stronger today than forty years ago.

So, we should not become too excited by our own propaganda about the need for additional funds to provide for more students. I remember reading in the *Proceedings* of this association a report of a 1921 survey committee of the University of Minnesota predicting enrollment for that institution in 1945–46 of 36,000 students, a figure certainly not realized. Predictions can be tricky. We have been meeting these problems of growth for a long time, and I don't see any reason to doubt that we can do so in the future.

Make the fecundity of the human race serve rather than defeat you. Look upon it as an asset giving you an opportunity to grow in curriculum and program. After all, you wouldn't know how to administer your institution unless it were growing.

Quit when you are ahead. Try to incite some irate taxpayer to take a gun in hand and make you a martyr; remember history's treatment of Lincoln. But, if you aren't shot, you can always resign when you're ahead.

The last maxim is, as is the first, Be lucky!

Epilogue

I wish to conclude with some sentences written at the turn of the century by my predecessor, a very wise man who understood the significance and destiny of the state university:

> What the people need and demand is that their children shall have a chance—as good a chance as any other children in the world —to make the most of themselves, to rise in any and every occupation, including those occupations which require the most thorough training. What the people want is open paths from every corner of the state, through the schools, to the highest and best things which men can achieve. To make such paths, to make them open to the poorest and lead to the highest, is the mission of democracy.

And so, we can all be thankful that the good Lord has given us the opportunity to help make these paths, to keep them open, and to spend our lives in a job that is great fun and is very important.

To you men who are beginners as presidents, I express the hope that you will have as much fun as I have had in the job!

Having been out of the presidency for seventeen years, I do not have, of course, the intimate knowledge of the working of the office that I had at the time these maxims were written. (I did spend a few months as interim president in 1968 at the beginning of the student troubles on our campus.) Since leaving the office, however, I have been closely associated with higher education in one form or another both in my institution and in other organizations. Looking back over these maxims, I see none that I would now eliminate but a few that I would reemphasize.

First, I wish to repeat the warning concerning proliferation. The proliferation of institutions, of which I warned on that May evening in 1962, has become a reality. The number of postsecondary educational institutions has grown astronomically; they have grown not only in number but also in variety. The latter seems to me to be desirable, for it enables the interests of a great range of high school graduates and adults to be served. Unfortunately some universities and collegiate institutions in search of new students from the dwindling supply have been tempted to try to be all things to all people. There is great danger in the dilution of resources by too rapid expansion of curriculum to meet the needs of various segments such as minority groups, business, labor, and the like. Many of their needs can be met by traditional disciplines, when administrators are made aware of the need and given a little time. The special requirements in nearly all areas can be encompassed within the framework of standard courses at much less cost than by creating separate departments and sections to deal with newly perceived neglect and newly found subject matter. Useful though novel instructional areas may be to particular segments, such activity on the part of a traditional institution tends to blur in the public mind the true functions of a university. It seems to me that the maintenance of high standards of scholarship and research are necessary, not only to fulfill the university mission, but also to distinguish clearly for the public a university from the welter of other types of postsecondary schools. In all probability coordination and cooperation among universities in curricular matters will become ever more important if money is not to be wasted. In fact, should the predicted decline in the number of available students occur, it will be necessary for institutions to be consolidated physically just as high schools had to be consolidated a decade or more ago.

What I was attempting to say about athletics in the section "On Legislative, Alumni, and Public Relations" might be clear if the maxim read, "The public-relations importance of athletic success is a figment of the imagination of sports writers and sophomoric alumni." I did not mean to denigrate the importance of the athletic program in university life. It is a delightful feature of the academic scene and we all feel better when we can win. A university should attempt to be first-rate in anything it engages to do. The importance of the athletic program—by that I mean not only the great spectator sports but also the sports with lesser participation as well as the whole intramural program—for the physical well-being and life of the students and faculty should likewise be noted. In fact, I should like to see my institution have more intercollegiate programs, rather than fewer, enabling more people to compete or participate. Also, additional programs would undoubtedly attract some students not now participating; for example, there are possibly students who should like to have the experience of being a member of a rowing team while they are in college, a sport that could be developed here.

That athletic victories are essential to the attraction of major private gifts is a figment of the imagination also. Winning teams do stimulate the flow of alumni contributions for athletic scholarships, which, of course, is desirable, but, so far as major gifts are concerned, rarely if ever in my experience have donors been motivated by athletic success or lack of success, by whether the university had winning teams or not. It is to be remembered that the University of Chicago, Harvard University, the University of Michigan, the University of California at Berkeley, and similar institutions are distinguished universities with great private endowments and large, private annual gifts. Although some of those institutions are occasionally successful in athletic competition, they attract gifts because of the quality of their faculties and programs. Of course, there is great pressure on athletic departments to produce winning teams because winning teams do increase the revenue from tickets. I regret, as I am sure does everyone in the athletic world, especially coaches and athletic directors, the fact that the spectator sports have to bear such a large proportion of the cost of the whole athletic program. Someday I hope that a way will be found to finance a first-rate program without such great box-office pressure.

Athletics perhaps should not be singled out in regard to misconceptions about public relations. Some enthusiastic fraternity and sorority members feel that Greek-letter organizations are essential to the public-relations image of the university. I would not deny that a good Greek-letter system is a desirable feature of university life and that it undoubtedly attracts certain students who would not otherwise come, but the same could be said of a good housing system or of any of the proper student facilities and amenities. Increased self-government and programs sponsored by the Indiana University Student Association, the Student Foundation and the Student Union activities, musical events—all have helped to create a campus ambience that is attractive undoubtedly to certain students and that is a useful and happy part of life in a university community. But to assign to them overweening importance, namely, that being first in any or all of these is a sine qua non of distinction, is to further the fantasies of the boosters in each of these areas.

There is much wailing now over the cost of bureaucratic proliferation at state and national levels. I am convinced that this proliferation has gone much too far and represents a cost beyond any good purpose it achieves. But I know no way to solve the problem other than to preach the gospel of the efficiency of freedom, to urge institutions to practice rigid self-discipline internally, and wherever possible to promote efficiency through regional coordination. Universities can serve as an example in this regard by avoiding bureaucratization of their own institutions if at all possible. There has been a tendency recently for administrators, sometimes even at the urging of a faculty committee, to solve each problem by the creation of a new office complete with a supporting staff. Few problems need to be solved by the addition of a new officer and staff. Given a little patience and time, most problems can be solved with existing machinery. But once the machinery has been added, it generally continues to encumber the organization after its need for existence has disappeared, the while attempting to find ways and means to justify its continuance.

Certainly the events of the 1960s and the mood of the 1970s underline my maxims that called for the president of the university to save time for contact with students, all types of contact, and likewise to allot time for both social and formal contacts with faculty members, individually and in groups. Just now this seems to be a more frequently voiced need on the part of the university community than I have known it to be before in my lifetime. There is simply no substitute for availability and visibility on the part of the president in his institutional relationships. Unfortunately, the sunshine laws and similar legislation and the insistence of the media on being a part of every formal session make it much more difficult to discuss policies and issues with either students or faculty members in confidence and have a meaningful two-way exchange. This situation seems to me, therefore, to underline the necessity of person-to-person and small, informal contacts to an even greater extent than was once the case. There was a time when we could discuss the most difficult questions off the record in faculty meetings and those attending would respect the confidence. They left the meetings feeling that they had had a part in arriving at solutions to difficult problems, as in fact they had.

My maxim about attending funerals was not intended to be flippant. The longer I live the more I realize that the officers of the university, including the president, have a real obligation to attend major occasions in the families of well-known and loyal alumni such as weddings, golden wedding anniversaries, and the like, as well as funerals. For a loyal alumnus there simply is no substitute for the presence of a president or a president's representative on these important—sometimes trying, sometimes happy—occasions. A loyal alumnus has the right to expect this kind of consideration, friendship, and courtesy to be extended by his institution whenever possible.

The maxims may need more amplification or modification, but in looking over them again I find them about as valid as they were at the time I gave them, half in jest, as a statement of the experience of a quarter of a century in the important office of the president.

⟦10⟧

O O O

Money, Money,
But Never Enough

FOR THE past 150 years faculties, students, and administrators of Indiana University have repeatedly lamented the inadequacy of the state's support for higher education generally and Indiana University in particular. Their complaints have had merit because there seems never to have been a time throughout the life of the university when the money made available to it from taxes and other revenues has been equal to its opportunity for effective use of resources on behalf of the citizens of the state.[1] The fact of the matter is that the opportunities available to a university for teaching, research, and public service are, for all practical purposes, limitless; as a consequence, it is improbable that sufficient money will ever be made available for an institution to realize all its capabilities in any given period.

From one standpoint this fact is not as remarkable as is the fact that the public supports higher education with tax dollars as generously as it does. Narrowly speaking, higher education directly benefits only those who have the opportunity to attend a college or university and receive training, and they constitute a relatively small percentage of the total population. Furthermore, there are always other highly desirable social goals dependent upon public support that compete for the tax dollar—highways, hospitals, and, in modern

1. Thomas D. Clark repeatedly makes this point in his three-volume history, *Indiana University: Midwestern Pioneer*, 3 vols. (Bloomington: Indiana University Press, 1970–1977). His presentation of the financial picture in volume 3 contains two misreadings of the situation, however, which need correction: (1) on page 184 the food-services building was an addition to the Indianapolis Union, not to IMU in Bloomington; and (2) the $25 million appropriation for construction, referred to on page 205, was actually a ten-year program adopted by the trustees but never implemented.

times, a vast number of social services in the areas of welfare, pensions, mental health, prisons, and the like. Although those of us who have spent our lives in the work of higher education are acutely aware of the inadequacy of the public support we have received, we remind ourselves of the fact that in most respects our governmental bodies make greater provision for higher education than do the governments in any other country in the world. A larger proportion of the college-age group is enrolled in college in this country than is true for any other country in the world, and a larger proportion goes on to advanced training here. There may be a few minor exceptions, but this is in general the case. So it does seem to me that the remarkable fact is not how little we receive but, in view of all of this, how much.

From the very beginning of statehood, the founders of Indiana expressed a belief that a free democratic society required support of public education for its realization. Unquestionably universities are essential to the development of society economically and politically. It is a fact that there are no highly developed nations in the world without highly developed universities. Nevertheless, the relationship between higher education and the total development and welfare of the state is a subtle and difficult one to comprehend. Many government leaders and informed citizens throughout the country have this understanding, but I doubt that the majority of the population has any comprehension of the relationship; yet year after year a substantial proportion of the tax dollar is spent for education at all levels including higher education.

Early in my administration I came to realize that the most we could ever expect to receive from the state were funds for the basic instructional work of the institution and for the basic instructional plant and that as a consequence we had to seek funds from other sources to finance complicated research programs and to build peaks of excellence throughout the institution. A state institution needs a wholesome balance between the two sources, namely, state appropriations and outside funds, and our financial policies were governed by that tenet throughout the years of my administration.

We attempted to keep the members of the Indiana General Assembly well informed, not only as to our needs, but also as to our operations. We used every possible technique available to us to accomplish this—visits to the individual legislators from time to time throughout their terms of service and invitations to the State

Budget Committee or, on occasion, the entire legislature to visit the campus and see firsthand what had been achieved with the tax money and what further support was needed. During the sessions of the General Assembly, rarely did I leave the state for more than a few hours because I wished always to be available for consultation with our legislative team or for making contacts with individual legislators. Our very effective legislative team through the years consisted of Ward Biddle, Joseph A. Franklin, Ross Bartley, Claude Rich, George Henley, the University's attorney, and Henry "Rosie" Snyder, a local attorney—Rich and Franklin throughout the entire period, and Biddle, Bartley, Henley, and Snyder during the years of their active service. These men were trusted by the members of the General Assembly and never betrayed that trust.

Through the years I formed great admiration for members of the General Assembly. They were men of integrity and of considerable talent, dedicated to public service. I felt that, with rare exceptions, they were attempting to do as well for the university as was possible in light of the other needs of the state as they saw them. We may have had a different evaluation of the relative needs of the state, but I always felt that the legislators were sincere and honest in their final judgments. Therefore it was our policy always to accept the money appropriated to us with expressions of appreciation and to request that we be allowed to use it as efficiently as possible where it was needed rather than to use it rigidly according to our original request. This policy was desirable because invariably our requests were substantially reduced and it was crucial for us to adjust according to our greatest needs rather than across the board.

In addition to attempting to secure as much financial support as we could from both state appropriations and private sources, we took other steps to try to improve the university's financial situation. One of the earliest of these was to relieve the university budget of the cost of indigent-patient care at the Medical Center. University hospitals customarily provide free medical care for indigent patients in order to furnish clinical training for medical students. The Indiana University Medical Center follows this practice, providing a large amount of indigent-patient care. I discovered at the beginning of my administration that the cost of this care had to be absorbed in the university budget. No other university hospital in the country followed such a budgetary custom. Here I am speaking only of adult indigent-patient care because there were endowments and certain legal provisions to reimburse unmet expenses of young patients at the James Whitcomb Riley Hospital for Children at the Medical Center. But the university received no reimbursement for its adult-patient care including even that which it provided for the inmates of the penal institutions. This was a tremendous drain on the university budget and particularly on the budget of the medical school. We made a decision to try to change the arrangement and were successful in securing legislation (passed March 13, 1947) that would allow us to bill the cost of indigent-patient care to the state auditor, who reimbursed us and in turn was reimbursed from the state treasury. The state treasury was then to be reimbursed by the counties from which the patients came. The net result was that the Medical Center was indirectly given considerable additional support and the general university budget given corresponding relief.

Another basic step was to break the vise in which the university budget was placed by the General Assembly's policy of appropriating equal amounts to Purdue and Indiana universities for operations and capital. We had about the same enrollment on the Bloomington campus as Purdue had on the Lafayette campus, or a little more, and yet we had to support another campus in Indianapolis and several extension centers out of the same amount of money—an intolerable situation so far as Indiana University was concerned, restricting its growth and making it nearly impossible for us to find the funds required for a quality program. At that time the alumni rivalry between the two schools was intense. This rivalry extended even into the state legislature and made it difficult for the General Assembly to do other than give each school the same amount regardless of the need. Achieving a more rational basis for appropriations was a long and painful effort.[2]

Breaking the parity involved the preparation of innumerable statistical studies and also meeting after meeting of the presidents of the four institutions and their staffs. At times it would seem that the cause was hopeless. We persisted, however, and finally were able to agree that the unique need of each institution should be the basis for its request but that the total would be circumscribed and deter-

2. The story of this process and its culmination is set out in considerable detail and clarity in a letter to Lytle J. Freehafer, then budget director of the state, dated November 15, 1950 (Thomas D. Clark, *Indiana University: Midwestern Pioneer. Historical Documents Since 1816* [Bloomington: Indiana University, 1977], pp. 579–84).

mined by a set formula.[3] An important corollary of this procedure was an agreement for the four institutions to bring to the General Assembly a joint budget request with individual budgets supported by all four and with the understanding that if any changes, upward or downward, were made by the General Assembly the percentage change would apply to each institution. This voluntary coordination was popular with the legislature for many years. It placed the burden of seeking an equitably allocated appropriation upon the institutions themselves rather than upon the state officers. The institutions naturally had more information available to assist them in arriving at an equitable distribution of the dollars to be spent for higher education than any state officer had. Furthermore, the combined request enabled the friends of all four institutions to join in supporting the request and made it possible for the four presidents and their staffs to make joint presentations, not only to the legislature, but also to all Indiana statewide organizations interested in the state budget such as the Farm Bureau, the Taxpayers Association, the state press associations, the state Chamber of Commerce, the Manufacturers Association, the leading newspapers, the State Teachers Association, and others. The achievement of a quadripartite budget through cooperative planning undoubtedly was the most important financial development that occurred in my administration.

Another effective policy initiated in the early years of my administration was to use in the budget request enrollment figures based upon a straight-line unit cost for each student enrolled for we believed we were entering a period of generally increasing enrollments. It was easy for the legislature to understand making an appropriation on the basis of a given number of students at so much per student. Moreover, this method frequently yielded an increment above actual cost because there is an element of decreasing unit cost up to a certain level as additional students are added to existing programs. We early established a policy of using this free increment for enrichment of graduate programs within our specific fields, for additional library support, for scientific equipment, and so forth. This practice did not represent any deception by the university because at the same time we refrained from requesting any substantial amount of money for new programs and new program development

3. See Clark's history, vol. 3, ch. 6. President Frederick Hovde of Purdue lent his full support to these efforts.

and informed the budget officials how we were using the free increment.

Another important financial policy that we initiated was the segregation of overhead received from grants into a special fund in the
Foundation and the use of this fund to prime the research program,
to furnish seed money for new programs, and to support the "peaks
of excellence" efforts. The importance of this practice is explained
in chapter 11.

We also followed the policy of trying to build for excellence
rather than breadth. We refrained from taking on whole new areas
of work such as engineering and a large number of new service programs just because somebody else was doing them and it seemed
opportune to follow suit. Instead we attempted to use our money to
strengthen in depth and quality our traditional fields. When the legislature mandated that we undertake new programs or fields, we
asked that these be funded separately because, if the basic budget
were to cover them, compliance would have meant skimping some
of our existing work. It was helpful that Purdue also followed this
policy.

We were never bound rigidly by salary scales or other internal
formulas. Instead we always sought the courage to make exceptions
when exceptions were in the best interest of the institution, regardless of how much temporary unhappiness the exceptions caused and
how much extra effort was required of the administrative staff to
handle them. Looking back over his administration, President
Bryan once said that his biggest mistake was treating every faculty
member and administrative officer the same in respect to salary.
There was one figure for deans, one for full professors, and so on
—a policy he came to believe had been counterproductive.

We studiously avoided the easy response of the administrator,
"Where is the money coming from?" when confronted with requests
by a faculty member who had a new project or an idea of importance to him. Rather we would compliment the colleague upon his
idea and discuss with him how much money would be required, the
possible sources of funds, and the time span envisioned. We used
these new ideas as a stimulus to try to find the money either from
outside sources or in savings from existing operations. It is remarkable how frequently with a little imagination a way could be found
to do something even though there was no apparent source of money.

In other words, we were willing to start big things in a small way, adopting a policy that President Bryan had followed throughout his career. But we went further, keeping in mind the big projects or ideas that had started small and trying to find the money and talent to realize them.

In budgeting, we practiced the policy of approximating as closely as we could what the departments needed so that they would not have an excess that they might spend ill-advisedly just to keep it from reverting. Once the reversions were aggregated, we sought to use them for constructive purposes—principally of an academic and sometimes of a dramatic nature. For example, with budgetary reversions, we acquired special books and collections and purchased scientific equipment. We had to be sure that those expenditures were sorely needed by the university and were not of a recurring type. Subscribing to one hundred new journals, for instance, would have meant a recurring cost and a future budget commitment, but acquiring special collections or specially needed equipment, adapting a space for a particular use, and providing the means for program initiatives were essentially one-time costs.

A university, like other large enterprises, has sufficient diversity to make creative budgeting possible, by which I mean using a combination of ingenuity and good financial practice to make available funds go as far as feasible, make them encompass in part what is desirable for the university as well as what is needed. Creative budgeting requires knowing what is possible, being willing to take risks, and, with due regard for solvency, viewing unawed the problem of balancing the budget.

Early in the days when funds became available from the Public Works Administration (PWA), the trustees of the university had made a decision to seek federal funding for expansion of the physical plant and to secure the matching funds required through bond issues, with the approval of the legislature. We adopted the same plan and later, with enactment of a federal graduate facilities act, followed it again. Without this policy we never could have achieved anything like an adequate physical plant within the direct-dollar appropriations that the General Assembly was able to make.

Another systematic approach that we took was to use such funds as we could find during World War II to purchase land for future expansion. Much of the land to the north and east of the central campus was acquired in this fashion. Land prices were very low then and there was no general comprehension of the fact that the university would be expanding rapidly after the war. Had we not applied funds to acquiring land during those years, our rapid postwar expansion would have been nearly impossible.

Not unlike that precautionary approach to land acquisition was a decision we made with the verbal approval of the governor and the State Budget Committee, but without a specific legislative appropriation, to incur a deficit in order to finance a large amount of temporary housing required by the returning veterans following World War II. The frenetic activity to obtain housing that took place at that time has been described elsewhere.[4] Suffice it to say here that the campus was dotted with Quonset huts and other relics of military installations. The incurrence of a deficit brought criticism from certain quarters, but it did enable us, for all practical purposes, to admit every returning Hoosier veteran who was qualified and who wished to come to the university following the conclusion of World War II. To overcome the criticism, we invited the whole General Assembly to the campus to see firsthand the reason for the deficit expenditure as well as the justification for other features of the budget request. As a consequence we received reimbursement for those expenditures and kept faith with the veteran students.

Our decision to accommodate returning veterans entailed considerable expenditure for temporary buildings because there was neither time nor suitable materials available to erect permanent buildings. We tried to expedite the contractors' work by making on-the-spot decisions about problems as they arose.

A crucial action, far-reaching in its effect, was the decision made in 1955 to attempt a major residential-hall program with borrowed money, a plan that was to accommodate an enrollment of at least 25,000 students. The buildings were to be constructed over a period of years and to be financed by pyramiding our indebtedness in such a manner that the holders of the later bond issues would be in just as secure a position as the holders of the first issues. The whole program was laid out in great detail by Joseph Franklin and his associates and presented in the course of a two-day Board of Trustees retreat at Camp Brosius in Wisconsin, after which the board courageously adopted it. From that time on we followed the plan consistently, building one student housing complex after another, accommodating both single and married students. The plan through

4. Ibid., ch. 8.

the years proved to be remarkably viable and was not modified in any basic respect except toward the end when two residence complexes (Eigenmann Hall and Forest Quadrangle) were added because enrollment went slightly higher than had been predicted. We felt that the residential program was necessary, not only to see that students were properly housed, but also to relieve the city of the unconscionable burden of accommodating the students privately and to make sure a lack of housing would not strangle the university's development.

During this period enrollments were rising rapidly and requiring a large amount of ever-increasing appropriations. We made it a policy to try to explain our budget request not only to the legislature but also to the presidents of the private colleges in Indiana so that they would be fully informed of what we were asking and would be aware that we were not asking for anything that would be prejudicial to them. In addition we were careful to explain our budget request to the representatives of the various important tax-paying groups, as I have mentioned before, and to describe it fully to the members of the faculty. On at least one occasion we held a student convocation to present the budget request to them just before they went home to family and friends for Christmas. It was our feeling that our own faculty and staff should understand the budget completely and that Bloomington leaders should understand it too because their friends from around the state would undoubtedly be asking them for their reactions and because members of the state legislature would seek their opinions of the need for our ever-higher, well-publicized requests. We therefore would invite representative townspeople to a meeting at which our budget request was explained in detail.

In our search for wherewithal, we attempted by every conceivable device to use what we had effectively and, as inspiration struck, creatively. We would use unconventional methods, if legal and sound, to achieve short-run objectives when it seemed to be necessary to do so. We actively sought efficiency, avoided any unnecessary expenditures, and stood ready for examination at any time. My own work in banking had acquainted me with the importance of being ready for the bank examiner without notification any morning at opening time, and we attempted to run the university in exactly the same way.

Concurrently with our efforts and initiatives to use public funds efficiently, we increasingly stressed the importance of obtaining outside funds from the federal government, from foundations, from private donors. The development of the search for additional sources of funds is treated in chapter 11.

[11]

○ ○ ○

The Private Sector:
Indiana University Foundation

A T THE TIME of Indiana University's centennial in 1920, a fund-raising effort was planned to provide for three badly needed structures that would also serve as a memorial to the sons and daughters of Indiana University who had lost their lives in World War I and commemorate those who had served in earlier wars. A centennial is a logical time for fund raising. The goals selected were for a Student Union Building, a stadium, and a building for women's housing and activities.

In August, 1921, William A. Alexander, an alumnus who had been serving as dean of men at Swarthmore, was brought back to Indiana to head the Memorial Fund campaign and was named university librarian to dignify his leadership of fund-raising activities. Under his direction a mighty campaign was organized. A team that included President and Mrs. Bryan and several student leaders journeyed with Alexander to Washington, Philadelphia, New York, Boston, and Cleveland, speaking to alumni groups on behalf of the campaign.[1]

A tremendous effort was made also to arouse the student body and the faculty, and as a consequence a substantial amount of money was pledged by these two bodies. In fact, the student campaign and the faculty campaign were responsible for most of the money raised, since, although in many individual instances alumni were generous, as a whole they were not oriented to supporting their alma mater. Edward Von Tress, who became alumni secretary in August, 1923,

1. The "Flying Squadron" included five students: Noble Butler, John S. Hastings, James S. Adams, Elisabeth Johnston, and Helen Coblentz.

traveled throughout the West and the South on behalf of the campaign; President Bryan carried it to our alumni in the East. Sufficient funds were raised to furnish financing for the first unit of the Union Building, for the Memorial Stadium—now called the Tenth Street Stadium—and for Memorial Hall, the first building of the Wells Quadrangle complex; however, the campaign in large part demonstrated that the university's fund-raising mechanisms were woefully inadequate and that the natural constituency of the university, composed of its alumni and friends, was ill-informed about the university's needs and the importance of individual giving.

In the course of the Memorial Fund campaign, the fund-raising activities of Indiana University were inevitably compared with those of the other Big Ten institutions and their equivalents throughout the country, usually to Indiana University's disfavor. Then the recession of the late 1920s and the deepening of that recession in the 1930s increased the university's financial problems, and the discussion of ways and means to stimulate alumni contributions to the university and to raise additional money to aid the institution grew lengthier and ever more insistent. Gradually some interested alumni began to perceive that only with outside funds could the peaks of excellence so desired and essential to the university's overall distinction be attained. Discussions and debates continued through the late 1920s and throughout the early 1930s. Certain alumni were especially interested in this subject, principally John Hastings of Washington, Indiana, and Uz McMurtrie of Indianapolis. They worked closely with George "Dixie" Heighway, the successor to Ed Von Tress as alumni secretary, and among them they kept alive the debate and discussion on the fund-raising issue. The early success of the James Whitcomb Riley Association served as a pattern and spur to their direction. The growing interest culminated in the decision to incorporate a nonprofit foundation affiliated with, but independent of, the university. The express purposes of the Indiana University Foundation were to stimulate alumni and other friends of education to make gifts and bequests to aid Indiana University over a broad field: to finance research, to subsidize publications, to establish scholarships and fellowships, to hold patents[2] and other property, and in general to aid the university in any undertaking

2. The Crest toothpaste patent is a later example of this advantageous provision.

for which funds were not otherwise available. The purposes of the Foundation were thus limited solely to the support and enhancement of Indiana University. They remain so today.

The foundation concept, as we know it, took form in the early years of this century through the humanitarian impulses of such pioneers as Andrew Carnegie and John D. Rockefeller. It was in the beginning a uniquely American creation with roots in the spirit of voluntarism that characterizes our culture. The combined contribution of the principal private foundations to the welfare of our nation and of the world is beyond measure; it stands as a remarkable testament to the capabilities inherent in philanthropy administered with the imagination, flexibility, and venturesomeness possible in a private organization.

Major state universities now typically have one or more affiliated foundations designed to help them better serve their students and their states. Through their foundations universities are able to achieve higher levels of excellence than otherwise possible by increasing the funds and options open to them for the encouragement of talent, ideas, and scholarship. State university foundations, it may also be remarked, are free to seek the donation of private funds, whereas states themselves are limited to obtaining funds through the compulsory route of taxation. An additional consideration favoring the development of state university foundations is the necessity of an instrumentality that has the flexibility to carry out functions that are special and essential to the work of a university but that are not customary in state government.

In this regard it should be mentioned that people who would not make a gift or a bequest to an agency of the state will give to a private body such as the Indiana University Foundation. Aside from fearing possible political influence in the disposition of the gifts, they are averse to having their gifts subjected to state restrictions. Also, some donors for good reason wish to remain anonymous: they may want to avoid being harassed by requests for money, to keep members of their family from knowing of the gift, or to prevent publicity that might lead to robbery and assault when it is known that they have money.

Gifts to the university directly are subject to state constraints that were not designed for an operation like the management of gifts and bequests. For instance, the state is limited by law in the kinds of investments it can make. In fact, although legislation would be needed to permit the admixture of university with Foundation gifts, the benefits of fiduciary management by a single office would be many: reduction of cost, uniformity in investment policy with some consolidation, greater diversification and security, and greater efficiency of management.

In 1936 the concept of the foundation was sufficiently new that, notwithstanding the strict limitation of purposes set forth for the Indiana University Foundation, some administrative officers of the university were a little fearful that the movement might represent an effort on the part of certain alumni to try to interfere with the operation of the university. As a consequence the provision was made in the Foundation's bylaws that the board of the Foundation should always include the president of the university, the president of the Board of Trustees, and two other trustees nominated by their fellow trustees.

The corporate charter of the Indiana University Foundation was issued by the Indiana secretary of state on June 15, 1936. The incorporators were Paul V. McNutt, George A. Ball, John S. Hastings, Ora L. Wildermuth, William Lowe Bryan, Hugh McK. Landon, Clair Scott, William A. Alexander, Albert L. Rabb, and Uz McMurtrie. The first bylaws provided for a board of directors not to exceed fifteen, nor to be less than ten, in number. The incorporators constituted the first board. These busy and, in several cases, eminent men were willing to serve partly because of their faith in the university's future but also because they were assured of freedom from partisan pressures and political influence in directing the Foundation as they saw fit. I joined the board upon becoming acting president of the university in July, 1937, one year after the board's inception, and have served on it ever since. During the period from 1937 to 1962 I held the dual offices of chairman of the board and president of the Foundation. When Elvis Stahr became president of the university, he was made chairman of the board of the Foundation, and I continued as its president. Among the administrative officers of the university who gave valuable service to the Foundation during this period were Ward Biddle, Joseph A. Franklin, John Hicks, and T. Edwin Randall. My responsibilities with the Foundation now include the offices of vice president and chairman of the Executive Committee, chairman of the Real Estate Committee, and president of Foun Farm, the wholly Foundation-owned corporation for the management of the Foundation's gifts of real estate, operated for profit. I am also a member of the Nominating Committee and the Investment Committee.

The articles of incorporation of the Foundation state that "the purposes for which it is formed are in general to promote educational and charitable purposes and objects; and specifically, but not in limitation of the foregoing, to receive, hold, manage, use and dispose of properties of all kinds, real and/or personal, whether given absolutely or in trust, or by way of agency or otherwise, for the benefit of Indiana University, and the educational and charitable activities and any or all of them that may be conducted by Indiana University or the trustees of Indiana University, or such corporation or body as may be established to succeed the trustees of Indiana University."

The initial funds for organizing the Foundation were contributed by George A. Ball of Muncie, then a trustee of the university. He gave $5,000 and stated that he expected his gift to be used as seed money to attract other funds that would sustain the growth. At the start George "Dixie" Heighway added to his duties as secretary of the Alumni Association those of executive secretary of the Foundation. Thus from a very simple beginning the present vigorous Indiana University Foundation has been developed.

Soon after becoming president of the Foundation, I began the expansion of the board. The first board was made up of alumni and friends solely from the state of Indiana, with the exception of Clair Scott, an alumnus from Chicago. As we expanded the board and finally amended the bylaws to increase its size to thirty members, we tried to achieve something of a national distribution of our board members. One of the strengths of having an auxiliary foundation to raise money for a state university is its board membership, and board interest therefore may be drawn from the nation or from the world, for that matter, rather than from the state alone.[3] The trustees of Indiana University must by statute be citizens of Indiana, even though our alumni are scattered all over the United States and the world. While the trustees of the university may be representative of the citizens of the state, it would be difficult indeed for them to be representative of the whole alumni body. The Foundation, on the other hand, gives us the opportunity to have a strong, national board working for the university.

3. Seventeen of the current directors live in Indiana and twelve are from out of state; see Appendix (F).

As I have suggested, the Foundation office staff in the beginning consisted solely of Dixie Heighway, who served on a part-time basis, and volunteers. In addition to his knowledge and understanding of Indiana University's great need for private money, he had a remarkable range of information about our alumni and about whether or not they were likely prospects for gifts. He also had many excellent ideas for fund-raising techniques. As the years went along and as new managers came and went, he continued to be the secretary and the important link with the past. An institution needs a memory.

By the mid-1940s we realized that we needed a man who could devote full time to the affairs of fund raising. We were able to secure the services of Lawrence Wheeler, an alumnus, who served the Foundation from January 1, 1944, to July 1, 1949. He was the first professional manager of the Foundation, having gained a broad background in money raising with the Ketchum organization in Pittsburgh. He knew all the techniques to be used and was a skilled writer, adept in the preparation of fund-raising materials. To his advantage, Lawrence Wheeler had a wide acquaintanceship and fine reputation among the professionals in his field, and he had a rare historical sense of the university's values as well as an ability to articulate its aspirations.

At Wheeler's retirement, Howard "Howdy" Wilcox was recruited. He had a good grounding in newspaper work and a natural flair for public relations. Howdy was innovative and energetic. The achievement of his period was remarkable, considering the shortness of its duration (1949–52). To interest students in the work of the Foundation and to make them aware of the university's needs, he organized the Student Foundation Committee, forerunner of the Student Foundation. Drawing upon the student leadership on campus, the executive director's office selected thirty-six men and women students, both organized and unorganized,[4] for the first committee. They received their appointments from me as the university's president and were honored a few days later at a dinner given for them by the Foundation. From the beginning the purpose of the Foundation was impressed upon them, as were the needs of the university and their role in interpreting those needs to other students. It was hoped and believed that they would carry this knowledge with them

4. Students who belonged to fraternities or sororities were spoken of as "organized," and others were referred to as "unorganized."

into their adult lives, when many of them might have the means and influence to have a major role in the Foundation's fund raising. The assumptions underlying this approach are necessarily speculative and as such dictated a cautious allocation of the Foundation's direction and resources to this development, but the concept of student involvement had the approval of the president of the Foundation and of the university.

Howdy Wilcox also launched a feature that was to become famous, the annual Little 500 bicycle race, patterned after the Indianapolis 500. The Little 500 has served as a rallying point for the activities of the Student Foundation Steering Committee. From the beginning the net proceeds from the sale of tickets have been used to provide scholarships for students who are working their way through school and need some help. The Student Foundation also sponsors other events such as Red Carpet Days for prospective students and the Telefund solicitation. Even after Howdy joined the Pulliam newspapers in 1952, he remained close to the Foundation and has for many years served as a very loyal and effective member of the Foundation's board of trustees. From 1963 to 1966 he was also an Indiana University trustee.

William S. Armstrong, a former sports newscaster and dairy company executive in Owensboro, Kentucky, succeeded to the Foundation directorship in November, 1952. He brought to the job a considerable experience in selling as well as enormous energy and enthusiasm. As an undergraduate Bill had been active in promoting university events along with Danny Danielson and Bill Menke, a powerful troika of student leaders. His devotion and dedication remained strong when he became an alumnus. Bill has given to the Foundation the valuable advantage of continuity of leadership. During this period, the Foundation has had its greatest growth—a period within which annual fund raising has become increasingly important, the Student Foundation has multiplied its program, and the Foundation itself has developed importantly as a factor in the support of university activities.

In the first decade and a half of the Foundation, the limited funds raised were mostly from private gifts and were applied directly to faculty use, to scholarships, to loan funds, and to the purchase of important collections for the libraries. A major effort was directed toward securing patents for faculty research products and, later, toward placing information about bequests and life income trusts in the hands of lawyers who might have as clients potential donors to the university. During the 1940s, the appeal for funds was organized into an annual giving campaign, and by the end of that decade the yearly drive was given visibility and impetus by the appointment of a national campaign chairman, Byron Elliott, with aides heading the solicitation in each state. Meanwhile the federal government became active in support of university research, and large private foundations stepped up their programs in direct aid to research. The Foundation, as a result, became increasingly involved in the field of grantsmanship and in the administration of grants.

The vigorous recruitment of new, research-minded faculty members at Indiana University in the late 1930s had stimulated a search for increased research funding from government agencies and foundations. In the period following World War II, from 1945 on, the Ford Foundation, the Carnegie Foundation, and the Rockefeller Foundation were all interested in supporting a variety of university activities, at home and abroad. The Ford Foundation, for instance, furnished much of the financing for the development of the university's Russian and East European Studies program. It also helped finance a variety of overseas activities. The Rockefeller Foundation was a source of funding for many projects in biology such as the addition of Herman Muller to our genetics team and the initial funding of Alfred Kinsey's Institute for Sex Research. Several other projects were financed by the Carnegie Foundation and Corporation.

At about this same period the federal government's increased interest in supporting research was evidenced at Indiana University in the Navy's grants for fundamental work in mathematics and in the support of physics, biology and chemistry by other departments of government. Our noted, bright new members of the faculty were energetic in pursuing research grants that, upon receipt, were channeled through the Foundation. For several years we retained in the Foundation that portion of every government grant designated for indirect costs so that these funds might be used flexibly as needed in the development of the university. In time we accumulated a relatively substantial sum of unobligated money through this means and allocated it where it was needed most in the university. We used it to seed new programs that in turn would attract more support. We used it for specialized equipment that would make it possible for the science faculty, particularly, to refine their research and even be more productive. We used sizable amounts of it for specialized library acquisitions, general library enrichment, and the purchase of special collections. Eventually we had sufficient funds to use as matching monies for federal grants to help in the construction of new buildings made necessary by our research activity and growing enrollment. All of this was done with the full knowledge of the faculty, to whom I reported from time to time on the use of these funds and from whom I received suggestions and comments. As I mentioned, had we put the indirect-costs reimbursement back into the General Fund, it might well have been dispersed too widely to be effective in any one way; instead, we used these funds for specific project objectives that were designed to enhance the quality of the university. The same policy was followed at the University of California at Berkeley during this period: the trustees of the University of California placed its indirect-cost money in a special fund that was drawn on for purposes similar to those for which ours were used. It was during this period that Berkeley made its greatest advance. I suspect that I may have learned this tactic from Robert Sproul, then president of the University of California. But, whatever the source of the idea, as I look back on it, it may have been the most effective of our administrative policies during that period in promoting the rapid development of the scholarly and research interests of the university.

In the development of an institution there is no substitute for a reasonable reservoir of money that can be used propitiously as opportunities present themselves. The university is no longer allowed by state authorities to follow that practice with regard to indirect-costs reimbursement and, as a consequence, undesignated funds have to be raised from alumni and friends for these opportune grants. The solicitation of undesignated funds is one of the most important functions the Foundation performs today, and it is devoting much of its energies to that work.

Those in university fund raising should like to respond to every request for funds from members of the University family. To do so is impossible for several reasons: the desires of individuals frequently conflict with each other; there is insufficient staff to attempt to meet all needs at one time even if the requests are equally worthy—phasing and priority determination are essential; certain types of needs should be met by the state, and it is not in the long-range interest of the university to relieve the state of doing so; and certain kinds of projects simply have no appeal to private donors, regardless of how eloquently the need or advantage may be presented. The staff charged with soliciting private funds and federal and foundation grants can be enormously aided by faculty understanding in what is involved in donor solicitation and by active faculty participation through sharing suggestions and ideas with the staff.

A quantum leap forward in the affairs of the Foundation came with the success of the 150th Birthday Fund drive in 1970. The purposes for which this fund was to be raised had been brought before the Faculty Council by President Stahr during the latter part of his administration, and the fund goal and the individual objectives had been explored with alumni and potential donors. The campaign was launched publicly on December 11, 1968. The announced goal set for the campaign was $25 million; by the conclusion of the campaign on July 28, 1972, we had raised $51,218,045.25 in cash, pledges, and pledged bequests, distributed among the goals of the campaign according to the designations of the donors (see Appendix [G]).

Such a major effort required additional staff who could devote themselves exclusively to the campaign. Fortunately we were able to enlist as the national chairman of the campaign Byron Elliott, a senior member of the board of the Foundation, a highly successful and respected insurance executive and alumnus, and, as already mentioned, the first chairman of the annual giving campaign. We were also exceptionally fortunate to be able to attract to the university Major General Joseph Butcher, who took early retirement from the Marine Corps in order to undertake the assignment as director of the campaign. General Butcher was a very loyal alumnus who had served as president of the Alumni Association and enjoyed a wide acquaintanceship with our alumni. He was ideally suited for this responsibility, which he performed remarkably well. The campaign was integrated with the university's Sesquicentennial celebration, which was the greatest academic and historical festival the university has ever had. It was very effectively headed by Claude Rich. The university's year-long celebration with its many important events and famous speakers helped to bring the campaign to the attention of alumni and other interested parties and performed an important role in assuring the drive's success.

The Sesquicentennial campaign benefited from several circumstances not present at the time of the centennial campaign. Among these were the fact that the annual giving campaign of the Foundation had helped to make our alumni more aware of the university's need for private gifts. Also, as an indirect result of President Bryan's policy of broadening the curricular base of the university, a higher percentage of alumni were in more remunerative fields than teaching. (The alumni body was made up primarily of teachers at the time of the Centennial.) Younger alumni, many of whom had been in Student Foundation activities, readily undertook the work of solicitation in geographical regions. Some of our older alumni who had been successful in their fields and had retained a strong interest in the university, in several cases serving on the Foundation board or as an Alumni Association officer, contributed handsomely. And, last, the growth of some family fortunes in Indiana (the Krannerts, the Lillys, the Balls, the Irwin-Sweeney-Miller family) made possible the generous gifts from these friends of the university that were a major factor in the campaign's success.

It is a truism in academic fund-raising circles that special campaigns must be conducted in addition to annual giving campaigns in order to stimulate the interest of alumni and friends. Therefore, at regular intervals appropriate occasions must be found for such campaigns. The 150th anniversary of Indiana University was, of course, an especially fit occasion for the launching of a campaign, and the university's need for certain facilities and resources that are not typically provided by the state furnished the rationale. The success of the campaign has had a marked influence on the activity of the Foundation. Since that date, the amount received annually by the Foundation, in part from the payment of campaign pledges, but in addition as a result of the aroused interest in giving to the university, has increased steadily during the past five years, as has the number of givers.

The rapid growth of the Foundation in assets and responsibility has necessitated additional executive personnel. Bill Armstrong has been fortunate in attracting a number of competent people for administrative positions in the Foundation, notable among whom are the two vice presidents, James Elliott and Jerry Tardy. Jim Elliott, trained both as an accountant and a lawyer, has remarkable competence in the financial field. Knowledgeable about taxes, he is a topflight investment man and an exceptionally capable money manager. These abilities aid him in successfully counseling major donors. Jerry Tardy is in charge of the annual giving campaign as well as the medical school campaign, but especially attends to the Foundation's administrative management as Bill Armstrong's able assistant.

Another personnel development that merits mention is the service of alumni who, after having had distinguished business or teaching careers, have elected to spend their retirement years in assisting the Foundation. Harold Lusk and Edward Von Tress were the first to demonstrate the value of this practice. Currently this role is being filled effectively by Eugene Fletchall, who is charged in part with the operation of the Well House Society. The Well House Society, launched two or three years ago, has as one of its main purposes the amassing of an unrestricted fund for the use of the president of the university to meet urgent needs.

The longer I live with the problems associated with the financing of the university, the more I realize that the peaks of excellence are provided typically by private money, as I have already remarked. The state, within the limits of its means, out of tax revenues, attempts to provide for the basic necessities of the institution: the campuses, the teaching staff, the classroom buildings, and the housekeeping—the heat, light, fuel, and so forth. But there is rarely ever enough money from this source to fund the exceptional, the special —areas unusually important in research and basic scholarship. They require outside money, outside grants, which make the real difference between simply a good teaching institution and a true university that must not only teach—and teach well—undergraduates but also provide graduate and professional education. To do so it must be heavily engaged in research. Needed funds for this purpose go far beyond the basic support provided by the state. It is for this reason that the Foundation's money-raising efforts and the other money-raising efforts to aid the university are of such vital importance. In addition to the Indiana University Foundation, the James Whitcomb Riley Memorial Association, which built the Riley Hospital in Indianapolis, has been one of the major sources of outside support to the university for research in children's diseases as well as for the Medical Center research of benefit to children.

As the result largely of individual gifts and bequests in the past, the Foundation is heavily engaged now in investment and property management, along with the administration of wills, trusts, and designated gifts. Possibly better than any other, this feature of the Foundation demonstrates the distance that the Foundation has traveled since its beginning. This feature, too, according to the way it is managed, is crucial in developing the confidence needed for individuals to entrust gifts and bequests to the Foundation for the benefit of Indiana University.

Another crucial component for future success is the attitude and interest of students and faculty. The members of the university community need to understand the importance of gifts and bequests for the maintenance and enhancement of the university's distinction in the future. They need to understand as much as possible the attitudes of potential private donors. With this understanding, in their many individual contacts they can tell the story of the university's needs and the special opportunities those needs provide for all who are interested in supporting youth and higher education. In addition they can help to bring prospective donors to the attention of Foundation officers.

Perhaps sufficient time has now passed to begin assessing the effectiveness of directing ever more attention and resources of the Foundation toward development of student leaders as the funding source of the Foundation. The Pacesetter Fund, or Armstrong Student Foundation Endowment Fund, a campaign honoring William Armstrong's twenty-five years with the Foundation, is designed to give a first answer to that approach. Meanwhile the annual giving campaigns will continue to profit from the accumulated experience of conducting yearly drives.

In 1986 the Indiana University Foundation will be fifty years old. It is therefore appropriate to mark that significant anniversary by concluding another major capital-gifts campaign, launched in good time and comparable to—or in excess of—the 150th Birthday Fund drive. Such an endeavor will furnish an ideal vehicle for recapitulating the record of the Foundation in service to the university for the information of students, faculty, alumni, friends, and the state. More important, it can provide funds for the critical needs of the university in the late 1980s and 1990s and inspire the rise to a new level of annual giving.

The first official portrait in my term as president.
(*Harris and Ewing*)

On the way to my inauguration, 1938, with Governor Henry
Schricker at my side and William Lowe Bryan behind me.

Bipartisan support at a football game in the 1940s—Charles Halleck on my right, appropriately, and Paul McNutt on my left.

Coach Bo McMillin and I rejoice over Indiana University's first Big Ten football championship, 1945. (*Allan Grant*)

On the chicken-and-mashed-potato circuit early in my presidency.

The president's office housed its share of returning
G.I.'s, 1946.

Celebrating James Whitcomb Riley's birthday with some
young friends, October, 1947.

Postwar German education as viewed with Frank Banta, 1948.

With J. K. Lilly at the groundbreaking for the Lilly Library,
March 7, 1958.

⌈12⌉

○ ○ ○

Academic Freedom and Tenure

EARLY IN my career as president of Indiana University, I was invited to speak at a forum sponsored by the Senate Avenue YMCA in Indianapolis on education in a democracy. It was in 1939, just prior to the issuance of the classic statement on academic freedom and tenure by the American Association of University Professors (AAUP), and I began by proposing that the principle of academic freedom is basic to education in a democracy. I pointed out that

> through all this more than a century, the university has actively worked for the preservation and advancement of American democracy by the method that is peculiarly the university's own, namely, fearless inquiry into every subject in search of the truth—fearless inquiry, not only in the "safe" realm of the physical sciences, but in the social sciences as well, even though they deal with the stuff of which human emotions and passions are made.

It must be remembered that democratic principles and individual freedoms were at that time once again threatened as they had been in World War I. With more and more foreboding we read of the horrors and conquests of Hitler's Nazi Germany, and many of America's educational leaders began to fear a recurrence of the violation of the academic sphere that accompanied World War I. The AAUP statement came in 1940. By the fall of 1943 it was felt advisable that Indiana University's consistent but unwritten policy on academic freedom be given formal expression, and on September 11, 1943, the Board of Trustees adopted the following statement, the first of its kind in the university's history:

> No restraint shall be placed upon the teacher's freedom in investigation, unless restriction upon the amount of time devoted to

it becomes necessary in order to prevent undue interference with other duties. No limitation shall be placed upon the teacher's freedom in the exposition of his own subject in the classroom or in addresses and publications outside the classroom so long as the statements are not definitely antisocial. No teacher shall claim as his right the privilege of discussing in his classroom controversial topics obviously and clearly outside of his own field of study. The teacher is morally bound not to take advantage of his position by introduction into the classroom of provocative discussions of completely irrelevant subjects admittedly not within the field of his study. The university recognizes that the teacher, in speaking and writing outside the institution upon subjects beyond the scope of his own field of study, is entitled to precisely the same freedom, but is subject to the same responsibility, as attaches to all other citizens.

The exposition of the university's tenure policy completed the statement.

Undoubtedly the greatest test of this principle of academic freedom resulted from some research that had been started in July, 1938, when Alfred C. Kinsey began the collection of sex histories from individuals. A respected biologist and Starred Man of Science, Dr. Kinsey became interested in the field of human sexuality when he discovered how little sex research was available to guide him in answering questions from his students. Employing the method of his longtime research on gall wasps, taxonomy, he launched an ambitious project to collect 100,000 sex histories of individuals. He knew, of course, that he would encounter opposition in gathering material on a topic involving the intimate lives of people. As he described it:

> There were attempts by the medical association in one city to bring suit on the ground that we were practicing medicine without a license, police interference in two or three cities, investigation by a sheriff in one rural area, and attempts to persuade the university's administration to stop the study, or to prevent the publication of the results, or to dismiss the senior author from his university connection, or to establish a censorship over all publication emanating from the study. . . . There were . . . threats of legal action, threats of political investigation, and threats of censorship, and for some years there was criticism from scientific colleagues. . . . Through all of this, the administration of Indiana University stoutly defended our right to do objectively scientific research, and to that defense much of the success of this project is due.[1]

1. Alfred C. Kinsey, Wardell B. Pomeroy, Clyde E. Martin, *Sexual Behavior in the Human Male* (Philadelphia: W. B. Saunders, 1948), pp. 11–12.

For me, there was really no question about support of Kinsey's research. I had early made up my mind that a university that bows to the wishes of a person, group, or segment of society is not free and that a state university in particular cannot expect to command the support of the public if it is the captive of any group. It must be a free agent to deserve the support of all the public, free of untoward influence from any group—business, church, labor, politics, and so on—and the only way to keep it free is to be willing to fight when necessary. We followed that policy, never yielding regardless of the pressures. It was not easy; there were hardships involved in sustaining this principle through public hearings, threats of legislative reprisal, and the disaffection of some faculty members who were squeamish about short-run consequences.

Observers of the American academic scene have called Indiana University's winning of its battle to protect Kinsey's Institute for Sex Research from those who would have eliminated it a landmark victory for academic freedom. So much has been written about this battle and the university's participation in it that I need not recount the experience in detail.[2] Rather, a few recollections of my own may be of interest.

In the very beginning I pointed out to the university trustees that the Kinsey study would be highly controversial and that we would be under great pressure to suppress it, but at that time I little realized the extent of the pressure that would come. In essence I told the board that Alfred Kinsey was a recognized scientist and that, although he was dealing with a highly emotional and explosive subject, he must be protected by the university and his right to carry on his research must be unimpaired if the university desired to be called a true university. Difficult and hard though this crucial test of the university's integrity might be, should we fail it, all hope for the achievement of real university distinction would be lost. I am proud to record the fact that, although the individual members of the board and the board as a whole were harassed and subjected to all manner of pressure, they never once wavered in their support of our policy toward the Kinsey Institute. They did not waver even when the board of the Rockefeller Foundation finally decided that discretion was the better part of valor and withdrew its support from the project.

2. See Thomas D. Clark, *Indiana University: Midwestern Pioneer*, vol. 3, *Years of Fulfillment* (Bloomington: Indiana University Press, 1977), ch. 10.

The Indianapolis *Star* (November 17, 1950) erupted shortly before a legislative session with a front-page story under the heading " 'Science' Says Kinsey: 'Dirty Stuff' Says U.S." The Indianapolis customs collector, Alden Baker, had opened a shipment of Japanese art work and seventeenth- and eighteenth-century French miniatures that he had gratuitously shown to the press and allowed to be photographed. His action was, of course, illegal. The trustees met the next day and I reported to them that the governor and certain members of the legislature were greatly exercised. The governor had called me in midmorning after he had seen the *Star*. "Herman," he had almost shouted, "what in the name of God do you mean by importing those dirty pictures?" I had tried to explain that one of the criticisms of Kinsey's first book had been that it was too statistical, that it failed to take into account the emotional and aesthetic aspects of sex that could be found in art and literature, and that Kinsey, as a result, had been attempting to build a library of erotica from which to correct his alleged neglect of the senses in his account. Even though it had been difficult to interrupt the governor's fuming for long, I had managed to point out that this material was to be used only by scholars in the field and would not be accessible to the public. The governor had continued to rage, growing more irate the longer he held forth. Finally, in desperation, I had said, "Governor, you are so angry, you're not listening to me. When you cool off, I will talk to you." With that, I hung up on him—the only time I have ever done such a thing and certainly then with considerable risk.

The Board of Trustees saw that I was still uneasy and in a quandary about the situation. To my surprise Merrill Davis, a board member, asked, "Do you mind if I attempt to handle this?" "Mind? I would be greatly relieved," I answered. Dr. Davis was not only a highly successful surgeon and friend of the governor, he was an art connoisseur as well, competent to appraise artistic quality and to identify the erotic manifestations that are frequently overlooked in familiar, famous paintings. Not long afterward, armed with several books containing illustrations of master painters' works that hang in the foremost museums, Dr. Davis called upon the governor. After a few pleasantries he said, as he later related, "Governor, I wish to show you some pictures I think you'll recognize." Then, leafing through the books, he began to point out the erotic details in each well-known painting. The governor, after observing and listening attentively for a few moments, suddenly grinned and said, "Oh, hell, Merrill. Get out of here!" And that was the last we heard from him about the Kinsey material.

Other members of the Board of Trustees spent endless hours then and at other times explaining the Kinsey project to irate friends, alumni, and legislators, and absorbing a considerable amount of personal abuse. During this period we would discuss the latest developments in their meetings, exchange ideas, and regenerate our courage and resolve to continue the battle.

The general administrative officers of the university were always trying to think of ways and means by which we could present the Kinsey program constructively to the public and to marshal our friends both inside and outside the university, in the public, and in the press to assist in this defense. I would be remiss if I failed to mention the numbers of persons with no direct connection to Indiana University who, convinced of the university's integrity and purpose, buoyed the spirits of the embattled university community. It was a great cooperative effort and a part of the task of the central administrative offices was to keep that cooperative effort in place, alive and vigorous.

For the most part the members of the faculty were highly supportive, although there were those who were frightened that the university would suffer reprisals and be harmed by the project and others who were opposed to the study for a variety of reasons, some professional and some emotional.

The students were on the whole interested and cooperative, and I am sure they were a helpful influence in their contacts with parents and friends throughout the state and nation.

Although many alumni expressed concern, their concern for the most part was expressed in an appropriate and constructive manner, that is, by seeking information. A few attacked us emotionally and beyond reason. But it must be recorded that throughout this entire period no official organ of the Alumni Association moved in any way to interfere. In fact, the officers of the association were supportive throughout, even though I know it must have been extremely difficult for them to live with the constant pressure created by the publicity.

Many clergymen upheld the project in a quiet way and found the Kinsey studies helpful to them in counseling their parishioners. However, some openly attacked the university. One of the most vicious attacks was that of Jean Milner, the influential pastor of the Second Presbyterian Church in Indianapolis, which included among its membership quite a few of our important alumni and many of the leading citizens of Indianapolis. In fact, Dr. Milner had more members of the power structure of the state—political, economic, and social—in his congregation than was true of any other church. He hurled a bitter broadside, even though confessing that he had not read the studies and did not intend to. Perhaps this confession blunted his criticism a little bit, but it was nonetheless a cruel blow.

Almost the entire Catholic hierarchy, the Archbishop of Indianapolis, and the Catholic press were uniformly critical. The most direct attack was made by the state division of the National Council of Catholic Women; their letter and my reply, which includes my earlier, official statement in support of the project, give some sense of the intensity of the battle:

August 24, 1953

Dr. Herman B Wells, A.M., LL.D.
President, Indiana University
Bloomington, Indiana

Dear Dr. Wells:

In the name of more than 150,000 women—most of them mothers, many of them with sons and daughters of college age—we, the Indiana Provincial Council of Catholic Women, seek some reassurance from you that Indiana University is still a place fit for the educating of the youth of our State.

How representative of Indiana University is the thinking of Dr. Alfred Kinsey? We have not, of course, read his latest book, but we have seen the sensational reports on it in magazines and newspapers, and these are frightening, indeed. Almost without exception, the writers, who have carefully studied Dr. Kinsey's book and have been thoroughly briefed by him, come to the conclusion that the Indiana professor considers our present sexual morals for the most part to be superstitious notions of an unenlightened and uncritical past. How dangerous such a teaching can be should be evident to you, Dr. Wells, as you know from many years of experience how difficult it is for youths to master themselves and learn to accept the demands that society imposes upon them.

But what of the practical conclusions young people themselves will draw from reading press accounts of the latest Kinsey report? A man presented to them by Indiana University as a distinguished scientist seems to advise them that to follow the accepted morals may lead them into preversions [sic] and that the chances for happiness in marriage may be in direct proportion to the amount of sexual experience they have as teen-agers. What will our youth make of this?

If you, Dr. Wells, do not recognize how dangerous it is to popularize incendiary suggestions like these, we tremble at what may happen to our sons and daughters entrusted to the care of Indiana University? For we acknowledge that in the past we have been happy in the assurance that whatever strange ideas individual professors may have propagated, you and the other authorities of the university staunchly supported Christian morality. We were shocked, therefore, to learn that you support Dr. Kinsey.

Convinced, however, that you cannot agree with his philosophy, we request a clarification. Will our sons and daughters be exposed to the ideas of Dr. Kinsey? Dare we risk placing them in the charge of a university that seems to be willing to degrade science for the sake of sensational publicity?

However far from the morals of our forefathers many Americans have strayed, most of us have steadfastly held that their ideals must remain our ideals, if we are to preserve our American way of life. Those ideals of the dignity and rights of man sprang from the firm conviction that there is a moral law determined by God. In recent years we have seen in Nazi Germany what can happen to men when the traditional idea of moral law is questioned and then scoffed at. Dr. Kinsey questions the worth of Christian morality; he comes close to scoffing at it. Does he represent your thought, Dr. Wells? Does he represent the thought of Indiana University?

We include among our numbers the mothers of no small segment of the student personnel of Indiana University and are, therefore, quite naturally perturbed at the thought that Dr. Kinsey's philosophy become the accepted ethics of the class room and campus of the university. We are appalled at the suggestion that premarital sex experience will make for a more happy married life. We are convinced that God is still the author and vindicator of the commandments and that, the pseudo-scientific deductions of Dr. Kinsey notwithstanding, a deliberate indulgence in the forbidden fruit may bring a passing sordid pleasure but it can never be the source of happiness.

As women interested in preserving our American way of life, as mothers anxious for the welfare of our sons and daughters, we seek the reassurance only you can give.

Mrs. Harold D. Brady
Indiana Provincial Director
National Council of Catholic Women

Mrs. Alfred C. Brown
President of the Indianapolis
Archdiocesan Council of
Catholic Women

September 2, 1953

Mrs. Alfred C. Brown, President
Indianapolis Archdiocesan Council of Catholic Women
Brookville, Indiana

Dear Mrs. Brown:

I am in receipt of the letter of August 24th signed by you and Mrs. Harold D. Brady in your respective official capacities in the National Council of Catholic Women.

In reply, I wish first to assure you that I have the highest respect and regard for the National Council of Catholic Women and its effective work and outstanding services. Therefore, I am happy to reply to your inquiry.

You ask for a clarification of the University's support of Dr. Alfred C. Kinsey's scientific research project. Perhaps you have not had an opportunity to read the entire statement issued August 21st in this respect, which said:

"Indiana University stands today, as it has for fifteen years, firmly in support of the scientific research project that has been undertaken and is being carried on by one of its eminent biological scientists, Dr. Alfred C. Kinsey.

"The University believes that the human race has been able to make progress because individuals have been free to investigate all aspects of life. It further believes that only through scientific knowledge so gained can we find the cures for the emotional and social maladies in our society.

"In support of Dr. Kinsey's research the University is proud to have as co-sponsor the National Research Council and its distinguished committee of scientists and physicians in charge of studies of this nature. With the chairman of that committee I agree in saying that we have large faith in the values of knowledge, little faith in ignorance."

The University never approves or disapproves the research findings of its experimental scientists. This is just as true of popular as of unpopular results. The verdict as to the validity of any finding can only be given by professional workers in the same field who subject all findings to continued examination, checking, and additional research. This final verdict frequently takes many years, perhaps decades.

The endorsement given by the University to the research project in question, or to any other, concerns the right of the scientist to investigate every aspect of life in the belief that knowledge, rather than ignorance, will assist mankind in the slow and painful development toward a more perfect society. To deny this right and this objective would seem to deny the belief in a divine order as it pertains to men and the universe.

This same conviction, I am sure, motivated the eminent scientists of the National Research Council, an agency of the National

Academy of Sciences. The Council not only has approved, but provides, the greater portion of the supporting funds for the Kinsey project. Moreover, it has provided for the project an advisory committee consisting of these distinguished scientists and physicians: George W. Corner, M.D., Chairman, Director, Department of Embryology, Carnegie Institution of Washington; Willard M. Allen, M.D., Professor of Obstetrics and Gynecology, Washington University, St. Louis; Clyde L. Kluckhohn, Ph.D., Professor of Anthropology, Harvard University; Karl S. Lashley, Ph.D., Professor of Psychology, Harvard University, and Director, Yerkes Laboratories for Primate Biology, Orange Park, Florida; C. N. H. Long, D.Sc., M.D., Professor of Physiological Chemistry, Yale University; Carl R. Moore, Ph.D., Professor of Zoology, University of Chicago; James V. Neel, Ph.D., M.D., Geneticist, Laboratory of Vertebrate Zoology, University of Michigan; and Milton C. Winternitz, M.D., ex officio Director, Division of Medical Sciences, National Research Council.

The search for truth is one function of all universities. Another function is teaching. Dr. Kinsey's research project is entirely divorced from the University's teaching function and he and his colleagues are assigned full time to research duties.

The University is proud of its teaching record. Last June it graduated 2,615 young men and women. This group, those who preceded them, and those yet to come will stand comparison with the graduates of any institution in the country as to morals, ideals, high-minded purpose, and integrity. This, I assume, you will not question. This the University will defend against any attack.

The churches, including yours, have contributed to this proud record of the University. On every Sunday during the school year there is a vast outpouring of students of the University into the churches of the community, crowding them to capacity and in some instances requiring several services for their accommodation.

The University has encouraged and invited the development of religious facilities adjacent to the campus in order that its students might have the continuing benefit of the spiritual guidance of their respective churches. The University is grateful to the churches of Indiana that they have responded to its invitation and desires to express through you great gratitude to the Catholics of Indiana for the beautiful new Catholic Church in Bloomington near the campus for the benefit of the student body.

I trust that what I have said will give you the reassurance which you sought with regard to Indiana University.

Cordially yours,
H. B Wells

This was not the first time Indiana University had been criticized by clergy and church representatives in a formidable manner. During his years at the university David Starr Jordan espoused the Darwinian theory of the evolution of the species and was bitterly attacked by the clergy of Indiana, but he did not yield. Instead he continued to stump the state and by overcoming his opponents established a precedent that helped to sustain us in the Kinsey battle.

It is difficult now to make vivid the steady national uproar that continued over a number of years as the Kinsey studies unfolded. But throughout we benefited from the sensitive cooperation of the embattled Kinsey, who, although he could be dogmatic and bitter in his counterattack and rightfully so, nevertheless cooperated with us in the many efforts that we made to see that the study was presented in the best possible light.

Great time and effort were devoted to the handling of the publicity with reference to the studies: the publication of the major studies was timed to follow shortly after a legislative session so that there would be a long cooling-off period before the next session started; and Kinsey helped by receiving delegations of legislators, showing them through his laboratory, and explaining his research procedures. We made it a policy to invite the bipartisan and influential state Budget Committee in its annual visit to the campus to tour the Kinsey Institute. The fact that this committee had visited the institute and found it to be not a den of iniquity but a highly antiseptic, scientific laboratory and the professionalism of Dr. Kinsey's own presentation to the committee were especially beneficial. I am confident that Dr. Kinsey's willingness to cooperate in various ways in handling the delicate public-relations problems posed by the study was a major factor in winning the battle. Without his help it could not have been done.

When we were unable to get the federal government to release the materials for the institute's library that had been impounded by Customs in Indianapolis, it became necessary to bring suit against the government. The Board of Trustees took the extraordinary action of volunteering to hire outstanding counsel for the university to appear with the Kinsey Institute as amicus curiae in challenging the government's policy. It was our great good fortune to be able to enlist at that time the state's most prestigious law firm—Barnes, Hickam, Pantzer and Boyd—to represent the university, and the case was assigned to the senior partner in charge of trial work, Hubert Hickam, an alumnus of the university. The firm had not accepted cases of this type previously but agreed to participate in the suit on an actual-cost basis. Later, members of the firm termed it one of the most interesting cases the firm had ever handled.[3] In my judgment, the trustees' action in this instance is among the proudest moments in the annals of the Indiana University Board of Trustees and in the history of Indiana University.

Because of the long duration of the pressure, because of its immensity, heat, and bitterness, I am sure that the whole university community from time to time wished the controversy could be ended. Looking back over the experience, I am now convinced that the importance we attached to the defense of the Kinsey Institute was not exaggerated. Time has proved that the defense was important, not only for the understanding of sexual activity, but also for the welfare of the university. It reinforced the faculty's sense of freedom to carry on their work without fear of interference, and it established in the public mind the fact that the university had an integrity that could not be bought, pressured, or subverted. I feel that the stand enormously increased the respect people had for the university, even those people who were bitter opponents of the Kinsey project. Over time, for a university's reputation nothing rivals courage, integrity, and impartiality in the protection of its scholars.

One sidelight on the story of the Kinsey battle that may be of interest occurred at the time of the fiftieth-anniversary celebration of the Rockefeller Foundation. The occasion, a formal affair, was held in the magnificent ballroom of the Plaza Hotel in New York City. All the Rockefeller brothers were present as was Dean Rusk, then U.S. Secretary of State, who had come from Washington to be the principal speaker. A great array of scholars from all over the world was present for the elegant, formal dinner. I was seated next to Robert Sproul, at the time recently retired from the presidency of the University of California. Looking about the room I tried to discover a clue to the guest list, since most of the guests for that kind of an affair are invited on the basis of a particular rationale. Neither Bob Sproul nor I knew why we were there. As we studied the crowd further, however, we came to the conclusion that the guest list for the most part had been made up of men who had conducted important scholarly activity for the Rockefeller Foundation through its first half-century and of representatives of institu-

3. The Institute employed Harriet Pilpel, a partner in the firm of Greenbaum, Wolff and Ernst, to represent it. The Institute received a favorable judgment, a decision important to the whole scholarly community.

tions associated with important Rockefeller Foundation projects.

At the end of the dinner I happened to see Robert Morison, head of the medical division of the Rockefeller Foundation, and told him of our discussion about the guest list. He confirmed the general hypothesis, adding, "Of course you were invited because the Rockefeller Foundation helped launch the Kinsey study." He continued, "Our medical division was asked to select its most significant projects in the past fifty years. I asked one of our young men to go back through the records and come up with a list. In due course he brought me the papers on the Kinsey Institute and asked, 'Does this rate as one of our important ones?'" Dr. Morison recounted that he had on his desk at that moment the latest textbook in gynecology, an excellent work. "I turned to a certain chapter and told the young man, 'This could not have been written before the Kinsey Institute studies. Does that give you your answer?' The young man responded with a smile, 'I think it does.'" Dr. Morison concluded, "We consider the Kinsey Institute one of the most important projects that our medical division has supported."

It is sometimes said that academic freedom can be maintained for faculty in private institutions alone. My own belief is that a state university not only has a greater need to be a free institution but also has the opportunity with proper leadership to become the freest of all academic institutions. A state university has responsibility to every segment of its society because it is supported through taxes by every segment of the state. Hence it has the same accountability to the Catholics that it has to the Protestants. It has the same obligation to business as it has to labor. It has the same responsibility to farmers as it does to manufacturers. Each sector of society is typically alert to any show of bias toward other sectors by a state university. With the pressures for recognition and service coming from everywhere, the public institution can be free and impartial because of these balanced forces. If the manufacturers pressure, for example, labor is a countervailing pressure. Under proper management and leadership the counterbalancing forces serve to offset one another and thereby to create in the center a vacuum of neutrality and freedom that makes it easier for a public institution to protect academic freedom than for a private institution to do so. Furthermore, since all the citizens of the state support the public institution through their taxes, it would be immoral for the university to favor one group over another.

I consider that the crucial questions of academic freedom raised during my presidency were related, first, to the Kinsey study and all its aspects, including the importation of erotic materials; second, to the recurring attacks by the American Legion and others against the university, culminating in the Legion's demand for investigation of the infiltration of the university by Communists, a charge that resulted from an informal petition signed by professors Bernard Gavit, Fowler Harper, and Howard Mann to the Indiana Board of Election Commissioners stating that, if the petition filed by the Communist Party (to be on the ballot) fulfilled the statutory requirements, it would be a mistake arbitrarily to refuse placement on the ballot; third, to attacks leveled against us over the development of the Russian and East European Studies program and specifically the importation of library materials essential to that study; and finally, to the attacks on us at the time of the importation of fugitive library materials dealing with the Hitler period in Germany while Professor Leonard Lundin and perhaps others were studying the Fascist phenomenon in Germany and elsewhere in Europe.[4]

Much was made of a stir in the mid-1950s, popularly known as the Green Feather incident, which I did not then nor do I now consider an issue of academic freedom. A small group of students with the commendable aim, in my judgment, of attacking the position of Senator Joseph McCarthy and McCarthyism generally sought to gain student support. Identifying themselves with Robin Hood's Merry Men, they made green feathers their symbol. In the course of their one-issue campaign they ran afoul of university regulations concerning recognition of student organizations and concerning political speakers on campus. Campuses in those days were not so open as they are now, and student activities were subject to many more regulations; since the 1960s changes have come about that make the situation in the 1950s difficult for present-day students to understand. In the case of the Green Feather incident, there was what many considered a righteous cause on the one hand, and on the other were regulations that, if waived or breached by the administration, would have been on behalf of the cause, thus destroying the university's neutrality.

4. The Federal Bureau of Narcotics asked the university, from time to time, to restrict Professor Alfred Lindesmith's research into drug addiction and to suppress publication of his findings. We of course refused all such requests. Although the pressure was great, taking several forms or approaches, the issue never became a matter of wide public controversy.

It is essential for the university as a corporate body to be completely neutral with regard to controversial public issues. By its neutrality it is strengthened in its ability to defend the freedom of the members of the university community to express their views in accordance with the established principles of academic freedom. Again and again I have seen universities get trapped into surrendering that position, greatly limiting their ability thereafter to take the position that the university provides a neutral and unbiased forum for the presentation of all points of view. In my judgment, in the so-called Green Feather case, the issue was contrived with the ulterior motive of trying to force the university to go on record for or against Senator McCarthy. There was good and sufficient evidence that forces off campus were manipulating the students in order to bring this about. I have no patience with an attempt of this kind to destroy the neutrality of the university even though, as in this case, I may happen to be personally in sympathy with the cause.

It is to be noted, however, that in the 1960s the same kinds of pressures to politicize were brought upon the university. Unfortunately, in some instances a number of faculty members joined in the pressure, urging a moral position as justification for the surrender of the university's neutrality. It has to be remembered that, in addition to the damage that the university's taking sides on controversial issues would do to its ability to defend its own position of neutrality and to protect thereby the academic freedom of faculty members, by taking a point of view on a controversial subject the university would make it extremely difficult for impartial research to be done on that issue in the future. It is the keystone of university policy that a faculty member is free to do research on any subject that he has the competence and interest to pursue. That freedom would be inhibited by the adoption of an official university dogma on controversial questions.

Incident During My Interim Presidency

The controversial issues of the 1960s had heated to a mounting agitation by the time I undertook the interim presidency in the fall of 1968. Very early some student activists sought to try me by confrontation over their "demands," based on largely spurious charges against the university. In effect they wanted all traces of the military removed from the campus: no R O T C, no recruiting, no defense contracts, no police training, no "security" surveillance of student political activity. To their vague and sweeping insinuations that Indiana University was fostering secret research for the war effort, we replied that we did not accept government funds for classified research, that faculty research funded by the U.S. Department of Defense was in each case initiated by a grant proposal from the faculty member to further his own particular research interest, and that the results were publishable and therefore in the public domain.

The militant students tried without success to refute our answers and continued their propaganda bombardment, hoping to force the university to terminate government-supported research. Their effort was a clear challenge to the freedom of inquiry, without which a true university cannot exist. Through the years I had had to defend academic freedom from attack by forces of the right, but this attack came from the opposite direction, the extreme left.

My first impulse had been to accept their request for a public appearance to answer their questions. The dean of students and our security officers objected, saying that the agitators would attend with bull horns and other disruptive noisemakers and make it impossible for me to be heard. It was suggested that instead we make a complete response, including a statement of university policy on freedom of research, and publish the whole in the campus newspaper, thus speaking directly to the entire university community. My colleagues and I worked hard to draft a comprehensive but unyielding statement, which was published and received a warm response from everyone except the agitators. So far as the research issue was concerned, it was settled. I am very proud of the document, which appears in the Appendix (H).

At the beginning of the agitation, I did meet informally with some of the activist students in front of the Administration Building and again in my office. I made no progress on either occasion, and I am sure that the course we followed was the wise one or at least the better part of valor. Still, I shall always wonder if I might not have faced the propagandists down in a large meeting, had I tried.

Some Thoughts on Tenure

Currently it is faddish on campuses to decry tenure. The general public has always viewed tenure with suspicion, frequently charging that tenure serves to protect the lazy and the incompetent. But now even some young faculty members have joined the call for abolition of tenure. They do so, I fear, for shortsighted reasons and without realizing the ultimate consequences of such a step.

I am a firm believer in the system of academic tenure that obtains in all reputable universities in America. I believe a strong tenure policy is essential to the attraction of first-rate faculty members. Moreover, the customary rules by which tenure is attained give the academic community the best possible method, if scrupulously observed, to determine a young scholar's promise and personal compatibility with colleagues. Once tenure is granted them, faculty members can make long-range plans for their research and personal development instead of dissipating their energies and abilities in a constant search for jobs.

I would have been very reluctant to be president of any state university that lacked a firmly fixed tenure policy. In fact, the development of such a policy was one of the first matters with which I concerned myself when I became president of Indiana University. Time proved this initiative invaluable to me in carrying out my responsibility toward the faculty during periods of stress.

We live in a volatile world. Issues arise that are highly charged with emotion. For many of them there are university experts—the best informed authorities in the fields related to the controversy—who can shed light on the subject and must do so, but in the heat of the moment opponents of their views may resort to demanding their dismissal. The administrator would first defend his beleaguered colleagues on the grounds of their merit and integrity as scholars, but sometimes passions are so aroused that he may find it necessary at last to raise the point of life tenure as an invulnerable defense. The protection that tenure affords the scholar in such an extreme is reason enough for its retention. To maintain their integrity and their usefulness to society, universities must have this tool that makes academic freedom possible.

There are those who think that the forces of ignorance and intolerance and the enemies of academic freedom are dead. It is true that we have had relative freedom from the extremes of those forces in recent years, but they are only dormant, not dead—in hibernation at the moment. For those who are unaware of the enormity of the battles for academic freedom in which Indiana University has been engaged, I would commend to them the reading of volume three (1977) of Thomas D. Clark's history, *Indiana University: Mid-*

western Pioneer, particularly chapter ten, "Sexual Behavior and the Kinsey Perspective," and chapter eleven, "In Pursuit of the Unicorn," which covers the McCarthy era and the continuing charges against the university of Communist activity during that period. Readers might then turn to chapter twelve in volume two (1973), which deals with the Ku Klux Klan's threats to the integrity of the university that were met in an earlier period under the leadership of President Bryan.

Having stated these convictions, I should probably comment on an argument that is used by some young colleagues who would rescind the tenure policy, the argument that because of tenure faculty members are retained beyond their productive years to the detriment of the university. Faculty members' careers peak at different times, unrelated to the moment of attaining tenure or of reaching a particular age. What we may forget is that on either side of the peak, not just on the side of descent, the performance of an individual will be lacking in some respects. Quite possibly there is a trade-off: wisdom for callowness, perspective for inexperience.

Quite aside from the hard question of establishing fitness, the argument as to productivity needs to be viewed from another perspective. The security of tenure has less effect upon productivity in a professional group such as academicians than contractual security is likely to have in other areas of employment. Faculty members are highly sensitive to the judgment of their scholarship by their colleagues. The need of this professional regard in almost every case acts as a stimulus to the older professor to carry on at as high a level of achievement as is possible long after persons in other fields would have begun to accept the lessening of their physical and intellectual powers.

The university traditionally upholds the ideal of human values in society. One would expect that the university, having had the benefit of the services of men and women at their peak, would retain them in their waning years. It is the totality of their service that should determine the reckoning.

Relation to Health of Economic System

Our founding fathers believed that freedom of thought and expression was essential to the development of our political system. This freedom is equally essential to the maintenance of the health and vitality of our economic system. Advances are made in the free enterprise system because talented individuals think the unthinkable and attempt the impossible: management makes advances only when it finds new ideas and new ways in which to direct the enterprise. Competition in manufacturing is sharpened by the ability of individual entrepreneurs to devise new and more efficient ways of functioning. In the beginning of the automobile industry, Henry Ford's revolutionary ideas not only made the mass-produced automobile possible but, and even more important, profoundly influenced every type of manufacturing. It is nearly a first principle of marketing that efforts must continuously be stimulated by new and fresh ideas. Indeed, successful companies regularly seek suggestions for improvement in their operating efficiency from those most familiar with the processes, their employees.

New ideas can much more readily be accepted in a free, competitive economy than in an economy that is nationally and centrally controlled by the state. The realities of the marketplace force their acceptance. An economy that is to be vital, competitive, and therefore increasingly productive must be fueled by fresh ideas, and those fresh ideas must be allowed to compete in a marketplace of commerce as well as in the marketplace of ideas in the university. Anything less than this results in a static, regressive economic state. Thus freedom of expression, freedom of ideas are essential to the maintenance of the vitality of the intellectual community and equally essential to the maintenance of the vitality of the economic community.

[13]

○ ○ ○

To Make Room for the Future

IN JULY, 1937, when I assumed the presidency, almost the whole of the Bloomington campus of Indiana University lay between Jordan Avenue and Indiana Avenue on the east and west, Tenth Street and Third Street on the north and south. All the academic buildings (except the Home Economics Practice House), the administration building, the library, the original Memorial Union Building, the President's House, a meeting and concert hall, all the sport and physical education facilities, the four residence halls, University School, the printing plant, the power plant, and two machine shops were situated in this quadrangle. Not all of the land within belonged to the university. Half of the sororities and fraternities had houses within these boundaries (many others were just across the street), and there were a number of private residences, particularly in the northwest section. Part was just open field belonging to the university and important in its planning.

Even though there was neither an east-west nor a north-south traffic artery through the campus, cars could travel east on Seventh Street to the Fieldhouse (now Wildermuth Intramural Center) or over a winding road that entered the campus at Fifth (Kirkwood) Street and exited down Sorority Alley (now a walk alongside Ballantine and Jordan halls) to Third Street.

The Self-Survey Committee, appointed early in my administration, reported that it foresaw no appreciable growth in the student body. Nevertheless, the time seemed to me appropriate for planning an orderly extension of the campus. We knew we had to move north and east because most of the undeveloped land lay there—north of Tenth and east of Jordan. We tried to place facilities that would be used by the whole campus as close to the center of the campus-to-be as we could then envision it. We picked the site for the Auditorium in 1939 with that thought in mind, and mentally we began to reserve the site north of it for the central library of the future, a building we knew was certain to come. The results of our planning for the university community can now be seen: buildings that are useful to the whole campus—namely, the Library, the Art Museum and Fine Arts building, and the Auditorium—are situated between the housing and the classroom areas of the university. Constructed earlier, Wildermuth fits into this pattern. Roughly speaking, we have housing and auxiliary services enveloping the academic core of the university in a partial crescent from Indiana Avenue east along Third Street to Union Street and then north on Union to Tenth, then west to Fee Lane. The plan also has a reserved area for the future development of research institutes and facilities that will be needed no matter how the student population fluctuates. A great university steadily develops its research and specialized activities and provides physical facilities for them without regard to student enrollment. It is highly desirable that these have proximate relationship to the library, the power plant, and similar central supply facilities.

The area between Indiana and Woodlawn extending from Seventh Street to the athletics complex has been earmarked for this kind of future development, and consistently through the years the university has been buying properties there as they became available at reasonable figures. Also in our campus planning it early became apparent that, as the university grew, intercollegiate sports would have to move to the periphery of the campus. The move was necessary to permit construction of the kind and size of athletics structures that would be called for, to provide adequate parking for spectators, and to give us room to develop a modern plant. Near the outset of our planning we realized that we must acquire the Faris farm of 160 acres, and we did; it now is the locus of the Stadium, Assembly Hall, and the Fieldhouse. In addition we began purchasing vacant properties to the east as they became available to serve for practice fields, track, and club sports. Fortunately we already had much of the ground required for a golf course, as it had furnished the watershed for the old university water plant, but additional ground had to be bought in that area. We also bought to the west of the watershed area (across what is now the Bypass) as much ground as we could get before it became unreasonably high-priced. These moves as a result of planning were among the most fortunate we made because we were able to acquire hundreds and hundreds of acres at near-farmland prices. We began this acquisition in the war years, when real estate was depressed anyway, and with faith that the university was destined to grow. Had we waited until the growth escalation became apparent, the cost to the state would have been almost prohibitive. The development of a modern academic plant in Bloomington was immeasurably facilitated by our policy of buying property very actively during the war years. I shall always be grateful to the faculty for their willingness to allow us to invest operating dollars in the future and to forego other needs that existed then.

We dreamed of a major building program and came to the conclusion that we should employ a distinguished architectural firm to coordinate the whole campus-plan development and to design future buildings. In the 1920s and 1930s two principal architects had been used. One was Carlisle Bollenbacher of the firm of Lowe and Bollenbacher (later Granger and Bollenbacher) in Chicago. Carlisle Bollenbacher was an Indiana University graduate who also had training in architecture; he had achieved a wide reputation as a designer of beautiful structures. That firm designed the original part of the Memorial Union Building, Memorial Hall, the Tenth Street Stadium, and Bryan Hall, the administration building. All these structures are in my judgment highly successful architecturally for their time and place. In addition to Bollenbacher the university employed from time to time Robert Frost Daggett, a well-known architect in his day and considered to be a sound and well-trained man, drawing good plans. He designed the President's House,[1] the original Music School Building on Third Street, the Chemistry Building, and perhaps others that I do not now remember.

Soon after I came to the presidency, Ward Biddle and I went to New York to inform ourselves about the leading architectural firms in America. From our interviews we hoped to form a judgment that would allow me to make a recommendation to our trustees. We saw McKim, Mead, and White and other firms, among them John Russell Pope Associates—later to use the names Eggers and Higgins and Eggers and Higgins Associates. For many years Otto Eggers had been the principal designer for John Russell Pope, a very noted

1. Edward James was the young draftsman for Daggett who drew the plans for the President's House.

architect of his time. Among the buildings for which Eggers had been Pope's designer were the National Gallery of Art in Washington, many of the buildings at Yale, including the famous and beautiful gymnasium, and other outstanding structures throughout the United States; he had also designed the addition to the Tate Gallery in London.

I found Eggers and Higgins interested in our building program and sensitive to the need to have Hoosier architects associated with it in order to maintain the good will of the architectural profession in Indiana and, more importantly, to provide knowledge of the local situation. Eggers and Higgins was quite agreeable to an arrangement by which it would be in general charge of the design and have associated with it local architects whom we would jointly select to execute the working drawings, subject to the approval of the New York firm. The firm's service with us began with the new Auditorium and continued over a span of more than thirty years. It subsequently designed all the new major buildings on the Bloomington campus preceding the Musical Arts Center. For many of these, the Indiana architects we used were in the firm of Burns and James, later the James Associates, well-known architects in Indianapolis, who formed a happy relationship with Eggers and Higgins, working in harmony and cooperation throughout that building development. The two firms shared similar tastes and standards, and altogether the arrangement was fortunate. Another Hoosier architect, A. M. Strauss of Fort Wayne, had just finished a design for the Business and Economics Building (Woodburn Hall) when we made our contract with Eggers and Higgins. Eggers and Higgins began by reviewing Strauss's design for that building and making some slight modifications in it. Strauss was the associated architect on the Auditorium, but the designs for the Auditorium, the Fine Arts Building, and later the Lilly Library were drawn by Eggers and Higgins. It was our plan from the start to try to preserve the traditional style of architecture on the old campus with as little modification as possible but, as we moved outward, to allow the buildings to conform with architectural styles currently in vogue.

Through the years Eggers and Higgins developed certain specialities, one of these being athletic facilities. Because no local architect had any particular experience or expertise in designing structures like our projected stadium and later Assembly Hall, Eggers and Higgins did the whole design and had its own representatives on the grounds to supervise the construction. The firm through the years developed a division dealing with hospitals and medical facilities. As it had designed a number of attractive medical centers and hospitals in various parts of the country, we used its services for most of the new structures on the Medical Center campus and especially for the new University Hospital, which, when phase three of its plan is constructed, will prove to be a building of great usefulness and outstanding design.

Early on we were fortunate to be able to attract for the university's supervising landscape architect Frits Loonsten of Indianapolis, unquestionably Indiana's leading landscape architect and gardener. As he was trained in Holland, one might expect him to be a specialist in the formal landscaping—flowerbeds and so on—that is characteristic of the Dutch. However, he had a great feeling for the natural, and through the years he landscaped new buildings on the Bloomington campus, keeping in mind the theme of the natural wooded area that we had early adopted as our ideal for the overall landscaping of the campus and tying in the newer areas with the older, wooded center. This scheme led to our setting aside three additional green areas to the east of the Old Campus: a small one behind Old College Row, the grounds around the President's House, and a larger expanse to be developed where the "temporary" Trees Center buildings are, ringed by Willkie, Forest, Read, and the Jordan River.

Loonsten was so expert that he was able to combine new landscaping with the old in such a way that it seemed always to have been there—the true mark of a landscape architect. We did develop a few formal spots, namely, that around the Showalter Fountain, the Sweeney Rock Garden to the north of the Auditorium, and the little sunken plaza in the west front of Ballantine Hall, as well as the garden of the President's House, which was begun in Dr. Bryan's time. But in general Loonsten emphasized that we should avoid flowerbeds and other such delightful ornamentation because they were out of character with the naturalness of the campus and were very expensive to maintain. Instead of planting what would have to be weeded and cared for all summer long, he advised that we preserve the wildflowers of the woodland campus. Loonsten was a happy choice and directed our efforts for many years. Much of the beauty of the campus can be attributed to his taste and expertise.

In the course of a building program of such size as we had on the Bloomington campus over a period of some thirty-five years, many peculiar and interesting things happened that were not anticipated. For example, right in the beginning Otto Eggers designed the Auditorium as the focus of the Fine Arts Plaza, with the Fine Arts Museum and Building on one side and a Greek theater on the other. His original design called for a centerpiece, a fountain it was hoped. A beautiful rendering of that scheme was drawn to be used in presentations to prospective donors. In due course the Auditorium, the Fine Arts Museum and Building, and the fountain were realized, but the alfresco theater bowl was not. By the time we were ready to build the theater, the public had become so accustomed to air conditioning that there was little desire for outdoor performances and assemblages. It seemed appropriate to use that site for the Lilly Library since it would certainly contribute its share to the fine arts.

From time to time, the cost of the planned building exceeded the money available and we had to make compromises. Eggers and Higgins was always willing to make compromises, perhaps too willing, in order to get the buildings under way. For example, the Geology Building, which is frequently criticized as being too austere, was not so designed; the original plans called for a handsome, heroic, metal sculpture on the south side that would have made the building much more aesthetically pleasing. The modifications of the plans for Ballantine Hall illustrate other compromises. The original design called for this large classroom building to have two stories fewer than it now has, but, as we moved along, there was pressure from the faculty to increase the size of the building, and, right at the last minute, two floors were added. Because the elevator facilities could not be expanded at that late date, they have not been as adequate as they should be. But perhaps the most questionable modification, made to save money, was the elimination of the escalators, replaced by a back stairway, for the first three floors of Ballantine. Had those escalators been retained in the plans, the bulk of the student traffic could be moved freely up and down and, even without the expansion, the elevators would have been adequate. Moreover, the two-story addition is exposed to the hot sun in the summertime and deprived of the cooling effect of the shade trees; unfortunately the space left for air-conditioning ducts has proved inadequate in spots for installing modern units.

In building the additions to the Memorial Union Building, Eggers and Higgins was very sensitive to the original design of both the exterior and the interior, although the construction took place in successive stages over about twenty-five years, I think. Every effort was made to blend the old and the new. The building is sometimes criticized as being too large because of the inclusion of the Biddle Continuation Center. We had the choice of adjoining the Continuation Center to the Union Building or placing it on the periphery of the campus. Michigan State had provided separate facilities, whereas Purdue had incorporated its continuing-education center in its union building. To have placed the Continuation Center on the periphery of the campus would have meant fewer parking and traffic problems, but a peripheral location would have deprived visiting scholars and professors of the use of rooms close to the departments with which they would be associated while on campus. Perhaps the greatest advantage of all in having the Continuation Center designed as it finally took form was that all dining facilities could be centralized rather than requiring a separate dining facility of major proportion in a new building off campus. The facilities serve faculty and student activities in the west section of the building and serve student, visitor, and conference functions in the east part of the building. All in all it has proved to be a satisfactory plan. Furthermore, facilities such as the bookstore, meeting rooms, and dining rooms are in juxtaposition to each other. The original plan was to leave a covered archway (as in Memorial Hall) between the bookstore and the next unit of the building because the students had made Woodlawn Avenue a major route of entry to the Old Campus and we thought that should be preserved. However, further study convinced us that the route could be enclosed; students could still enter from Woodlawn, pass through the building, and be exposed to the building's facilities and amenities on their way to the Old Campus. This plan has worked reasonably well and would have worked superbly had we not eliminated the down escalator in that area. I still think that the down escalator should be installed and the Woodlawn entryway be made a bit more important than it now is by lighting and furnishings to attract students through it. Of course, with the building of additional dormitories to the north and east, the heaviest student traffic into the heart of the campus is along other routes.

In the latter part of my administration, there began a transition from natural ventilation in the summer to air conditioning. Some planners were urging that we air-condition all new buildings as soon as air conditioning was available. We followed a different policy for several reasons. In the first place, air conditioning was at that time generally regarded as a luxury. Few people had air conditioning either in their homes or in their offices. If we had air-conditioned all buildings, as wise as it now might seem, it would have been considered an extravagant expenditure of public money and it would have seriously impaired our relationship with the legislature. In the second place, university operating funds were then very meager; summer-school attendance was not large in those days, and the additional cost of air conditioning would have put a strain on the operating budget for the benefit of a relatively few students and faculty. Third, where there was some functional reason for air conditioning—for example, in certain laboratories, in libraries, in surgeries, and so forth—we used it as soon as it was available. We made a special point of not air-conditioning the administrative offices in Bryan Hall because we felt we had no right to make the administrative staff comfortable unless all areas of the university were similarly comfortable. During this transition period, however, we did ask that buildings be so planned and constructed that, when and if it became feasible to air-condition them, the ducts would be in place and no extensive amount of construction would be necessary. The architects and builders carried out this policy in many of the buildings, but in a few instances, as in Ballantine Hall, the duct space has had to be enlarged.

With the energy crunch and the pressure to reduce energy consumption, we may now have come full circle. At least it now seems there will be a reversion to more use of natural ventilation for much of the summer, except in the most extreme weather. Our buildings, in contrast with some on other campuses, are so constructed that, with rare exceptions, windows and doors will open.

Except for Eigenmann Hall, none of the residence halls is air-conditioned.[2] The reasons for omitting cooling units from the plans were similar to those for academic buildings. Although many of the halls are not open in the hot summer months, those used by summer students and conference participants are from time to time

2. Two apartment buildings considered to be married student housing because of the predominance of student residents (Campus View and Tulip Tree House) are air-conditioned, as is the Union Building. The dining rooms in the residence halls are also air-conditioned.

uncomfortably warm. Incidentally, the Greek-letter houses built in that period did not have air conditioning.

The housing of students was planned as carefully as were the academic buildings. When I was an undergraduate, Indiana University had no dormitories nor residence halls, except for a building called Alpha Hall on Third Street, rented from Colonel T. J. Louden and managed first by Florence Bond and then by Alice Nelson as a dormitory for women. Fraternity and sorority houses, most of them converted family residences, were scattered throughout the residential area of the town.

Since from time immemorial organization houses have on occasion "entertained" and that entertainment has frequently been noisy, there was constant friction between the student groups and neighboring householders. When I became president, I discovered that one of the most frequent complaints we received at the president's office concerned the sleep-disturbing din from fraternity and sorority houses. Rather than try to suppress the spirits of youngsters who gave parties and dances and, particularly in the spring and the fall, entertained on their lawns into the wee small hours of the morning, I early began thinking about what could be done to locate the Greek-letter houses away from the homes of more sedate citizens. I felt it desirable to try to congregate the Greek-letter houses in one area so that the only neighbors they would disturb in their exuberant manifestations would be fellow Greeks.

During my undergraduate days there were no suitable vacant lots available for purchase by Greek-letter organizations. Hence they had to buy an existing structure and either remodel it or demolish it in order to build. As Greek-letter organizations had a reputation for being "easy marks," owners typically placed a very high price on their properties. Moreover, few properties were available and certainly few in appropriate locations. A private developer with experience in construction of fraternity houses at the University of Wisconsin attempted to solve this problem in 1926. Beginning with Indiana University, he hoped to sell his plan to all of the major midwestern universities, a plan that made him responsible for the design, financing, construction, and furnishing of ten to twenty fraternity and sorority houses on each campus. This entrepreneur, Ralph S. Crowl, developed the Jordan Avenue quadrangle (Delta Chi, Delta Gamma, Theta Chi, Chi Omega, Phi Mu, Alpha Chi Omega, Sigma Alpha Epsilon, Zeta Tau Alpha, Sigma

Kappa) as well as the Kappa Sigma house on Third Street. Because of the heavy financing involved for the organizations, the scheme was especially vulnerable to the effects of the Great Depression; the resulting problems gave fraternities and sororities the reputation of being poor financial risks.

As we began planning the expansion of the campus and purchasing additional land for future development we kept in mind the housing needs of Greek-letter organizations. To make the land north of Tenth Street useful for university growth, we bridged the Illinois Central Railroad and extended Jordan Avenue northward. This improvement enabled us to offer attractive building sites to Greek-letter organizations at cost. We charged for each building site the raw ground cost, which was very cheap, and its proportionate share of the cost of roads and utilities. Organizations were then able to acquire spacious and attractive building sites at much less expense than would otherwise have been possible.

More than reasonably priced sites were required to stimulate the Greek-letter organizations to relocate and to build modern housing. Financing was needed, and lenders, wary of making mortgage loans on chapter houses, increased interest rates to offset the presumed risk. On the other hand, since the full credit of the university was involved in borrowing for construction of residence halls, it could obtain money at low rates. As the cost of financing had to be absorbed in the charges to students, the Greek-letter housing efforts were at a comparative disadvantage. To overcome this in part, we evolved what came to be known as the Indiana Plan, famous throughout the Greek-letter world. Briefly stated, the plan consisted of a three-way contractual arrangement among the university, the fraternity or sorority, and the lender that was designed to eliminate the risk factor for the lender and thus reduce the rate of interest to the borrower. The tripartite contract required the university, in case of a default, to purchase the house and the fraternity or sorority to sell for the amount of the delinquent, unpaid balance, the proceeds to be used to pay the lender in full.[3]

3. Several colleagues were active in creating the Indiana Plan. A committee, headed by Professor Harold Lusk of the School of Business, was formed; members included Mary Maurer, a trustee, Colonel R. L. Shoemaker, Dean of Students, Professor Edward E. Edwards of the School of Business, Lloyd E. Setser, University Real Estate Manager, William Henry Snyder, a local attorney, and J. A. Franklin (ex officio), Treasurer of the University. They received assistance from Theodore Dann, an Indianapolis attorney, and J. Dwight Peterson, former university trustee and president of City Securities in Indianapolis.

The Indiana Plan was highly successful from the beginning, stimulating construction and reducing rates. Defaults through the years have been negligible, and in all instances the chapter houses have been successfully refinanced or sold to another organization. The composite debt has been steadily reduced until it is now small in comparison with the value of the properties. The one objective insufficiently realized in the working of the plan has been a fully compensating reduction in interest rates; at least I feel the rates should have been reduced more than they typically have been.

Some other universities tried to assist their Greek-letter organizations by building the houses, using university credit, and leasing them to organizations at a rate designed to defray the cost over a period of years. This method seemed to us to be paternalistic, robbing the chapters of a measure of their autonomy and also depriving them of the experience of fiscal management.

The rather spectacular fraternity and sorority row on North Jordan Avenue, including the extension beyond Seventeenth Street, came into existence as a result of the Indiana Plan. To keep the planning within bounds, a fraternity was limited to a building cost of $5,000 per student member. In the beginning certain of the Greek-letter organizations were reluctant to take advantage of the sites made available because the location seemed to them too far from the center of campus. They, and particularly their alumni, were simply unable to envision the future growth of the University. The Sigma Nus were the first to buy on North Jordan. They were persuaded to give up the site that they had bought earlier for a new house: the corner now occupied by Wright Quadrangle. That broke the resistance on the part of the organizations. Slowly and then more rapidly many others followed until at the present time the majority of the fraternities and sororities are housed on Jordan Avenue, from Third Street almost to the Chi Omega gates at the Bypass. Those organization houses which elected to stay adjacent to the campus on Third Street and on Seventh Street have been relieved of private neighbors as the university has purchased bordering houses and has generally turned them to university uses.

As we had early determined that we must offer an option to those students who wanted group living other than in Greek-letter organizations, we developed residence halls for the independent (non-affiliated) students. The first residence halls, those constituting the present Wells Quadrangle and Men's Residence Center (M R C), were constructed close by the academic campus. But particularly in the case of M R C, private homes stood all around and we had some of the same problems we had had with the fraternities and sororities, namely, students disturbing worthy householders. Soon, therefore, the wisdom also of grouping the residence halls on the periphery of the academic campus became apparent. We then began the development of residence halls on Fee Lane and eastward into the Smithwood area, placing them around the postwar temporary dormitories that in due course would be eliminated to leave a green center surrounded by permanent living units. We now have a majority of students residing in Greek-letter houses or university dormitories ringing the academic core of the university and away from private residential districts.

One night recently I drove around the student-housing areas at the end of the first week of the school year. The students were all swarming about, rejoicing in being together again—a small world of happy youth. Because their housing was apart, they were not disturbing their elders who were, by that time of night, either in bed asleep or burning the midnight oil.

Planning the residential hall system extended, of course, beyond matters of location and construction to considerations of financing and incorporating a concept of living. The state had taken the position that residence halls must be self-financing. Our answer, self-liquidating bonds, required that a charge for bond retirement and interest would be added to each student's bill. Essentially this amounted to a fee charged each user for the availability of such housing.

We were keenly aware of the need for these residence halls to be made superior places for study and for the self-educating advantages of group living, if possible. In addition, we believed that the lounges and public rooms should be beautifully furnished as a way not only of making them attractive to the students but also of displaying a standard of taste, which we considered to be an important part of the student's experience. We would have preferred private rooms for most students, but the rate would have been generally prohibitive. We were able, however, in the beginning to have some suites available where, say, three students who wished to be together could share a living room but each would have a private bedroom.

To accomplish these attractive features and at the same time keep the cost bearably low (even with furnished sites) required very careful architectural planning that incorporated all of the experience we had gained and all the information we could gather from other schools with longer experience in dormitory construction. Here Alice Nelson and her staff were an invaluable aid. She had a great sense of the practical and great courage, which served us well. The dormitories had to be attractive, not only on the inside, but on the outside as well to enhance the whole campus.

The very first dormitory to be self-liquidating was old South Hall, now Smith Hall, which was built right after World War I; successful financially, it did not, however, furnish a satisfactory model for future buildings. We continued the policy of issuing bonds for the cost of construction. The buildings were carefully phased so that the earliest buildings would be well along with their financing before the final buildings had to be constructed. We thus kept our equity at such a level that the security brokers were willing to sell our bonds. There was likewise provision for setting aside depreciation and reserve funds to meet the bond issue if a catastrophe should deplete the residency occupation for a year or two. From a financial standpoint, the significant factor was that we laid out in the beginning a plan that encompassed all of the huge dormitory development to come, with the exception of the final two, Eigenmann and Forest. The enrollment grew so rapidly in the 1960s and the residence hall system was in such good financial shape that it was possible to piggyback financially two additional structures on those originally planned.

We are now reaching a period in which many of the older dormitory structures will have to have major updating. One of our original ideas was that, if we could ever afford it, when the buildings were paid off and modernized, many of the double rooms, really rather small, would be converted to single rooms. We also had a feeling, especially in regard to the complexes built for approximately a thousand students that seemed to be an economical operating unit from a dining-room standpoint, that, if the time ever came when we could drop the occupancy back to 500 or 750 (not every student wants a single room), there would be sufficient nonassigned space to permit operation of the unit to some degree as a residential college with classes and tutorials conducted in the building. Planning of the buildings included this development as a possible eventuality and, who knows, it might come some time. There are signs that the idea is alive at the present in, for example, the intense in-house intellectual activity at the Living-Learning Center in M R C and also the increasing number of classes being taught in the recreation rooms or special lounges of the residence halls. The day may come when the idea will be realized fully.

The trauma of the late 1960s and the early 1970s and the general decline in standards of public decorum have largely obliterated the dream of providing lounges that would give students a taste of gracious living.[4] This ideal seems to have been replaced by a utilitarian emphasis on furnishings that are impervious to the abuse to which students subject them. Curious to record, the only exception to the student structures so abused is the Indiana Memorial Union. Its management has worked persistently and imaginatively to make it a social center with amenities that would leave a mark upon the students throughout their lives.

When we started on the major program of dormitory building, we envisioned the possibility that a time would come when the university's academic enclave ought to include what is now Wells Quadrangle and the M R C. They might be needed to establish residential colleges, we thought, or, more particularly might be used for academic purposes since they are in the central-campus area. Were these two complexes to be converted to academic use, there would then be an equality of location for all university student housing on the periphery of the campus.

One aspect of the dormitory building plan called for gradual phasing out of the many temporary structures that had been relocated here following World War II. These frame, two-story War Surplus buildings had been brought from the Bunker Hill base and set up south of Seventh Street between Jordan Avenue and Union Street in a section that came to be known as Trees Center. With the indispensable assistance of a local contractor and alumnus, Cecil Harlos, who assembled a crew of eight hundred men, the structures were made habitable for the influx of students after the war, many of them G.I.'s. Governor Ralph Gates aided materially in this housing emergency by providing some money from a Postwar Reconstruction Fund, partially obtained from a gallonage tax on alcoholic beverages.

Earlier, when the gallonage tax law was modified to provide a

4. As this goes to press I have learned that a plan for restoring the lounges to their former graciousness is being implemented.

distribution of the yield that included the state universities, I reported this to my fellow university presidents in the Council of Ten at our spring meeting. It was customary for this group, after we had taken care of matters concerning athletics, passed some resolutions and conducted other routine business, to have a roundup with each president reporting on what success he had had with his legislature. Referring to our state's new source of money from the gallonage tax, Ed Elliott, president of Purdue, shook his head and in his inimitable way declared, "Herman and I are not afraid of tainted money." Quick as a flash Alec Ruthven of Michigan retorted, "Trouble is, 'tain't enough."

The Indianapolis Campus

The planning and development of the Indianapolis campus were governed by circumstances and requirements different from those of the Bloomington campus. The ruling conditions were in large part the functions to be performed in the various buildings, their relationship to each other, the limited growth of the student enrollment because of fixed ceilings for each of the three professional schools—medicine, dentistry, and nursing—but at the same time provision for expanding outpatient services, for increasing hospital operations, and for rapidly growing research programs. In addition, space had to be found for important facilities such as the Veterans Hospital, the Krannert Heart Research Institute, the headquarters and laboratories for the State Board of Health, and the expanded City Hospital (now Wishard). Since in the beginning we were desperately short of hospital beds, these affiliated hospitals were essential to our teaching function. Still, it was necessary to reserve space for a major teaching hospital of our own, which was in due course realized.

As all buildings had to be accommodated within a relatively small tract, the arrangement had to be very compact. Fortunately, most of the students lived in town and we were freed from the responsibility of providing more than minimal residential facilities. We did, however, plan and develop two first-rate apartment buildings for married students and allocated a portion of the Union Building there for student residence.

With all of this in mind, we early began to acquire property to the east of the campus as it became available. Thus, by the time

the Indiana University-Purdue University at Indianapolis (I U P U I)
organization had been effected and the Indianapolis campus was
joined with Bloomington to form an axial core of the university,
we had acquired most of the property extending from the old Indianapolis campus for some blocks to the east. Much of this property was tenement rental property. The Hoosier Realty Corporation
was invaluable in these transactions, buying property when it became available and selling it to the university as it was needed. Surprisingly enough, we found out that, if we bought consistently in an
area over a decade, we were able to acquire property at a buyer's
price. I am proud that we had the vision, in Indianapolis as in Bloomington, to pursue an aggressive program of land purchases, which
makes the expansion of the Indianapolis campus now more readily
possible than would otherwise be the case and which fosters the
vision of congregation we had for the gathering of our schools and
divisions in Indianapolis on one campus.

Such a compact campus as that of the Medical Center affords
little opportunity for landscaping, but we were able to preserve a
green area in the core of the campus and to establish pleasing landscaping around the Riley Hospital.

In our extension centers, since we had to operate with little
help from the state legislature in the beginning (as I have described
elsewhere), we began operations in shared quarters with the high
schools. Our classes were held for the most part in the late afternoon
or early evening, the hours when high school facilities were unused.
Thus there was little additional direct cost, and the arrangement
resulted in an extra utilization of expensive public plants, a socially
desirable policy. However, there was some resistance by students
to the use of high school classrooms. As soon as possible we began
to build our own plant, overcoming the student distaste for the earlier arrangement and allowing us to operate throughout the day.
In some instances we acquired existing buildings and made the required adaptations. Where we were able to build new structures,
we built with limestone to emphasize the ties to the mother campus
as well as to provide beautiful quarters for our evening students and
faculties. In time we had to abandon limestone because of the cost,
but we attempted to find attractive campus locations, landscape them
appropriately, provide room for the future, and follow where appropriate the policies that have made the Bloomington campus notable. Those policies have helped to achieve a number of beautiful

center campuses and at least one, Southeast, that is spectacularly successful.

The Importance of Specialized Structures for the Future of the Mother Campus

Every great university has fine libraries and teaching museums, and most of them have attractive student and faculty amenities such as union buildings, faculty clubs, and the like; practically all have extensive recreational facilities for faculty and students. Harvard, for instance, has some of the worst classrooms in the world, but it also has the Houghton Library, the Widener Memorial Library, the Littauer Center for Public Service—highly specialized and elaborate structures for their purposes.

My basic principle in seeking certain specialized buildings for the Bloomington campus was that the concentration of such facilities makes the campus an effective center for specialized study and performance. To disperse them throughout the system would be very costly and inefficient. Such structures as the University Library, the Musical Arts Center, the Art Museum, the Lilly Library, the Glenn Black Laboratory, the University Museum, the Auditorium, the Cyclotron, Assembly Hall, and Memorial Stadium make it logical for the Bloomington campus to continue its function as the historical flagship of the Indiana University system. This is the reason why I believe the development of specialized facilities, which represent the adornment of a great university and which all great universities have, should be a high priority. Indiana University continues to make progress in this respect.

[14]

○ ○ ○

Student and Alumni Relationships

I HAVE LONG greeted freshman students with, "So you are a freshman. Great! Freshmen are very important people. Without freshmen there soon would be no seniors or, in fact, a university, and I like it here."

With rare exceptions I had happy relationships with the students during my days in the president's office. I saved time for contact with them; I tried to accept their invitations even though in some instances it was not particularly convenient to do so. I recognized the fact that they invited me to their many functions in the best spirit, evidencing their interest in Indiana University and their friendliness toward me. Many times student dinners are a bit stiff and awkward, but the youngsters are learning the art of entertaining, a useful part of their whole learning experience. By keeping close to students, one is reminded that they are a major reason for the existence of the university and certainly the major reason why the state supports the institution. In the quality and spirit of these youngsters is to be found the future of the state and nation. They and their parents are making sacrifices in order to realize an individual and family dream, seeking the mobility and self-fulfillment that can come with a collegiate and professional education.

I not only spent a great deal of time in responding to student social obligations, but as well tried throughout my career to schedule open office hours regularly for student visits. At the beginning of the academic year, I set aside a period each month during which, it was announced, students were invited to come to my office without making appointments to discuss any subject they wished. In this way I tried to overcome any reticence that students might have about breaking into the calendar of a busy president. Needless to say, students did come, and came in large numbers, particularly at the beginning of each year. But after a month or so, their numbers would dwindle. Possibly it was because I was unable to make the sessions interesting enough for the individual student, or perhaps, when the students found out that they had ready access to the presidential ear, they were satisfied, unless they really had some important reason for wanting to be heard.

In the early days of my presidency the university's enrollment was predominantly undergraduate, but as the years went along the graduate and professional enrollments increased dramatically both in numbers and in relation to the rest of the student body. Graduate and professional students often have a maturity that makes them academic colleagues in the true sense of the word, and one can be stimulated by them and learn from them. On the other hand, even to this day I find meeting the shy, naive freshman or sophomore one of the experiences I most value. It is so refreshing to talk to these youngsters, to learn that each succeeding generation of students is facing life in much the same way that their predecessors did, then to try to help them by giving them perspective and encouragement, knowing that they will, if they persist, find their way as so many have done before them.

The beginning of my administration was before the time of the organized Help Weeks project that Colonel Raymond L. Shoemaker as dean of students was later to inaugurate. Nevertheless, from time to time, the students on their own quite spontaneously developed projects in which they demonstrated their interest in the university's welfare, addressed the needs of some of the town's unfortunate, or otherwise attempted to meet their civic responsibilities in the society of which they were temporarily a part.

Throughout most of my presidential years, there was high student morale on the campus, at both the graduate and the undergraduate levels. The morale was reflected in the students' attitude toward the university and in their reports concerning it to their parents and friends throughout the state. A satisfied student body is, after all, the greatest public-relations asset a university can have. In fact, it needs no formal public-relations program if the members of the university community, students and faculty alike, believe enthusiastically in the institution and proclaim their belief in it throughout the state. The voice of administrators or even the voice of trustees could never approach the force of the combined chorus from the host of students and faculty members as they spontaneously and informally express their views of the work and the program of the university.

Of course, the students who came after World War II were a very special lot. For the most part they had had to interrupt their education or delay it to serve in the armed forces throughout the world, had had bitter and brutal experiences, and, in the case of many of them, had married and begun a family. So they came to college determined to make the most of their opportunity. I suppose we will never have a more diligent, determined, and remarkable group of men and women than those who came to us in the late 1940s, motivated and tempered by their wartime experiences. The university tried to respond by doing its best, with limited resources of staff and plant, to make sure that no qualified student was denied access to this opportunity. It is a great tribute to the students that they were tolerant and patient about the physical inconveniences they had to bear in their housing and living arrangements and about the inadequacy of many of the classroom and laboratory provisions arranged rapidly to absorb overwhelming numbers of students. They were an inspiring lot to all of us, and by their own determined spirit, sacrifice, and enthusiasm they sustained us in the nearly superhuman task of meeting the onrush of veterans.

One of the most time-consuming and important responsibilities relating to students that occurred during my administration involved the effort to shake off our previous university practices that discriminated against Black students—in essence, the effort to make Black students full-fledged members of the university community. First, a little background is necessary.

Bloomington has long enjoyed the benefit of a substantial number of Black families, some of whom came here from the South before the Civil War, many soon after, and quite a few of whom have remained for several generations. As a consequence they are now among the town's oldest families, well established and well respected. They early began to send their children to the university, and one, Preston Eagleson, became a highly regarded halfback in football and pitcher in baseball on the teams of 1894 and 1895. Graduates among the children of these local families have had a proud record of achievement in teaching, in legal scholarship, and in other professions and fields. There has never been to my knowledge any discrimination against the admission of Black students, and because until the 1900s the university furnished no living or dining facilities for students—white or black—discrimination on the basis of race was not an issue at that time. In those days there seems to have been relatively little racial tension present on the campus.

Seemingly with the coming of the Ku Klux Klan and its activity in the local community following World War I, absurd barriers of segregation were erected by the university. For example, when I became president, Black students had been barred from the use of the university swimming pools. Also, the university physician, using the device of a medically certified handicap to exclude them, automatically exempted Black male students from the compulsory R O T C program on the pretext that they all had flat feet. There were segregated tables for Black students in the Commons dining room of the Memorial Union Building. Black students were not admitted to university residence halls.[1]

Partly to meet the need thus created and partly as a result of their own initiative, some local Black entrepreneurs developed housing and dining facilities for Black students. A most dramatic example of this entrepreneurship was provided by Sam Dargan, a graduate of both Indiana and Purdue, who for nearly a lifetime was curator of the law school here and who came to own, by acquiring it piece by piece, a considerable amount of property adjacent to the campus. His property was adapted to student housing, one rather large house and annex for women with a housemother to meet the university requirements for chaperonage. In later years he built a substantial brick dormitory for men. One of the women who had property near the campus, Ruth Mays, ran a boarding house for Black students, and her place became a social and counseling center (older students took responsibility for younger students) as well as a dining club. The churches of the Black community were active in welcoming Black students who came to Bloomington and helped to provide social life and activities for these young men and women. Kappa Alpha Psi, a Black fraternity, was founded here in 1911 and, having now spread throughout the United States, has become a powerful national organization. Soon there developed some Black sororities as well. Kappa Alpha Psi was started in part because Black

1. Even though there was discrimination, we had more Black students than did any other collegiate institution in the state.

students knew each other and wished to have their own social organization and in part because by that time the predominant, white organizations either had discriminatory clauses in their national constitutions or simply practiced discrimination by not offering membership to Black students.

As we began to break down the barriers of discrimination, occasionally individuals who had been providing services for the Black students were less than cooperative because they felt that, by lifting the barriers, we were eliminating their source of livelihood in callous ingratitude for the investment that they had made to provide the only services Black students could hitherto obtain. I suppose the local Black community approved the removal of these barriers in principle, but some individuals were not exactly happy about the result in practice. The state NAACP and prominent Black alumni in Indianapolis and elsewhere, by maintaining constant pressure for change, were helpful by supporting our moves in the face of varying forms of resistance.

In taking the steps required to remove those reprehensible, discriminatory rules, we tried to make a move if possible when the issue was not being violently discussed pro and con on the campus. I felt that making the moves in this manner would, and in fact it did, prevent any backlash that might set the whole program back. For example, one of the earliest steps we took was to remove the reserved signs from certain tables in the Commons. Everyone knew that these reserved signs on the tables meant that the Black students were to sit there. One afternoon when the place was deserted, James Patrick, then manager of the Union Building, went with me to the Commons to look the situation over. I turned to him and said, "Pat, I want you to remove all those signs. Do it unobtrusively and make no mention of what you've done." He followed my instructions explicitly. It was two weeks before anyone discovered the fact that the signs were gone and then, of course, the absurdity of the previous situation was apparent.

The denial of the men's swimming pool in the old gymnasium to Blacks had to be handled in a similar fashion. It had long been the policy of the football coaches to welcome Black players, some of whom became relatively famous. This provided my clue. One day I asked Zora Clevenger, the athletic director, to come see me. Our conversation went something like this: "When is the swimming pool most heavily used in the afternoon?" He answered, "Generally from

3:00 to 4:30." "Who is your most popular Black athlete?" I asked. He quickly replied, "Rooster Coffee." Rooster Coffee was a well-known football player with a wonderful personality who had won the heart of the campus. I then inquired, "Is Rooster around here in the afternoon?" He said, "Oh, yes, he's here regularly working out." I told Clev, "Some afternoon next week when the pool is quite full, go down on the floor, find Rooster, and tell him to strip in the locker room and go jump in the pool." (Swimmers were required to swim in the nude for sanitary reasons.) He asked, "Do you mean it?" to which I replied, "Yes, and don't tell anybody, even Rooster, what you're going to do in advance." A few afternoons later, when the situation was just right, he spoke with Rooster and Rooster co-operated completely—stripped and jumped in, swimming with abandon for a half hour or so. He was so cordially greeted, I doubt that anyone realized a policy had been changed. That was the last of discrimination against Blacks in the use of the pool.

At that time there was an informal understanding among the basketball coaches that they would not recruit Black basketball players, a practice that now seems incredible. There was some kind of mumbo jumbo about the fact that the sport included too much bodily contact to make it feasible to mix the races. One afternoon along in the spring some of my Black friends from Indianapolis, most of whom were alumni, showed up in my office to say that if our basketball coach, Branch McCracken, would play Bill Garrett they felt that they could persuade him to come to Indiana University. Bill Garrett had a fabulous record as a high school player, and his team had just won the state tournament. I said, "That would be great. Let me see what we can do."

I again consulted with Clevenger, who said, "The basketball coaches have an understanding on this, and, if we were to violate that understanding, we'd probably have a hard time getting a schedule, but, if Branch wants to do it, I'll back him." So I asked Coach McCracken, "Branch, how would you like to have Bill Garrett on your team?" His reply was enthusiastic. "That would be great. He's a magnificent basketball player already and we sure could use him, but you know I probably would be ostracized by all my fellow Big Ten coaches if we took him." "Let's take him," I urged, "and if there's any conference backlash against it, then I'll take the responsibility for handling it." To convince him I added, "In the first place they won't dare make a public issue of it, and if they harass you in private I will, through the Council of Ten, bring the pressure of the other nine Big Ten presidents to bear upon the coaches." Bill Garrett did come here and made a great record as a basketball player and student. So far as I ever knew or heard, the other coaches capitulated and began to scramble for good Black players. It just took one school to break that vicious circle. We had somewhat similar experiences in other sports with the same happy outcome. Although of course we had had Black football players before the turn of the century, as I have said, in golf and baseball as well as in basketball, we were the first Big Ten school to have Blacks on the team.

Our efforts to end segregation hit a snag with the development of on-campus housing. The administrators of our housing units were apprehensive that, if we admitted Black students, there would be objection, not necessarily from white students, but from their parents to the extent of seeking other housing for their sons and daughters. This fear did not prove to be justified in the case of male students, but with women students it was another matter. The pressure from that direction against having Black students in the residence halls was sufficient for the trustees to become fearful that integration could not work just then. As a consequence, in order to achieve our goals, we had to take an intermediate step, which was to create a residence hall for Black women that was nevertheless a university facility. Sometime before, when the Kappa Alpha Theta sorority had built its new house, the university had bought its rather fine old house on Sorority Alley to be used for university housing and called Lincoln House. Now we decided to remodel it, make it into an even better facility but retain its name, Lincoln House, and bring in a skilled interior decorator from Cincinnati to decorate and furnish it. Then we placed one of our most able counseling couples in charge and transferred one of our topnotch cooks to head the kitchen force. It was perhaps the best-appointed and most comfortable housing facility that the university has ever provided for any students, black or white. Although the rates were the same as for other housing units, Lincoln House was filled for only two years and then the number of its residents declined and the house became a financial burden. The year after Lincoln House opened, the dormitory administration and I were able to persuade the trustees to let us admit Black women to whatever dormitory they wished to enter, and by 1952 there was no longer a need for segregated housing.

The situation with regard to barbershops was another difficult one. As the Black student population grew, some local members of the barbers union tried to get agreement among their members not to cut the hair of Black students, at least during regular barbering hours. The need was met by a Black-owned barbershop on the west side of town, but only after regular hours. We solved that problem with the cooperation of Ed Correll, an influential member of the local barbers union, who was the proprietor of the popular Varsity Barbershop across from the Administration Building. Through his wife, who was in charge of the University Archives in my office, he understood the university's abhorrence of all forms of discrimination. We decided to lease the handsome barbershop in the Union Building only to an operator who would cut the hair of both Black and white students, and Ed Correll offered to undertake the operation of the shop on that basis with the promise that, if he could not hire barbers who would follow the policy, then he would serve the Black students himself. We accepted Ed's offer, and later the other barbershops one by one began to accept Black patrons.

One of the most dramatic confrontations that we had was with the local restaurant association. Practically none of the downtown restaurants would serve Black students. Some of the students, aided by faculty members, sought to be served and threatened legal suits against the restaurant owners if they were not served. The faculty members and students knew that there was a statute that made it illegal for public restaurants to discriminate on the basis of race. The issue generated considerable heat, and before long I was invited to meet with all the restaurant owners in the back room of one of the downtown restaurants. There I was informed that, unless we persuaded the students and their faculty supporters to remove their demands for service, the restaurant owners were prepared to close all downtown restaurants, thus depriving many students as well as the downtown community and travelers of their customary places to eat. Prior to the meeting I had taken counsel with Harold Jordan, director of the Union, and when I received this ultimatum I simply called their attention to the fact that they were engaged in procedures that were not just immoral but also illegal, and, therefore, although we wanted to cooperate with downtown businessmen, in this instance our cooperation would have to take the form of expanding the facilities in the Union Building to feed all their displaced customers indefinitely. It was pointed out that many of their customers did from time to time dine at the Union Building, where we served

Blacks on the same basis as whites after desegregation of the Commons, and those same customers seemed not to resent service under such conditions.

This was an unexpected response from the university and was, I am sure, very startling to our downtown friends. The issue had grown to intense heat, involving a lot of public statements, editorials, and so on. Our ultimatum in response to theirs resulted in the evaporation of the whole issue, and most restaurants began to serve Black customers as well as white. There may have been a few holdouts, but they were not of sufficient importance to concern the Black students very much.

Through no fault of our own the restaurant issue involved outright confrontation, which we had sought to avoid wherever possible. Once I was accused by a young minister in the town of being a traitor to the cause of equality. It was his belief that the greatest progress would be made only by bringing all issues to a state of confrontation. My reply to him was simply that I wanted to win each issue and not lose one; consequently, wherever possible I thought it best to proceed as we had been doing. Looking back now over those results and others, if I had it to do over again, I would proceed in the same way.

It took a long time to get the discriminatory clauses out of the national charters of the Greek-letter organizations. Many alumni were actively attempting to do so. I attended several Grand Chapters of my own fraternity, Sigma Nu, in order to work to remove racial discrimination in that fraternity. Not only had Sigma Nu discriminated against Blacks from the time of the founding of the fraternity right after the Civil War, it had also added an Oriental clause at the time of the so-called Yellow Peril scare after the turn of this century, a clause that had been pushed by the West Coast chapters. Later, some chapters, unaware that the Oriental clause existed, had initiated Orientals, and other chapters wished to do so with the admission of Hawaii to statehood and with the coming of many talented Oriental athletes to the United States. Just so, when Black athletes became prominent, some of our chapters were eager to pledge Blacks also. Still, the southern and the western chapters were adamant, and it took several sessions of our Grand Chapter before we could get a sufficient vote to eliminate the offensive clauses.

By the time the Greek-letter organizations had cleansed themselves, ironically the Black leadership had begun to spread the "Black is beautiful" philosophy, which tended to deter Black students from accepting invitations from predominantly white fraternities and sororities. In fact, Black students who did accept such invitations often were subjected to considerable pressure by their fellow Blacks. As a consequence the move toward resegregation, whatever its merits, did have as one of its effects a lost opportunity for actual desegregation of the Greek-letter houses.

From the beginning of my presidency to the present day, I have sent a Christmas treat to the staff of the *Daily Student* each year to indicate to them my appreciation for their efforts. In the early years, in addition to this contact with the *Daily Student* staff, I attempted to attend as many individual Christmas parties in the halls of residence and in the Greek-letter houses as possible. Following World War II, in 1948, the Association of Women Students (A W S) and the Union Board decided to stage an all-university Christmas party for students, faculty, and their families before the students went home for Christmas. It was called Christmas Eve on Campus and began with the "Chimes of Christmas," a musical program in the Auditorium that is still held annually. Following it the Union Board and the A W S held a party in Alumni Hall and elsewhere in the Union. It was for this occasion in 1948 that I was first asked to play Santa Claus. When it was determined that no ready-made Santa Claus costume would fit very well, the Union Board obtained a suit pattern from my tailor and had a company make the costume for me. It fit perfectly and has continued to be used right up to the present. When we arrived at the Union after the "Chimes of Christmas" program, I was taken to the suite in the Union tower, which then contained hotel rooms, and with the aid of some members of the Union Board changed into my Santa Claus suit. In the *Daily Student* and elsewhere much had been made of the fact that a mystery Santa Claus would visit the Union Board's Christmas party. Headlines in the *Daily Student* proclaimed: "Saint Nick is campus bound today—mystery Claus to visit Union Christmas party."[2] Coming down to the lobby floor of the Union, I was met by several waiting members of the A W S board and the Union Board who were dressed as elves and carried bags of candy canes. The music was stopped in Alumni Hall and a fanfare was struck. Then I proceeded

2. Someone at the Gables, the student hangout, clipped and modified the headline and posted it so that it read as a Gables bulletin, "Nick is campus bound." Nick, who was very popular on campus, was one of the Poolitsan brothers, owners of the Gables.

through the packed crowd in the hall throwing candy canes in all directions even after I reached the stage. By prior request of the committee, I next asked for the crowd's attention and delivered a Christmas message to the university family, expressed my good wishes for their holidays, and admonished the students to drive carefully to and from their homes. Of course, the crowd under the circumstances was warm, friendly, and responsive. I continued throughout the entire time of my presidency to speak to the campus celebrants on this cheerful, affectionate, sentimental occasion.

I still make appearances for the Union Board in their Santa suit at Christmastime, but their party has been radically changed. It is an all-day affair in the South Lounge, refreshments are served, and Santa Claus appears for an hour or so to visit with students and children individually in quite a casual way.

The question of desegregating the sexes in the residence halls was not a live issue during my service as president. In the mid-1940s, when we were designing the halls that became Wright Quadrangle, our plan called for women to occupy one wing and men the remainder, and the women and men to share the lounge and dining facilities with the idea that this arrangement would contribute to the social development of the students, that is, make them conscious of their appearance, improve their manners, and assist them in cultivating some of the social graces. Because when Wright was completed we were in urgent need of rooms for men, this early intent to have side-by-side units for men and women was not carried through. It was a decade later before Teter Quadrangle, composed of three buildings for women and two for men, opened and inaugurated coeducational lounges and dining rooms without fanfare or a single objection that I can recall.

But by the time I had become interim president in 1968, students were actively seeking an end to the university's policy of "in loco parentis," agitating for elimination of curfew hours for freshmen women in the dorms, and pressing for open guest hours in student rooms. Many people in the state were alarmed by what they considered a backing off by the university from its responsibility for supervision of student conduct but what the students insisted instead was long-overdue recognition by the university of individual responsibility. (It was probably not by chance that such a feeling had manifested itself soon after the national call-up of youth to bear a large share of the responsibility for the American defense of Vietnam.) Still, a vocal segment of the public saw nothing but evil intent and outcome in these proposals to entrust students with responsibility for their social conduct.

The president of the student body at the time, Ted Najam, now a prominent local attorney, had staked his leadership on seeing these issues through to a successful conclusion. Capable, bright, and fastidious, he was a persuasive protagonist. Even though a brief trial period of open guest hours in the spring had failed to produce the dire consequences predicted by opponents and even though a summer survey of parental attitudes toward open visitation had shown surprising support (about 40 percent), the Board of Trustees was for the most part reluctant to approve the measures. A committee of the board met with student leaders, several faculty members, and administrators at my home prior to the board's official session. It was pointed out that students could and did live in apartments that were not segregated by sex and that the whole system we had inherited was in many ways absurd. Moreover, any differentiation in practice between rules for men's rooms and those for women's rooms could not be sustained under the force of such logic. At the board session that followed, motions approving open guest hours under specified circumstances and freeing students from living in university housing if they preferred off-campus arrangements passed by narrow margins. Since students from then on could live where they and their parents pleased, including certain residence halls reserved for those who did not wish open guest hours, the board's action provided all the options that could be desired.

Indiana University was the first school in the state, public or private, to move in this direction. Dire predictions of legislative reprisals and parental boycotts of the university or its residence halls followed. No serious repercussion occurred, although an alumnus in the legislature tried to make a hot issue of the guest-hours privilege in the next session of the General Assembly. It would have been prudent for the students to have deferred their proposal until after the General Assembly met, as I advised them then, but they were impatient. Considerable heat was generated, but in the end the legislature did not penalize the university for its action. As I look back now, I feel that this recognition of student responsibility was long overdue, and I am happy that it came about when I was the president, though briefly, for any stigma associated with the decision rightly attached to me rather than to my successor. Unfortunately for him, that distinction was not always made by critics of the university, but the outcry soon subsided.

In nearly every instance during my career, I enjoyed the cooperation and support of student leaders, which I tried to reciprocate fully by meeting their requests and program ideas whenever possible. However, some of the changes through the years, particularly with reference to eliminating the in loco parentis stance, have resulted in the employment of more expensive and less efficient means to achieve virtually the same end.

For example, for many years the university maintained an inspection service of off-campus housing and kept a list of approved rooms and apartments. A university staff member inspected the rooms and apartments, noted their adequacy in furnishings and arrangements, and placed the approved ones on a list that was made available to students for their use in finding space out in town. For some reason, during the 1960s this procedure caused quite an uproar among activist students, who termed it paternalistic, discriminatory, and unnecessary. Not many years after the procedure was abandoned, students, finding themselves at the mercy of landlords, began clamoring for the Bloomington City Council to pass ordinances requiring the inspection of rental rooms. That inspection proved to be an endless, ineffective, and expensive procedure, involving considerable bureaucracy instead of the lone university staff member who accomplished the inspection as only one of his duties when the out-in-town students were fewer in number.

Much the same kind of costly substitution for in loco parentis has taken place in the field of counseling, where now an elaborate program, clearly and strongly paternalistic, is continually being expanded to meet the needs of special groups as well as of the student body as a whole.

A happy student body translates itself into a happy alumni body. One of the greatest assets that the university enjoyed in the 1930s, 1940s, and 1950s, as I observed in my presidency, was the active, loyal, and interested support of our alumni throughout the state and the nation. In a typical county-seat community in Indiana the majority of leading businessmen, the majority of the physicians, the majority of teachers, nearly all the nurses, and nearly all the lawyers and civic leaders have attended Indiana University. As one goes about the state, one is always enveloped in the interest and affection of these men and women. So it is with the alumni throughout the country. Many of our men and women have, because of the nature of our society, found their careers beyond the borders of the state with the result that we have in nearly every population center throughout the United States a group of distinguished leaders in their professions or activities who are Indiana University men and women, and they rally to the support of the university whenever called upon. It is true in Washington, New York, Boston, Chicago, San Francisco, Los Angeles, and so on. In fact, I believe that Indiana University furnishes a disproportionate share of political leadership relative to the size of its total student body, as compared with the total student body of the state.

Through the years two delightful types of extracurricular activities have been outstanding at Indiana University: one, the search for either a husband or a wife and the record of success in that regard; and the other, the university's service as a spawning ground for political leadership to such a degree that a very high proportion of the political leadership—national, state, and local—that has come from Indiana has had training in political organizations and in political student activity on this campus.

A distinctive characteristic of the alumni scene at Indiana University throughout all the years of my presidency and to the present has been the highly constructive leadership of the Alumni Association. As an official body the association has been diligent and persevering in its support of the university, dedicated to the university's welfare, and unusually understanding in times of university crisis. Although individual alumni would occasionally attack us bitterly during the Kinsey period, never once throughout all those years did the Alumni Association as a body fail to back the university's policies. The same steadfastness has been accorded the athletic program. In some universities the alumni association is so attuned to football victories that a string of defeats swings the association to an antagonistic view toward the administration of the university. We did not have that kind of opposition to contend with during my years. There were alumni who were disheartened, discouraged, and sometimes bitter when we lost more than they thought we should, but such attitudes were never expressed in a destructive or organized manner. The alumni of a great university often have first loyalty to their individual colleges, divisions, or professional groups, whereas one of the areas of interest common to all is that of intercollegiate athletics. So the lawyer, the doctor, the schoolteacher can all share the desire for winning teams and the sorrow over losses. We had during this period strong alumni secretaries, George Heighway and Claude Rich, who were able to interpret to other alumni the fact that we were striving to do our best, using all of the skill and ingenuity we had to succeed in every area of the university's life.[3] As a result we always had the official cooperation of the Alumni Association.

We tried to reciprocate this support by taking the alumni into our confidence in every way conceivable such as confidential meetings with the officers of the Alumni Association, the appointment of alumni visiting committees, and a never-ending effort to carry the story of university activities directly to the alumni in their meetings throughout the country. In the second year of my presidency, under the astute and skillful guidance of George Heighway, I spent many weeks speaking to alumni clubs from Boston to Seattle and from Minneapolis to Miami, crisscrossing the country. There were some fifty-odd alumni meetings in which we attempted to lay out the program that we envisioned to ensure scholarly growth and distinction, and we invited alumni to back us in that mighty effort. They responded magnificently, and I shall ever be grateful to them and their leadership for the help that we received in trying to build a more distinguished university in which they could take pride and that would enhance the value of their degrees. Conversely, the university was always conscious of the fact that in the success and achievement of its alumni lay the true measure of the quality of its own work and service to youth.

Because of their invaluable assistance and support during my administration, George Heighway and Claude Rich deserve a special word. George "Dixie" Heighway was a knowledgeable and perceptive alumni secretary and executive director of the Indiana University Foundation. Aware that I was not known to the older alumni when I became president, he set to work immediately to ease the transition from President Bryan's leadership to mine among those longtime alumni and to establish a relationship between them and me, assisted throughout by Dr. Bryan himself. Only a person keenly attuned to the perceptions of the older alumni and at the same time frank with me could have advised me, as he did on one occasion,

3. George Heighway served from November, 1925, through December, 1947. Claude Rich became alumni secretary on January 1, 1948, and left the post on May 1, 1968, to direct the university's Sesquicentennial celebration.

to seek a better tailor. I did. Claude Rich and I have known each other since we were children and, as distant cousins, attended the same family reunions and visited back and forth with our families. Claude proved to be a vigorous and effective leader of the Alumni Association, raising it to new heights in membership and activities. Quite early he became my trusted, indispensable advisor, with whom I discussed every major issue affecting the alumni or the public. As the years passed, he helped to involve the alumni in our legislative activities and became an effective agent in interpreting our needs to the newly elected and incumbent members of the General Assembly and to our friends throughout the state.

A considerable part of the Alumni Association's program is carried on through the active constituent alumni societies of the schools and divisions. These groups—for instance, those of the dental school, the business school, the law school, the medical school, education, and journalism—are the counterpart of the traditional city and county clubs throughout the state, the nation, and abroad. Another innovation in this period was the establishment of the Distinguished Alumni Service Award (DASA), five of which are bestowed annually, and the formation of the DASA Club, composed of the awardees, which meets during Commencement weekend. Under the able and entrepreneurial leadership of Frank B. Jones, the award-winning Alumni Association has continued to expand its programming to involve more and more alumni in such activities as travel, family camps, and the Mini-University.

Through the years of travel I have met alumni in every state of the Union and in many foreign countries, both Americans living abroad and alumni who have returned to their native countries. Regardless of where I would travel, on whatever kind of business, I have had the happy privilege of coming upon alumni, sometimes in wholly unexpected places. Not always would I recognize them, but they recognized me and a warm reunion would ensue. In time I came to realize that our alumni are everywhere; in fact, the sun never sets on the world of Indiana University alumni. Moreover, throughout the world and often in strange circumstances I have found some link with Indiana University through the activities of the extended university family, as is illustrated by the following story.

In the spring of 1974 I accepted an assignment to go to Nigeria to conduct a survey for the Public Service Review Commission of that country. I was recruited to conduct a study of the ability and willingness of the existing Nigerian universities to train people for the development function of the nation. Nigerian political leaders were charging that the universities were interested only in traditional education, hence were neglecting the training of people to lead the work of developing the "new Nigeria."

I arrived in Lagos on May 15 and was assigned a room in the new section of the New Ikoyi Hotel, the best hotel in Lagos. My room looked down on a large and beautiful swimming pool presided over by a Nigerian named Dada. Dada was a handsome chap who was, I should say, about forty and who had a brother with the permanent delegation of Nigeria to the United Nations.

It was steaming hot in Lagos at the time, very humid. Although I had an air-conditioned office as well as an air-conditioned hotel room (when the air conditioning worked), the heat and humidity were debilitating. To combat these, I developed a habit of swimming about twilight before going to dinner. Dada was fascinated by the fact that a white-haired guest of the hotel would elect to swim each day, so after a while we struck up an acquaintance. When I was delayed in coming down at the end of the day, he would invariably telephone my room to say, "You haven't been down to swim yet. You must get down here." The water was warm but refreshing, and my swimming companions were lots of happy Nigerians as well as members of the international colony then resident in Lagos. Recorded music blared out across the pool. The tunes were of an ancient and honorable vintage—such songs as "It's a Long, Long Way to Tipperary," "Margie," and other World War I songs.

Late one afternoon I was resting by the side of the pool after swimming and Dada was there with me. We were discussing a whole variety of topics. He always addressed me as "Papa," the way Nigerians address a white-haired man; a woman is addressed as "Mama." These are titles of respect. We had a good deal of fun with "Papa" and "Dada." In the morning when I would go down to breakfast I would say, "Good morning, Dada-Dada-Dada-Dada!" and he would reply, "Good morning, Papa-Papa-Papa!" On this particular occasion, the evening was calm and delightful; the sun had just set behind the dense, black-green foliage at the end of the pool, sinking suddenly as it does in the tropics. I looked up at the sky and, seeing that it was filled with fleecy white clouds, I said to

Dada, "That's a buttermilk sky. You probably don't know what a buttermilk sky is because you don't have buttermilk here. A friend of mine, a college classmate, wrote a song called 'Old Buttermilk Sky.' He lives in Palm Springs, California, fifteen thousand miles from where we are. Of course you wouldn't know about him, but I thought you might want to know what a buttermilk sky is and that there is a song written about it." Dada grinned almost from ear to ear, and I could tell that he was about to deliver a coup de grace. He loved besting me. After a moment's hesitation, he broke into song, singing Hoagy Carmichael's "Old Buttermilk Sky" from start to finish. I could not have been more surprised or pleased. It gave me an eerie feeling, hearing "Old Buttermilk Sky" in that circumstance, long distant from the day when Hoagy had composed it and far away in the depths of tropical Africa, sung by a native Nigerian. Of course, it was a striking demonstration of the universal appeal of Hoagy's songs. Dada was delighted to have been able to cap my story.

⟦15⟧

○ ○ ○

Culture to the Crossroads

THE INDIANA UNIVERSITY system of main and regional
campuses grew from an early and continuing policy of its administrations to take education to the people if the people could
not come to the institution. At first, two or three faculty members
traveled to the cities from which requests had come for classes
in certain courses. Subsequently extension centers were established
when the demand and favorable circumstances warranted. Ultimately there developed the vigorous regional campus system that,
with the Bloomington and Indianapolis campuses, constitutes Indiana University as we know it today. Robert E. Cavanaugh has
written a detailed history of this development.[1]

Why did the development take that form rather than that of a
public junior college system, a two-year extension of high school,
in the state? One reason was the future of several junior colleges
that were begun. Another, more telling reason was, I believe, a realization of the clear advantages to be gained from association with
an established university. The benefits of full integration with a parent institution such as sharing its administrative and library resources, prestige, and academic maturity while forming its own
individuality as a smaller, more locally oriented educational center
undoubtedly were persuasive elements in the decision of a civic
group to seek establishment of a branch of Indiana University in its
community rather than found an independent junior college. The
efficiency and economy that result are advantageous both to the
state and to the student. The viability of the branching system is one
evidence of the remarkable variety, diversity, and flexibility of higher
education in America.

---

1. Robert E. Cavanaugh, *Indiana University Extension: Its Origin, Progress,
Pitfalls, and Personalities* (Indiana University Extension, 1961).

It is not well known that both our Gary and Kokomo campuses were originally public school–connected junior colleges, which had been in existence for some years but which, after their initial success, had languished. Community leaders in each city approached us, requesting that we consider taking over the junior college as it then existed and converting it into an extension center (later called a regional campus) in the Indiana University system. We proceeded only after being assured that the public school administrators as well as the civic and business leaders were in favor of the affiliation. Since these communities could be justifiably served by Indiana University, both having sent many students to the Bloomington campus through the years and having a large number of alumni resident in their areas, we decided that it was an appropriate move for us to make. In both instances the takeover of the existing programs by the university resulted in a rapid and immediate increase in student interest and enthusiasm and therefore in a much more successful operation than had been possible before. So far as I can tell, this resulted not because the programs had been poor before, for they had not been, but because having Indiana University's imprimatur for the courses made students in the communities much more interested in enrolling and much more willing to undertake their college work at home.

Through the years many communities approached us asking us to start extension centers. In each instance we responded to the request with reasonable interest. We did so by making a careful survey of the community—its potential, its high school graduates, the presence or absence of a private institution either in the community or nearby offering collegiate work for the high school graduates—and on this basis decided if we should or should not establish a campus there. We were sometimes charged with a desire to spread everywhere, but in actuality we turned down far more communities than we entered. If we learned that the volume of student interest was too small to make the operation viable or if we thought its needs for collegiate training for high school graduates could be served by existing private colleges in the vicinity, we declined the invitation accordingly. One of the benchmarks we used in deciding upon a new location was whether or not it would injure any existing private institution.

The use of this benchmark is illustrated by two incidents. Once upon a time Evansville College had fallen upon bad times: its en-

rollment was dropping; its financial situation was desperate. Finally
its president and board of trustees came to us to say they had no
choice other than to ask us to take over the college and to establish
on its campus a branch of Indiana University. This of course was
attractive to the university because Evansville would normally have
been a place that we would feel some obligation to serve and that
could be served quite expeditiously from the Bloomington campus
of the university. However, following our custom, Ward Biddle and
I made a journey to Evansville and spent a few days carefully sur-
veying the situation with the faculty members, the officers of the
college, and the downtown power structure. We came to the conclusion that it would be entirely feasible for us to establish a branch
on the existing Evansville College campus, but we also believed that
it was feasible for Evansville College to continue. Our study indicated that, with a little greater support from the business and civic
leaders of the community and a more sympathetic concern for the
life of the institution by the Methodist Church, with which it was
affiliated, the college could be made viable. One of the curricular
needs that the institution had was for master's-level courses in certain
fields such as education and nursing that we could offer. We suggested to the Evansville College officials that they regroup and move
ahead rather than capitulate. We agreed to assist them by sending
some top-level faculty to Evansville for a few semesters to teach
courses the college could not afford to offer. In addition, we
spoke to some of the leaders of the local business community such
as Charlie Enlow, telling them we thought it was shameful that the
community was not supporting the college better and that, if they
would get behind the college, it could be made successful. We also
sought out some of the leaders of the Methodist Church, including
the bishop, repeating our appraisal to them. As a result of these
initiatives, Evansville College did regroup and, with increased support from downtown businesses and the church, was able to begin
an upward climb that has resulted in university status and its present
highly successful and valuable work.

One of the unhappy events in this story, however, is that Indiana
State University at Terre Haute, breaking all agreements that the
four institutions had had concerning branching and with total dis-
regard for Evansville University's welfare, did a few years ago establish a branch campus between Evansville and Mt. Vernon, and
with vigorous promotion considerably damaged Evansville Univer-

sity's future growth possibilities. We are proud of the fact that we put the welfare of that institution first rather than the aggrandizement of Indiana University.

Another illustration of our policy of coordination and cooperation with the private colleges comes from our relationship with Earlham College. The community of Richmond was asking Earlham College for certain courses of a professional and vocational nature and also asking that they be given in the evening. Earlham was not interested in undertaking such offerings; however, its plant was largely unused from midafternoon through the evening hours. President William C. Dennis of Earlham invited me to meet with him one day. In the course of this meeting he suggested that we work out an arrangement for a joint Indiana University-Earlham College center to serve the vocational, professional, and evening-class needs of that community. Our agreement roughly called for Earlham to supply the plant and for Indiana University to meet the cost of the instruction, the faculty, and the administration of the program. Both Boards concurred, and for many years the plan functioned very successfully until Earlham College decided to discontinue the arrangement. Later, the present Indiana University East campus was established with Earlham College's blessing. But at the time of the agreement, it was an unparalleled arrangement between a state university and a private liberal arts college to offer an evening program and is an excellent example of what can be accomplished to the mutual advantage of each when two institutions join in a program better to serve the youth of an area.

When we were invited, indeed urged, to come into South Bend we first sought to ascertain the attitude of Father J. Hugh O'Donnell, the president, and the other officials of the University of Notre Dame. They cordially welcomed our entry with our type of program, which would help to relieve Notre Dame of the pressure of providing the kind of courses that we were proposing to offer to the youth of that community. Notre Dame wished to maintain its integrity as a national university drawing its student body from everywhere rather than having a disproportionate number from the local community.

Our system as it finally evolved, with some additional branches that Purdue University established after a time, brings the four years of college training within twenty-five miles of 95 percent of all high school graduates in the state. In making this statement, of course, I am including the offerings of the private colleges as well as of the public institutions. So far as I know this is an unparalleled distribution of collegiate opportunities in any place in the United States, and I do not exclude California with its much-publicized state college and junior college systems.

I am not unaware of criticisms that have been leveled against a satellite system such as ours. As the regional campuses mature and develop their own individuality, often a desire for autonomous decision making also grows: to set their own standards, to obtain the amenities of the core campus, to have their own athletic teams, and so on. Although understandable, aspirations of this nature, if fully realized, would lead to a multiplicity of state schools all seeking ever-increasing appropriations from the state legislature and, since there is a limit to state spending for higher education, ending in a struggle to stay alive. The present administration of Indiana University has maintained a viable balance, it seems to me, between the aspirations of all its campuses and the realities of state funding.

As we began to develop our branches throughout the state, one of the difficulties we encountered was Purdue's practice of insisting that any branch operations had to be supported from the general legislative appropriations of Indiana University. This meant that any money spent on the branches, or extension centers, had to be squeezed out of an already inadequate Bloomington-Indianapolis budget. But Purdue was adamant, stating its belief that all the centers should be approximately self-supporting from student fees. Purdue continued to press the point until circumstances made it expedient for it to begin establishing branches, and at that time its officials retreated from their previous position. I can only assume that their earlier policy, when they had no branches, was based upon the probability that funding of Indiana University's branches would break the parity of appropriations between the two institutions. Another reason for their eventual willingness to allow us to seek money for our extension centers probably was that, by the time of Purdue's branching, parity was already broken and appropriations for the centers were no longer at issue.

As Purdue began to enter the field we attempted to eliminate competitive factors as much as possible by a number of devices. One was the host-guest relationship. In an area where we were already established and had a sizable offering, we would become host, providing Purdue the facilities necessary for it to offer some courses.

We did so in Jeffersonville, South Bend, Kokomo, and Indianapolis. Purdue in turn played host to us in its Michigan City branch. In recent years we have evolved a joint administrative structure when both institutions are established in a community as in Fort Wayne and in Indianapolis. In Fort Wayne, Purdue handles fiscal matters for the whole campus and each institution carries on its own academic program. The reverse is true in Indianapolis: we handle all fiscal and general administrative matters for both Indiana and Purdue programs.

I think that, all in all, the system as it evolved offers to the state of Indiana the best possible program for the benefit of the students and all citizens of the state. It not only gives them a widespread coverage of academic opportunities, but does so with the least possible duplication and with the greatest efficiency involving the least cost per credit hour delivered.

⟦16⟧

○　○　○

The University Looks Abroad

FROM 1945 ON, American universities were increasingly engaged in technical-assistance programs for developing countries funded both by the major foundations, especially Ford, and also by the federal government. Indiana University was deeply involved in this effort for several reasons.

First, we recognized that in the early years of its development Indiana University along with other American universities had been greatly assisted by the older, European universities, particularly the German and French. Even as late as my undergraduate days there were men on our faculty who had won their Ph.D.'s abroad prior to the time when most American universities were equipped to offer the doctorate. So the American university, now among the strongest anywhere, had an obligation to repay its debt to the world of scholarship through extending assistance to the new universities in the developing lands.

Second, we realized that by our taking an active part in these international projects the benefits would be two-way: while lending whatever help we could to institutions abroad, we would be greatly enriching the store of experience, knowledge, and professional competence of our faculty participants in the assistance programs, who, upon their return, would bring to the campus a comparative view that would stimulate the atmosphere of learning in the university.

We were somewhat motivated also by a missionary impulse to spread the American ideals of democratic higher education throughout the world. There is a bit of missionary zeal in all of us to propagate the ideals in which we believe. Pope John Paul I, in one of his few public statements, advocated mutual understanding in international life and social progress to "overcome hunger of body and ignorance of the mind," especially in underdeveloped countries.[1] I suppose, in the final analysis, we were imbued with the conviction that our efforts might contribute to such a high purpose.

Indiana University's technical-assistance efforts spanned the globe. Through the years we undertook official university projects in Korea, Indonesia, Thailand, Pakistan East and West, Afghanistan, Ghana, Nigeria, Yugoslavia, Brazil, Peru, Chile, Colombia, Venezuela, and the Philippines (see Appendix [I]). American universities engaged in technical-assistance contracts were criticized from time to time because of their unwillingness to make a total institutional commitment to the work they had undertaken to perform in their contracts. Some were accused, for instance, of being unwilling to recruit from their own departments for service abroad, hiring instead men from other institutions derisively referred to as "academic mercenaries." From the beginning we adopted the position that, if we undertook these contracts, we should attempt to perform them abroad to the best of our ability and we should commit whatever resources of the university were needed to the work in the field.

Another problem had to be met. Faculty in various schools were said to be reluctant to accept foreign assignments lest they be forgotten by the promotions committees and officers of their home institutions and thereby miss the opportunity for advancement. Too, they feared they would have difficulty in reentering the academic community when they returned. We attempted to solve both problems by making a commitment to those who went abroad that they would receive appropriate credit for their accomplishments there and would not be forgotten at home. We undertook to recruit our best rather than those of whom we wished to be rid and soon were able to have an understanding on the part of the university community that service abroad was honored by both the general faculty and the administrative officers. This assurance was necessary for other reasons: persons who went to developing nations frequently worked under very difficult circumstances; there were many problems of a professional nature and hardships in living arrangements, schooling of children, and so on. It was easy for them to begin feeling forlorn and isolated.

All the overseas contracts called for periodic review by appropriate individuals from the campus and made financial provision for the trips. Thus it was feasible for the general administrative officers

1. *International Herald-Tribune*, Paris, August 28, 1978.

(the president, vice presidents, deans, and even occasionally trustees) to visit the field from time to time to offer encouragement and support to these bootstrap operations, particularly when discouraging developments had occurred. We also visited the field to help in negotiations for new or renewed contracts or to participate in official celebrations on the occasion of significant milestones of achievement. On these trips we scrupulously observed the ritual of making ceremonial calls on officials ranging from key bureaucrats to cabinet ministers, prime ministers, kings or heads of state. We used those occasions to assure the officials that we fully backed our project staff, that the resources of Indiana University were behind the project, and that we wanted to be as helpful as possible. In turn, our visits gave the officials an opportunity to air any objections or opinions that they were reluctant to express to our own people there.

Apart from official university contracts, many of our specialists undertook technical-assistance assignments abroad as individuals. I undertook four of these myself during the years: (1) a consultancy to the Pakistan Commission on National Education in 1959; (2) membership on the Advisory Committee to Haile Selassie for the development of the national university in Addis Ababa, a committee that was created in 1966 and carried on its work for a few years thereafter; (3) a mission for the Ford Foundation to Peru in 1967, when the head of the Ford office in Lima was Peter Fraenkel, as an advisor to the Inter-University Council on planning for the further development of higher education in Peru; and (4) in 1974 a study for the Public Service Review Commission of Nigeria of the readiness and ability of the Nigerian universities to train students for the development function of the country.

Over the years it so happened that the university had a series of contracts with two countries in particular: Pakistan and Thailand. Descriptions of the projects in each of these countries may serve for all the rest to illustrate kinds of university involvement in technical assistance and the nature of my own participation.

The projects in Pakistan were financed for the most part by the Ford Foundation, and through the years this situation enabled us to achieve a felicitous working arrangement with Ford Foundation officers in New York and with its staff in Pakistan. The Foundation had selected Pakistan as one of the developing countries where it wished to concentrate its efforts, and Indiana University was chosen to play an important role in realizing the Foundation's program.

The first project there was a contract to assist with the development of the Khyber Medical College of the new University of Peshawar. This was the first Pakistani medical college to be administratively part of a university rather than under the Ministry of Health. The experience of the late Paul A. Nicoll, Chief of Party and Professor of Physiology, at Peshawar led to the establishment of the Postgraduate Basic Medical Sciences Institute at the University of Karachi. We also undertook to assist Punjab University at Lahore in establishing an Institute of Education and Research for the improvement of teacher training and eventually in building a new teachers' college campus; to assist in the development of the Institute of Business Administration at the University of Dacca for the training of master's and doctoral students; and to play a major role in the creation and building of a national university for graduate students at Islamabad, the new capital of Pakistan.

To make the need for technical assistance in Pakistan understandable, it is essential to describe conditions after Partition in 1947. The partition of India into two entities, one Hindu India and the other Moslem Pakistan East and West, created one of the great social upheavals of modern times. There was extensive migration of Hindus from the Pakistan areas into India and, conversely, migration of Moslems from India outward to the Pakistani territories. A new nation of approximately seventy-three million people was created overnight, so to speak. This nation, already an old society, had some of the physical structures of a developed society such as railroads, shops, factories, farms, and so on, but almost in a matter of weeks the people had to organize their own monetary system, government, postal system, social services, and an educational system tailored to the needs of the new nation. What they had inherited had been cast in the British-Indian mold, and not only were their social institutions radically disrupted by Partition, they were also wholly inappropriate and inadequate to serve in the new context. It is one of the miracles of the century that the Pakistani people were able to accomplish so much in so little time and to establish a major nation that began to function notwithstanding the ruptures and fragmentations produced by the new geographical boundaries and the new political necessities of independence.

In education the situation was especially critical. The educational system that the Pakistani inherited had been instituted by the British in the eighteenth century and was designed to produce civil servants to manage the country under the direction of their British rulers. Moreover, as all instruction was in English a major part of the population was barred from entry into the school system even at the beginning level. A few young men of great promise were sent abroad for advanced training with the expectation that they would come back to help meet the professional and technical needs of the subcontinent, but too frequently they remained abroad and so became a brain drain instead of a brain bank.

To further complicate the situation, after Partition nearly all the Hindu teachers, and there had been many in the Pakistan areas, migrated to India and hundreds of thousands of Moslem students moved from India into Pakistan. With more students and fewer teachers the resources of personnel, buildings, and facilities were wholly inadequate. It is a great wonder that the system did not fall into complete chaos but instead kept going somehow.

As would be expected in a society whose members had been starved for education so long, there was popular pressure for rapid expansion. Universities were quickly founded between the years 1947 and 1953 at Hyderabad in the Sind, at Karachi and Peshawar in West Pakistan, and at Rajshahi in East Pakistan. Each of these had a number of affiliated colleges such as agriculture, engineering, medicine, liberal arts, sciences, education, law, and commerce. All were established in such a rush that there was really no time for adequate planning and preparation, and many problems arose.

There had been criticism that the system Pakistan inherited did not concern itself with the critical requirements for the economic and political development of the society and that it was unconcerned about the cultural and religious aspirations of the new nation. As thoughtful leaders viewed this churning, rapid growth, they recognized the great urgency for a national study to identify necessary reforms and especially to chart the course for an educational system that would meet the needs of the new nation. Thus the President's Commission on National Education was appointed in December, 1958, and installed on January 5, 1959, by the president of Pakistan, General Mohammad Ayub Khan.

Heading the commission was a remarkable Pakistani educator, S. M. Sharif, the education secretary of the government in West Pakistan, a man who had had important educational and ministerial experience in both India and Pakistan. The secretary of the commission was Raziuddin Siddiqi, who at that time was a founding member of the Pakistan Atomic Energy Commission with special responsibility for developing nuclear science. Dr. Siddiqi had been the vice chancellor of Osmania University in Hyderabad, India, and then founder and vice chancellor of the University of Peshawar. He is perhaps the most remarkable leader of education in that part of the world, having made an unparalleled contribution to the whole field of education in both the subcontinent and the developing world. Other members of this distinguished commission included M. K. Afridi, vice chancellor of Peshawar University and later head of the World Health Organization; R. M. Ewing of the Forman Christian College at Lahore,[2] a man from a family long dedicated to missionary educational work in India; General Mohammad Khan, Director of Army Education, who was a psychologist and a man of exceptional ability; and Atwar Husain, a member of the faculty of Dacca University, one of the persons with whom we were to continue contact through the years.

The commission sought the aid of some outside consultants: from the United States, John Warner, president of the Carnegie Institute of Technology at Pittsburgh, and me. We each spent about a month full-time there. Two eminent Pakistani scholars then teaching abroad, I. H. Qureshi at Columbia University and Abdus Salam (co-winner of the 1979 Nobel Prize in physics) at Imperial College, London, were brought back for consultation.

The commission worked with great intensity. In the beginning its members traveled to all sections of Pakistan, both East and West, to conduct hearings at which a variety of citizens had been invited to express their views. For me it was a revealing experience to listen firsthand to the views and attitudes of the people of Pakistan and to see a considerable portion of the country in the process. Pakistan at that time was just beginning its great development and still was extraordinarily picturesque. Even in the port city of Karachi, the streets were filled with a curious variety of traffic: occasional flocks of sheep, herds of water buffalo, now and then a heavily loaded camel train, pedicabs, and pedestrians. Once in a while we spotted a relic of the British rule—an aging Rolls Royce—being steered in and around the moving stream.

One interesting incident that occurred during my service with

2. The Forman Christian College at Lahore was recognized as one of the best of the teaching colleges in Pakistan. The list of commission members illustrates the quality that was mobilized for this work.

the commission in Karachi may be worthy of recounting. In the course of our deliberations it was reported that President Ayub Khan was unhappy that rich Pakistanis were not contributing financially to the development of education, especially higher education. His unhappiness arose in part from reports of the generosity of American individuals to their universities. I pointed out to the commission that a powerful factor stimulating personal philanthropic gifts was the provision by our federal government that allowed these gifts to be tax deductible. In due course I was summoned to meet with President Ayub Khan, who asked for my advice as to how Pakistanis could be stimulated to give to worthy causes including higher education as rich people in the United States did. I repeated to him what I had said to the commission about tax-deductible gifts. He grasped the idea, questioned me closely about it, and in time, I was told, he pushed a similar provision through the Pakistan government.

After our hearings throughout the country, we settled down in Karachi and worked steadily many hours every day. I joined the commission in mid-March and left in mid-April. President Ayub Khan had requested the completion of the report in six months because of his urgent need to have its recommendations. Although the deadline was not met, the final report was presented to him before the end of the summer.

The printed report comprises a sizable volume of more than three hundred pages and is remarkable in its extent and quality, considering the time allotted. It has come to be known through the years as the Sharif Commission Report, and it is now viewed, in light of the perspective of twenty years, as one of the best presentations on higher education and education in general in that part of the world—in fact, in any of the developing nations during that era. It can be quite accurately described as the bible for educational reorganization and direction in Pakistan.

It was that commission's recommendations concerning higher education, graduate education, and the development of research potential in the country that in time led to the movement to create a national graduate university at Islamabad, the new capital, a project with which I was to be personally involved over a period of years and through which I had the privilege of being associated again with Dr. Siddiqi, this time as a collaborator, and of having further contact with that admirable senior statesman, Mr. Sharif. The creation of the university at Islamabad was the means selected to try to achieve the goals and objectives recommended by the Sharif Commission. It was so conceived that it eventually came to represent a new initiative and an example of the so-called higher higher education in the Third World. Because the project as it unfolded involved nearly every segment of Indiana University including many of my colleagues, a description of the effort may be of interest.

The part of the Sharif Commission Report dealing with postgraduate studies and research concluded that this area had not been developed properly in existing Pakistani universities. It had not flourished for a number of reasons: lack of equipment and resources, lack of tradition, and, mainly, lack of a faculty competent to offer that level of work. The specialists were just not available largely because some of the best and the brightest, after being trained abroad, stayed abroad. The commission had noted that resources were not sufficient to develop every university into a center of excellence. Eventually it was decided that the government's effort should be concentrated in the beginning on a single, new, unitary university devoted solely to postgraduate studies.

The next decision was to locate the experimental institution at Islamabad. It was to be supported by the national government and the hope was that in time it would be surrounded by national institutes of research. The university was to be selective in enrollment, drawing its students from the brightest graduates of the other universities, and by its high promise to lure back top Pakistani scholars teaching abroad. It was an ambitious, innovative, and daring experiment that caught the imagination of those interested in educational improvement in the developing nations all around the globe. Dr. Siddiqi was able to project a great dream and his idea caught fire internationally. I sometimes have explained what he with his helpers was attempting to do by pointing to the special genius of Johns Hopkins University and what it did for American higher education. Johns Hopkins was founded as a graduate institution with high standards for admission. As aspiring students of other institutions sought to qualify for admission to Johns Hopkins, they in effect forced upward the standards of their own schools. The planners hoped that the University of Islamabad would have a national impact, raising standards throughout as well as training highly competent Ph.D.'s for the nation's leadership.

The starting of a new university of the highest rank required hard currency, that is, foreign currency. Pakistani currency was in short supply, was blocked, and could not be used for the purchase of many things required to bring a university into existence. Thus the United Nations Development Fund under the leadership of Paul Hoffman joined the Ford Foundation in some funding, and Unesco gave a little help, principally with personnel. These funds, dispersed through the Indiana University Foundation, paid for the travel of Dr. Siddiqi and Mr. Sharif throughout the world as they examined graduate institutions. Hard currency also paid for the cost of architectural designing and for consultants to go to Pakistan to assist with the planning. Professor Edward Najam of Indiana University and I secured top consultants from Europe and throughout the United States to work with the planners in Islamabad.

A beautiful site overlooking Islamabad was selected, and the distinguished American architect Edward Durrell Stone was engaged to design the buildings of the campus as an integrated unit with an architecture indigenous to the region and on an international level of distinction.[3] Several members of the Indiana University faculty and staff, acting as consultants to the architect, helped to plan the facilities; for example, Harold Jordan was a consultant on the student union building, Cecil Byrd on the library, Lynne Merritt and others on the physics and chemistry laboratories, and Stanley Hagstrom on the computer center.

Academic work got underway in temporary quarters while the new plant was being built. Dr. Siddiqi went to country after country recruiting outstanding scholars for his faculty. The boldness and originality of the plan caught the imagination of Pakistani scholars living abroad, and Dr. Siddiqi was a very energetic and persuasive recruiter. He rather quickly realized one of the major objectives of the plan, namely, the repatriation of Pakistani scholars. In fact, approximately fifty first-rate men agreed to return from various pursuits in which they were occupied. This feat perhaps represents the only really successful reversal of the brain drain in the Third World.

From the very beginning he was also able to attract first-rate students from all over Pakistan East and West—not in large numbers, because he was very selective, but in sufficient quantity to validate the objective he had of stimulating promising students to

3. Stone also designed the capitol at Islamabad, as well as other principal buildings there, and the U.S. embassy at Delhi.

achieve well in the established universities with the goal of being admitted to Islamabad.

In time the institution moved from its temporary quarters to its new campus, which included not only teaching facilities but also residential quarters for both faculty and students in handsome and functional structures. I was privileged to attend the elaborate dedicatory ceremony, held on October 5, 1971. President Ayub Khan, who had been one of the principal supporters of the institution, had retired by that time and his successor Yahya Khan presided.

The institution was already off to a promising start when Dr. Siddiqi, having reached the mandatory age limit, retired as vice chancellor. Then with the coming to power of a new socialist regime under President Bhutto, the original concept for the university was all but abandoned, and soon it began to operate just as any other university without regard to its special mission.

Both Dr. Siddiqi and I think that the idea behind it was sound, that the dream that inspired it was prophetic, and that eventually the institution will be restored to the role for which it was created: as a research center and producer of leaders for Pakistan and as an example for the rest of the developing world. I spent a great deal of time as a consultant on this project and as a catalyst for Indiana University's participation, during which the resources of our institution were more broadly utilized, in my estimation, than by any other of our technical-assistance projects with the possible exception of the one in Kabul.[4] It was an exciting and stimulating adventure.

Another example of our technical-assistance effort abroad is to be found in Thailand, one of the most interesting countries in the world. To the best of my memory, our very first contact with officialdom of Thailand occurred in October, 1948, when His Excellency the Permanent Under Secretary for Education in the Ministry of Education, Mom Luang Pin Malakul, visited here. He had become interested in Indiana University because two Thai students were working for advanced degrees in audio-visual education under Lawrence Larson. Malakul, in the United States on a round-the-world trip to a Unesco conference in Beirut, stopped to see them. I enjoyed my visit with Mom Luang Pin from the moment of meet-

4. The Kabul contract involved a substantial number of people, but dealt with a more limited range of problems, principally related to administration.

ing. He was handsome, imaginative, and congenial. Trained at Oxford, he was the most powerful Thai leader in the educational field, greatly respected for his experience, professional competence, dedication, and wisdom. His wife, Khunying—now, Tauphuying (titles conferred by the king)—Dusdi Malakul, who was related to the Thai royal family, was an influential figure in women's and civic affairs. He was received by Indiana University as an official guest and accorded the courtesies that his distinction deserved. I spent much time with him, entertaining him, showing him the university, describing its resources, and discussing the problems in educational development that he foresaw in Thailand. This was the beginning of a personal friendship that has continued to this day.

By fortunate circumstance Willis Porter, then a member of the faculty of the State Teachers College at Oneonta, New York, had been recruited by the International Cooperation Administration (ICA), predecessor of the Agency for International Development (AID), to have a look at the state of teacher education in Thailand and to recommend a course of action, if needed, to expand and modernize the system. In due course he formulated an ambitious program and forwarded it to Washington; Indiana University was in turn asked to consider undertaking it. At about that time Walter Laves, who was soon to join our faculty as head of the government department, stopped in Bangkok enroute to Burma on Unesco business, learned about the program, and briefly explored what training there was for public administration in Thailand. John Ashton, one of our vice presidents and dean of our graduate school, made a trip to Bangkok to meet with Dr. Porter; soon thereafter Dean Wendell Wright of the School of Education, also a vice president, spent ten days in Thailand discussing the program with the people in the Thai ministry. While there he was able to persuade Dr. Porter to remain in Thailand to direct the project, which we had decided to undertake, but we asked that he resign his position at Oneonta and become a tenured member of the Indiana University faculty, in line with the policy we had formed to have all our technical-assistance projects directed by regular members of our faculty.

In brief, the contract called for us to assist in the development of a national school of teacher education to train teachers for the whole of Thailand. The base was to be a recently founded, small College of Education at Prasarn Mitr in Bangkok, and the program envisioned its complete rehabilitation and major expansion. In time

the contract was broadened to include assistance to the Division
of Teacher Education at Chulalongkorn, the first and most important university at the time in Thailand, located at Bangkok. Porter
helped to guide the development of this small division of education
at Chulalongkorn into a strong professional college. Provision was
made not only for us to advise and assist with the College of Education at Prasarn Mitr, but also for promising young men and women
to be sent to the United States—principally to Indiana University—
for training as future faculty members in Thailand.[5] We were to
furnish personnel, representing a variety of fields, who could assist
in expansion and modernization of the curriculum, in the preparation of teaching materials illustrated with objects and customs indigenous to Thailand, and in the planning and development of the
buildings, including particularly a major library. To this project
Indiana University unstintingly committed its resources, and during
the eight-year life of the contract a firm and sound foundation was
laid by the Thai-American effort to strengthen teacher training in
Thailand.

The effort was fortunate in attracting some remarkable Thai
leadership, and it was greatly facilitated by the sympathetic and
sensitive help of Bhunthin Attagara, who occupied strategic positions first as director of external affairs and later as director general
of teacher education. The first president of the college was Saroj
Buasri, who had been trained in the United States and was familiar
with modern practices in teacher training. Its vice president, likewise trained in the United States, was Khunying Ubol. She was importantly involved from the beginning, and her husband, Malai
Huvanandana, was until his death in 1979 to play a significant role
in a later project undertaken by the university.

We assigned thirty-two staff members to the Thailand project
for periods ranging from several months to a few years, only three
of whom were recruited from outside the Indiana University faculty.
The men and women for the most part were senior, mature members
of the faculty, leaders in their respective specialties. Their willingness to enter into this endeavor was heartening; I think that it was
the nature of the program that made our people willing to interrupt
their careers here and spend some time in Bangkok.

Progress at the College of Education was steady and certain

5. Four Thai alumni of Indiana University are now college presidents in
Thailand.

from the very beginning. Today the main campus of the College at Prasarn Mitr is handsome, well equipped, and enriched by a major library, and the institution has branch campuses throughout Thailand.[6] Objective observers testify that the college has been a major influence in raising the level of instruction of the school system of Thailand and in so doing has made a fundamental contribution to the educational advance of the country.

While we were involved with the College of Education, we began negotiations for our program in public administration, a project that Walter Laves had developed as a result of an interest dating from the earlier visit to Bangkok. Indiana University's responsibility under this contract was to provide professional personnel to advise and to aid in the training of staff for the new Institute of Public Administration to be located at Thammasat University. We were also to advise concerning its organization and its methods of teaching, its research and consultative services, conference and training programs, training aids, professional associations, publications, and library development.

The formal relationship between Indiana University and Thammasat University, begun May 3, 1955, originally was to have lasted three years, but the period was later extended, terminating in October, 1964. For assisting Thammasat University to train men and women for government and public service, Indiana University made a major commitment of personnel. In all, forty-five faculty and staff members were sent to Bangkok for service, including two who were later to become presidents of Indiana University, Joseph L. Sutton and John W. Ryan. Generally the families of the faculty members accompanied them to Thailand. In turn, during this period forty-one carefully selected Thai men and women were sent to this country for advanced degrees, thirty-five of them to Indiana University and the other six to institutions for curricula we did not have. Toward the end of our relationship Thai leaders began to feel the need for greater expertise and sophistication in the broad field of development administration. Whereas the Institute of Public Administration had been providing training for the public sector, it was now thought that this base of training should be broadened; with that

6. In 1975 the College of Education was named Srinakharinwirst University by royal decree. Its present president is Sasidorn. Of the eleven vice presidents at the parent and regional campuses, the majority are Indiana University graduates including my friend Vichitr Sinsiri. The enrollment is 25,000, the largest university enrollment in Thailand.

idea as an impetus, the National Institute for Development Administration (N I D A) was established by royal proclamation on March 23, 1966, and given university status shortly thereafter. N I D A was a cooperative effort by four bodies: the Thai government, the Ford Foundation, the Midwestern Universities Consortium for International Activities (M U C I A),[7] and Indiana University. It had a somewhat broader base than the Institute of Public Administration. In fact, the program of the Institute of Public Administration at Thammasat was merged into this new center and became the School of Public Administration within N I D A. In addition to the School of Public Administration and the School of Business Administration, N I D A had a School of Development Economics, a School of Applied Statistics, a Research Center, a Training Center, a Development Document Center, and an English Training Center. It was officially designated a graduate school and granted authority to give master's and doctoral degrees. The contract for the program was with M U C I A, but the Indiana University Graduate School of Business was selected as the administrative agency for the grant because of our involvement and experience in Thailand.

The project was fortunate in its leadership from the very beginning. Bunchana Atthakor, a highly respected figure, was the first rector. The second rector was Malai Huvanandana, a man whose warm relationships with Indiana University were continued through the years by personal visits and through his children who became Indiana University students. He had been dean of the program at Thammasat. Choop Karnajanaprakorn was the vice rector and in N I D A's formative period he and Malai shared their responsibilities, with Dr. Malai concentrating on external affairs while Dr. Choop concentrated on the academic organization. Dr. Malai, an influential figure in Bangkok, was able to secure support for the building of an efficient and attractive physical plant. Dr. Choop, who had been trained at Indiana University as a participant under the Thammasat contract, was an excellent academic leader. With the retirement of Malai in 1972, Choop became rector, and thus we had in the beginning years of this project continuity of leadership, a very important asset. The chief of party for the Ford Foundation in Bangkok, first George Gant and then Howard Schaller, gave the project

7. MUCIA was incorporated in 1964 by the University of Illinois, Indiana University, Michigan State University, and the University of Wisconsin to improve their technical assistance abroad and the academic benefit to each campus from their overseas activities.

warm and intelligent support. Howard Schaller eventually resigned from the Ford Foundation and became chief of party of the M U C I A-N I D A project. He had been a professor in our business school prior to going to the Ford Foundation and is now back at Indiana as associate dean for administration in the business school.

Altogether, some forty outstanding Thais were recruited through N I D A to come to the United States for advanced training, four of them at Indiana University. N I D A's progress was vigorous and sustained from the beginning and all evidence indicates that the institution has made a major contribution to research and to the training of personnel for the development process in Thailand. Especially in the field of business administration, the influence of its M.B.A.'s is being felt increasingly in the private sector, and these graduates are rapidly assuming positions of economic leadership.

I made a number of trips to Thailand during these years to give encouragement and assistance to our staff as best I could and to renew friendships with the Thai leaders who had been influential in support of our programs. Included among these, in addition to individuals already mentioned, were Nob Palakavansa, Sudchi and Maria Laosantara, Field Marshal Thanom Kittikajorn, Prince Wan Waithayakon, Prince Dhani Nivat, and His Majesty King Bhumiphol Aduldej, who, from my first audience to the time I received from his hand an honorary degree from the College of Education, evidenced warm support for and a keen interest in our collaborative efforts. I especially treasure my Thai friends. They are a talented, attractive, sensitive people, and, in the work of modernizing their ancient society, they deserve every possible measure of success.

Throughout all these years Willis Porter and Walter Laves were active, energetic entrepreneurs, participants, interpreters, and ambassadors of these successful programs. In the early years, until his death in 1961, Dean Wright also was an active participant. This Thailand–Indiana University relationship, begun in 1954 and continued through the early 1970s in formal ways, now is maintained by warm personal ties and continuing enrollment of outstanding Thai students at Indiana University. The regular influx of students from Thailand and their return to serve their country have given us the largest alumni group in any foreign land, men and women who are now rapidly assuming positions of leadership. Of Thailand's seven provinces, four have been governed at one time or another by an alumnus of Indiana University. In those days we sometimes referred to the "Bloomington-Bangkok axis," and I indeed am proud of the linkages, personal and professional, that were created during that period.

Typically our technical-assistance contracts for aiding institutions or nations abroad with their educational systems made provision for personnel from these institutions to be sent to Indiana University for specialized training to lead the pattern of change being developed in the home country. From time to time we undertook also to train here personnel in whose countries we did not have an institutional base. For example, in 1956 we entered into an ICA program to train teachers from Belo Horizonte, Brazil—members of an elementary-teacher-education faculty. The beginning group of nineteen arrived in 1956; twenty more came in each of the three succeeding years. In 1956 we also undertook a twelve-month's program of training for twenty-five Puerto Rican teachers of English, who were given courses in English, government, and linguistics.

A contract was awarded us by ICA at approximately the same time for our Audio-Visual Center to train in its specialty twenty-nine students from thirteen countries. Following their yearlong stay on the Indiana campus they returned to their own countries to positions of leadership in the audio-visual and mass-communication fields. Participants in this program were from Afghanistan, Brazil, Egypt, El Salvador, Ethiopia, Indonesia, Iran, Iraq, Panama, Thailand, Uruguay, and Vietnam. Because of the large number of countries involved, this contract had special complexities that had to be dealt with.

One of our very rewarding student-training programs was undertaken by the School of Business. Working under a subcontract from the American Association of Collegiate Schools of Business, in cooperation with ICA, the business school brought nine teachers from various European countries—West Germany, France, Italy, Greece, and Turkey—to study here in January, 1956. These men were selected by the European Productivity Agency as potential leaders in a movement to modernize and update the training for business in Europe as one phase of the mighty effort that grew out of the Marshall Plan. The program continued for six years with approximately sixty participants, and time has proved it to have been unusually successful, for the men who were trained here returned home to become leaders not only in business education but also in major industries and government bureaus dealing with economic matters. As a group these men occupy a remarkable position of influence in the European community and remain loyal, active Indiana University alumni.

The 1950s were a period of such intense activity in the international field that by 1959 I could say in my State of the University address, under the general title of "The University Abroad," after having reported on several new contracts entered into during the previous year, that

> these contracts not only contribute richly to the development of their respective countries, but also serve to spread the fame and name of Indiana University throughout the world.
>
> Science and scholarship are truly universal. American universities are called upon in increasing measure to make them so. During the past year individual scholars from our institution were busily engaged in research and scholarly activities in more than twenty countries around the world. Our students were drawn from sixty-five nations, and our alumni were living and practicing their professions in every part of the globe. Truly, the sun never sets on the work of a great university.

During this time, in addition to our technical-assistance projects, collaborative arrangements were made with other universities and, as I've mentioned above, professors undertook consultancies in their special fields under contracts with governments or foundations. Indiana University over a period of years established teaching centers for our students abroad in Germany at the University of Hamburg, in France at the University of Strasbourg, in Spain at the University of Madrid, in Italy at the University of Bologna, and in Peru at San Marcos University.[8] It was a period also of sweeping curricular enrichment in our university system through introduction of non-Western and other international studies in response to the internationalization of higher education then taking place throughout the country. The dislocations of the great wars and the development of rapid air transportation and worldwide communication systems had produced a comprehension that our world was shrinking or that, in the words of our distinguished alumnus Wendell Willkie, we truly live in One World.

8. At present the study centers abroad include the Catholic University of Peru, Lima; University of Sao Paulo, Brazil; the universities of Strasbourg, Hamburg, Bologna, and Madrid; the Hochschule für Musik, Vienna; the Hebrew University, Jerusalem; and the University of Kent, Canterbury, England.

This mighty impulse toward internationalization, this realization of the universality of knowledge and the importance of that recognition in our teaching, research, and service are unlikely ever to be diminished or discounted. I am pleased that the university under the leadership of President John Ryan continues to be deeply involved in overseas technical-assistance and other international programs. President Ryan, himself an expert on Asian matters, sets an example by frequent participation in international conferences dealing with Asia and by service on a number of committees and commissions in this field.

It seems to me, however, that another fifty years will be needed to assess with any degree of accuracy the true value of the strong technical-assistance efforts made by the universities, the foundations, and a variety of church and international organizations in the postwar era on behalf of the developing Third World nations. That these nations have made great economic progress is already apparent. Yet to be seen, however, is how stable their political institutions will become; and yet to be discerned, it seems to me, is whether or not the endeavors of the American universities and of many of the universities and governments of Europe made a contribution in both short-term and long-term results.

⁅17⁆

○ ○ ○

Academic Ferment

I N H I S history of Indiana University, Tom Clark told of the agony of the era. I remember more vividly the ecstasy of 1937–62.

Personal agony there was aplenty—the agony of shattering crises, of fourteen-hour days, of grinding drudgery with every minute scheduled and utilized and rarely a vacation, of disappointingly unrealized ambitions, of weariness beyond description. But these are dwarfed by the achievements of my talented, dedicated, and determined colleagues through nearly superhuman effort.

The years from 1937 to 1962 were filled with strenuous effort. Problems that almost defied solution had to be solved in order to make the adjustments required by the dislocations of World War II, the flood of returning veterans, the booms and recessions, and the military effort of the Korean War. The struggle to secure the necessary funds for operations and to expand the plant and facilities to meet what seemed to be inexhaustible needs was constant.

In addition during this period I undertook to be a good citizen by doing my share of civic activity at home and abroad from Bloomington to Bangkok, all of which demanded incessant travel around Indiana and from coast to coast in the United States, and innumerable crossings of the Atlantic and Pacific for meetings and missions in Europe, Latin America, Africa, the Middle East, and Asia. Nevertheless, administration had first claim upon my time as we attempted to take full advantage of all the opportunities opening up. Administrative activity per se, however, was not the most exciting aspect of the era.

There was abroad on the campus an extraordinary esprit de corps that engendered the courage to attempt the impossible in scholarly effort and achievement. Gradually we all became imbued with the belief that we could be the equal of any of our contemporaries and, in certain fields, could excel them. The inferiority complex that had plagued Indiana University until the 1930s was completely dissipated, and in area after area our distinguished academic teams boldly aspired to reach the top.

Early on, with Dean Payne's help, a group of distinguished geneticists had come to join us—men such as Cleland, Sonneborn, Muller, Luria, Ebert, and others—and soon they had won for the university the top position in their field. Postdoctoral students from all over the world eagerly sought to work in their laboratories. Once on an Atlantic crossing I was with Warren Weaver, of the Rockefeller Foundation, who had been selecting outstanding young European scholars for postdoctoral fellowships in the United States. During the voyage we discussed on several occasions the difference between scientists in Europe and those in the United States. With great seriousness he told me that Indiana University was very troublesome to him. Startled, I asked why. Then with a smile he explained that all the brightest scholars in the biological field wanted to come to Indiana and that the Rockefeller Foundation naturally could not send them all to a single institution.

Under the leadership of Ralph Shriner and Frank Gucker, the chemistry research program blossomed and attracted scholars throughout the world. Department heads such as Moffat and Sutherland—later Mueller—were not only building their departments, but also were contributing sound, balanced, universitywide faculty leadership. Mitchell, Langer, and Konopinski were pioneering in nuclear research, and under their aegis one of the early cyclotrons was built here. They drew research physicists and noted mathematicians to the university. Kinsey's intrepid research in human sexual behavior is now universally recognized to be of epochal importance.

Languages, always a strong field at Indiana University, became even stronger by the addition of many new offerings. Interesting changes were taking place at the time, in part because of the development of area studies, but even more because of the impact of the National Defense Education Act and Indiana University's campus-based military contingent of language specialists. Wartime emphasis on rapid language training aroused an interest in new methods, created a need for an array of "informants" with different native tongues, and prompted the formation of the Indiana Language Program to encourage language training in secondary schools.

In 1947, with the support of the Rockefeller Foundation, we began to develop our first area studies program, Russian Studies, and soon afterward the Department of Russian Studies was initiated with Michael Ginsburg at its head. After the mid-1950s, under the leadership of Robert Byrnes, the program quickly came to occupy one of the top two or three positions in this field in the country and amassed a library collection the largest of its kind among American universities. In the mid-1950s a Ford Foundation grant spurred further development in language studies. East Asian Languages and Literatures became established here under Wu-chi Liu; Sebeok and his colleagues introduced such exotic newcomers as Uralic and Oriental Languages; and Slavic Studies became Slavic Languages and Literatures. From standard language offerings, we grew to a complement of thirty-six, and the resulting cosmopolitan infusion helped change forever the nature of our faculty body.

Meanwhile the Department of English enjoyed a remarkable flowering under the leadership of James Work, followed by William R. Parker, until my friends at Yale were quite ready to say to me without attempting to be flattering that they considered our department one of the most, if not the most, competitive departments in the United States. Side by side with the strengthened literary scholarship came a burst of creative writing by Samuel Yellen and William E. Wilson and their students, the social histories of Herbert Muller, the rise of the Writers' Conference and the transfer of the Kenyon School of Letters to Indiana University, and the publication of a poetry series by the Indiana University Press. All stirred a lively interest in the creative field.

Beginning earlier but nonetheless closely allied to all of this growth was the burgeoning folklore field under the inspired leadership of Stith Thompson whose name is known all over the world and whose disciples, Dorson and Sebeok, were to earn their own positions of scholarly renown. With the coming of the Voegelins the allied field of anthropology began to thrive and these two disciplines have continued to go from strength to strength.

Newton Stallknecht brought a brilliant young scholar, Norwood Russell Hanson, to the campus. He was soon joined by Michael Scriven and in a brief time they formed a new department, the History and Logic of Science, since renamed the Department of the History and Philosophy of Science. In what seemed a remarkably short period, the university began to win an enviable reputation in this field and to attract attention not only in the United States but in England and the continent as well.

This omnipresent sense of heightening achievement or renaissance was aided and abetted by the rich influx of distinguished scholars from abroad during World War II and the period immediately following as a result of the upheaval in Europe or because the academic life in America seemed more attractive than in Europe, bringing us such brilliant additions as Hlavaty, Artin, Brendel, Haurowitz, Kaufmann, Nettl, Hopf, Tomasic, Pounds, Apel, and Benes. This emigration of scholars to the United States enriched the whole of American higher education but we at Indiana University were unusually fortunate in those who chose to come to us. Our existing faculty, among them the few much earlier emigrés such as Agapito Rey, welcomed them cordially. These men and women from abroad added impressive scholarly repute and an exciting international dimension to our academic family.

Equipped with a new theater in a wing of the Auditorium, the inimitable Lee Norvelle and his talented colleagues made unusual strides in the field of drama. Given its independence from the English Department, Speech and Theatre grew in enrollment and student productions attracted an ever-widening audience. Lee was not only a dynamic administrator but also a good manager of money. Through his own initiative and with funds amassed from ticket receipts, he launched the Brown County Playhouse and later was able to add the Showboat Majestic as another outlet for the display of student talents. Because of their excellent training and the encouragement they received, alumni of the Speech and Theatre Department have had an enviable record of success in commercial theater, radio, and television. Too, students had the advantage of classes from one of the best known historians of drama, Hubert Heffner.

Astronomy made rapid strides with talented men such as Edmondson, Wrubel, and Cuffey. The department became a major producer of Ph.D.'s, made possible through the magnificent gift by Dr. Goethe Link of his excellent observatory located on a high, secluded hill between Bloomington and Indianapolis. It provided hitherto unavailable research facilities for graduate students in astronomy. This facility was later to be augmented by another research observatory constructed in the Morgan-Monroe State Forest. The department's eminence was recognized by the invitations to sponsor and operate along with six other universities the great Kitt Peak

Observatory in Arizona financed by the National Science Foundation, and later the Cerro Tololo Inter-American Observatory near La Serena, Chile. The group incorporated in 1957 as the Association of Universities for Research in Astronomy and was joined soon afterward by Yale and Princeton.[1]

One of the exceptionally strong teaching and research departments was Government, now Political Science. With men such as Oliver Field, Ford Hall, Walter Laves, and Ed Buehrig providing leadership, the department attracted an increasing number of graduate students who subsequently received advanced degrees here. Among them was John W. Ryan, the future president of Indiana University.

Dynamic events were taking place in the School of Music. Wilfred Bain, building on the strong foundation created by deans Merrill and Sanders, was attracting to our faculty men and women of national and international distinction as scholars, teachers, and performers in their respective fields. Using the medium of opera, which Dean Bain believed was the most useful and comprehensive activity around which to build the applied music fields—orchestra, stage direction, voice, scene design, ballet, and so forth—and with the help of men and women such as Hoffman, Kuhlman, St. Leger, Lipton, Kaskas, Busch, Manski, and many other notables, he had developed within a relatively few years a school of international fame. He accomplished this through the rare spirit he was able to engender, not by an infusion of funds, for he was allocated much less money than he could have expected on the basis of the School of Music's rapidly rising enrollment.

The School of Business under the unusually astute and tireless leadership of Dean Weimer and with the help of lieutenants such as Edwards and Mee was not only meeting the demands of a rapidly increasing enrollment and the claims of the business world for its services, but also was making the important transition from a mainly undergraduate business school to one predominantly graduate in emphasis, until in an amazingly short time it became second only to Harvard in the production of top quality D.B.A.'s.

It was an exciting period in the School of Law, too. Horack, Fuchs, Harper, Hall, Clifford, Wallace, Gavit, and others were meeting the problems of growth and at the same time updating the cur-

1. The founding universities of AURA, in addition to Indiana, were California, Chicago, Harvard, Michigan, Ohio State, and Wisconsin.

riculum to train a generation of lawyers in tune with the new social order created by the revolutionary social and legislative changes of the Roosevelt New Deal. The law school faculty members were active university citizens as well, furnishing leadership for all-university committees and, in their professional capacities, providing public-service initiatives in the state and nation.

The graphic and plastic arts had the great good fortune of having as their head Henry Hope, a man of extraordinary taste, vivid personality, and rare ability. A distinguished scholar in his specialty and an administrator with flair, he had the virtue of being able to make up his mind and to achieve great things with small resources. He developed a strong faculty with art historians such as Otto Brendel, Albert Elsen, and Ted Bowie, the sculptor Robert Laurent, the jewelry designer Alma Eikerman, and others.

The Library was growing apace under the leadership of Robert A. Miller, the university's first professionally trained head librarian, and his able assistant, Cecil Byrd. We were giving priority to building the collections of books, journals, and manuscripts, and this policy was immeasurably enhanced by J. K. Lilly's gift of his rare book collection, at the time said to be the greatest collection in private hands, which became the basis of the distinguished Lilly Library of rare books and special collections, now one of the notable scholarly manuscript and rare-book libraries in the United States. Lilly's gift was the forerunner of major and significant additions to the Lilly Library.

During this same period under Dean VanNuys's administration the medical school was making the transition from mainly a teaching and treatment center to a teaching, treatment, and research center, which necessitated not only a greatly expanded plant but, more importantly, a major shift from a largely part-time faculty to a geographical full-time clinical staff. VanNuys's adroit leadership, guided and aided by the extraordinary wisdom of men such as Ritchey, Winters, Kohlstaedt, Irwin, Hickam, and others, made this transition, which was not without some serious difficulties, on the whole less painful than, to my knowledge, any similar transition was ever made in the United States. Problems there were, heartaches there were, but they were overcome in the process and left few permanent scars.

A like change was taking place in the dental school under the leadership of first Crawford and then of that extraordinary administrator and academic entrepreneur, Maynard Hine, who met the problems of growth, of developing quality rapidly, and of attracting postdoctoral fellows from all over the world so well that the school eventually was ranked among the first five dental schools in the United States in anybody's rating. Since American dental schools are the best in the world, it had a similar rating internationally. While an international reputation attained in many subject areas may be little known outside the profession, even the man in the street recognized the usefulness of the development of Crest toothpaste by that genius, Joe Muhler, building on the basic work in chemistry upon which he, Nebergall, and Day collaborated.

The School of Education was blessed with a strong and experienced faculty who were highly respected by the teaching profession in the state. As a consequence they were called upon to make innumerable management studies and to perform a wide variety of public services for state and local units of government. The School of Education was one of the most active in the international technical-assistance field as well. Dean Smith had been a pioneer leader in international education at the elementary and secondary levels. Dean Wright followed in his footsteps and broadened the base of interest to include the university level as well. Technical-assistance programs staffed by the School of Education with men such as Porter and Jung and by Larson, Stevens, and Pett from the Audio-Visual Center spanned the globe. Few faculties could have been their equal in developing a comparative understanding of the various educational systems of the world.

This period of seething, fruitful ferment was brought about for the most part with small means. Never were our appropriations even close to our needs, but, as our faculty began to achieve national and international recognition, we attracted more funds from the outside that were essential for this developing process. But progress came primarily out of the daring, the courage, the determination of an inspired group of scholars. They knew they were as good as any in the world, and they set about to prove it by their research and writing and their acceptance of positions of national and international scholarly leadership. Soon national and international societies looked to Indiana University for men and women of achievement. An increasing number of our faculty members were elected to the American Philosophical Society, the National Academy of Sciences, the American Academy of Arts and Sciences, and similar prestigious societies abroad. The campus community was electrified when Herman Muller was named to receive a Noble Prize. We rejoiced when Hlavaty won acclaim for solving the Einstein equations on unified field theory, when Sonneborn won the Kimber Genetics Award, and when Haurowitz won the Paul Ehrlich Award.

Although quite a few persons have attributed the glow of the 1940s and 1950s to the addition of amenities and handsome buildings, I feel that the excitement year after year, so real that it was almost tangible, came from the inspired spirit of the members of the faculty as they successfully pursued their dream of making this a university of the very first rank. Throughout the period this explosive intellectual renaissance had the support of exceptionally capable, understanding, sympathetic trustees—men and women who knew what a university should be and readily perceived the prime claim on resources to be for intellectual and scientific achievement, who were willing to support this faculty effort in every way possible and to defend against all critics the transformation that was taking place. I doubt that a university has ever been more fortunate than we were to have had three such dedicated and knowledgeable board presidents as Ora Wildermuth, John Hastings, and Willis Hickam.

The faculty effort was undergirded by the talent of what I believe to be the most amazing team of general administrative officers ever assembled—Briscoe, Biddle, Franklin, Collins, Merritt, Wright, Ashton, Braden, Bartley, Rich, Nelson, Kate Mueller, Shoemaker, Shaffer, Fraenkel, and Reed—and such other remarkable academic administrators as Payne, Cleland, Bain, Weimer, Gucker, Gavit, Hine, Irwin, and Thompson. Byrum Carter was a junior administrator during part of this time, giving an early indication of his later outstanding administrative service.

Similar periods of rapid change and renewal have been known to encounter stubborn alumni resistance. Just the opposite was our experience. First under the guidance of George "Dixie" Heighway and then of Claude Rich, the Indiana University alumni on the whole did not oppose the ferment but welcomed it, abetted it, and rejoiced with each new objective won.

It would be untruthful to allege that the students of the era had a revolutionary change of attitude toward scholarship, but they too were affected. The ordinary undergraduate began to take pride in the academic achievements of the faculty and in the university's increasing stature. When Herman Muller spoke at an all-university convocation upon returning from Stockholm, where he had received the Nobel Prize, the auditorium was packed to the rafters with students. Of course, the returning veteran students, the G.I.'s, helped set a more mature tone for the campus. They were perhaps the most demanding and appreciative students in the university's history, undergoing some real personal hardship with surprisingly little complaint. Candid and constructive in criticism, they were nevertheless quick to respond to opportunities to make their contribution to the advancement of the campus. During the period from 1945 on, the percentage of graduate and professional students was increasing, bringing a new stratum of cultural and intellectual concern. But all segments of the student body—undergraduate and graduate, veteran and nonveteran—contributed to the stimulating spirit of the campus.

The supporting staff, which responded magnificently, won praise for their services so essential to maximum efficiency and achievement in winning goals and reaching for aspirations. The building and grounds staff became imbued with a sense of pride in the beauty of the campus and found ways beyond the call of duty to make the campus a more beautiful place in which to live and learn.

How did it happen? I really do not know. Perhaps, as Shakespeare says in *Julius Caesar*, "There is a tide in the affairs of men, which, taken at the flood, leads on to fortune." But if I had to explain it, I would say simply that occasionally a group of superior men and women, dedicated to a common high purpose, come together and become inspired by that vision to achieve both individually and collectively to the utmost of their abilities. To have been a part of that community and that effort was a rich and rewarding experience, an experience that makes one realize the nobility of great human beings of integrity, talent, and generous spirit.

National and
International Service

[18]

○ ○ ○

A Trip and a New Awareness

PRIOR TO 1941 the only foreign countries I had visited were Mexico and Canada. My first opportunity for extensive travel abroad came when I was invited by Hubert Herring, the executive director of the Committee on Cultural Relations with Latin America, Incorporated, to participate in the Institute on Inter-American Affairs, which traveled throughout Latin America from late July through mid-September, 1941. The trip was organized so well that I gained an amazing amount of information about Latin America in a relatively short period, but, more importantly, the experience enlarged my perspective in a way that was to have a profound influence on my view of Indiana University's province. All at once I became conscious of the world scene.

People were beginning vaguely to perceive Latin America at this time as of much more significance to the United States than had previously been recognized. Rumors of the Nazi infiltration in Latin America were rife, and suddenly, because of the war pressures, we began to realize the importance of Latin American raw materials such as rubber to our own economic health. As a result, attention focused on Brazil, which was in the process of developing rubber plantations.

Hubert Herring was an authority on Latin America, had written several books about it, and in the course of his many travels there, had become acquainted with the outstanding personalities in nearly every field—journalism, government, education, business, the military, and the intelligentsia. His reputation was so well established that he was able to arrange conferences for us with the most important people in each of the countries, that is, people who could give us the best insight into and interpretation of their particular country in relation to what was happening overall in Latin America. Herring had invited to go with him as a part of the seminar group eleven others, selected to represent journalism, labor relations, education, business, religion—in fact, the whole gamut of the social and political concerns within the countries.

Part of the group assembled in Miami and it was joined by the rest in Panama, our first stop. I had my initial view then of the little country that has been so much of a factor in the political arena from that time to this because of the Canal and its real or imagined strategic importance to the welfare of our country. Although I described in the log I kept of the trip the Hotel Tivoli and my impressions of a drive through Old Panama, previous experience still formed my frame of reference:

> There are many Oriental shops run by Indians and other types of Orientals. The contents of the shops are not so good as those in Mexico City except for the food stores, but the general effect is one of much greater well-being and cleanliness than any place in Mexico except the fashionable portion of Mexico City.

From there we went to Bogotá, Colombia, and began our intensive study of that country. Among others we had a long session with Spruille Braden, the U.S. ambassador to Colombia. He stressed the danger of the Nazi infiltration into the political life and economic structure of South America, which he believed and, as we discovered later many others believed, was intended eventually to place the whole of Latin America under a Nazi-oriented leadership that would be both an economic and a military threat to our country's safety.

In Colombia we began a schedule that was replicated as we went from country to country. We met successively the U.S. ambassador and leaders of various professional and political groups. We were briefed by the ambassador and entertained at the U.S. embassy for dinner. Hubert Herring always arranged to have us briefed also by any members of the embassy staff whom he considered particularly outstanding; for instance, if the commercial attaché in a country was especially acute, he too would brief us. Also, in each country, if the ambassadors from other Latin American countries were of a very high quality, Herring arranged for us to see them as well. Often, to cover various conferences in a city, we divided our forces along the lines of our individual interests and exchanged information when we reassembled.

I might mention that we had recently become somewhat interested in encouraging foreign students to enroll at Indiana University. Prior to leaving for South America, I had been authorized by our Board of Trustees to award fellowships to two South American students of my choice, and several fraternities had agreed in principle to house the holders of these fellowships once they were selected. Everywhere I was besieged by eager young scholars hoping to come to this country. In one way or another I was able to facilitate the migration of several to Bloomington, a few more than the two to whom I could offer fellowships. In fact, Hubert Herring jokingly called me a pied piper and asked, after I returned, just how many students had followed me out of Latin America.

In Bogotá I observed the beginning of a trend in Latin America that has since spread, namely, the movement of the national university from the middle of the city to the outskirts, drawing faculties scattered throughout the city into a single location known as the *cité universitaire*, or "university campus."

From Bogotá we went to the beautiful, provincial city of Cali—the city of eternal spring—a place that has lingered long in my memory. It probably has as desirable a climate as any city in the world, and I remember also the exuberance of the architecture—part Mediterranean, part Spanish Colonial, and part pure modern experimental. We next flew to Quito, the capital of Ecuador, departing from Cali at 6:00 A.M., an hour typical of our morning flight schedules. As airports at that time were not yet well developed and were without lighting, flights to nearly every country had to be made in daylight hours. Since Latin Americans entertain and dine quite late, there would be only two or three hours between our last social engagement and the scheduled time for us to leave for the airport, usually set two hours prior to flight departure because of the red tape to be undergone and the distance from the hotel to the airport.

Quito was the most picturesque of the old colonial cities, fortunately little touched by time. It seemed almost like a museum, with magnificent churches and monasteries, which we visited, some of them filled with treasures of art work and old manuscripts, wonderful library materials about the explorations and settlement. The buildings were Spanish Colonial. In Quito especially and in other west-coast cities, I was impressed by the omnipresent music of the church bells, everywhere church bells, the beauty of the eucalyptus trees, and the distinctive fragrance of smoke from eucalyptus wood being burned for heating and cooking.

I had been struck by the poverty I saw everywhere, the number of beggars, for instance. Late one night in Quito, as I went for a walk, I met a mother and a little boy. Her face was pinched and she wore a dark ramboso over her hair. He was a nice looking boy. They were searching for food in the gutter, but a dog had gotten to it ahead of them and left very little. I gave them some chocolates and I keep recalling the lad's cry of exultation as he ran to his mother: "Dulce, dulce, dulce"—candy, candy, candy. But they did not eat it immediately. Trying to get ahead of the dog, they kept on looking for food in the gutter. I called them back and gave them a coin. At that, they went happily chattering away, she limping slightly. The beauty of Quito and its opulence contrasted dramatically with the poverty of this mother and child.

In Quito I met for the first time a great figure, Galo Plaza, who had been born in our country when his father was ambassador to the United States. Galo Plaza was then a young, handsome, bright leader, much interested in scientific agriculture, which he had studied at the University of Maryland. He had already held a number of high government posts. Everyone thought he was destined to have a great career, a perception that proved to be accurate. He became president of Ecuador, ambassador to Washington, director general of the Organization of American States, an active figure in United Nations affairs, and chief of a number of international missions. One of the delightful excursions that we had and also one of the most illuminating was at the invitation of Galo Plaza. Arrangements were made for us to go from Quito into the high Andes to Otavalo, a provincial city with a famous Andean market. Galo Plaza's great hacienda, or cattle ranch, was our destination, as I recounted in my diary:

> Saturday morning. Left at 5:00 A.M. for Otavalo, a high Andean market, 25,000 Indians participate. Enroute stopped at a lake for a second breakfast brought from his ranch by Sr. Galo Plaza. Huge bowls of cereal with cream and scrambled eggs. [Galo Plaza had arranged this breakfast with considerable thought knowing that we would by this time be hungry for cereal, which we would not have had in any other circumstance nor would we have been served

cream. The cream came from his own dairy.] The market was magnificent, and the mountain drive beyond description. Afterward we drove to the hacienda of our host for lunch. The buildings were erected in 1600. Farm of 4,000 acres, 400 families of Indians. Paid 2 ½ sucres for five-day week, 17 cents. He furnishes chapel, school building, each Indian five to ten acres, and they can have grazing land for their stock and also medical and dental care. He also loans them money without interest and sells them stock at a discount. The house was a charming place with thick walls. Lunch was very simple and informal: sliced tomatoes and cold meat, potato cakes made with cheese with peanut sauce and avocados with hot sauce. Then Heinz beans and hot dogs because the cook thought we should have some American food, and the host humored her. Had bananas and cream for dessert.

He raises cattle, 2,000 head of sheep, some hogs, has a dairy. The milk is made into cheese and he also grows wheat and corn. They farm right up the mountain side in an incredible fashion. The soil is very deep black loam and seems inexhaustible. There was a high wind and much dust. The sight of farm life in the high Andes far far away from civilization was unforgettable. The Indians were pleasant, quiet, simple little people that seemed to blend into the landscape with their flocks of sheep and cattle. . . .

In Quito we attended the Rotary luncheon. Wherever possible, Hubert Herring had arranged for us to attend Rotary or Kiwanis luncheons, which gave us easy and informal contact with the area's business and professional community. We also met Rene d'Harnoncourt, the famous anthropologist and expert on Indian art, later to be for a time director of the Museum of Modern Art in New York. He was arranging an exhibition of Indian art for the museum at the time we saw him, an exhibit that was to win enthusiastic reviews. On occasion I have since then discussed problems of the development of Indiana University's art resources with him.

Our next stop, in Peru, provided an unusually rich experience, as revealed in a letter to my parents:

We had an amazing time in Lima. It is a very beautiful city. Broad avenues filled with trees and flowers notwithstanding the fact that it is winter—there are flowers everywhere—and they are magnificent. Everywhere the embassies entertain for us and everybody else wants to follow suit. We never have time to sleep, but it doesn't seem to matter for I am feeling exceptionally well.

Yesterday we did the world-famous Inca and Pre-Inca museums, then went to the site of one of the excavations with the famous archaeologist who is in charge. The contents of the museums are so remarkable that I believe they alone are worth a trip to South America.

I was referring to Julio Tello, a friend of several Indiana University faculty members in zoology. Dr. Tello was one of the most respected scholars in all of South America. The Inca museum of which he was the director contained a sequestered section of erotic art that was later to be tapped in Alfred Kinsey's research. Dr. Tello was generous with his time and in helping us understand the complex nature of a continent with so many natural geographic barriers that it would be difficult ever to unite it.

Dr. Tello arranged for our pleasure a typical Peruvian feast: a *pachamanka*—a type of barbecue said to be derived from the Incas, and Indians are always the cooks when the modern version is offered. The *pachamanka* is done in this manner: Stones are heated in a fire until they are red hot. Meanwhile a big pit is dug. First a layer of stones goes in, then a layer of banana leaves, next a layer of whatever meat is available at that particular time and place— such meats as pork, beef, lamb, chicken, goat, and various kinds of game—another layer of banana leaves, and then vegetables—corn in husks, onions, and the local vegetables that are available. The entire procedure is repeated until the pit is filled, when it is covered with a mound of straw and dirt to keep the heat in. The cooking goes on for some hours.

In due course the food is pronounced done, the pit is opened, and the food is brought out and served on large tables out of doors. While preparing the food or at the time it is served, *aji*, the red hot spice of the highlands, is used liberally. As *aji* induces a desire for something cold to drink, *pisco*, the local homemade beer, flows plentifully. We enjoyed tremendously this taste of an allegedly good reproduction of Inca cuisine.

In Peru I met for the first time Dr. and Mrs. Virgil DeVault. A highly successful surgeon and alumnus of the Indiana University medical school, Dr. DeVault was treating in his British-American hospital patients from all up and down the west coast of South America. He had been the surgeon for one of the oil companies earlier, but then had set up an independent practice in Lima and was more or less the head of the Hoosier group there. He left Latin America to become the medical director of the Foreign Service in the U.S. State Department, establishing the clinics abroad that are now attached to our embassies. More recently he has been the international secretary general of the International College of Surgeons.

We also visited picturesque San Marcos, the oldest university in the western hemisphere. To have missed it would have been like visiting a head of state and failing to visit the tomb of the unknown soldier. Although San Marcos is unique in its antiquity, age has not benefited it as it does wine. San Marcos was modeled after the medieval University of Salamanca in Spain, which, along with the early French universities, influenced the structure and objectives of many older Latin American universities. By the time of our visit, however, ideas for modernization and reform inspired by the example of our North American system were beginning to be heard. Some educational leaders were advocating greater democratization of the system of admissions and a greater curricular emphasis on technical and vocational subjects in order to equip the institution and its graduates to contribute to nation building. Most of South America at that time was economically dependent on a feudal agriculture and on mineral mines operated by foreign companies. At every one of our meetings with educators and cultural-institute groups, the subject of university reform was introduced. The ensuing discussion usually involved a spirited comparison of the strengths and weaknesses of the United States system versus the French, German, English, or modern Spanish system as a pattern for the future of Latin American institutions. Day after day, therefore, I found myself defending our system and extolling its virtues. It was a good exercise in the comparative analysis of divergent systems of higher education, a subject to which I was to devote considerable attention in future years, during my ten years on the Executive Board of the International Association of Universities, while participating in many personal and Indiana University–Third World technical-assistance efforts, and in the course of my several years as chairman of Education and World Affairs.

Our visit enabled me to renew my acquaintance with a chap whom I had known as an undergraduate, Alberto Arca-Parro. He had directed the first census of Peru in modern times and had come to be one of Peru's most respected social scientists. Later he was to serve in the Peruvian congress, where he won equally high esteem.

Arca-Parro was one of the most distinguished of those who came from Latin America to gain their education at Indiana University and then returned to serve their country.

To illustrate the range of the kind of people we met, I think it important to tell the story of our meeting with Victor Raul Haya de la Torre, who was the principal spokesman for the Peruvian Aprista Party, founded in 1931. He had been active on the political scene since about 1924. The Aprista Party came to be called the "Party of the People" because it purported to represent a "United Front of Manual and Intellectual Workers," that is, the workers, field laborers, students, professionals, merchants, proprietors, and so on. The Party considered itself democratic, antifascist and anticommunist. Haya de la Torre thought of himself as a Peruvian Franklin D. Roosevelt. When we were there, the Aprista Party had been banned, as I recall, and Haya de la Torre himself was in exile. But it was a pleasant form of exile: he could hide out in the suburbs just as long as he did not surface. No one was supposed to know he was there. But, of course, Hubert Herring was aware of his whereabouts and arranged a meeting with him and his cabinet for about midnight. We were led through a long, circuitous route down back streets and alleys, up hill and down dale until we finally arrived at his hiding place. For an hour or so he poured out his heart, giving us the opposition's view of the regime in Peru at that time. He particularly wished us to carry the message to President Roosevelt that he was a liberal, antifascist, anticommunist force trying to bring about in Peru the same kinds of reforms that Roosevelt was initiating in the United States. He wanted help from the United States if he could get it.[1]

In Peru we met still another memorable figure, the Honorable Moises Saenz, the Mexican ambassador to Peru. His name was frequently mentioned in the world press during that period because of his remarkable achievements as Mexico's minister of education. He had originated a program called "One Teach One" that by then was quite famous. Each literate person was asked to teach an illiterate person. The program was so successful that the rate of Mexican literacy increased dramatically in a single decade. He was a delightful host, a charming man who had a keen perception of Latin American affairs, and we were fortunate to be able to spend time with him.

From Lima we traveled to Arequipa in order to take the train

1. Haya de la Torre died August 2, 1979.

A matter of pride—the personal signature of the president
on every diploma.

A working session with Alfred Kinsey and George Corner, chairman of the National Research Council's sex research committee.

A contest with Governor Schricker at the Sigma Chi Melon
Mess held annually in Dunn Meadow.

A painful moment for the spectators
during a football game.

Harold Macmillan, then Chancellor of the Exchequer, Great Britain, just
after award of an honorary LL.D. degree from Indiana University, 1956.

Selecting the background music for a party in Woodburn House.

John Foster Dulles presents commissions to Irene Dunne and me as
delegates to the Twelfth Session of the United Nations General Assembly.

With Irene Dunne and other members of our delegation at the United
Nations General Assembly, 1957.

Table decorations ranked with the sandwiches and cookies in importance
as we prepared to receive our numerous guests.

up to Cuzco. Arequipa is the most important southern terminal for the railroad line that runs from the Pacific coast to Cuzco in the highlands. It is a beautiful city, its buildings constructed for the most part of white volcanic rock with magnificent Mt. Misti, an inactive, snow-covered volcano, as a backdrop. Arequipa is the center of a thriving agricultural region served by an irrigation system that had been developed at the time of the Incas. It grows some of the world's finest alfalfa, which is pastured green year round. At the time of our visit, American industrial enterprise was making its first inroad with a Carnation Milk plant in the process of construction.

Our host at Arequipa was Carlos Gibson, rector of the University of Arequipa and second vice president of the republic, who met us at the airport. He was a descendant of one of the old Scottish-immigrant ranching families, which through the generations had developed a factoring enterprise that stretched throughout the whole of southern Peru. It included commercial installations serving the farmers and ranchers, banks, and many exporting and importing operations. Rector Gibson, who was eager to develop his university, asked many questions about universities in North America as he conducted us on a tour of his facilities. It was my first view of a provincial Latin American university, and I was startled by the meagerness of its resources. We were accompanied by the rector's son, who was a graduate of Cambridge and Harvard.

We were delightfully housed at a famous hostelry, the Quinta Bates. In the early years of the century an adventuresome girl from Missouri had married a Britisher and migrated to Peru. The husband turned out to be ineffective, but his wife, forced to struggle for a living, gradually developed a unique hostelry famous throughout all of the west coast of South America. It was the preferred stopping place, not only of Peruvian v i ps and political leaders, but also of international travelers. The establishment was known for its great food. Tia, or Auntie, Bates ran the place with an iron hand. She accepted only guests of whom she approved and woe to anyone who stepped out of line, for she was noted for the most profane vocabulary in the region. A shrewd businesswoman, colorful, warm-hearted, childless herself, she adopted in the course of her lifetime twenty-seven children of various races and nationalities, and reared and educated them. No one who had the good fortune of meeting her will ever forget her.

Our trip to Cuzco had to be made by train; no plane service

could then fly into Cuzco because it was so high in the Andes. In fact, at the highest point we had to put on oxygen masks because the air was so thin. Since I was young and inexperienced, the landscape and the activities everywhere made a vivid impression upon me, as the following passage from my diary illustrates:

> Friday by train to Juliaca. At the top of the climb we were nearly 15,000 feet. There were no trees. The houses all of unplastered adobe with thatched roofs. The native[s] look definitely Oriental. There are no trees so they burn a sort of dried cedar brush. At a stop along the way, all the passengers got off for lunch. The women of the village had wide tables and sold soup, chicken, bits of beef heart cooked on a spit over a little brazier.
>
> The scenery was magnificent, snow-capped peaks, mountain lakes, and on the plateaus, herds of sheep, llamas, alpacas, and occasionally cattle always attended by shepherds, usually women or boys, and of women always spinning by hand. Everywhere they are, the spinning never ceases. At the high altitudes, they grow beans, a type of mustard that has a quality like oatmeal, and other types of grass crops. A little lower between Juliaca and Cuzco, they have eucalyptus trees and a more diversified agriculture. Everywhere their methods are most primitive. They thresh with oxen or even with flail, plow with primitive wooden plows and oxen.
>
> Costumes vary, but in general they wear homespun. The men wear neutral trousers with a gay poncho in beautiful red with magnificent Oriental design. The women wear several layers of homespun skirts, frequently blue, ornamented blouses, a bright-colored bundle or baby sack, a funny, high-crowned straw hat, or a hat with flaps hanging down from the sides. The men frequently wear rude sandals, and the women generally are barefooted, though occasionally they wear old-fashioned high-top shoes.

A private car was added to our train when we left Juliaca that morning. We did not know who was in it, but we were told by the train crew that it was the private car of the president of Peru and that some distinguished visitor was on board. At each station, as my notes mention, he was greeted and generally a band played; then there were speeches back and forth while the train waited. Occasionally a woman got off with him, and in due course we learned that the mysterious passengers were Axel Wenner-Gren and his wife. He was, at that time, at the height of his power and prominence as one of the Swedish matchkings and owner of a number of important enterprises throughout the world including Servel at Evansville, Indiana. He had just founded the Wenner-Gren Foundation for Anthropological Research, Inc. Mrs. Wenner-Gren was so exotic-looking I immediately imagined her as coming from a romantic background, perhaps that of a Balkan opera singer.

Wenner-Gren was making this trip as the start of a scientific expedition into the upper Amazon region, which reaches into Peru, and so the Peruvian government was eager to facilitate his trip in every way. We had gone to Cuzco, not only to see the magnificent old Inca city, but also to visit the ancient university there, particularly its wonderful library filled with antiquarian treasures. To our surprise, several of us received invitations to attend a convocation the following day at which Mr. Wenner-Gren was to be given an honorary doctorate. In Latin American terms I was a visiting "intellectual," that is, a person connected with a university, and was due the courtesy of an invitation. The next afternoon at six, which is the standard time for such ceremonies in Latin America, I and two or three others of our party went to the university—a beautiful old colonial quadrangle—and witnessed an impressive ceremony. The rector spoke and conferred the degree; Mr. Wenner-Gren replied appropriately. After that we adjourned to the magnificent Great Hall, which is a feature of every Latin American university for use on formal occasions such as this. There we enjoyed champagne and biscuits while a band played intermittently. As I started down the reception line to be introduced to Mr. Wenner-Gren, I kept trying to dredge up some French phrases out of my memory, hoping that French would be a way to communicate with his beautiful foreign wife. Wenner-Gren, who spoke good English, as almost all Swedish do, greeted me cordially, adding, oh yes, he knew of Bloomington because he owned the Servel plant in Evansville, and they went there frequently to have a look at it before going to French Lick. Then he said, "I want you to meet my wife." I was still groping for the elusive French phrase when, in the broadest Midwestern twang I have ever heard, the subject of my desperate effort exclaimed, "Why, you are from Indiana? From Bloomington? Well, I am from Missouri, St. Louis." She went on chatting amiably about living most of the time in the Bahamas and invited me to stay with them when next I visited Nassau. I cannot remember having had before or since a flight of my fancy so disappointingly grounded.

Our next destination was La Paz, Bolivia. It had a good American school, the American School of La Paz, and some of the brightest students in the school were assigned to us to be guides. One of

these was Peter Fraenkel, a high school sophomore or junior, whose
father had emigrated from Germany to escape the Nazis. When
I visited the faculty of the school, one or two drew me aside to tell
me that they thought Peter Fraenkel was a lad who deserved a better
education than was possible at the university in Bolivia, and they
urged that I find some kind of aid to enable him to study in the
United States. As it turned out, he did come to Indiana University
on a scholarship, completed his work here, and his career was coin-
cident with mine for many years, as recounted in chapter 20. It was
really a very fortunate meeting for me.

At Santiago, the capital of Chile, we had the privilege of visiting
with Ambassador Claude G. Bowers, who entertained us at the embassy and who was most helpful. Bowers, a Hoosier, had been the
ambassador to Spain before being assigned to the Chilean post,
which he occupied for another decade, and he was a noted author of
historical narratives as well. We also met the rector of the University
of Chile, Juan Gomez Millas, whom I came to know better through
the International Association of Universities, and Salvador Allende,
who became president in 1970.

Chile at that time was certainly the most advanced of the west-
coast countries. It was vital and progressive: it had the best school
system on the west coast, a relatively low rate of illiteracy, a well-
developed university with forward-looking leadership, and a firmly
launched program of technical education. Especially Chile and the
Argentine, but all the rest of Latin America as well, had the problem
of a concentration of wealth in the large estates. The landowning
groups still represented the backbone of the conservative opposition, and any criticism of the current order was automatically labeled
communism. The German influence was very strong there at the
time of our visit and was later evidenced by the fact that Chile did
not declare war against Germany until the closing months of World
War II.

We were entertained in Argentina by Victoria Ocampo, editor
of *Sur*, one of the foremost literary magazines of Latin America.
She was a rich woman and an intellectual in every respect. She lived
in a beautiful family mansion with magnificent grounds, and she
presided there over a sort of literary salon. She entertained people
in whom she was interested from all over the world as they traveled
through Buenos Aires, and she corresponded with many of the major

literary figures of her time: Albert Camus, Virginia Woolf, T. S. Eliot, Stefan Zweig, Marcel Proust, George Bernard Shaw, Archibald MacLeish, and many others.

We visited not only the University of Buenos Aires, but also the University at La Plata, which was reputed to be the most liberal in Latin America, its rector, Risieri Frondizi, being a socialist senator and a superior man. Over the years our paths continued to cross, especially in connection with the activities of the International Association of Universities which he helped to organize.

I wrote in my diary:

> On return [from Buenos Aires and La Plata] stopped at a large *estancia*—37,000 acres of deep, rich black soil. Four huge mansions on it. Enormous truck farms, carpenter shop, blacksmith shop, electric generating plant, etc., 500 to 800 employees. Most of it in pasture that is green year-round. Lots of it is in alfalfa. The young bulls were the finest I have ever seen, and they are reared like children. A record of their monthly weight is kept. The *estancia* also has sheep and fine horses. Drive from the gate must have been two miles anyway. Acres and acres are developed and kept in park-like fashion around the house, trees from all over the world, flowers in profusion, beautiful green lawns, well kept roads, and a large, private chapel. Large supplies of fowl are raised, and many bees are kept, and a few hundred acres are in garden, fruit, and forage to supply man and beast on the *estancia*.

Here I learned that beef cattle were fattened solely by grazing rich, green alfalfa year-round. I was told a top-grade steer could be produced in this manner for four cents per pound. I found the quality of the beef at least as good as our top-grade, grain-fed cattle. The Argentinians were convinced that United States legislation banning the importation of fresh Argentine beef, ostensibly to prevent the spread of hoof and mouth disease, was in fact passed because the high quality and low cost made Argentine beef too competitive with our own. Since agricultural products were Argentina's principal exports, the ban was bitterly resented.

We had the privilege while we were in Buenos Aires of attending the opera, which probably was the best in South America, and hearing a very good *Figaro* with Kipnis singing the title role in fine form. Since we were going to entertain the Metropolitan Opera at Bloomington in the spring, I made a note in my diary that I might use my experience of Kipnis in Buenos Aires as a publicity story to stimulate sales of tickets as he was to sing the role of Figaro again in Bloomington.

From Buenos Aires we went to Rio de Janeiro, Brazil, where we were to have another rich experience lasting more than a week. Rio is considered one of the world's most beautiful cities. Its reputation derives in part from its incomparable setting. In 1941 its natural beauty was being enhanced by man. Young architects were beginning to design some imaginative new structures that attracted international attention. The broad, tree-lined streets with beautiful old Spanish Colonial buildings on either side contained many plazas and fountains. Adding to the beauty were its incomparable beaches. It was a gracious, relaxed, happy city of great charm. On a recent visit I was saddened to see most of the lovely colonial structures replaced by modern skyscrapers: a forest of concrete, steel, and glass with little breathing space remaining. While based at Rio we made a trip to Sao Paulo and its progressive university, which at that time was receiving substantial Rockefeller help and was internationally acclaimed as the leading university in Latin America.

In Rio I had a notable meeting with the under secretary for foreign affairs, Mauricio Nabuco, head of the Ministry of Foreign Affairs for Brazil and recognized as one of the most perceptive diplomats in all of Latin America. He later was ambassador to the United States and earlier had held other ambassadorships. When I had my conference with him in September, 1941, he spoke to me very earnestly, saying:

> You must know that I am very favorable toward the United States and the West. I was educated in the United States, my father was ambassador to the United States. I am very favorable to the West in this struggle that is now going on. I want to make a prediction [Remember, this was before we were in the war!]: when this great European war now raging is over, there will be just two powers in the world. England will be spent, France will be devastated, Germany will be wrecked, and the two major powers remaining will be Russia and the United States. If the West is to survive, it will depend upon the leadership of the United States. As much as I admire and love the United States, this worries me because I am not sure that the United States will have the resolve to fulfill this mission, and, furthermore, I am not sure that the United States has learned that the making of foreign-policy decisions must stop before the precinct level. Foreign policy cannot be made at the precinct level to serve local political ambitions and purposes.

I have thought of this remarkable prediction many, many times since and quoted it again and again. I am sure few other men at that time had his vision.

After a memorable stay in Brazil, we went by way of Belem (with its glimpse of the Amazon jungle) and Trinidad to Caracas. There we were entertained by the rector of the university as well as by the U.S. ambassador and others. The rector of the university was in the midst of moving his university from downtown to a new, suburban campus, an example of the same phenomenon that I had observed in Bogotá at the beginning of the trip. Several persons inquired about Meredith Nicholson, Hoosier author and diplomat, who served as envoy and minister to Paraguay, Venezuela, and Nicaragua successively from 1933 to 1941.

From there we went to Trinidad and on to Barranquilla to catch the flight to Miami, arriving on September 16. I stayed in Miami a few days to get my bearings before returning to Bloomington and the pace of the new school year.

Strenuous as the trip had been, it had given me an uncommon opportunity to learn much about South America in a short period of time. In fifty-odd days we must have met, talked with, and had conferences with hundreds of leaders in government, economic life, education, and cultural activities. In addition, we had visited universities, schools, industries, public institutions of all kinds. In each country we had met with the United States' highest-ranking officers, an able diplomatic corps, as well as with high-ranking nationals. We had talked with labor leaders, and, wherever possible, we had spoken with peasants. It remains to this day the most culturally and intellectually rich experience abroad in a comparable period of time that I have had.

Since I had done so little traveling before, the whole trip seemed to me incredibly colorful and picturesque. We had visited every republic in South America except Paraguay, and I have long wished to remedy that omission. The trip demonstrated to me what I have observed again and again in my travels: with an effort at serious inquiry and with arrangements to make contact with intelligent and well-informed observers abroad, one can come back enriched in understanding, not only of the country or countries visited, but also of their countrymen's perception of us and of the problems and relationships evolving between their country and ours.

From this venture I gained great enthusiasm for enlarging the international dimension of Indiana University, a new conception of the strength and values that international studies might offer us, and a determination to continue encouraging our foreign-student program, bolstered by the several Latin American students who came to Indiana University as a result of my contacts during the trip.

Despite the mound of work that had accumulated on my desk, I was able to speak on South America to a total of almost four thousand people around the state in the two months' time following my return. By sharing my experience in this manner, I hoped to broaden the benefits of my trip. Thereafter it became part of my general philosophy about international travel and exchanges that the persons involved should undertake to be cultural ambassadors, extending understanding of our country abroad and, upon return, of foreign nations among our various constituencies.

Some Observations on the Trip

Besides being my first extended trip abroad, this trip was my introduction to countries other than Mexico that constitute what we call the Third World, that is, countries characterized by political immaturity and by a dependence upon agriculture and extractive industry such as mining and timber for exports. The social pattern was colonial with the wealth concentrated in the hands of a few. The rigid class structure consisted of a dominant oligarchy of wealthy landowners, a very small middle class—except in Chile and Argentina—and a large, poverty-stricken lower class. There was a great deal of underemployment as well as true unemployment. I was impressed by the vast gulf between the very rich few and the indigent multitudes. Here I observed for the first time certain economic, educational, cultural, and political characteristics that I was to find in other sections of the world in the years following World War II when Indiana University became involved in technical assistance for educational development in Third World countries in Asia, Africa, and Latin America.

The universities had certain characteristics in common, varying in degree from institution to institution and from country to country. A major factor in Latin American universities was the different pattern of faculty service as compared with American universities. A large majority of the members of the faculty spent a minimum of time devoted to their university duties. They attended mainly to their personal affairs: the practice of their various professions, property management, business, or similar activities. They maintained personal offices away from the campus and could usually be found there. The excuse was the low pay of university professors, but the pay was offset by the high prestige that society accorded a university professor, a real advantage. However, faculty in general had little time for pure research, and they were fairly inaccessible to the students for counseling, guidance, or individual tutoring.

I was impressed by the richness of the university libraries and the archival holdings of rare colonial manuscripts and books in the older universities. Each was typically a treasure house that made me realize the poverty of Indiana University's library in this respect. Since then we have acquired the magnificent Mendel collection and have benefited from a vigorous program of Latin American accessions.

Unfortunately, the Latin American libraries were totally disorganized with much of the material uncatalogued and unavailable for use. They had very little staff, and what staff they had considered it their function to guard the collection from usage. Modern librarians believe their function is to promote the materials in the library and assist the scholar in their utilization. (Rumors had it that the books were so valuable that they disappeared from the libraries and reappeared in the rare-book market. In this respect, maybe the protective attitude was justified.)

The universities were strong in the humanities and classical languages, and weak in sciences. Technical and vocational education in such fields as engineering and agriculture was nearly nonexistent or just beginning, with the exception of Chile, Argentina, and Uruguay.

I was awed by the richness of the formal reception halls or senate chambers of the ancient universities. In these quarters formal university affairs were transacted, distinguished visitors received, and important convocations and receptions held. The rooms were a joy and added great dignity and impressiveness to formal occasions.

I was struck on the other hand by the absence of student amenities. The classrooms and laboratories were very poor—and there was a paucity of restrooms, study areas, and rooms for social gatherings. Practically no provision was made for student recreation or exercise. In most of the Latin American countries other organizations, including municipal and government agencies, sponsored both individual and spectator sports. Much of Latin America, even at that time, had huge stadiums for soccer, adaptable for other kinds of sports. They were among the largest in the world. Most of the countries had beautiful race courses, some with pavilions of strikingly modern design. Of course, there was always a handsome jockey club for the elite. And everywhere flowers, flowers, flowers.

Here I first became aware of the presence of "professional students," that is, students who made much of their life work attending the university, taking a minimum number of courses, but devoting themselves to agitation and the organization of demonstrations on behalf of one group or another, frequently on public issues. It was alleged that most of these students were paid and supported by various political parties.

Another phenomenon that made it possible for professional rabblerousers to be effective was the fact that the university charters made the university premises off limits to the police and army personnel, therefore making university authorities solely responsible for the maintenance of order on the campus. It was the lesser of two evils, and I sometimes think it might be a good policy for us.

⟦19⟧

○ ○ ○

A Glorious Experience in the Springtime of My Career

FOLLOWING WORLD WAR II Greece was in a state of political turbulence. It had gone through a four-and-a-half-year period of dictatorship during which usual political activity was forbidden, followed by the Axis occupation, and then more than a year of civil strife between the forces of the Left and the Right. It was alleged that the Communists were pouring a good deal of money and support into the country in order to try to take possession of it. Historians and Russian experts agree that a longtime objective of Kremlin policy had been to gain an outlet and a year-round, warm-weather port on the Mediterranean, and Greece offered the best possibility for this. After all, one of the southernmost Soviet republics, the state of Georgia, is partly of Greek origin and the Georgians are closely allied with the Greeks in culture and attitude.

The Greeks were convinced that a democratic election had to be held soon and that they would need help from the outside to ensure the fairness of the process. Already the Soviets were charging the British military in Greece with intimidation and covert activities. At Yalta the Allies had pledged themselves to help the liberated countries reestablish their democratic institutions. In line with this pledge and upon the invitation of the Greek government, the United States, France, and Great Britain agreed to create a tripartite commission to observe the Greek election and to report to the world on its fairness and adequacy. The South Africans associated themselves with the observations as an international gesture and because of the large number of Greek immigrants in South Africa. The Russians, though pledged at Yalta, nevertheless de-

clined to participate, using the excuse that the mission would interfere with the sovereignty of an independent state.

Henry Grady, whom I had known in Washington and who later
became president of the American President Lines, Ltd., was named
chief of the United States Mission with the personal rank of ambassador, and I was invited by Acting Secretary of State Dean
Acheson to join it. The U.S. Mission consisted of six men in addition to Ambassador Grady and me: Harry J. Malony, Major General, U.S.A.; Joseph Coy Green, a State Department career officer;
Walter H. Mallory, executive director of the Council on Foreign
Relations; James Grafton Rogers, a lawyer, educator, and former
assistant secretary of state; William W. Waymack, editor of the Des
Moines *Register and Tribune*. Each of us was given the personal
rank of minister for the duration. It proved to be a congenial and
effective team.

Our official instructions read, in part, as follows:

> It has been agreed among the participating Governments that
> the three national groups will be organized into an Allied Mission
> to Observe the Greek Elections and that the observation will be con-
> ducted as a combined Allied operation. . . . During a period of three
> weeks prior to election day these teams will inspect and report on
> the status of the electoral registers and of the provisions made for
> the election. On election day the teams will be sent to a sufficient
> number of representative polling places throughout Greece to give
> a valid sample of the effectiveness and integrity of the polling.

We were advised that we were going there to observe and to
report, not to supervise. We were cautioned to be fair and objective
in our reporting and to make sure that the Greeks themselves ran
their election as free from intimidation as it was possible for an
election there to be run.

The members of the U.S. mission were assigned a substantial
staff of experts drawn from the State Department and from the ranks
of scholars specializing in the Greek world. Our preparation began
in Washington, D.C. on January 14–15, 1946. The six of us were
briefed by the experts in the various government departments: State,
War, Commerce, and so on. We were also given a stack of background papers to absorb. At the conclusion of the intensive briefing,
we were asked to meet with President Truman in the Oval Office. We
all went expecting a perfunctory kind of meeting, a mere well-wishing
on our appointed task. The opposite proved to be the case. After

we were ushered in, introduced and seated, the president gave a brilliant review of the historic political aims of the Russians and the geopolitical significance of our undertaking. He did not refer to a single note nor did he hesitate for a word. We learned more in that hour than we learned in all our briefing sessions and from reading our background papers. In fact, he expounded what came to be known as the Truman Doctrine for the Eastern Mediterranean.

Outside the Oval Office, we looked at each other in amazement. The man we had met seemed utterly different from the person that the press had depicted as a bankrupt haberdasher from Kansas City who occasionally made extravagant statements and fussed with the music critics over their criticism of his daughter's ability as a vocalist. The press at that period seemed to be intent on picturing him as a petty, impulsive, and weak president. History has now proved how wrong that appraisal was, but for us the discovery occurred in our session that afternoon.

We departed Washington on February 15, 1947, about 4:30 P.M. on an air-transport command plane, as I remember it a D C 4, which others characterized as "old groaners" because of the peculiar groaning sound of the motor. At long last I was to visit Europe, even though just one small part of it, and my anticipation was high. It was also my first transatlantic crossing, and by air at that. Ambassador Grady, an old hand, having already made eleven such flights, counseled, "Now, Herman, since you're new at this business of international air travel, I want to give you some advice. There are two indispensable aids to maintaining health and efficiency when changing time zones rapidly. They are sleeping pills and milk of magnesia. With them you can make nearly immediate adjustment to any new time zone in which you find yourself." That has been one of the best bits of practical advice for travel that I've ever had. Of course, since that time I've made innumerable trips across the Atlantic by air and by ship, more than a hundred by now, and also many trips across the Pacific, all of which have involved great differences in time zones.

After a journey that included stopovers at Bermuda and Casablanca, where we were treated to superior hospitality and sightseeing visits to historical and scenic spots, we arrived in Naples, Italy. There we were billeted on the waterfront at Parker's Hotel, operated by the U.S. Army. Our junior staff and our support staff, consisting of military personnel still stationed in Europe, were quartered just outside Naples at the Bagnoli military base. The military had been charged with furnishing the logistical support for our stay in Greece. The hotel, like all in Italy at the time, was cold; only in the lobby was there a little heat. The tile floors in the rooms intensified the chill.

Busy days followed for us—attending lectures in the morning, doing some sightseeing in the afternoon. We were even able to crowd in an attendance at the opera, where we sat in the royal box. I remember that the performance of *Carmen* was surprisingly good, considering the times. I found Naples quite picturesque. The magnificent stone buildings faced in pompeian colors, the crooked streets, the little shops with meat hanging in the open, Vesuvius looming over the bay—all were a delight to me. I took special pleasure in the sights, sounds, color, and smell of Naples because this was, as I mentioned, my first exposure to the beauties of Italy and of Europe. One afternoon we drove to Pompeii with just enough time to have a quick look at the ruins. Even that cursory viewing made a profound impression on me. The only discordant note was the threadbare state of the Italian people, who no doubt were hungry as well because of the terrible inflation. At that time shoes cost about fifty American dollars, and other necessities were proportionately high.

On the fifth day of our stay in Naples, we drove to Rome to call upon our ambassador to Italy, the Honorable Alexander Kirk, a longtime career diplomat. Leaving early in the morning in the company of Ambassador Grady, we had a beautiful drive through the countryside, seeing the olive groves, spring crops, and some quaint villages, which contrasted sharply with others that had been ravaged by the war. We arrived at the Excelsior Hotel in Rome about noon, and I had my first view of that admirable establishment, enhanced by lunch in Ambassador Grady's suite. A drive around the city afterward introduced us to the principal sights including the Colosseum, St. Peter's, the Forum, the Borghese gardens, and other spots. These sights were thrilling to me then, as in truth they still are after many subsequent visits.

That evening we all dined with Ambassador Kirk at the Barberini Palace, which was then the U.S. embassy residence, one of the most imposing of the ancient palaces in Rome. Because of wartime austerity the dinner could not be elaborate, but the setting was magnificent—a beautiful table with elegant china, crystal, and silver, and a huge staff to serve the dinner. As I remember, a footman stood behind every chair—or perhaps every two chairs.

There was much talk of the geopolitical situation in Southern Europe and of the plans for reconstruction and rebuilding of Europe after the tremendous devastation of the war. Also, there was a great deal of discussion of our Greek assignment because, during part of the war, Ambassador Kirk had been assigned to the king of the Hellenes in exile and therefore was fully informed about the complexity of Greek politics and the importance of establishing a stable and representative government in Greece.

On our return from Rome we took another route, via Monte Cassino, where we had a glimpse of the terrible destruction that had occurred when Italy was liberated. The drive back was otherwise a great pleasure because everywhere were little gay carts, horses with tinkling bells, people strolling along the roads, fields green with spring planting at the base of majestic mountains—an indelible experience.

After our planning and orientation in Italy, the mission was moved to Greece on February 25. Greece was prostrate after the war, economically bankrupt, politically disorganized, and filled with tensions and rumors. "In every village," I wrote at the time, "there are those who hate others until it is almost impossible to weld any village into a cohesive community." The Germans had done their work of setting class against class with diabolical cleverness. It had been ten years since there had been an election, and hardly anyone could remember how an election was conducted. Even simple things such as registration and poll books were nonexistent so it was an immense undertaking.

The general headquarters of the U.S. mission was set up in the Grande Bretagne Hotel in Athens, and the French and English counterparts of our general staff were housed in separate quarters. The country was divided into five districts with a central board in Athens, and personnel were assigned to each of these regions. I was selected from our mission to be in charge of northern Greece at Salonika, which was the area of greatest unrest. The United States had the great good fortune to have initially as the secretary general and counselor for the embassy at the central board Foy D. Kohler. Kohler was then a young Foreign Service officer, later to have a distinguished career in the State Department, serving as ambassador to a number of major foreign countries including Russia, where he earned a reputation as one of our great Russian experts. He was already revealing by his industry and knowledge the qualities that were to carry him to the top of the Foreign Service. Our group included two scholars who later joined the staff of Indiana University: Jim Clark and B. R. Davidson, Jr.

At Salonika I was chief of our mission, as I mentioned, and there was a chief for the French, Roger Fabre (who had to leave in late March because of the death of his father), and one for the British, J. W. Horan. This was the pattern for each region, except that in Salonika we had in addition a South African representative, Major P. J. Strydom. We were to coordinate our efforts as best we could. I was aided as well by the very competent U.S. consul general in Salonika, William M. Gwynn, a career man who knew the region well. My personal assistant was Peter William Topping. He had come to Salonika nearly a month prior to my arrival to organize our arrangements there and particularly to select interpreters and other staff members with Greek-American competence for our headquarters office. His complete mastery of the Greek language was an enormous benefit, and along with it he had qualities that made him an admirable aide and colleague: an amiable temperament, a regard for accuracy, and a habit of close attention to detail. He was in fact my right arm during my stay in Greece. Since then he has had a notable career in the field of scholarship, in recent years as Charles Phelps Taft Professor of History and Later Greek Studies at the University of Cincinnati, and now senior research associate in the Center for Byzantine Studies at Dumbarton Oaks.

Many of our physical needs were cared for by the American Farm School, located outside Salonika, which had been largely dismantled during the latter years of the war but which was beginning to resume its program of training Greek youths for life on the peasant farms. We were fortunate to be able to have fresh eggs, good milk, cream, butter, and produce furnished us as needed from the American Farm School. We reciprocated by channeling to the school such surplus items of transport and other useful equipment as were available. There was in Europe so much surplus matériel, which was impractical to send back to the United States, that we could take care of many of the American Farm School's urgent needs without difficulty. Also, some of our young soldiers were interested in assisting the school and in off hours helped to put the buildings and the farm back into operation.

I was quartered on the fifth floor of the American consulate building, which was located on the waterfront promenade in Salonika. The apartment was quite comfortable, and the scent of the powder and perfume of the occupant just before me still lingered in the rooms: Gracie Fields, the famed British comedienne, had stopped there during a tour through Greece to entertain the soldiers.

The war had been hard on Salonika. The city was largely in ruins, and the waterfront harbor was filled with sunken ships. Since Salonika had been one of the important shipping points for supplies to Yugoslavia and the Balkans, the harbor had been bombed until it was useless. By the time of our arrival, however, men were in the process of clearing the harbor sufficiently to allow relief supplies for the Balkans to be shipped there, then to be loaded onto trains and sent to Belgrade and elsewhere, following the historic supply route.

Protocol demanded that I make certain calls upon my arrival. First, I made contact with the U.S. consul general and then, under his direction, arranged to call upon the principal leaders of the community: the governor-general of northern Greece, the mayor, the governor of the department of Central Macedonia, the top leaders in each of the political parties including the Communist Party, and finally the archbishop. In Greece the custom in formal calls is for a host to send for Turkish coffee immediately upon his guest's arrival. This very strong coffee is passed around and consumed in little cups ceremoniously. Because my calls were made seriatim in one day to avoid the appearance of favoring one person over another, I had about a dozen cups of coffee in a relatively short period of time, two or three hours, and found that this kind of coffee drunk in such quantities can be nearly as intoxicating as alcohol. I remember little of the personalities I called on that day except for Archbishop Spyridon, one of the most noted and influential members of the Greek Orthodox hierarchy in the country. A handsome old gentleman, he had a beautiful white beard and was splendidly robed. In addition to coffee, he offered me the other traditional gesture of hospitality, a spoonful of delicious candied fruit in syrup.

After I finished these calls, protocol required that I return immediately to my office, there to await the return calls of each person visited that morning. They came one after another to my office. I assured each of the privilege we felt in being in Salonika, of our awareness of the importance of the election, and of our dedication to being impartial observers and reporters to the world.

Early in the development of the mission, it had been decided to send with us to Greece some young American scholars who were in the process of developing a sampling technique for polling public opinion. This now common procedure was then in its infancy and its accuracy was as yet unproved. One of the leading exponents of this method was Raymond J. Jessen from Iowa State College, who headed our technical team and brought with him a number of men who were trained in this system of data gathering. It is my understanding that the poll they conducted in Greece was the first widespread use of public-opinion polling by the sampling technique. Their work proved to be invaluable to us, and their predictions, as I shall relate, to be quite accurate. We brought with us also a number of distinguished archaeologists and scholars in the field of Greek language and literature who knew Greece intimately. The archaeologists were particularly helpful because of their knowledge of the countryside. Scholars such as Carl Blegen of the University of Cincinnati and his associates, Frank E. Bailey of Mount Holyoke College and Shirley H. Weber of the American School of Classical Studies, Alison Frantz, a leading member of the agora excavation in ancient Athens, and others gave us valuable insight into the Greek character and into the land that had helped to form it.

We quickly went about establishing our apparatus for the observation of voting places, which was an urgent matter since the election was to be held within less than four weeks after we arrived in Greece and since I had a staff of only 1,200 to cover the whole of northern Greece. We also attempted to assist the Greeks with their election machinery without in any way intruding upon their politics. As the weeks went on we began to feel that our observation system would be adequate and effective. Of course, all our efforts had to be coordinated with our partners in the French and the English missions. The working relationships among us were easy. The other missions had very small staffs and relied on our field staff for the most part.

In due course we started to take soundings of public opinion through area sampling. Sampling teams were sent into the remotest villages, many of which were far from roads. At that time, only 1.5 million of the 7 million people comprising the Greek population lived in cities and the remainder in villages. There were then about

10,000 villages in all, and for the most part the families in these villages had lived in the same place for centuries and thus had come to know each other intimately. Many villages had been consolidated into one precinct or polling place, and at the time of the election there were approximately 3,400 of these in all of Greece. The sampling teams talked to leaders of the different parties in the villages concerning the adequacy of the registration lists and the possibility of fair elections. The teams then selected names randomly from the lists and sought to find out whether those individuals were current residents.

The sampling results, which made us feel hopeful for the democratic forces, we kept to ourselves lest they might in any way influence the outcome of the election. However, the Communist forces began to be observably more active. Then some incidents of terrorism took place within the district. The territory that was my responsibility stretched all the way from Kavalla to the Balkan borders and was in the mountainous, relatively wild part of Greece that was inclined to be turbulent anyway. The turmoil increased, however, and looked suspiciously as though it were being inspired by the Communists as a way to scare people away from the polls when election day came. The Communists may well have realized that the tide was running against them. Predictably, a week or so before the election was to be held, the Greek Communists ceremoniously announced to the world that the election was being rigged and urged all Leftists to abstain from voting. Their statement created a great deal of tension, but the Greeks pressed ahead with their election. On the appointed day, March 31, the democratic forces won a clear victory.

On election day the sampling teams observed the polling places, and after the election they checked to find out whether people voted or refrained from voting as indicated by the registration lists. They then tried to ascertain from the nonvoters the reasons why they had not participated. The results of the observation and sampling led our Allied mission to the conclusion that, whereas there were serious difficulties with the election, as there were bound to be under the circumstances, nevertheless on the whole it expressed the will of the people.

From our observations and polling we could report reliably on important aspects of the election. As many as 71 percent of the names on the registration lists had been found to be valid. Electoral preparations had been reasonably adequate. There had been freedom of the press throughout. Of eligible voters 93 percent were registered and 60 percent of these had voted. Although the Left claimed all of the remainder, we found by our checks of registered voters that only 9.3 percent abstained for party reasons, that 22,000 votes were cast illegally, and that only 11,000 persons were prevented by intimidation from voting. Since the British officers and troops had been confined to quarters on election day, they could not be accused by the Left of intimidation. Intimidation by both Rightists and Leftists did exist, and there was much squabbling related for the most part to old feuds, but the general atmosphere on election day was largely one of dedication to patriotic duty.

We had some reason to be confident of the statistical accuracy of our findings, moreover, because on the night before the election our teams had reported to us that 1,100,000 citizens would vote the next day; the estimate missed by less than 10,000—an amazingly accurate prediction. It was evident that the political machinery in Greece had been rehabilitated and reconstructed along democratic and representative lines.[1]

Not all was grim, determined pursuit of a fair election. On the eve of the election, I gave a party for the Greeks who had helped set up our election machinery in appreciation for their efforts. The air was that of a group cautiously optimistic because of the soundness of their effort.

On election day, Sunday, March 31, Peter Topping and I, accompanied by Major Strydom of South Africa, spent the day observing for ourselves exactly what was happening in certain representative polling places. In the morning we drove to Hagia Sophia, Nea Menemeni, and Eykarkia. In each of the three places, voting was quiet and orderly. In the afternoon we observed two more city polling places and then visited one in the outlying village of Aden-

---

1. The official report of the mission concluded thus:

"The Mission finds that the proceedings of election day were orderly and satisfactory. The registration lists in large areas contained irregularities but there was no significant amount of illegal voting. Intimidation existed in some degree, from both extremes, and was even on occasion given countenance by members of the gendarmerie, but it was not extensive enough to affect seriously the election. The practice of deliberate abstention did not reach large proportions.

"The Mission therefore concludes that notwithstanding the present intensity of political emotions in Greece conditions were such as to warrant the holding of elections, that the election proceedings were on the whole free and fair, and that the general outcome represents a true and valid verdict of the Greek people."

dron. I remember still the care being taken by those in charge of the polling places to carry out their duties impartially and meticulously.

Throughout the work of our mission we maintained central direction and coordination in Athens. Our contact with headquarters was by regular flights between Athens and Salonika, which carried dispatches and information. I attended staff meetings about once a week in Athens.

On one such trip to Athens, I took occasion to visit the great dam that created the Athens Waterworks. It was built of marble and was a beautiful sight to behold. By reason of its creation, Athens had one of the few pure water supplies then available in that part of Europe. The dam had been built by Henry Ulen, a poor boy from Lebanon, Indiana, who left to seek his fortune after finishing high school and who had become a great international contractor for the building of waterworks, railways, bridges, and so forth in various parts of the world. He also was quite a wizard in financing those projects in the New York money market. Late in life he retired to Lebanon, Indiana, founded the suburban village of Ulen, and started the Ulen Country Club. The Greeks all knew the Ulen name and revered and honored it. They were grateful for and proud of their great marble dam. In contacts with Greek friends, I could say that I was from Mr. Ulen's home town in Indiana and knew him. Thus I acquired a bit of prestige that I would not otherwise have had.

I also visited the Gennadeion Library in Athens. Shirley Weber, director of the library, who guided Peter Topping and me on a tour of the collection, called my attention to a copy of *Histoire Picturale de la Guerre de l'Indépendance Hellénique, par le général Makryjannis,* which he said was a rarity and available at the excellent price of one hundred fifty dollars. As he felt certain our Indiana University Library would not have a copy, I purchased it and upon my return presented it to the library.

Northern Greece being mountainous, with many inaccessible villages and with what few good roads there were having been either neglected or largely destroyed during the war, transport in the countryside was very difficult. However, I had been assigned a comfortable car that could be used in the city, and in the country we traveled for the most part by jeep or by a small plane, a c 5 I think it was, that could land in almost any pasture. In this way I saw much of northern Greece, a beautiful and interesting area, all the way from Yannina to Kavalla. On occasion I was also able to fly to some of the Greek Islands. I remember particularly visiting Crete just before our departure from Greece and seeing some of the magnificent archaeological ruins there. I had hoped to get to Mt. Athos, which was in my assigned district, but such a trip proved to be impossible because of lack of time.

I well remember a drive from Kavalla on the Aegean Sea, the center of the tobacco-growing industry of Greece, back to Salonika. It was an early spring day, late in the afternoon, and the drive, as I described it then, was especially beautiful:

> Out across the plain, the freshly plowed soil was a chocolate brown, splashed with the bright green of new wheat and the pink of blossoming almond trees. You could see people with their donkeys silhouetted against the horizon, and furnishing a backdrop for it all was the beautiful, snowcapped mountain, Mt. Pangaeus, from which Philip of Macedon, father of Alexander the Great, obtained the gold to finance his conquests. . . .
>
> As you drive along the country roads, you can see the shepherd with his flocks, tending those flocks in exactly the type of costume his ancestors of two or three thousand years ago wore.

I think I have never seen a more captivating spring scene, made all the more so for me because of the fact that I was traveling the exact route that St. Paul had followed when he landed at Kavalla and then proceeded to Salonika to bring his gospel to the Philippians.

Salonika is an important center of Byzantine churches and antiquities. Peter Topping arranged for Professor Xyngopoulos of the University of Thessaloniki, an expert on Byzantine antiquities, to conduct us on a tour of Salonika's treasures, accompanied by his colleague, Professor Kyriakides, dean of the Greek folklorists, who spoke highly of the work of Indiana University's Stith Thompson. As I had decided that I should call at the University of Thessaloniki before I left, it was arranged for me to meet with the rector and the university senate on April 2. Prior to that visit, a delegation of students had waited on me complaining about their lot at the university. In particular they were incensed by the poor quality and high price of the food and by what they considered to be insensitive treatment of students by the faculty. I related this incident to the university senate and told them to their amusement that these student complaints were so similar to what I would be hearing if I were at my university, I felt right at home there in Salonika.

Another reminder of home came with the arrival on March 11

of the December issue of *Life* magazine. In it was a picture of Alvin "Bo" McMillin embracing me after Indiana University had won the Big Ten football championship the previous fall. This different glimpse of the American-in-charge in Salonika caused a stir as the magazine was passed from hand to hand for everyone in headquarters to see. A fortnight later we held a reception for some U.S. reporters and a *Life* photographer. Among the guests was M. W. Fodor of the Chicago *Sun,* then one of the leading international journalists.

The University of Thessaloniki was at that time second only to the University of Athens in importance in the country and now has grown to such preeminence that it is perhaps the most important university in Greece. I shall always remember my call at the university. It was early spring, it was cold, there was little heat indoors, and much of the university was in shambles. Nevertheless, the university senate had assembled in full regalia in the beautiful, formal senate room, where the members received me with appropriate greetings. I replied as best I could, identifying my educational background and pointing out that my visit had been enriched by association with some of their colleagues. They asked me many questions and were deeply interested in our mission's undertaking.

Another of my treasured memories of Salonika was the spirit of youth. The apartment that Peter Topping and I shared looked out on the great esplanade on the waterfront with a full view of evening activities there. It was a custom at night for the Greek youth to parade back and forth, especially on pleasant evenings and on moonlit nights of spring. They sang songs the words of which I could not understand, but I enjoyed the melody—singing, singing, singing until the wee hours of the morning. They were probably cold and hungry, and their town was devastated, but the eternal spirit of youth that is part of the Greek heritage was expressing itself in exuberant song.

An amusing incident, which has helped me to maintain a realistic view of what is possible in international communication and to remind me that good intentions are not enough in the establishment of international harmony and peace, is worth recounting. Toward the end of our stay in Salonika, one of our young career officers came to me to say that the harbor had been cleared sufficiently to allow the docking of a freighter filled with wheat for the relief of the Yugoslavs and the Balkan region. It is to be remembered that, while the rail route through Salonika to Yugoslavia was an important supply line before the war, historically there had been great tension between the Thessalonians and the Macedonian Yugoslavs, the largest remnant of the Macedonian culture.

The officer said that the wheat would be loaded onto freight cars and on a certain day in the following week the train was to move over the rebuilt tracks to the Yugoslav border to deliver the wheat. The one workable passenger car still in the yards at Salonika was to be attached at the end of the train to carry our official personnel to the border, where there was to be a ceremony, involving the official Yugoslav personnel on the one side and the American and other international personnel on the other, to mark this important event: the delivery of the first United Nations Relief and Rehabilitation Administration (UNRRA) wheat. The officer stated that if I were free he would be happy to include me in the official party. As this participation seemed to offer an interesting prospect, I joined the party for the trip. While the train went chugging along through Greece, we enjoyed the beauty of the countryside and the comforts of our combination diner and parlor car, a relic of the famed Orient Express, which had operated in prewar times through Salonika.

When we arrived at the border, protected except for the actual track itself by high barbed wire, we found a great many Greeks on the Greek side and a great many Yugoslavs on the Yugoslav side. Bands on each side were trying to outplay each other. At intervals, when the bands were not playing, the Greeks would hurl insults at the Yugoslavs, and the Yugoslavs would hurl insults at the Greeks. Ironically, traditional rivalries were manifesting themselves in the midst of this dramatic gesture of international cooperation and friendship.

Just as the train pulled up to the border, a young Yugoslav colonel who had been sent down from Belgrade to greet us came into our car to check our papers. Since I had been added to the United Nations party at the last minute, the necessity of my having papers had been overlooked, or perhaps it had been assumed that I would not need any. When the Yugoslav officer, very much impressed with his authority and the importance of the occasion, found that I had no papers specifically for this event, he announced that the car could not cross to the Yugoslav side where the ceremony was to be held and the luncheon to be served. This incensed our

State Department personnel, who pointed out that I was the highest-ranking American official in the entourage; they had tacitly agreed that a refusal to let me participate in the ceremony would be an insult to the United States, an insult they were not prepared to accept. To ease the situation I offered to get off and mingle with the Greeks, allowing the ceremony to proceed. But the young State Department staff members—our diplomats-to-be—were as adamant as the young Yugoslav. Their indignation was all the greater because it was American wheat that the U N R R A mission was delivering for the relief of the Yugoslavs. The argument went on for at least half an hour and finally it was resolved in the following amusing fashion:

Our railroad car was pulled across the line, half resting in Yugoslavia and half remaining in Greece. The Yugoslavs sat at one end of the car and the United Nations personnel, including the Americans, sat at the other. The ceremonial speeches were given, toasts were drunk, and we enjoyed a delicious five-course luncheon. The honor of the United States was upheld, the dignity and authority of the young Yugoslav colonel were preserved, and all was sweetness and light. Afterward, a Yugoslav engine came to pull the wheat into Belgrade, and our engine returned us to Athens. This little incident out at the periphery of diplomatic and strategic events in retrospect still brings a smile.

My stay in Greece as well as the intensive briefing that I had received in Greek matters stirred the beginnings of my long love affair with Greece, its history and its people. I gained a new appreciation of and friendship for our Greek-American colony in Bloomington. While I was in Greece I visited some members of their families.

Somehow on my returns to Greece through the years I had not managed to visit Salonika again. However, in February, 1975, after attending a meeting of the board of trustees of the American University in Cairo, I decided on the spur of the moment to stop over in Greece and spend a few days exploring what I wished to see, without notice to any friends there, even those in the American School of Classical Studies. I had visited the school on other occasions because we had established a warm bond with the staff and because some Indiana University people had worked there, but this time I wanted to visit Greece on my own terms and in my own way.

I particularly wanted to see one of our Indiana University excavations, although I knew it to be closed at this season, and I wished to revisit Salonika.

I made the trip to the excavation and relished the on-site view of the dig. I visited numerous places on my own and absorbed again —quietly, without the distraction of others—the sights and atmosphere of that beautiful land. As before, it was early spring, so early that hardly any tourists were around. In due course I flew up to Salonika and spent a long and gratifying day there. I was astonished to see that the city had been completely rehabilitated and had grown enormously; only a few old landmarks remained. It had become a handsome, modern European city. In fact, I know of no European city in which the extent and quality of its postwar rebuilding have excelled Salonika's. There were not just fine-looking new apartment houses, business buildings, streets, beautiful parks, an impressive new university campus, and a completely rebuilt modern harbor, but also a handsomely designed new museum specializing in the antiquities that are being recovered from the archaeological excavations in that area. Greece has set a policy of establishing regional museums to receive artifacts from within each region as they are unearthed. In this setting one gains an added sense of the significance of the artifacts. The disadvantage of such a system is that, to view very many of the treasures, one must travel throughout Greece; yet, if the artifacts were all gathered in Athens they would lose something of their regional significance, and their very mass would make it difficult for the public to appreciate them in the way that smaller displays in the regional museums allow.

I found the new museum in Salonika, which I visited with a good Greek guide-driver—a young woman who had just graduated in archaeology from the University of Thessaloniki—fascinating. She was a superb interpreter of the region and intensely interested in my earlier experience there from a period that she was too young to have experienced but that she knew of from her reading. We concluded the day by a visit to the American Farm School, which was flourishing again, and to the girls' school affiliated with it. I was delighted to see that these excellent institutions were again thriving and teaching young Greek boys and girls scientific ways of agriculture that are adaptable for the peasant farmer to use.

My initial experience in Greece not only gave me a new comprehension of the historical, political, and social forces at work in that part of the world and of what can be accomplished by peaceful diplomatic means, but also it broadened my acquaintanceship. There were, of course, new friends among the Greeks and even more among the American professional diplomatic corps and the young men and women in the U.S. Army who were later to make their careers in the diplomatic arena or in the international organizations that were then in the process of being formed. Through the years, as I have had other international experiences, I have been delighted to find from time to time acquaintances that I had made on the Greek mission serving in the United Nations Central Administration, in career positions in international organizations, and in United Nations offices elsewhere.

The Greek experience also heightened my respect for archaeology as a science and as a scholarly discipline. I think our mission could not have been successful without the knowledge that the archaeologists imparted to us about Greece, both ancient and modern. In truth, American archaeologists became our most important informational resource in observing the Greek elections. The happy outcome of this delicate and significant task represented America's first diplomatic victory on behalf of the West in the series of Cold War events, diplomatic initiatives, and skirmishes that have characterized the period from World War II to the present between the forces of Communism and the forces of the free world.

I am sure that my own interest in and support of Indiana University's efforts to engage in archaeological work grew in no small part out of my Greek experience. I found the Greek antiquities indescribably beautiful and awe-inspiring. Coming early in my life as this experience did, when I had had little exposure to cultures other than my own and had not traveled at all in the ancient world, it made a profound impression upon me. It helped to make me conscious of the importance of our cultural heritage from the Greeks and the necessity of preserving and protecting it.[2]

I also found the Greek people a joy. They are handsome, tal-

2. I gained a great respect for our American classical scholars and the work of the American School of Classical Studies. Late in my career as president I rejoiced at the opportunity to encourage Professor Norman Pratt, chairman of the Department of Classics, to expand into classical archaeology and accept the invitation of the University of Chicago to become a partner in the excavation of Kenchreae, one of the harbors of ancient Corinth. I recently represented Indiana university at the opening of the new regional museum at Isthmia that houses the artifacts from the excavations, including glass panels from an ancient sunken ship that represent a unique contribution of our effort.

ented, vivacious, and gregarious. They have a natural love of politics; wherever two Greeks are together you can be sure that they will be engaged in an animated discussion of some matter, most likely politics. The emigrés from Greece to the United States have greatly enriched our culture and have introduced into the American population structure highly desirable qualities. They have helped promote the economy, support cultural activities, and develop a vigorous professional class.

In remarks I made to the Indiana Bankers Association on May 16, 1946, shortly after resumption of my university duties, I described a moving experience I had had just before leaving Greece:

> Just after we had finished our report and were waiting for a plane to bring us home, the great *Missouri* came to the harbor of Athens, and Admiral Hewitt gave a small reception one afternoon. We went out to that reception and when it was over we started back. Night had fallen, and as I looked up at the city of Athens, I saw that the Parthenon had been flooded with lights in honor of the *Missouri's* visit. There the Parthenon stood silhouetted against the black sky. It is perhaps man's most perfect physical expression of all that is good in him, of his eternal search for truth and beauty. There that beautiful building stood, looking down upon Athens as it has now for two thousand years—land of ancient achievement, land of promise for tomorrow!

[20]

○ ○ ○

With Clay
in Occupied Germany

THE PROBLEMS of Indiana University immediately following World War II were very great, perhaps as challenging as
any set of problems faced by the university in a similar period of
time. We had an overwhelming increase in the number of students
year after year. It was very difficult to construct housing fast enough
to accommodate them. Much of the structure of the university had
been fractured by the absence of many key members of the faculty
and staff on war assignments. The Indiana General Assembly, the
governor, and the entire state felt as we did at the university that the
task of providing for the education of returning veterans whose
education had been interrupted by service in the war was a matter
of high priority. It was later to be our proud boast that we had accommodated all veterans who were qualified and who sought to
enroll.

But those were strenuous days—days that put enormous pressure upon the staff, the faculty, the administration, and the Board
of Trustees. In view of these problems, some members of the board
had lingering doubts about the wisdom of having granted me leave
of absence for the Greek mission. Too, my enthusiasm about my
Greek experience may have caused apprehension among them that
I might find work of that type sufficiently attractive to entice me
away from the university permanently. Whatever the cause, the
board suggested that I not accept any long-term commitments away
from the campus thereafter unless they were connected in some way
with education. This informal policy I respected and until my retirement breached only once, namely, when I accepted appointment
as a member of our delegation to the Twelfth General Assembly

of the United Nations. That particular post, however, was one of such prestige and indirect importance to the university, and matters on campus were sufficiently in hand, that the board fully approved my acceptance of the invitation.

But, to return to the period of immediate postwar problems— in its midst I was approached by a representative of the United States Military Government in Germany with the request that I head the new Education and Cultural Affairs Branch of the Oc- cupation. Some serious organizational and staff problems had de- veloped within the military government's education branch, and it was felt that improvement of the situation required an outside person.

When I made this request known to the trustees, they were not favorably disposed and for good reason. Neither were the governor and some members of the legislature. However, with their approval I accepted General Lucius Clay's invitation to visit Germany briefly for the purpose of meeting the personnel, seeing the organization, and getting some sense of the problems to be solved and what might be done about them. At the conclusion of my visit I made some recommendations to Clay that he countered with a question: would I consider becoming his personal adviser on educational and cultural affairs? As such I would have responsibility for advising not only on the entire German educational system within the American sec- tor but also on associated cultural activities. General Clay was not to get an answer on my availability for more than two months and then only after extensive debate and editorializing in the state fol- lowed by telegrams from Clay to Governor Ralph Gates and to the president of the Indiana University Board of Trustees, Judge Ora Wildermuth (see Appendix [E]).

On October 17, the Board of Trustees having arranged for an administrative committee composed of John Hastings[1] as chairman and deans Herman Briscoe and Wendell Wright and Joseph Frank- lin to discharge the duties and responsibilities of the presidency, I was granted leave for six months with the concurrence of Governor Gates. I joined Clay a month later. My stay in Germany, from No- vember 21, 1947, to May 27, 1948, was punctuated by two neces-

---

1. Judge Hastings, chairman of the Board of Trustees, possessed a remarkable understanding of the university, a facility in working with people, rare wisdom and common sense, and a gentle sense of humor. Had he chosen to go into educa- tion instead of law, he would have made a masterful university president. He later resigned from the Board of Trustees when he was appointed to the U.S. Court of Appeals for the Seventh Circuit.

sary visits home and other absences on behalf of my mission. From the very beginning I had made it clear to General Clay that my stay in Germany could only be temporary and short-term because I felt I could not be away from the university for a long period. This he had accepted since he wished primarily to accomplish an administrative reorganization of the division and to have me recruit someone of competence who could undertake the task for an extended period of time.

I was able to persuade Peter Fraenkel to join me as my assistant. Peter was of German background, had a degree with honors from Indiana University, and was at the time in Harvard's graduate school studying for his master's degree. I could not have made a better choice. As he, too, was a bachelor, it was an easy matter for us to maintain a common living and working arrangement in Berlin. He early proved himself to be very perceptive about political and educational matters and was invaluable to me from his arrival in mid-January onward. In fact, he stayed on for some months after my departure to close the office and, upon his return, as I mentioned in chapter 18, became my assistant in the president's office, where he served in a highly effective manner for about fifteen years. He next had a long career in international activities with the Ford Foundation before becoming assistant to the current president of Indiana University, John Ryan.

When I arrived in Berlin in the late fall of 1947, the city was still in ruins. I was told by persons who had been present three years earlier, at the time the German forces surrendered, that every aspect of the German society had completely collapsed.[2] There was no responsible government—national, state, or local. The men who participated stated that, as the U.S. Army took one town after another, it had to organize fire departments, police departments, and even the collection of garbage. Industry was at a standstill, agriculture was disorganized, and trade and commerce were nonexistent. Schools were closed and children roamed the streets. Looters robbed bombed-out homes and stores. The people were sullen, disappointed, dispirited. Germany was truly a beaten nation.

All the important cities were from 50 to 75 percent destroyed. I often traveled through streets in which the rubble on both sides

2. The substance of the following observations on Germany at the time, somewhat modified here, was presented in a speech to the Indiana Library Association on October 28, 1948, in Indianapolis.

was piled higher than my car. Blackened, broken concrete and twisted steel were ghostly reminders of war's toll on government buildings, hospitals, museums, factories, and apartment houses. On the streets one could observe bitter-faced people dragging behind them small carts loaded with stumps of trees dug up in the woods for fuel, women standing in long lines to buy a small piece of meat or the first pair of shoes in eight years, and teenagers, who wore made-over Army uniforms, selling American chocolate and cigarettes on the black market. Although there was less physical destruction in the rural areas, they had not escaped the effect of war; as in the urban centers, the shortages were acute and the disintegration of social institutions was complete.

Despite the war-wrought destruction and the loss of millions of lives, Germany had 10 percent more inhabitants when I arrived than in 1939. The population of the United States zone had increased 18 percent in the same period. Millions of refugees from the territory east of the Oder Neisse River and now under Polish administration and further millions of German expellees from Germany's eastern neighbors were crowded into the farm houses and into the towns and villages of the west. Of course, the mere fact that these villages had not been leveled served to attract the influx. The once-symmetrical age-sex structure of the German population, as well as the religious and social composition of German society, was upset by the destruction of male youth in the war and by the huge influx of the newcomers who added to the confusion, friction, and unrest. German society had been shaken to the core and a tremendous readjustment had to be made. This readjustment, of course, had to be made under the severe economic handicaps resulting from the dismantling of German industry, production, and trade.

My title was that of cultural affairs adviser to the military governor, one of four advisers who constituted an informal cabinet that reported directly to Clay in the Berlin headquarters. This was a staff position. In addition, I was acting director of the Education and Cultural Relations Division of the Office of Military Governor for Germany (U.S.), or OMGUS. This was a line, operating position. Because the civilian advisers were given the simulated rank of two-star generals, they had considerable authority in carrying out their work. OMGUS had charge of the American zone throughout Germany, but the American sector in Berlin had a status similar to that of the *länder,* or "states," in the field and was under its own director,

Colonel Frank L. Howley. Those of us in general headquarters shared responsibility for the whole of the American zone in Germany. Our office was located in one of the buildings of the former Kaiser Wilhelm Institute in Dahlem, and Peter and I were assigned a comfortable four-story, twenty-four–room house in the suburbs at 24 Am Kleinen Wannsee. It had been the home of a former German movie magnate and was a typical upper-class German home: spacious, comfortably and completely furnished, and graced with a delightful formal garden. There was a good staff to operate the whole, including a splendid executive housekeeper, Helene Schuster, of whom we became very fond. She served to make our stay in Berlin agreeable.

I moved immediately to learn from the existing staff all that I could about the problems that needed to be solved. The principal figure in the education section was Thomas Alexander, a recognized authority on German education, on leave from Teachers College of Columbia University. He had moved from the position of deputy director of the Education and Religious Affairs Branch to that of acting director when John Taylor, the previous director, had left to become president of the University of Louisville. For many years Dr. Alexander had taken his graduate students in comparative education to Germany for study and was acquainted with the personalities in German education as well as with its structure and its strengths and weaknesses. He was a brilliant man from whom we learned a great deal, but he was not especially gifted as an administrator and his view of the Germans was troublesome. Not only was he dogmatic, he could sometimes be vindictive as well. He believed, as did a sizable group in the United States, that we should follow a very hard line in attempting to restructure the German educational system, since he felt that the structure that had existed had been responsible in no small part for the fact that the Germans had been the aggressor in two successive world wars. Our official policy, however, was a little less rigid, and my own point of view was that the Germans had to be responsible for their own reforms and that the best we could do was to aid the reform by suggestion and persuasion rather than by order and decree. We believed that this was the only way to achieve a lasting reform, and we certainly had no desire to impose the American system on the Germans, an attempt that would have been self-defeating. Although Alexander was not generally in accord with this point of view, he welcomed us heartily, cooperated with us, and was a tower of strength to us in all of our work. I had great admiration for him and the friendship we formed there lasted as long as he lived.

We likewise moved promptly to acquaint ourselves with the headquarters staff, with the staff in our various länder in the American zone by visiting them in the field, and also with our opposite numbers in the French, British, and Russian zones. Many policy decisions were supposed to be made on a quadripartite basis, and a great deal of time and energy of the headquarters staff had to be devoted to preparation for quadripartite meetings and to the effort to reconcile the points of view of the various occupying powers. The meetings went on endlessly, for the Russians were especially difficult. They of course had an entirely different educational philosophy from ours and also a different attitude toward the Germans. Had they had their way, the entire educational system would have been restructured along Russian lines, and all subject matter content revised to conform to the current Communist-Marxist point of view. As a result, in nearly all matters, it was necessary for us to move in our zone independently of the Russians. There were some differences with the English and French, but they were minor by comparison.

A further complication in our work was the absence of agreement on the part of our own U.S. personnel within and without the Education Division as to policy, timing, and procedure. Reflecting the conflict of opinions among the educational and political leaders at home, the O M G U S personnel were split between a desire to keep Germany weak and a feeling that a rebuilt Germany would furnish the Western world a bulwark against communism. The education staffers were, in some cases, traditionalists and, in others, Dewey progressivists.

In our field visits we soon discovered that we had many dedicated men and women of high competence and superb background, although there were a few spots in which we found weak personnel whom we had to transfer, and we did so as rapidly as we could. We tried also to gather from our field staff as well as from the headquarters staff their views of what revisions should be made in American policy and what actions needed to be taken by O M G U S headquarters in Berlin. It was then our task to carry these recommendations to the proper source at the general headquarters, which from time to time meant carrying them to General Clay himself.

We had not been in Germany long before we realized that there was a communications problem between the military men and the education specialists. They did not understand each other's language. One of my duties, therefore, was to interpret to the general, in a manner comprehensible to him and his staff, the substantive concerns and tensions within my division.

I early learned to have great respect and admiration for General Clay. He was a brilliant man and a superb executive with a sound vision of our responsibilities and our tasks as an occupying power in Germany. He was a man of courage and determination and well able to hold his own when challenged by the other powers on major issues, as he dramatically illustrated later by his defiance of the Russians at the time of the Berlin blockade. He had great concern for achieving results in the fields of education and cultural affairs and demonstrated his concern by giving me excellent cooperation during my entire tour of duty. Clay had recruited me principally to help bring order out of considerable chaos in the cultural affairs branch, and therefore my assignment was essentially organizational and administrative. It can be briefly stated in terms of its four parts.

My first assignment was to assemble cultural activities in a single division and to arrange to have them administered under a unified policy in contrast to the somewhat divergent policies that had been followed in some divisions previously. Thus the Education and Cultural Relations Division was created. Elementary, secondary, university, and adult education; religious affairs; youth activities; women's affairs; theaters; music; the coordination of cultural exchanges; and the allocation of textbooks and materials—all were brought under the management of a single unit of the military government. Provision was made to include in this unit also, but at some later date, the indirect media of education such as publication, press, and radio.

The second responsibility was to attempt to create an agency in the United States to serve as a cultural liaison between the American people and the new Education and Cultural Relations Division in Germany. This agency was to feature a number of technical advisory panels corresponding to the main cultural activities of the military government in Germany. An earlier visiting committee had recommended formation of the panels, which was accomplished a few months after my return to the United States.

The third task called for us to try to stimulate appropriate military-government divisions to enter reorientation work. It was felt that nearly all branches of the military government could make some contribution to the work of reorientation if a harmonious policy could be established and that they could be encouraged to assist in the work of educational reorientation.

My fourth and most important task was to recruit top level personnel for the key positions in the new Education and Cultural Relations Division in Germany and in the stateside organization, when and if it could be created. The major objective was the recruitment of some educator to take my place because, as I have mentioned, my assignment was understood to be of limited duration. One of the reasons Clay had sought me for this job was that he felt I would be able to attract the kind of person he wanted to take the position for a more or less indefinite period of time. How I went about this and with what success I describe later in this account.

I shall not dwell here on the substantive problems and their solutions, for they are set out in greater detail in the speech I made immediately upon my return.[3] However, to understand the nature of our task, a picture of the German situation when O M G U S began its operation is necessary.

The task of occupation is not an easy one in any situation, I suppose, and it certainly was not easy in ours because we were attempting to reconstruct, encourage, and reorient the whole of the educational and, to some extent, the cultural life of Germany along democratic lines. The days were filled with staff meetings, visits with members of the staff, visits to the field, visits with German educators, officials, and churchmen, and endless discussions with our experts on what to do next. I attempted to absorb as much as I could about German life, its philosophies, its organization, and its potential. Every waking moment was spent in study or in discussion with informed individuals. In time I began to feel that I had some grasp, although fragmentary at best, of the German scene. A few incidents and anecdotes that remain in my memory may add to the information contained in the formal speech, which is a part of the record.

Because of our interest and their importance, we attempted to maintain as close contact as possible with leading German scholars

3. "The United States and the German Problem," Convocation Address, Indiana University, June 23, 1948.

and with rectors of the principal universities. In mid-May the University of Frankfurt held a major convocation to celebrate the centenary of the 1848 revolution. The university invited Robert Hutchins, then president of the University of Chicago and a leading critic of American education, to come as the speaker for the occasion. Because Hutchins was a traditionalist in education, arguing for the classical curriculum with great rhetorical license, his selection was a strategem on the part of the conservative professors who opposed our efforts toward reorientation and democratization in German education. General Clay was invited to attend the convocation, but he declined and delegated me to represent the military government and to serve as host for Hutchins, who was to be in Germany for a few days.

I went to Frankfurt and Bob Hutchins and I had a delightful visit at the Castle Kronberg, where he was staying. I remember at this particular time he was not very well and was under some personal stress. Nevertheless, he made a brilliant speech at the convocation, and the university put on an impressive show. It was the first major academic festival following the conclusion of hostilities, and all the German universities were represented, their rectors in their magnificent robes and others in beautiful academic costumes. The whole affair was brought off with great pomp and circumstance. Bob's speech that day, although it gave some aid and comfort to the conservative element, did no serious harm to our efforts.[4]

Another incident is especially clear in my memory. It was our custom to hold open house at our home in Wannsee on Sunday afternoons and evenings for students, scholars, German intellectuals, and other interesting personalities. On one such afternoon a number of German students from the Technical University of Berlin, located in the Russian sector of the city, came with some young newspaper friends to state that they were being stifled in their studies by the Russians' insisting on a Marxist orientation for all scholarship

4. The wife of one of our senior advisers in headquarters was also present on that occasion. She had once been an editor of *Vogue* and a designer. She asked me whether the robe I wore as president of Indiana University was as gorgeous as the one worn by the rector of the University of Frankfurt, who was addressed as "Your Magnificence." When I replied that our robes were very sedate and plain, she began drawing on her imagination to design a robe for me. As I recall it, she would have had the robe crimson, decorated with a liberal amount of white ermine and with corn stalks and hogs rampant embroidered in gold thread on either side of the robe's front. Obviously in her mind Indiana was strictly an agricultural state. It would have been great fun to have had her design executed and to have worn the robe on some occasion. But I am indulging in fantasy.

and on censorship of class materials. Their plea was for the Americans to sponsor the establishment of a free university of Berlin, free in the sense that students might have the freedom to study that a true university accords. The discussion went on for some time, and the students, very earnest and persuasive themselves, were supported by Kendall Foss, a young American newspaperman who accompanied them. I finally agreed to take the idea to General Clay. I had no sense of how he would react, but I thought the proposal deserved a hearing.

One could get in to see Clay easily on Sunday mornings, when typically he was in his office by eight, refreshed, without pressure because few people were willing to get up that early on Sunday, and ready to listen. Taking advantage of that circumstance, I presented the proposal for a free university of Berlin to him and, I think perhaps to my surprise, his reaction after considerable questioning was positive. In fact, it was so positive that it startled me. He said, "It's a fine idea and I think we should accept it and act at once." He added that we should plan to have the university open by the next fall. That took my breath away. I explained that starting a university is a complicated business, that we had to have a faculty, a library, laboratories, and so on. I was sure that we would have plenty of eager students, but I was not sure that we could accommodate them in such a short time. He brushed aside all my doubts, said it could be done, and asked me to put the machinery into motion. When I reminded him of the need for space in a city that was practically devastated, he suggested that we commandeer part of the space at headquarters, where the buildings had originally been devoted to education and research since they were all buildings of the Kaiser Wilhelm Institute. I gingerly mentioned the fact that each building had in it, very comfortably situated, top-level military personnel who would not be much impressed by my suggestion that they vacate on behalf of a university. He replied that when we needed the building he would order the place vacated. It was from this initiative that the Free University of Berlin sprang. I did not stay long enough to do more than start the machinery to establish it, but the university opened the following fall after I had returned to Bloomington. It started with almost two thousand students and became a powerful influence for freedom and democracy in German higher education for a number of years.

On one occasion it was necessary for me to go to Paris to see

Julian Huxley, the director-general of the United Nations Educational, Scientific, and Cultural Organization (Unesco). We felt it desirable to have Unesco's understanding of what we were attempting to do in Germany and to secure its cooperation if possible. I had a satisfactory visit with Huxley about our problems and received his pledge of cooperation, but first he wanted to ask me about some of the friends he had made on several visits to Bloomington. His first question was, had I heard from the Tracy Sonneborns recently? Then he inquired concerning the Herman Mullers, and after two or three other inquiries he asked, "Well, how is Kinsey?" I said, "Quite well, I think." He paused for a moment, reached into his desk and pulled out a recent issue of the *New Yorker* that had in it the now famous cartoon of a character inquiring of his wife, "My dear, is there a Mrs. Kinsey?" Huxley showed me the cartoon with a chuckle and after another pause said, "Well, *is* there a Mrs. Kinsey?" I assured him that there was, that she was a wonderful lady, the mother of three fine children, and that the Kinseys enjoyed a happy married life.

Another incident that I remember quite well involved Clay's readiness to make decisions and to back our work. Our staff became increasingly convinced that it was time to begin a major exchange of students and scholars between Germany and the United States. A mission headed by George Zook, president of the American Council on Education, had surveyed the educational activities of OMGUS during the month of August, 1946, and had made many recommendations, one of which had called for the beginning of a wide-scale exchange program and for enlisting the support of the private sector in the United States for such a program. As a result of this recommendation and no doubt also because of the keen interest of Henry Kellermann, then in the State Department with responsibility for formulating government policies relative to education and cultural affairs in the Occupation, the State-War-Navy Coordinating Committee on March 31, 1947, issued a directive announcing the decision of the United States Government to "permit and encourage the revival of visits of Germans to the United States . . . and of persons from the United States to Germany."[5]

5. SWNCC269/8, which in turn cited the MacLeish Committees' Long-Range Policy Statement on German Reeducation incorporated in SWNCC269/5 (August 21, 1946). See Henry J. Kellermann, *Cultural Relations—Instrument of Foreign Policy, U.S.–German Exchange, 1945–54* (Washington, D.C.: U.S. Department of State, Bureau of Educational and Cultural Affairs, 1978), p. 20.

Even though such exchanges had become an official policy of the United States, there were many operating problems on the German side as well as very limited funds, since the government had not included in the Occupation budget any allocation for this purpose. In fact, in all of 1947 there were only eighty-one persons traveling on government funds, and most of these were specialists going to Germany or German leaders going to other countries. Although no students or trainees traveled on government funds, there were perhaps fifty German students attending a variety of American universities under private auspices. It was against this background that I undertook to express to Clay the belief of our staff that the time had come for widespread introduction of German-American exchanges of student scholars, which would of course require appropriation of funds to finance the movement of the Germans to the United States and of the Americans to Germany. I took this idea to Clay early one Sunday morning and found him quite interested in it, but skeptical of its practicality. In fact, he said he believed it was too soon to begin such exchanges; in his opinion American collegiate student bodies, which included a high proportion of veterans, would be antagonistic to the reception of Germans and unpleasant incidents would probably occur. I stood stoutly for our position and finally he said, "If you believe it's not too early and you can get Congress to insert the necessary funds in the appropriation bill for OMGUS, I will support it."

Accordingly, I made a trip to Washington and, with the help of friends in the American Council on Education (ACE), was able to get a modest appropriation put into our budget that enabled us to begin the movement of German students and scholars to American campuses the following September.[6] I am convinced that the successful launching of a widespread exchange program this early in the Occupation was due in large part to the vision and sensitive and astute leadership of Henry Kellermann. There was a rapid increase in the number of exchanges sponsored by the U.S. government, from the 81 in 1947 that I have mentioned to 354 in 1948, of which 232 were Germans going to the United States, 214 of them German exchange students. Clay's fears were not well founded. In fact, the Germans were welcomed wherever they appeared, and the process

6. Clay wrote on my report of the trip to Washington: "Dr. Wells: A lot done in a short time. Thanks again. Please follow Washington developments closely and let me know if you receive any 'flack.' "

of German-American scholarly exchanges, which had been a very important part of the American university scene prior to World War II, was resumed and has continued at an increasing volume ever since. When the Federal Republic of Germany did me the honor of conferring upon me the Commander's Cross of the Order of Merit in 1960, that recognition came in part, I am convinced, because of this initiative. Objective observers believe that the German-American exchange program helped to achieve the cordial relationship that has existed between Germany and the United States in the postwar era. It also was the prototype for the postwar expansion of foreign scholarly exchange as an instrument of American foreign policy. Many of Germany's present political, financial, and academic leaders are alumni of the program.

My other important assignments for that Washington trip were to recruit personnel for our organization in Germany and also to attempt to find the right man to direct the newly reorganized division. We had many vacancies throughout the organization. I addressed a general session of the American Association of School Administrators in Atlantic City, where there were more than ten thousand in attendance, and made a plea for cooperation in our work, explaining to them something of the opportunities and requirements of service in the Occupation. Lieutenant Colonel Irwin of the Civil Affairs Division in Washington accompanied me, and following the speech we were flooded with questions, applications, and requests for interviews during the remaining days of the convention. My speech was reported widely in the United States and thus stimulated many other inquiries. As a result we were able to find people for our vacant positions. The most important task, however, was to find a director of the new Division of Education and Cultural Relations. In pursuit of the proper person, I made contact by letter, personal interview, and long-distance telephone with nearly one hundred persons who I thought had special competence to nominate candidates and to evaluate their qualifications. In this way I accumulated a prospect list of about fifty men. In the course of the recruiting endeavor, a few men were suggested over and over again, principal among these being Alonzo Grace from Connecticut. He paid us a visit in the spring and we were able to recruit him for the position, which he occupied very capably for some two or three years.

My trip to Washington had still other objectives. One was to get some clarification of budgetary matters dealing with the Education and Religious Affairs Branch and the Information Control Division in the reorientation section of the OMGUS budget. I also carried with me proposals to the Rockefeller Foundation requesting funds for certain cultural reorientation projects that had been developed by our staff in Germany. Furthermore, I attempted to initiate a stateside organization of private agencies for the promotion and support of cultural exchange with Germany. George Zook, who had headed the mission previously referred to, at our request called a conference on education in the American zone in Germany to which were invited representatives of the leading associations in education. The conference was held in the National Education Association Building in Washington on February 19, 1948. Out of that meeting grew the Advisory Committee on Cultural and Educational Relations that was formally created in the fall of 1948 under the auspices of the ACE and financed by a grant from the Rockefeller Foundation. It later was renamed the Commission on Occupied Areas and I was from the beginning its chairman; Harold Snyder, a member of the ACE staff, became its executive director. The commission continued for some years under my chairmanship, enabling me to maintain contact with the activities in Germany and perhaps be of help from this side.

I had an unpleasant brush with the Russian military. On one Sunday afternoon, Peter Fraenkel and I had driven into the Russian sector of Berlin to deliver a CARE package to Peter's childhood nurse. Before he and his father had emigrated to South America, Peter had been cared for after the early death of his mother by an old German nurse, whose present welfare concerned him. Berlin, as is well known, was divided into four sectors—American, English, French, and Russian—but, by a four-power treaty, all sectors were open to personnel of all four powers. Enroute home about four in the afternoon from delivering our CARE package, we saw a brightly lit shop in the otherwise dark Potsdamer Platz near the boundary of the American zone. I asked our driver, PFC Wade Ferris, to take us over to see what was going on. Later we learned that it was a fence run by Russian soldiers for antiques taken from German houses. All innocent, Peter asked a Russian soldier nearby if the store was open. The soldier shook his head and, as Peter returned to the car, detained us with an order to halt, reenforced by a gun. We asked repeatedly why we were being held—as we sat in the car, while we were guarded in a building to which we were led, and after we had been taken to headquarters by a young Russian captain. The soldier accused us of driving round and round Potsdamer Platz taking pictures in a manner unfriendly to the Soviet Union. Though it was evident that the charge against us was fabricated because we had no camera, it was two hours before we were released into the custody of an American Military Police captain. We were never in real danger, I suppose, but the detention was discomfiting and unpleasant.

The next morning I went in to report the incident to Clay, who had already learned of it from Intelligence sources. There had been several baseless arrests of American personnel, which were thought to be a method of trying to harass us and to soften us up for the blockade that our intelligence told us the Russians would try to impose. Clay told me that the American newspapers were making much of my arrest because of my rank, and it was being interpreted as a deliberate signal that something was about to happen. He asked me for my assessment of the incident and I replied that I felt it was a green Russian G.I. who had seen an American military car come into Potsdamer Platz and had thought "This is the enemy," hence he should do something about it, and he had stopped us. Clay agreed with my analysis, noting that a regiment of green Russian troops had just arrived in Berlin, many of them from Asiatic Russia, who had never seen a big city before and who hardly knew what to do. He said, "We will have Howley protest vigorously and see what happens"—Colonel Frank L. Howley being the American director of o m g u s for the Berlin sector. Howley did make a strong protest concerning our arrest to his opposite number in the Russian sector of Berlin, who called upon Howley in about two weeks to make a formal apology. The American newspapers barely mentioned the apology, but actually it was more significant than the arrest. Although I was not the only staff member of the American military government ever arrested up to that time, the subsequent apology from the Russians was certainly a rarity.

Another interesting incident involved a number of leading German industrialists who came to lunch at my house one day with Walter Hallstein, rector of the University of Frankfurt and a distinguished economist, supportive of the American Occupation. Hallstein had been a prisoner of war in the United States in Texas and had grown to have a great admiration for Americans because of the treatment he received there. He later was to become the first president of the Commission of the European Economic Community and played a very important role in postwar German and European recovery. At this luncheon, the conversation turned to the dismantling of German industry then in full sway. I remarked that I regretted the fact that our policy might cripple recovery and the future welfare of the German economy. Their response was surprising to me. They smiled and said, in essence, "We are not truly disturbed by this move although we have been protesting loudly. Actually what is happening will be of great benefit to us for the future. You are dismantling our obsolete and worn-out machinery and plants and sending them to our principal competitors in Europe—the Belgians, the French, the Dutch, and the English. As soon as that has been completed you will undoubtedly furnish us capital with which to rebuild our plants, and we will rebuild them incorporating the latest technological advances and consequently have plants of far greater efficiency than those with which we will have to compete. So we will be able to compete as never before." I have thought of that conversation many times since. Nothing could have been more prophetic or accurate. Germany has been able to compete as never before in international trade, in no small part because her factories were all rebuilt along the most modern and efficient lines.

It would be inaccurate to leave the impression that my life in Berlin was too full of serious matters to allow enjoyment of my stay. In my letters home, along with the weather I always mentioned the sights—particularly of flowering trees and blooms—and the sounds. On December 21, I wrote, "During my walk this afternoon, I saw scores of children out coasting with their homemade sleds. Their shouts of joy seemed to fill the air." A few days afterward I entertained some Berlin children in my home and wrote to my parents about it:

> Now I will tell you more about our Christmas party held the day before Christmas. We gathered the children up in the car and brought them to the house. They ranged in age from five to eleven —about half boys and half girls. Before dinner, they looked at magazines such as the *Saturday Evening Post* and *Life* with keen interest because all German children are eager to see the pictures in our magazines. They were extremely well behaved and of course filled with expectancy. We had a turkey dinner with all of the trimmings: soup, turkey, dressing, vegetables, cranberry sauce, fruit cake, and ice cream. There was also all of the milk that the children could

drink. Since the food nearly all came out of army cans, it didn't compare in quality with the dinner I know you had at Aunt Rosie's (she sent me the menu), but it tasted good to the children. They ate and ate. They took small bites to make it go farther, and, until they realized that they could have more than one glass of milk, they sipped it very carefully. The little five-year-old didn't want to eat his turkey. He didn't know what meat was and consequently wasn't sure that it should be eaten.

After dinner, the tree was lighted with real candles and the children were led into the room. The room (in the front parlor) had been closed before dinner and so they saw the tree in all of its glory and surrounded by many gaily wrapped packages. The boys got shoes, the girls dresses and beads, and then all of them received toys, books, packages of cookies, apples, oranges, candy, and nuts. They really had fun. One lad half-way through the opening of his presents said, "My, but I was lucky to get to come." They were so appreciative that I am afraid that I was a little misty-eyed when they told me goodbye. Smitty, my G.I. driver, had located the children and helped organize the party, get the consent of the mothers, etc. He had dinner with me and the children. The maid, the cook, and the gardener also helped generously and joined in the fun around the tree.

Many competent men had been recruited by Clay to help with the complex job of occupation and of helping the Germans to begin the process of restoration and recovery. George McKibbin, a successful Chicago lawyer, who as a young man had been assistant to the president of the University of Chicago, his alma mater, became a close friend. He was Clay's adviser on governmental administration but was always interested in the work of the education division. Robert Murphy, then in mid-career, was the top diplomatic officer in the occupation as political adviser with the rank of ambassador. He was a born diplomat, keen, courteous, and very likable. Later he was to cap his distinguished public career in the post of under secretary of state for political affairs under President Eisenhower. A brilliant young political scientist by the name of Edward Litchfield was in charge of the Civil Administration Division. He became dean of the Cornell School of Business and Public Administration, and finally chancellor of the University of Pittsburgh. (We were to travel to Russia together shortly after he assumed the Pittsburgh post.) I also met for the first time Ruth Woodsmall, a member of a prominent Indianapolis family and an alumna of Indiana University. She was head of the women's affairs section in the Office of Public Affairs. For many years she had been general secretary of the World's Y W C A Council in Geneva and as a byproduct of her travels and investigations had written the definitive book on the status of Moslem women.

There were many other outstanding men and women on the staff, and interaction with several of them has continued from that time to this. Here, too, I first met Landrum Bolling, who was covering the Occupation as a newspaperman. I was subsequently on the board of Earlham College and of the Lilly Endowment, which Bolling headed in succession. Young Frank Banta, now a valuable member of the German department at Indiana University, was in the Education and Cultural Relations Division of O M G U S as acting chief of the Cultural Exchange Branch. Two other Indiana colleagues were with us at that time, Robert Ittner of the German department, who had served for a time as my assistant in the president's office, and A. E. Zucker, then from the University of Maryland but formerly chairman of our German department.

My service in the Occupation was a mindstretching and stimulating experience as well as a very strenuous one—strenuous because of the very nature of the work, strenuous because of my initial unfamiliarity with many of the problems, and strenuous also because of the constant necessity of maintaining some contact with the affairs at Indiana University. Moreover, in addition to the work in Berlin it was necessary for me to come to the United States twice for congressional contacts and to transact other business in connection with the Occupation. I had to return for personal reasons, too. My father became ill during the middle of the year and declined very rapidly. I was called home to be with him and stayed as long as I could but felt I had to return to Germany. Within a week or so after I was back in Berlin, he died tragically and I returned to the United States once more. This, of course, was the most difficult feature of the year. I adored my father and I had a sense of guilt that I had not been able to be with him when he may have needed me most. I had some feeling that, had I been with him, his death could have been avoided. It is difficult even now to accept that event philosophically. My father, mother, and I were a very close-knit family and I felt guilty also about being unable to help Mother during that difficult period. But I had to go back to Germany right away. By late May the principal tasks that we had been assigned were accomplished, and I returned in time for the June Commencement at Indiana University and the opening of summer school.

General Clay had requested that my leave be extended for another six months but, with the G.I. surge onto our campus and the attendant problems of accommodating the influx, my responsibility clearly called me back to the university. It was nevertheless a source of regret that I did not have a longer time to assist with new and emerging problems, but I was gratified that we had had some success in accomplishing my original assignment. General Clay wrote of that effort:

> I am grateful for your letter of 24 July and even more grateful to you for having put our Cultural and Educational program on a sound basis. I can already see the returns.
>
> I am not going to fill the post of Cultural Affairs Adviser for the moment while I watch how Mr. Grace works out. I may call on you for recommendations later though. I do want to count on you for help there and in a consulting capacity here if the need arises.
>
> I know your work here can bring you little returns except in your own satisfaction in having contributed to a great American experiment. That contribution was of high order and, even more important, of lasting effect.
>
> If I can ever be of service, it would be a pleasure to have you call on me to give me at least the opportunity to show in small measure my sincere appreciation.

{21}

○ ○ ○

One World or None

For almost two decades I undertook intermittent assignments related to the United Nations. They began prior to the San Francisco Conference while I was dividing my time between Indiana University and the U.S. State Department at the beginning of the 1940s, and they concluded, for personal reasons, in the waning weeks of 1960. So crucial an initiative for peace as the United Nations concept offered, it seemed to me, deserved what time I and others could afford it. I have never begrudged the days, weeks, and occasionally longer periods I devoted in service to that ideal.

The UNRRA *Conference*

An international conference of forty-four nations was convened on November 10, 1943, at Atlantic City to formulate the program and organization of the United Nations Relief and Rehabilitation Administration (UNRRA). Since I was at that time doing wartime duty four days a week in the State Department as deputy director in charge of liberated areas in the Office of Foreign Economic Coordination, I was chosen to be a member of the U.S. delegation to that conference. It was headed by the assistant secretary of state (for economic matters), Dean Acheson, later to become secretary of state and an increasingly powerful figure in the world of diplomacy and politics.

The headquarters of the conference was at the Claridge Hotel, the newest on the Boardwalk. Offices and rooms of the administrative officers were also at the Claridge, but many of the delegations and the support staff were housed elsewhere. All nations then actively engaged in supporting the war against Nazi Germany had been invited to Atlantic City, and most of them, including our wartime ally Russia, participated. The war, of course, was in full swing and the outcome yet in doubt. Nevertheless, it seemed necessary to begin planning for the relief of the invaded nations after they were liberated. We were in Atlantic City three weeks, and the resulting organization was widely hailed as an important step in planning for the future and for the rehabilitation of areas devastated by the war.

Dean Acheson was made the chairman of the conference, and Herbert Lehman, who had recently left the office of governor of New York and joined the State Department as director of Foreign Relief and Rehabilitation Operations, was elected director general. The choice of Lehman was a popular one with the delegate nations because he was well known and noted for his humane and generous instincts. Although sometimes labeled a poor administrator, he was undeniably distinguished, a man of great ability and, I think, an ideal choice for the position of director general. In that role he carried on the great tradition that had been established by Herbert Hoover in directing relief for Europe following World War I, but Lehman's task was much more important and much more difficult since he had to work with an international organization.

A good deal of political maneuvering and debate attended the formation of the working machinery of the organization. It was dimly realized that, since this was the first of the international organizations to be formed for functioning after World War II, it would probably furnish precedent and pattern for the others and particularly for the United Nations organization itself, which the allied leadership had already begun to dream of and plan for. The spirit of the occasion was partially revealed in the presentation of the delegates, as I wrote at the time in my notes on the conference:

> Over and over again, the speeches voiced determination to make the program work and to cooperate without reservation to that end. Underneath was the realization that internal political problems were involved for most of the countries—for the receiving countries, problems arising out of the certainty that the people will expect more than their leaders can get for them; for the contributing countries, problems occasioned by the fact that the people will resent further or continued restrictions of their own supplies in order to be able to make their contribution. So there is an understanding on the part of all the representatives that genuine cooperation is essential to the building of an international organization that will help absorb some of the internal pressures.

I was assigned to cover three subcommittees of the First Committee, "Organization and Administration," and was made directly responsible for one as the American representative on the conference subcommittee that fashioned the formula for apportioning UNRRA's expenses. This was a hot issue, of course, with every country hoping to be allocated as small a percentage as possible since each would be assessed likewise for the cost of the relief, to be paid either in currency or in kind. The Latin Americans were especially reluctant to accept the formula that was proposed, but they finally did so,[1] and the formula adopted there was incorporated in essentially the same form in the organization of the United Nations at San Francisco. For many years it remained practically unchanged as the formula for assessing the cost of running the United Nations organization and some of its specialized agencies. Although the subject matter was not one of great ideological importance, I found this diplomatic exercise broadening and interesting, revealing the nuances of international relationships and character as expressed in the representatives' reaction to the obligation of paying for the cost of an international humanitarian relief agency.

Many of the nations were represented by relatively young fig-

---

1. An account in my notes made at the time about the Latin American participation is pertinent:

"The Latinos display the same lack of seriousness of purpose in an international conference that they do in civic affairs at home. They are full of speeches and of elaborate phrases of cooperation, but, unlike the other delegates, are likely to spend most of the night in the bar and consequently to miss the early morning sessions. Dean tells the amazing story of how the highest-ranking Latino, a Cuban who is second to Batista, 'lined up' the Latinos on the financial plan. He called them all into a room one day and said, 'Now, we are Latinos together. When matters of principle and expressions of cooperation and so on are of concern, we like to walk in the front door with the greatest display, very obviously and ostentatiously, and make pretty speeches. But when anybody speaks of paying anything, we all run out the back door. Now, if we "belly-ache" all week, we won't get anything adopted, we won't have any plan at all, and we will go home with nothing. I don't think my country will pay the one per cent called for by the present proposal—in fact, I don't have any idea that it will or can—but I am going to recommend it, and I want you all to do the same.'

"The value of the good neighbor policy is thus demonstrated in a most striking fashion. Each of the little Central and South American countries has a vote, and, by and large, all of them follow the United States out of gratitude for and interest and confidence in our intentions toward them. As we go into an era in which there will be more and more international organizations dealing with matters of grave concern to us, the vital significance of the good-neighbor policy becomes more apparent. The eighteen votes represented by these countries are invaluable to us in our position in the world."

ures, then unknown, who were destined to become men of national and international importance. I recall several but shall mention only a few. Jan Masaryk of Czechoslovakia made an indelible impression on me. He was a delightful, charming, witty, and talented man who would have been outstanding in any group. Later he was to have a tragic end when a Communist coup d'etat drove him to what was alleged to be suicide but was felt by many to be murder at the hands of the Communists. Here I first came to know Lester B. "Mike" Pearson of Canada, who took a leading role in the U N for some years, heading several Canadian delegations to the U N after it began functioning in the postwar world and later becoming prime minister of Canada and a world figure. He was always a delightful companion, and we frequently met for a friendly Scotch in the late afternoon. Also I saw the distinguished Sir Girja Bajpai, who was then agent general of India in Washington, D.C. Since India was still a colony of Great Britain, he could not have the title of ambassador, but he was nevertheless a figure of truly ambassadorial prestige and influence. He was Oxford-educated, eloquently articulate, and impeccably groomed. He was an impressive man, for whom I had great admiration. Another memorable figure was Edward G. Miller, Jr., one of Dean Acheson's two top aides and a specialist on Latin American affairs. He was long active in the eastern intellectual establishment as a lawyer and, from time to time, was a member of other important national and international committees and commissions. I had already met Jean Monnet in Washington, but here I saw more of him. He became one of the greatest international leaders in the postwar world and the eloquent and successful exponent of the European community. He was a man of great vision and extraordinary talent. At this conference also I first met Paul-Henri Spaak, Belgium's foreign minister, later to be president of the U N and a dominant figure in international activities for a long time following World War II. Here also I met Carlos Romulo, whom I mention later.

Andrei Gromyko, the U.S.S.R. ambassador to the United States, served as head of the Russian delegation until a delegation arrived directly from Moscow. I had been at meetings with him from time to time in Washington but came to know something of him at this conference. Always guarded in his contacts, he was a man who could be completely charming when socially relaxed. (He prided

himself on the quality of the dry martinis he mixed.) Later I was
to see a great deal of him when I served on the American delegation
to the UN and he was head of the Russian delegation.

Attendance at the UNRRA conference was an excellent experience for me, uninitiated as I was in international conferences. Not
only did I learn how things could be accomplished in an international
gathering, but my acquaintanceship was widened, particularly among
international personalities. In addition, there was the satisfaction
of participating in an organization that seemed destined to become
a very important postwar agency for relief, rehabilitation, and heal-
ing the wounds of war.

Some of the behind-the-scenes activities lent color to our experiences. I recorded several in my notes, one of which is possibly helpful in its glimpse of the Russian mode of operating:

> An amusing incident occurred toward the end of one of the
> afternoon sessions, when the member from Czechoslovakia arose to
> suggest that the council express appreciation for the work done and
> the results achieved at the Moscow conference by Mr. Hull, Mr.
> Molotov, and Mr. Eden. The day previous, the member from Hon-
> duras had proposed that greetings and congratulations be sent to
> Mr. Hull, who had just returned to Washington from Moscow. (The
> Russians were disturbed by the omission of Mr. Molotov from the
> statement and, as a consequence, had brought pressure upon the
> Czechs to present another proposal, which would include him.)
> The issue was delicate because of the tension between the Poles and
> the Russians. Mr. Acheson handled the situation admirably by di-
> recting, when the Czech had concluded, that there be entered on the
> record the statements made by the Honduran and the Czech and the
> fact that they represented the sentiments of the council. He thereby
> avoided the embarrassment of a vote.
>
> Later, Masaryk told me the story, in his inimitable style, of his
> participation in the occurrence. He said that Gromyko, the Russian
> ambassador, who always looks as though he had eaten a very large
> sour pickle, came to him and asked if he would not undertake to
> introduce a resolution thanking Mr. Molotov. Masaryk objected
> slightly, saying that the member from Honduras had opened the
> subject and asking, "Why not let him rise and mention all three
> powers?" Gromyko replied, "Honduras??? Honduras??? It is a very
> small country."
>
> Masaryk also told me that he always did his best, in talking
> with the Russians, to keep reference to the Allies' small losses out of
> the conversation. In that connection, he said that a day or so before

Gromyko had made a remark about "the Italian campaign of two miles," referring, of course, to the distance the American troops had gained that day.

A further observation about the Russians in my notes will be recognized by anyone now experienced in the field as standard practice for U.S.S.R. delegates:

> The Russians are personally charming and are surprisingly young for representatives of a country in which all the young men are supposed to be in the army. Most of the delegation appear not to exceed their middle thirties, and many seem even younger. They are the least talented linguistically of any of the groups and have had to use interpreters rather extensively. I am of the opinion that, politically, they are not yet skilled. They certainly do not understand the give and take of the legislative process; they have had no experience in making those minor adjustments that smooth the progress of debate and yet at the same time do not affect vital principles. When they come into a meeting, they come instructed on certain points, even though the instruction, as revealed by their conversation, indicates an improper understanding of the point at issue, making their objection invalid. Nevertheless, they do not alter their position. This does not render them helpful partners in committee deliberations and thus does not enhance their popularity with their colleagues. The Russian delegation is the only one of which this is true. All the others appear to understand committee and legislative deliberations and to be skillful in participation in them. Part of the inadequacy may grow out of the difficulty with the language. The Russians' enemies, however, insist that they use interpreters even when they do understand, to give them greater protection and longer time for thought. The feeling between the Russians and the Poles is intense and manifests itself at every turn.

The work of the Conference was widely acclaimed in the press at the time and the record of U N R R A in the postwar world fulfilled most of the dreams and ambitions that were held for it at the meeting in Atlantic City. It may be of interest to learn how I viewed the results of the conference at the time:

> As the conference completes its work, there is agreement on all sides that a practical and comprehensive machinery has been devised. If the executive work is as good as the legislative, the success of U N R R A is assured. Likewise, the essential wisdom of the move becomes evident. A system is provided by which the resources of

the entire world are mobilized for most effective use wherever needed, and the burden of sacrifice is distributed. What is even more significant, countries are given an opportunity to work together toward an immediate practical objective and in so doing may learn how easy it is to cooperate in international programs. An organization dealing solely with principles and policy would find it more difficult to function in the beginning, just as any group finds it more difficult to deal with the abstract than with the concrete and the immediate.

Another feature of UNRRA that to me is significant is that relief policies and programs are kept under the jurisdiction of each of the recipient countries involved. There is no patronizing benevolence, no opportunity for well-intentioned but misguided persons of missionary zeal to try to reform and remake countries by performing good-will activities in connection with relief. Individual mores and outlooks will be adequately protected under the system as organized. In my judgment, this is one of the important respects, perhaps, in which this effort differs from the last, and it represents a triumph for our State Department's policy of nonintervention in the business and affairs of other countries. It represents likewise the practice of the department of avoiding the old game of power politics, the sophisticated interpretation of meddling in the affairs of other countries.

In organizations, persons find an opportunity to express themselves and receive the stimulation to put forth their best efforts. Countries react in the same way. This truth was aptly stated by the member of the council from Canada in the evening session of the fifth plenary meeting. "The will of nations," he said, "like the will of peoples, is best aroused and expressed through the workings of responsible and representative organs." Hence, UNRRA probably will stimulate even invaded countries to take a more active part in making their surpluses, wherever they have such surpluses, available for the needs of others. All in all, events, coupled with knowledge of human reactions, augur well for the future.

If one might judge by this conference, he can be led to the belief that international cooperation does not present as many difficulties as might be expected. I am impressed by the fact that the points of similarity and agreement here are greater than the points of dissimilarity and disagreement. Much has been said in the past about the difficulties of legislation in international affairs because of differences in backgrounds, ideals, and languages, which influence our thinking. These differences are more apparent when we see people in their own settings than when we see them in a common setting. In my judgment, this group would have seemed perfectly at home in London, Paris, New York, Indianapolis, Buenos Aires.

The closing session was impressive. It had been well organized by the steering committee and the program arranged and presented to the council in closed session. Unity and harmony were the dominant notes. The feeling was genuine. Various countries had been defeated in proposals that they had advanced during the session but had accepted their defeat gracefully. The conference was a triumph for the democratic process, which involves giving and taking in good spirit. It demonstrated beyond question the feasibility of international deliberative assemblies where there is a determination on the part of all persons to achieve a common purpose. Any international problem could be settled under such circumstances—settled as wisely as the capabilities of the assembled delegates would permit, just as is the case with any legislative body.

The cynic might say that this was an idealistic expression of a naive person, but, even in light of the experience of the past thirty-five years, I still believe in the truth of this conclusion.

My next work with the United Nations came about as a result of my service as chairman of the American Council on Education and is therefore recounted in that section. Suffice it to mention here that I was a consultant at the San Francisco Conference in 1945 and later participated in several Unesco-related bodies.

Service with the United Nations

From the beginning of the U N it has been the policy of the United States government to select representatives to each session of the General Assembly from various walks of life. The thought was that lay representation on our delegation would promote better public understanding of the aims and purposes of the U N. These men and women in turn were given the backup services of professional international civil servants and diplomats. In the early summer of 1957, I was invited by Secretary John Foster Dulles to meet with him to discuss the possibility of my becoming a delegate to the Twelfth Session of the United Nations General Assembly, to be convened in September. As I had been present at San Francisco and had had several international assignments since then, I found the idea exciting, but I told him that I would have to consult with the Indiana University Board of Trustees. The trustees generously granted me permission to undertake this assignment, so from early September until nearly the end of December I served as a member of the U.S. delegation. In this instance again, I attempted to carry on part of my responsibilities at home, a plan that in retrospect I am not sure was wise. It meant that I spent five days in New York and Saturday and Sunday in Bloomington, trying during the weekend to deal with all of the university's problems that needed my attention. I could not have followed such a schedule except for the fact that I had a remarkable team of colleagues who carried on admirably all week and who were ready for consultation and conference over the weekend. Yet managing the two jobs, even though done imperfectly, was an exhausting experience and I probably did not perform my university work as well as I should have on the one hand, nor gain as much from the U N experience as I otherwise might have on the other.

The U.S. delegation was headed by Henry Cabot Lodge, the United States ambassador and permanent representative to the U N. There were five delegates and five deputies on the American team. In addition to Ambassador Lodge and me, the delegates were George Meany and two members of the U.S. House of Representatives, the Honorable A. S. J. Carnahan, and the Honorable Walter H. Judd. It was the custom to alternate between the Senate and the House; one year the House had two members in the delegation and the next year the Senate had two. The deputies were Ambassador James J. Wadsworth, Philip Klutznick (who recently was appointed secretary of commerce in the Carter cabinet), Genoa Washington, Mary Pillsbury Lord, and Irene Dunne.

My deputy was Irene Dunne, the distinguished actress and movie star from California. She was originally a Hoosier, having been born in Madison, Indiana, and I found her a delightful colleague. Although she had not been active in movies in recent years, she was well known to the delegates from abroad because they had seen and admired her pictures. She was a woman of great charm and intellect who had been active in President Eisenhower's campaign in California and whose husband, Francis D. Griffin, had been a successful dental surgeon in California but was said to have become in more recent years a prosperous real-estate operator. An admirable husband, he accompanied Miss Dunne to New York and was with her on every social occasion, attempting whenever possible to guard her against overexertion. Although in quite good health, she was a bit fragile. She was a delight to have as a member of our delegation.

Each delegate who lived outside New York was housed in a suite in the Vanderbilt Hotel not far from the office building in which the headquarters of the American delegation was then located. Ambassador Lodge resided in the top-floor suite of the Waldorf Towers, which for many years has served as the embassy residence for U.S. ambassadors to the U N. It was here that he frequently entertained and carried on the usual social functions associated with an ambassadorial post.

For the first week of the session Secretary Dulles was in New York and met with us. It was customary for the delegation to assemble each morning at nine with the secretary, Cabot Lodge, and our advisers and, after the first week, with Cabot Lodge as the presiding officer of the meeting. During that meeting, which typically lasted about an hour, we were briefed upon the issues that were likely to arise during the day's session and were given instructions about what the United States' position would be on the issues and questions. Also, the work load for the day was assigned then. These sessions were especially interesting during the week or ten days in which the secretary was on hand, for he attempted to share with us as much as possible the broad outlines of American policies. At these morning sessions, in addition to any instructions required for that day's work in the General Assembly, we were given reports on special problems that had arisen in the past twenty-four hours and were assigned to the day's social functions.

The custom was for each country to give a reception for the delegates from the other countries. Representatives of minor countries could afford to miss some of these affairs but the United States, because of its prominence, was expected to be represented at every official social gathering as well as to be present in force at any reception or social function hosted by the United States. Part of the morning routine, therefore, was a review of the list of parties to be given that evening and a call for volunteers to attend them. As a rule all of us received written invitations to each affair, but it was not expected that every member of the delegation would appear, except in a few instances. The congressmen were usually quite busy and a bit blasé about social events. Since George Meany lived in New York and had his own active office to run, he was generally too busy to attend the evening affairs. Miss Dunne was in great demand, but she was always such a popular figure at receptions that they were very wearing experiences for her, and she felt that she could appear only infrequently. Mary Lord, who carried on an active social program of her own, entertaining delegates at her Park Avenue apartment, would usually be unavailable. Thus frequently

Cabot Lodge would look over at me and say something like, "Herman, you're a university president and accustomed to standing in line. You go." As a consequence, at the end of a long and exhausting day in the General Assembly, I found myself nearly every evening with an assignment to attend from one to three receptions. These would be huge receptions held in hotels, ballrooms, in the reception areas of the UN, or at those embassies of the UN members that were located in New York. Mercifully, transportation was provided and, starting about six o'clock, I would go from one affair to another, in each instance staying long enough and working through the crowd sufficiently to make sure the host and others knew that the United States was represented there. Then I was off to the next one, following the same procedure, and finally after the third, which would end about ten, I would be driven to the Oyster Bar in the Grand Central Station, where I would have oyster stew before going on down to the Vanderbilt and falling in bed exhausted. Hand shaking, conversation, and representation left no time for food or drink during the social affairs. On these occasions one frequently could pick up bits of useful information to report to our delegation the next morning, and so the affairs were useful, not only in getting the delegates acquainted with each other, but also in providing a means for informal communication. Occasionally the cocktail-reception routine was broken by an assignment to attend a black-tie dinner given by an important organization in one of the New York hotels that was of a nature to require the attendance of some member of the U.S. delegation.

Each delegate with his alternate was given a regular committee assignment and sometimes special, ad hoc committee assignments for shorter periods of time, but my particular assignment for the whole of the session was Committee IV, which dealt with trusteeships including non–self-governing territories. Also I was one of five delegates appointed to serve on the Special Political Committee, which helped to share the work of the First Committee. The First Committee was concerned with political and security affairs, including the regulation of armaments, and thus had more work than could be done by a single committee. But for the most part my duties were connected with the Fourth Committee, which had on its agenda for the session particular items: the treatment of Indian and Pakistan minorities in the Union of South Africa; the whole question of southwest Africa, a question still very much in the arena;

the future of French Togoland; the boundary dispute between Ethiopia and Italian Somaliland, an issue that is somewhat active yet; and, above all else, the African territories' severance of their colonial ties with Europe and the creation of independent states.

Work that went on in the Fourth Committee eventuated over time in the creation of several of the smaller African states. The pressure for liberation and independence was enormous, and during the 1950s and early 1960s country after country severed its colonial ties, redefined its borders, and became members of the UN. We realized at the time that a number of these new so-called countries were in each case simply the territory of a particular ethnic or tribal group. The former national lines had been drawn arbitrarily by European conquerers in the last century without regard to homogeneous populations. Moreover, many of these units were quite small, and there was a question in some quarters whether these countries could be both economically and politically viable once they acquired independence. Yet the pressure for independence, supported by world opinion, was so strong that nothing was likely to halt the creation of the new countries. Now, in retrospect, it can be clearly seen that we have a number of nonviable units in Africa as well as in Oceania and elsewhere in the world. In time these units may find it desirable to regroup by confederation or some other method into larger units that will be economically and politically viable.

To return to the morning briefing—after it was over, we went off to our several assignments at the UN headquarters building, taking our seats with our delegation when there was a plenary session, but more frequently taking our assigned seats in the particular committee session scheduled for the day. In addition to participating in the work of the committees, we occasionally had to speak for the United States in the Great Council Chamber of the UN on some issue growing out of a committee recommendation to a plenary session. I had that experience on one occasion and found it awesome and nerve-racking. However, there was one advantage. We did not have to write our own speeches on such occasions. The official positions of the United States were arrived at by a procedure that began with a discussion among our delegates in their morning session. There we received as background the information that the delegates had picked up from speeches in their respective committees. This information was forwarded to Washington where the official position of the United States was formulated and where a speech was written to be presented by the assigned delegate on the committee or in the plenary session. This was the manner of proceeding for all the important policy questions. Of course, on minor questions we were free to speak within the limits of what we knew policy to be, but for the most part policy was formulated in Washington and sent to us daily, which was as it should have been. Otherwise the United States government's position could not have been consistent and would certainly have been puzzling, to say the least.

The work of my own committee was extremely interesting because of the very nature of the material, the topics with which we dealt, and the problems and questions to which we were asked to address ourselves. It was made delightful as well by the fact that our presiding officer was Thanat Khoman of Thailand, ambassador to the United States and a member of the Thai delegation. He later became world famous as the foreign minister of Thailand. Having become a good friend, he came to Bloomington to visit from time to time, occasionally to speak or simply to play golf and later to see his beautiful daughter, Thavida, when she was a student at Indiana University. I have valued his friendship through all the years since those U N days. Khoman's secretary and adviser was Hans Wieschhoff, formerly of the University of Pennsylvania, an authority on the problems of Africa particularly and consequently a valuable resource in directing our deliberations.[2] He too became a fast friend. I made many friends among the delegates on that committee, and soon a good deal of camaraderie developed among us; we became a sort of special fraternity with loyalty to the Fourth Committee and to each other. This made our deliberations easier, especially when we were dealing with delicate problems.

At the beginning of the session controversy arose over who would be elected president of the General Assembly. Sir Leslie Munro, New Zealand's ambassador to the United States and permanent representative to the U N, was chosen president and served admirably. The secretary general of the U N, a distinguished Swedish scholar-diplomat, Dag Hammarskjöld, was very impressive in his role. I soon became acquainted with him and had the privilege of dining with him at his apartment from time to time. On those occa-

---

2. H. A. Wieschhoff was the acting director of the Department of Trusteeship and Information from the Non–Self-Governing Territories. He was listed as one of two secretaries of the Fourth Committee.

sions he loved to talk about academic and intellectual subjects as a relief from the day-to-day problems of the U N. Four years after this session he was killed in an airplane accident on a U N mission in Africa. He was accompanied on that occasion by Hans Wieschhoff, whose daughter was then at Indiana University, and it was my sad duty to tell Virginia that her father, whom she adored, had just died in a tragic accident along with the secretary general.

Always at the right hand of the secretary general as executive assistant and under secretary was a remarkable Hoosier, Andrew Cordier, who for many years had been a professor at Manchester College in the fields of history and political science and who had also taught concurrently most of that time at Indiana University's Fort Wayne extension center. During his active career as a teacher in Indiana, Cordier had been one of the leading voices throughout the state in the promotion of international cooperation. He had made hundreds and hundreds of speeches at luncheon clubs, women's clubs, and the like on the subject of international relations. He first entered the national political scene by becoming a speech writer, along with Ross Bartley, for Alfred Landon during Landon's unsuccessful bid for the presidency, but from that task he went on to serve as a technical expert with the U.S. delegation to the San Francisco Conference for the formation of the U N and continued with the U N until he reached retirement age. Then he became dean of the new Graduate School of International Affairs at Columbia University and later served two years as president of the university. When we met at the U N I had known and admired him for many years. He was gracious and helpful to me during my U N service. It was comforting to me to see his lively and interesting presence on the platform next to the secretary general at every plenary session. He was the man to whom the secretary general and the presiding officer turned for parliamentary advice or for the answer to some question of fact. He knew more about the U N than any other individual and played a major role in holding the organization together and keeping it alive during its formative years.

To return from this tangent—as delegates we had an enormous amount of work to do. I have already mentioned the day-after-day attendance at meetings frequently lasting for hours and the exhausting round of social affairs. Moreover, the social side of the assignment called for entertaining groups of U.S. citizens from all over the country who came to visit the U N. Their visits frequently required that some members of the U.S. delegation meet them in one of the rooms in the UN building set aside for such a purpose and explain to them the work of the current session. I remember speaking to several groups from Indiana and to one from Louisville. I suppose we were assigned to this chore according to the nature of the group.

Being a delegate required a tremendous amount of study. Prior to the opening session heavy documentation had been prepared for our understanding and for background on the major issues that were expected to arise. Documentation continued to flow to us from Washington and from the UN Secretariat daily during the session. Just to keep up with the paper work would have been a hard, full-time job, but reading had to be crowded in with everything else. Fortunately we had a very able team of career State Department advisers, for the most part young men who were bright, alert, and well versed in all the technicalities of the questions before us. I grew to respect and admire them. One for whom I formed a special liking was Thomas Bartlett. During the session he confided in me his desire to become a college president. He had already won his Ph.D. degree and had reputable scholarly credentials. In due course he was able to achieve his ambition when he was chosen president of the American University in Cairo, and I had the privilege of being one of his trustees during part of his tenure there. He resigned from that position to succeed President Everett Case at Colgate University, where he had a successful career in educational administration. The diplomatic service suffered from his defection to education, but education has gained greatly.

Of the U.S. delegation I found each member interesting and worthwhile. It was my first opportunity to observe George Meany at close range, for whom I formed great respect. I developed affection and admiration for Mary Lord, with whom I worked in a variety of causes until her death in 1978. She was one of the most public-spirited and interesting women of our generation. It was a privilege to be associated with Philip Klutznick, a remarkable business leader from Chicago who has given much of his time to public service and to major responsibilities in B'nai B'rith. I formed an excellent opinion of Henry Cabot Lodge. He is a man of intellect, courage, and great ability. As chairman he was incisive and articulate. All in all he gave us excellent leadership and spoke on the principal occasions for the United States' interest in a courageous manner. He was then at the center of the controversy (the cold war) we were having with the Russians.

The Russians were housed in a handsome mansion on Park Avenue and entertained frequently. Andrei Gromyko was the head of the Russian delegation at that time. Since we had known each other slightly in Washington during the war, he would always recognize me when I went through the receiving line. He had given two parties and at each of them I had been the single UN delegate to appear. On the third occasion, as I went down the line, Gromyko, obviously conscious that the rest of the delegation had cut the previous two parties, looked at me with a somewhat sardonic twinkle in his eye and said, "You here again?" As he was normally an impassive man, I chuckled to myself and related the experience to Cabot Lodge and the delegation the next morning for their amusement.

In addition to the formal sessions, the formal meetings of the committees and subcommittees, and the plenary sessions, and in addition to the formal social affairs, a great deal of business was transacted by the delegates in the Delegates' Lounge outside the General Assembly chambers. In this respect, the UN is similar to the U.S. Congress or, I suppose, to legislative bodies any place in the world. It was necessary to spend some time in the Delegates' Lounge in informal conversation over a cup of coffee or a drink to iron out some misunderstanding in a committee discussion or to gather information that would be useful for the next committee session and in this way advance one's work.

There were only 82 members of the UN at the Twelfth Session in contrast to the 150 or so members at the present. Nevertheless, the annual meetings of the General Assembly attracted to New York the leading world figures of the day: kings, queens, prime ministers, top journalists, intellectuals, representatives of various international organizations—all made their appearance in the UN, either in the corridors or in formal sessions during the weeks that the General Assembly met. Every day was a colorful scene regardless of what was going on. The delegates themselves were for the most part men and women of prominence in their own countries. Some countries followed our policy of having lay delegates, some followed the policy of having only professionals, but all countries whether or not they had professionals as official delegates had some of their principal statesmen there for all or part of the Twelfth Session. The opening statement for the United States at the General

Assembly is made by the president or the secretary of state. Frequently the heads of state of other countries came to New York to make their delegations' opening statements for the session, each enunciating the aims, purposes, and ambitions that his or her country held for that session. This provided a rare opportunity to see the great and near-great of the world in action, to hear them speak, and frequently to meet them.

I found my contact with many of the delegates stimulating and interesting, men such as Prince Wan of Thailand, tall, handsome, distinguished in appearance, warm and humane, universally recognized for his wisdom and experience. He perfectly illustrated the fact that small countries could make an uncommon contribution to the work of an international body by reason of the quality of their representation. In other words, it is not necessary to represent a major country to make an important contribution to world thinking. General Carlos Romulo of the Philippines, an old friend of mine, was also an active and influential figure among the delegates. After many years of diplomacy, he served as president of the University of the Philippines but is now again in public service as his country's secretary of foreign affairs. He is one of the most durable of the statesmen of the World War II period.

A great deal of color and drama is present at a session of the General Assembly: the beautiful building in which the work is carried on; the cosmopolitan group of delegates representing now every conceivable corner of the globe, many of them very colorful and distinguished people, with their staffs; the appearance of top leadership on significant occasions. I remember the queen of England, speaking for the United Kingdom at the Twelfth Session, as did the king of Morocco for his nation. All of this imparts a sense of drama and importance, and inspires awe. The five months were provocative, enlightening, and exciting, but also very strenuous. I became convinced from my inside view that the reporting of the work of the UN is very inadequate and that therefore only the few people who have the opportunity to see the internal workings come to understand something of the UN's nature. It is not a perfect instrument; as it is a relatively new agency still, anything like perfection would be miraculous. The only power that it actually has is the power of persuasion through world opinion, and we have seen such power effective on several occasions, though ineffective on others. I gained increasing respect for the UN as I became more familiar with it. It

With Karl Detzer, distinguished Hoosier author, just before he is
awarded an honorary LL.D. degree by President John Ryan
at Commencement, Fort Wayne campus, 1979.

Peter Fraenkel saw Mother and me off to Europe on the *Queen Elizabeth*, July, 1963.

At the board meeting of the International Association of Universities at the University of Moscow, 1964.

Members of Mortar Board with Mother, who was made an honorary
member in 1964.

I still enjoy playing Santa Claus after a third of a century—and
the suit still fits!

As surrogate for President Joseph Sutton, Commencement, Southeast campus, 1969.

At a chilly Little 500 race.

Congratulating Thomas D. Clark on completion of his history of Indiana University.

A pleasant privilege of my chancellorship is the reception of distinguished visitors, here the ambassador from Mali.

Hosting the Shenyang Acrobatic Troupe in Indianapolis, 1972.

A summer's walk to work, with a pedometer registering the mileage.

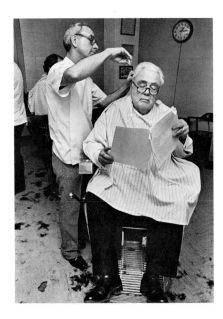

A haircut at the Student Union Barbershop, 1980.

certainly facilitates quiet personal diplomacy along with public debate. I honestly believe that, given time and the support of the nations of the world, it can do much to build a peaceful and better world community.

Lay delegates are rarely reappointed to the delegation of the U N. Perhaps it was unfair to Indiana University for me to have undertaken this assignment at a very dynamic period in the life of the institution; it would certainly not have been fair to my vice-presidential and other administrative colleagues to have extended this burden on them for a second year. Moreover, this service in a strict sense violated a principle enunciated by the university's trustees that I should take on outside duties only if they were concerned with education. However, because of the special nature of this invitation, the trustees had been quite agreeable to my serving.

I maintained contact with Dag Hammarskjöld until his death and active personal contact with Andy Cordier until his death recently, and throughout the years with Thanat Khoman. I also kept in touch with others with whom I had made friends there. My only other official work for the U N, however, came when the secretary general, Dag Hammarskjöld, asked me to join what was designated as the Committee of Experts on the Review of the Activities and Organization of the Secretariat and to make recommendations as to how the U N Secretariat might function more effectively. This work began on May 17, 1960, and continued till 1961.

Committee of Experts to Review Activities and Organization of the United Nations Secretariat

Considerable criticism of the U N arose among member governments during the 1950s. The Russians, the English, and the Americans were especially critical of the lack of efficiency of its operation and its cost to member governments. As a consequence the Fourteenth Session of the General Assembly passed a resolution on December 5, 1959, requesting the secretary general "to appoint a committee of experts composed of six persons," later made eight, "with broad and practical experience in various aspects of administration, chosen with due regard to geographical distribution in consultation with the respective Governments, to work together with the Secretary-General in reviewing the activities and organization of the Secretariat of the United Nations with a view to effecting or proposing further measures designed to insure maximum economy and efficiency" in the work of the organization and especially the Secretariat.[3] The committee was to report to the secretary general, and it was expected that the committee would have provisional recommendations ready for the next session (the Fifteenth) of the UN General Assembly, and the final recommendations were to be made to the Sixteenth Session.

The four countries that sponsored the resolution—the U.S.S.R., the United Arab Republic, the United Kingdom, and the United States, were asked to send representatives, as were Colombia, France, Ghana, and India. Several months after the resolution was adopted, Andrew Cordier phoned and notified me that the State Department had submitted four names from which the committee member representing the U.S. would be selected and that I was one of them. Cordier hoped that I would be selected and, in that event, that I would accept. In due course Secretary General Dag Hammarskjöld, after consulting with our State Department and particularly with Cabot Lodge, invited me to join the group. I did so reluctantly because I was already committed to attend the third general conference of the International Association of Universities in Mexico City during early September and, following that, preparations were necessary for the Indiana General Assembly session from January to March.

The committee made an interim report on schedule to the Fifteenth Session of the United Nations General Assembly. However, at that session a new element was injected into our work. The Russians made an all-out attack on the Secretariat, its location, and the structure of the UN. Nikita Khrushchev, speaking for the Russians, declared that the single post of secretary general had outlived its usefulness and that the executive body of the UN should be made up of three persons: one representing the military blocs of the Western powers, one coming from the socialist states, and one from the neutralist countries. The Russians further recommended the UN should be moved to another location—perhaps Switzerland, Austria, or even the U.S.S.R. Our interim report helped to relieve some of the pressure for an immediate response to Khrushchev's call for change, but this new turn of events entailed an expansion of the committee's study and report for final action.

3. Resolution adopted by the General Assembly [on the report of the Fifth Committee (a/4336)] on December 5, 1959.

With our charge broadened, I felt I could not afford to give the resulting increased amount of time to the work of the committee and thus resigned in February, 1961. My replacement was L. M. Goodrich, professor of International Organization and Administration at Columbia University, who was an expert on the Charter of the United Nations and therefore admirably competent to deal with the newly raised questions on the structure itself, an entirely different matter from what our original charge had been, namely, the efficiency and operation of the Secretariat in its existing form. Other representatives also felt they had to resign at that time, but some original members continued, and a final report was made to the Sixteenth Session. I should add that the change in the nature of the work of the committee would have made it undesirable for me to continue to serve, even if I had had the time. I was completely out of sympathy with the Soviet recommendations and I could not have been an impartial participant.

For a year or two I maintained some personal contacts with the Secretariat and with members of the permanent delegations by stopping in occasionally at the Delegates' Lounge and the General Assembly as long as the doorkeepers recognized me and thought I belonged there. But after a time my visits dwindled and then ceased. I doubt that I could find a doorkeeper who would recognize me now.

[22]

o   o   o

An Unusual Mission
to the U.S.S.R.

M Y AWAKENING interest in Russia and its people grew
     steadily as I came to know individual Russians at the UN
San Francisco Conference and later on at UNRRA and Unesco
committee meetings and in the UN General Assembly. Some of my
colleagues here at Indiana University visited Russia in an effort to
activate a U.S.-Russia exchange of scholars, and I learned from
them something of the Russian scene. All of these contacts with
Russian diplomats and American experts on Russia whetted my ap-
petite to see Russia itself and to try to learn something, if I could,
about that enormous land and society so different from our own.
Russia was not hospitable to mere tourists and did not have the facilities to handle them. However, as part of its propaganda effort,
it did spend a considerable amount of money and time on officially
sponsored visits, mainly by delegations from Third World and Communist Bloc countries, which came in large numbers.

In the summer of 1958 I was offered an opportunity to visit
Russia that would be of benefit to the university as well as to me.
At that time, Edward H. Litchfield, who had served with me on the
staff of General Lucius Clay in Germany, was chancellor of the
University of Pittsburgh and also chairman of the board of the Governmental Affairs Institute in Washington, D.C. A resourceful man
with many international contacts, he had been able to arrange for
a group of seven university presidents, in company with six other
persons, to visit Russia. Litchfield's mission also included Franklin
D. Murphy, chancellor of the University of Kansas; Deane Malott,
president of Cornell; T. Keith Glennan, president of Case Institute
at Cleveland; Harry D. Gideonse, president of Brooklyn College;

Gaylord P. Harnwell, president of the University of Pennsylvania; H. Philip Mettgers, vice president of the Governmental Affairs Institute; Frank H. Sparks, president of the Council for Financial Aid to Education; Alan Scaife, president of the board of trustees of the University of Pittsburgh and Fellow of Yale University. Four wives including Mrs. Scaife accompanied us, adding an element of charm and grace to our party.

Our trip was undertaken because of the enormous curiosity, aroused by the success of Sputnik, on the part of the American people and especially American educators to learn more about Russian education. We viewed our visit as an opportunity to observe the Russian system carefully and, upon our return, to report formally to the higher educational community as well as to other interested segments of the American population. The report that we published on our return did receive widespread attention, both in the press and in educational circles, and, I believe, served its purpose well.[1]

It was the custom of the Russians to arrange trips such as ours as exchanges: that is, having invited us, they expected to pay our expenses in Russia and, in return, have a group of Russians invited to the United States with all of their expenses in the United States paid here, thus overcoming the Russian handicap of a shortage of dollar exchange. Since we wanted to be as independent as possible, to have our trip as little monitored and circumscribed as we could manage, we declined the hospitality of the Russians and did not have to reciprocate with similar sponsorship on this side. Our offer to pay our own way was unprecedented in the experience of the Russians. Though hesitant to accept an arrangement that departed from their acceptable pattern of visits, they eventually agreed.

We were able to be financially independent because of the generosity of the Scaife Foundation. Its officers, who were also two of its principal donors, accompanied us on the trip. Both Alan and Sarah Scaife were deeply interested in higher education. Both liked exotic and even difficult, out-of-the-way places. Although they were not professional educators, they knew enough about the field and about the world to be stimulating members of our group. They were delightful traveling companions.

Prior to our leaving, Litchfield had been able to negotiate successfully with the Russians for a rather extensive trip to include

1. *Report on Higher Education in the Soviet Union* (Pittsburgh: University of Pittsburgh Press, 1958).

not only Moscow and Leningrad, the usual objectives of visitors, but also Tbilisi, Samarkand, Tashkent, and Alma-Ata. Although our visit was privately financed, we had the status of an official American educational mission, which was valuable to us in gaining access to information. Our sole objective was to have a look at Russian higher education; we were the first group of university presidents to do so after World War II. We were well briefed before we left and the mission was carefully organized. In each city we divided ourselves into teams of one, two, or three, and each team took a different assignment. Although our trip lasted only 15 days, by hard traveling and careful planning we managed an accumulative total of 150 observation days. The effectiveness was increased as we shared our observations with each other.

We were received cordially, both officially and privately, everywhere we went and were shown what we asked to see, except for the Party schools, that is, institutes that train young Communist Party leaders. Not only were the students there given a complete political indoctrination, they were trained in executive management as well. Thus the Party schools were in a particular sense comparable to the executive-development institutes run by American universities for both industry and labor. Graduates of the Party schools were placed in factories to ensure political conformity and, importantly, to stimulate production to meet government goals. (One was placed in every faculty senate for similar reasons.)

We early learned that the years of misunderstanding and propaganda had produced many misconceptions about American society among Russians in general. We were asked frequently about the treatment of the American Indian, racial segregation in the schools, starvation and unemployment, and the hard lot of the American student. The propaganda line of the Party concerning our economic and social order had been implanted in the average Russian. Yet, surprisingly, the individual Russians we met without exception were friendly to us and were interested in learning all they could about America, particularly about its music and authors.

We had accurately anticipated that education, Russian style, or at least research had a very high priority in the U.S.S.R. because of the dramatic evidence of it just nine months earlier when the Russians startled the world by launching the first Sputnik on October 4, 1957. The high importance granted education in Russia was in a way illustrated by the principal facility of the University of Moscow. Just completed, this imposing building was then the highest in all of Europe and contained thousands of rooms and a library of 5,500,000 volumes. Other construction was underway and, on my last trip to Russia in 1975, I observed that there were many additional buildings located on the spacious grounds of the university. In the nine years preceding our visit in 1958, more than $200 million had been invested in the physical plant.

We devoted quite a bit of time to the University of Moscow, which we found awesome because of the immensity of its physical plant, the extent of its scholarly resources, and the quality of its faculty. We were told about the massive outlay, not only for buildings, library facilities, and technical equipment, but also for scholarships that made it possible for 80 percent of the students to attend the university at the cost of the state, if their academic credentials warranted. We learned that teaching at the university level is one of the highest-paid professions in the Soviet Union and that a faculty-to-student ratio of one-to-ten prevailed. It was quite apparent that, because of education's high priority, a people that formerly had great pockets of illiteracy had become almost wholly literate even in the remote provinces. There was an extensive array of facilities for training in certain specialties that U.S.S.R. officialdom seemingly deemed most important to the state. Yet, impressive as all this was, we were mindful that only 20 percent of the students completing secondary school were permitted to continue their education.

It should be said that we were also made aware of official Soviet interest in outshining the United States in conspicuous aspects of higher education: buildings, research facilities, faculty salaries, and financial support. Contrary to a general impression, the Russian bureaucracy encourages competition—competition to excel, to be productive, to achieve designated standards, and to better previous performance. For such accomplishments there are nonfinancial rewards in the form of various recognitions spelled out in advance to stimulate maximum effort.

We found one of the principal differences between the Soviet system and ours to be the fragmentation of their curriculum in higher education. There were at that time thirty-nine universities and between seven and eight hundred technical institutes, that is, specialized professional schools. Nearly all the specialties, with the exception of law and journalism, were offered in individualized institutions. For example, the Institute of Agriculture was connected with the Ministry of Agriculture, and the Institute of Medicine was part of the Ministry of Health; even the Institute of Music had bureaucratic ties through the Ministry of Culture. But in every case the curriculum, the admissions policy, textbooks, and numerous other policy matters were decided by the central Ministry of Higher Education. Of course, this fractionated system of training specialists made cross-fertilization of ideas between members of different faculties and student bodies difficult, and from an administrative standpoint it seemed to be a rather expensive system, running up a very high overhead cost. Additionally, students would find it prohibitively difficult to change fields. As far as we could ascertain, there were great gaps in the curriculum—for example, in the behavioral sciences —as might be expected in such a system.

Every university we visited had extensive library holdings that included a large section of up-to-date foreign journals. Apparently reading is a popular pastime among the Russians as bookstores were crowded, and we were told that there was a flourishing black market in new paperback editions of both contemporary and classical works. Correspondence study is widespread, and industry provides workers released time to go to the campus for study and examinations, all expenses paid. Abundant use is made of museums as an educational resource.

Of course, education was clearly geared to the needs of the state with resulting overspecialization, rote learning, rigidity punctuated by sudden changes, intellectual isolation, absence of a community of scholars, and no real academic freedom. In this regard, the number of women in higher education (51 percent of all students) should be mentioned. In some fields such as pedagogy and the arts (78 percent), medicine (69 percent), agriculture (44 percent), and technical institutes (39 percent), the percentage of women students was much higher than in comparable fields in America. Women held positions as directors and rectors, and more than a third of the faculty and the researchers were women. But at the highest level, members of the Academy of the U.S.S.R. and Doctors of Science, less than 10 percent were women.

Continuing from secondary schools, there was an emphasis on language training within the universities and specialized institutes as well as in the institutes dealing solely with languages. We learned that all university students must take work in professional education and be prepared to teach if, after graduation, they were assigned to a teaching post. A graduate is more or less obligated to accept a proffered post no matter where it is located. As the rector of the University of Moscow expressed it, the student was not forced to accept the post; he could refuse if he wished to—refuse and starve. The stress on science, which has now become well known to all the world, did not surprise us, but we were impressed by the great encouragement and support of certain of the humanities. They are nurtured and developed on an unprecedented scale, especially music, drama, theater, opera, ballet, radio, and television. For some reason physical education is important to the Russian bureaucracy, and each student was required to take a total of 136 hours of it in the first two years of higher education. We observed a strong interest also in history—history rewritten in terms of Russian ideology— and we noticed considerable activity in the field of archaeology. In the years since then, Russian archaeologists have made great discoveries and valuable contributions to that science.

An incident during our Moscow visit may be of interest. Before leaving Bloomington, I had been charged by my colleague, Roy Harris, the late distinguished American composer then on the faculty of the Indiana University music school, to carry recordings of some of his recent symphonies to the eminent Russian composer, Dimitri Shostakovich. Harris and Shostakovich had corresponded through the years, had met, and they had high respect for each other professionally. Soon after I arrived in Moscow, I told our Intourist representative that I wished to see Shostakovich and I told him the reasons why. The young man first said that would be impossible but upon my insistence agreed to inquire. He came back the next day to say that Shostakovich was out of town, but I continued pressing the fellow and finally I had a favorable answer: on such-and-such a day Shostakovich would receive me in his apartment.

At the appointed hour we went to the apartment, which was in one of the new apartment buildings in Moscow (they all look alike), and took the rickety elevator up to the fifth floor, as I remember it. In Moscow at that time the elevators only carried passengers up; they had to walk down. The minds that had created Sputnik could have mastered this relatively simple technical principle had anyone thought it important to do so. I was received by a maid and invited into a room that apparently served as a combination sitting-dining room. I suppose the closest counterpart in American life would be the "family room." We sat around a big table that I am sure was used also for dining. Shostakovich entered after a few minutes, obviously quite nervous at receiving me. Although he had received the Lenin Award, had received the title People's Artist of the U.S.S.R., and was held in high esteem, he seemed frightened to have face-to-face contact with an American, a condition that saddened me. I could only assume that he feared a black mark against his record because of my visit. Through an interpreter we had a pleasant conversation about music, and I delivered the records with Roy Harris's cordial greetings. Tea was served, and at the end of about half an hour or so we left.

I had a chance to have a glance at the apartment. It was much more spacious, I am sure, than the typical Russian apartment, but it was furnished in a very plain and humble fashion notwithstanding the fact that its tenant was a man at the very pinnacle of the Russian musical world. I was told that he had in addition to this apartment a country place that he frequented, and as a star artist he must have had adequate income, but, unless he really preferred simple surroundings, it would appear that there was little he could buy with his rubles. This revealing glimpse of how a world figure, a man among the artistic elite, lives in Russia lingers hauntingly in my memory of that trip.

I should say here that the contrast between public buildings and private accommodations was startling. We observed that homes and apartments were meager to modest, that people had few clothes and personal effects, and that there were very few personal luxuries. "On the other hand," as our report stated, "they have quite extraordinary public facilities. The theaters are elaborate and in some cases most attractive. The drama, choral, ballet, and opera groups which perform in the theaters are very good indeed. Schools, libraries, museums, parks, and similar public facilities are distinctly superior. They are very extensively used and appear to be deeply appreciated."[2] Russia is a land of collective glamour and individual austerity.

It is also a land of amazing paradoxes: a common roller towel in the most modern of jet airplanes; streets filled with automobiles, but a driver pours water on the engine of his car to cool it; in a jet plane a woman sitting on her baggage in lieu of a seat; great scien-

2. Ibid., p. 12.

tific and technical accomplishment and yet poor, disorganized service everywhere.

Our next stop was Leningrad. Moscow had impressed me as drab, somber, and uninteresting, and our hotel there was Grand Central style on the inside and Atlantic City on the outside. In contrast Leningrad is a European-style city—pleasanter and brighter than Moscow—and our hotel was of European type. At the University of Leningrad we had the privilege of meeting with the faculty senate and found this a stimulating experience. Leningrad is also a very distinguished university, typically a little less rigid in its ideological position than is the University of Moscow. The farther we got from Moscow, the more relaxed the societies and universities seemed to be. We found Tbilisi beautiful and the Georgian people a joy. Notwithstanding the fact that it was Stalin's home state, the Georgians seemed to be quite uninterested in what went on in Moscow. According to my notes made at the time, the city has "lovely parks, cool and shaded fountains, two beautiful stadia, beautiful formal walks and flower beds—cool shaded areas. A toy railroad for the children run by the children and given an educational twist." Baku I remember as simply a great oil center, but Samarkand was interesting because of its historical background and the contributions that had been made there to science. Tashkent we found quite rewarding; there we met with the equivalent of a city council as well as with university representatives, and we asked questions and were answered freely.

While at Tbilisi, we spent a day at a collective farm 150 miles away. There we were greeted quite hospitably by farmers and their wives. The grape harvest had just been concluded, and the new wine, fermented only a few days, was ready for testing. Our visit coincided with the typical new-wine festival they celebrated. They had spread under the vineyards and fruit trees, for our enjoyment and their own, great tables laden with all kinds of Russian foods—fish, chicken, goat, suckling pig, salads, cucumbers, tomatoes, cheese, bread, and yellow cherries—and there were huge kegs of the new wine to be consumed. We ate and we drank and we had a great time discussing agriculture and education and our respective ways of life. They were particularly interested in farming, about which Deane Malott and I could talk a little, more perhaps than some of the others. As the afternoon wore on, it became evident that there was to be a contest between the Russians and ourselves as to who could consume the most new wine. Alan Scaife and I early determined that we would not let the Russians beat us, regardless of what the drinking did to us. So with toast after toast and our arms intertwined in Russian fashion, we drank the new wine. All our people except Alan and me dropped out early, and the Russians gradually dropped out too, one after another, until in the end Alan and I were the only persons still drinking and we were declared the victors. It was a Pyrrhic victory at best as was evident soon after we had taken our farewells and were out of sight of our hosts, but Alan and I had been in no mood to cede anything to the Russians.

As we came back to Tbilisi in the evening, most of our party went up to a funicular to have a look at the city from the air. I went on to the hotel, since I am not exactly addicted to funiculars, and there I found our young Intourist representative greatly agitated. He reported that Moscow had just phoned to say that Khrushchev was coming to Tbilisi the next morning and that the plane we were to have taken at ten A.M. had been cancelled. As a consequence, we would have to leave at four A.M. I told the young man that the plan was quite impossible: our party had not packed and would probably not get back to the hotel until about midnight. It would be impossible for us to leave before the regularly scheduled time. He became even more agitated, insisting that it was absolutely necessary for us to get out of the hotel since Khrushchev's party would need our rooms when they arrived in mid-morning. As I suspected that this was a change made merely for the convenience of the transportation system, I repeated that the arrangement was impossible. I also advised him that, if the regular plane had been cancelled, he should call Moscow and have a special plane sent down —that we should be glad to charter a plane to take us away at the regularly scheduled time the next morning. By then the young man was thoroughly upset and arguing that he could not do that—that there was no system of plane chartering in Russia and that it simply could not be arranged. He then began pleading with me, "Dr. Wells, if you will tell the group when they come in at midnight that they have to leave at four A.M., they will do so." I flatly refused, adding, "It's your problem. We'll not leave the hotel until time to go to the airport, which means we'll be here until about nine o'clock, and you can work it out however you wish." He went away in a state of great distress and, so I was told, telephoned Moscow that he had a group of crazy Americans on his hands who would not leave and that something had to be done. Well, just as I had suspected, the authorities could and did arrange for a plane to pick us up at the scheduled time the following morning. Between ten and eleven a special plane arrived from Moscow and we were its sole passengers enroute to Baku, Samarkand, and Tashkent over a wild and barren land. This was one of the first of my several brushes with Russian bureaucracy, all of which have amused and, in a way, delighted me.

At Alma-Ata we found a delightful, nearly pioneer city, only 150 miles from the Chinese border. We were enthusiastically received by faculty of the university, who seemed a world apart from their colleagues in Moscow. The university was of some size but obviously did not receive the kind of support that Moscow received. We learned that a faculty position at Alma-Ata was considered to be a hardship post, so professors were paid more there than at the universities of Moscow and Leningrad. Even so, few faculty had wished to leave Moscow, seemingly because it was the seat of power and preference. We visited the Astro-Physics Institute, set in a beautiful spot, where the students were observing Sputnik III with great pride. The vice-director asked to be remembered to Frank Edmondson of Indiana University's astronomy faculty. It was the judgment of our group that, if we were to teach in Russia, we would prefer to be at Alma-Ata. The place reminded me of our Northwest: it was an orchard-growing country and a very productive agricultural region. Many of the people in Alma-Ata were of Oriental background, and there were numerous students from China in the university as exchange students.

Our hotel offered some surprises. As I noted then, "General bath is very clean and bright, thank heaven. All showers, however, are two floors below. Beds are small and hard but again, thank heaven, single rooms and everything is bright and clean and the pillows are soft and of reasonable size. There is a table, a lamp, a vase for flowers, teakettle and radio in the room."

While in Alma-Ata we also went to the opera house to hear the state symphony orchestra, a delightful experience, for the players were talented and beautifully trained. (Incidentally, every Russian city of any size has a well-equipped opera house and frequently also a concert hall.) As we entered the theater to take our seats, we were startled by applause. Our first thought was that we were late and that the applause was for a completed number. But in a moment we realized that the applause was for us. They had held up the performance, waiting for us to enter, and we were greeted in this cordial and friendly manner because the community felt highly honored to have a group of visiting university presidents from America. The young conductor, obviously Oriental and impeccably clad in white tie and tails, led with great verve an orchestra with an unusual combination of both Eastern- and Western-style instruments in a fine program of Beethoven, Bach, and Brahms. At the intermission we were nearly mobbed by students trying out their English and asking questions about America.[3]

Throughout our trip, surprises and paradoxes abounded. At Alma-Ata, for instance, the air terminal was an elaborate building with crystal chandeliers, overstuffed furniture, and vast reception lobbies. Notwithstanding this impressive structure, the air runways were undeveloped and, as there was very little traffic, the terminal seemed largely deserted. The explanation we were given was that one bureau controlled the building of airstrips and another controlled the building of air terminals. The air terminal bureau was ahead of the strip bureau and, as a consequence, Alma-Ata had a magnificent palace to receive passengers but only grass runways for the planes.

Our hosts there, who were unexpectedly well informed about the United States, were very hospitable. The rector entertained our group in his spacious house with its lovely garden and fountain. There were forty at dinner but more could have been accommodated in the dining room. The dinner—excellent, elaborate, and served with a sense of decorum—consisted of many cold dishes—meat, salads, fish, paté—chicken and cauliflower, fish with excellent sauce and potatoes, ice cream, raspberries, strawberries, cakes, and candies, all accompanied by a great variety of beverages.

The plane that was to come for us was very late; our departure was scheduled for between eleven and twelve o'clock, but the plane

3. During this intermission we decided that we should present flowers to the soloist, who was to perform in both the first and second portions of the concert. We sent someone for flowers from a nearby flower shop and we were prepared to go on to the stage to present them at the end of the concert, but this opportunity was not offered. Instead we went backstage to make the presentation to the prima donna, who was buxom and formidable in size in the best operatic tradition. When I presented the flowers to her on behalf of our group, in my enthusiasm I remarked that she was tremendous—meaning, of course, that she had given us a great performance. Her eyes sparkled and, observing my corpulent figure, she smiled and through the interpreter said to me, "That, from *you?*" Rarely have I had a better lesson in using care in word choice when addressing a lady.

did not arrive until two A.M. Our host committee accompanied us to the airport and would not leave until they saw us safely aboard. I shall always remember the picture of us gathered together under the stars—it was a beautiful summer night—singing songs to pass the time. The Russians, surprisingly enough, sang the songs in English, such oldtime favorites as "Swanee River," "My Darling Clementine," "A Long, Long Way to Tipperary," and so on. Not infrequently the Russians knew the words better than some of us did.

I have made three other trips to Russia for meetings of the board of governors of the International Association of Universities (I A U) and for one of the quinquennial conferences of the I A U. On another occasion I stopped there briefly enroute to Islamabad. Even with all the changes and improvements that had taken place by the time of my last trip to Russia, in 1975, I still found traveling in Russia arduous. It is a vast, amazing country, difficult for the Westerner to comprehend. It is even more difficult for the Westerner to understand the apparent acceptance by the great mass of the Russian people of their type of government and the censorship and restrictions under which they live.

This memoir is not the place for a detailed description of the political ideology and the educational philosophy and practice of the Russians. But I am grateful for the opportunities that I had to have some exposure to them and so to have, in viewing the problems of the world, reading the day-to-day news, and greeting the Russians who now come to the States more frequently than in the past, some better understanding of Russian society and the shaping of its attitudes.

In the published report of our mission there appears a thoughtful comment about "the dynamics of the atmosphere" present in most aspects of Soviet life and a caveat on inferences about Russians that may serve as a corrective to other impressions of our visit: "There is a noticeable conviction as to progress, an apparent feeling of success, a pride and a sense of destiny which is inescapable. Whether the individual is right or wrong in feeling as he does, the fact remains that the prevalence of this dynamic provides a general stimulation for the people which is of tremendous importance. Anyone who has assumed a role of leadership in creating change in either a single institution or in a major segment of society is aware of the fundamental significance of the development of such a dynamic."[4]

4. *Report* . . . , p. 7.

⸨23⸩

○ ○ ○

Education and World Affairs

NO ONE could have foreseen that during the last few months of my university presidency and from 1962 to 1970 an organization called Education and World Affairs (E W A) would absorb a large portion of my time. The genesis of this organization, its purpose and how I came to be involved in it have a claim on this record.

During the 1950s American institutions of higher education began to shed their parochialism and slowly to embrace the concept that the world is education's parish. One after another, universities became involved in international activities, generally with Third World countries, in the form of technical and advisory assistance. Yet that development was in a sense haphazard, without coordination, and characterized more by good will than by wise planning. Both in government and in the private sector, the feeling grew that the higher-education community should be making a more impressive contribution to alleviation of international problems than so far had been the case. Secretary of State Christian Herter, through his special assistant for educational and cultural affairs, Ambassador Robert H. Thayer, convened a meeting of representatives from government, private foundations, universities, and the business and professional worlds. Out of it came the recommendation that the Ford Foundation be asked to form a committee of influential citizens to study the involvement of universities in international affairs and to suggest what could be done to improve their contribution.

J. Lewis Morrill, who retired as president of the University of Minnesota in 1960 and became a consultant to the Ford Foundation, chaired the committee that was subsequently appointed.[1] With

1. Other members of the Morrill Committee were Harold Boeschenstein,

the help of an able staff, the Morrill Committee conducted an intensive and thorough review of the international activities in which universities were engaged. Its report, published in late 1960, was distributed widely in the United States and abroad, and influenced the thinking of people in education, government, and world affairs.

In addition to ideas and proposals for improvement of the universities' performance in the international field, the Morrill Committee Report included the recommendation to establish an organization as a center for coordinating the universities' activities through planning, conducting studies, holding conferences, and gathering and dispersing information on American higher education's role in world affairs.

Under the continuing leadership of the Ford Foundation, along with representatives of other foundations, meetings were held to discuss the implementation of the report, particularly concerning the nature and operation of the proposed central organization. The result was appointment of a task force of five university and college presidents to suggest the manner and form of the implementation. Franklin Murphy of the University of California, Los Angeles, was chosen to head the task force composed of Robert Goheen of Princeton University, John Hannah of Michigan State University, Douglas Knight of Lawrence College (later of Duke University), and me. We met during the spring and summer of 1961 and decided that a new, separate organization, which should have a role as far as possible distinct from what other organizations in the field were doing, was needed. We proposed a beginning budget for the year of $650,000, to be supplied by the major foundations.

President Henry Heald of the Ford Foundation and President John Gardner of the Carnegie Corporation, in concurrence with our proposal, suggested that the members of the task force be the nucleus of a board of trustees for the new organization and that we name additional trustees up to a total of fourteen. To provide the financing, the two foundations soon approved five-year grants —$2,000,000 from Ford and $500,000 from Carnegie—payable after the organization's incorporation. By spring of 1962, we had

president of Owens-Corning Fiberglass Corporation; Harvie Branscom, chancellor of Vanderbilt University; Arthur S. Fleming, secretary of HEW; J. W. Fulbright, U.S. senator from Arkansas; John W. Gardner, president of the Carnegie Corporation; Franklin D. Murphy, chancellor of U.C.L.A.; Philip D. Reed, former president of the General Electric Company; and Dean Rusk, president of the Rockefeller Foundation.

succeeded in persuading seven others to join us on the board: Ambassador Ellsworth Bunker, U.S. representative on the Council of the Organization of American States; Ray Eppert, president of the Burroughs Corporation; T. Keith Glennan, president of the Case Institute of Technology; Kenneth Holland, president of the Institute of International Education; David Lilienthal, former chairman of the Tennessee Valley Authority (TVA) board and of the U.S. Atomic Energy Commission and since 1955 chief executive officer of the Development and Resources Corporation, whose wise and provocative questions were to serve as a stimulus to educators on the board; Frank McCulloch, bureau chief for China and Southeast Asia, Time-Life Foreign News Service; and Logan Wilson, president of the American Council on Education.[2]

During the organizational period Murphy and other members of the steering committee, knowing that I was leaving the presidency of Indiana University, had tried to prevail upon me to take the position of chairman and chief executive officer full time. Although I was deeply interested in the purposes and believed profoundly in the potential of the new organization, I did not wish to sever my ties with the university and with the state of Indiana. I had agreed with Elvis Stahr when he succeeded me as president of the university that I would take an active role in the affairs of the Indiana University Foundation, continuing as president while he assumed the office of chairman of the board. It was proposed that I devote myself largely to stimulating our giving program and particularly to working with major donors who were interested in Indiana University. Moreover, throughout my professional life I had resisted all requests to leave Indiana University to take other positions, several of them in New York. I frequently stated that I preferred to carry on whatever outside work I did from a Hoosier base rather than to surrender it and establish a new one.

In the end, William Marvel, executive associate of the Carnegie Corporation, was named president and I was made chairman of the board under an arrangement whereby I was to give 40 percent of my time to the New York office, commuting from Bloomington where I attended to my responsibilities with the Indiana University

2. At one time or another such men as Vincent Barnett, Jr., President, Colgate University; Edward Mason, Lamont University Professor at Harvard University; Frederick Seitz, President, National Academy of Sciences; Sol Linowitz, distinguished diplomat; and Robert McNamara, President, World Bank, served on the board.

Foundation. For the following eight years I devoted a substantial amount of my time to the work of E W A, commuting typically weekly to New York or at least every other week and spending three or four days there unless I was on an E W A assignment elsewhere. It had been agreed that I would take no additional salary for this effort, but, since I was being paid by the Indiana University Foundation, the E W A would compensate the Foundation for the time I spent on E W A work.

My association with E W A made for exciting and rewarding years. We had a talented staff of highly experienced younger men who brought to the work extraordinary enthusiasm and dedication. In addition to Marvel himself there were such colleagues as Ralph Smuckler, Maurice Harari, John Scott Everton, Howard Reed, Henry Russell, Preston Schoyer, Ebba Corcoran, Allan Michie, Peter Gillingham, and several others.

Unquestionably, one of the signal successes in the formative days of E W A was the quality of the persons who agreed to serve on its board—men of great experience and accomplishment in their respective fields. As planned, they took an active part in discussions of the principal issues, kept themselves informed about E W A's programs, and made themselves available to advise in matters of policy and practice. In other words, the trustees did not perform in a perfunctory manner, but rather as a vital intellectual resource, deliberating on the issues and developing the policies of the organization. On at least two occasions their sessions were held in Washington rather than in New York in order to consult with Ambassador David Bell of the Agency for International Development (A I D); Leona Baumgartner, assistant administrator for Human Resources and Social Development; Lucius Battle, assistant secretary of state for Education and Cultural Affairs, and others.

I found contact with this talented board a stimulating experience, and to serve as their chairman was challenging and demanding. The board discussions were of a very high order and really constituted the policy bible for the work of the organization. It was my first experience in the development of an entirely new organization of considerable size and national importance. President Marvel and I and members of the board worked for many months with the complicated legal and practical problems of bringing the organization into being, recruiting a staff, and finding a location for our work. After working in temporary quarters, we finally acquired a permanent home at 522 Fifth Avenue, which proved to be adequate and desirable for our purposes.

In certain ways, these years were very demanding ones for me. The personal problems involved in living and working in two locations were considerable. In addition, it seemed undesirable to give up membership on a number of national committees and boards with which I was already connected. Fortunately, several of these met in New York and attendance at their meetings was in part facilitated for me by my having a New York base.

One of the ambitious initiatives that was felt essential to enable the new organization to operate effectively as early as possible was carried out within its first full year. E W A held regional conferences at Sante Fe, New Mexico; East Lansing, Michigan; Hanover, New Hampshire; Pebble Beach, California; White Sulphur Springs, West Virginia; and Princeton, New Jersey in order to bring the program of E W A close to the educational leadership in each area. Those conferences brought into the E W A a large number of scholars and administrators particularly who began to look to E W A for guidance in their international concerns. E W A had an active program of conferences, seminar studies and reports, consultations with colleges and universities, consultation on international educational policy making, and an active, functioning program of committees and councils dealing with specialized problems.

Early in the development of the E W A program, it was determined that two operational services would be useful and could best be discharged by divisions of E W A. As a consequence the Overseas Educational Service (O E S), sited in our E W A office in New York, and the Universities Service Center, sited in Hong Kong, were established to provide new services to the American educational community.

In the 1950s many American educators and technicians were abroad carrying out technical-assistance contracts, pursuing studies, or acting as consultants. The logistical problems they faced were substantial: for example, difficulty in obtaining extended leaves of absence, differences in salaries at home and abroad, unusual living conditions, slow reentry into the U.S. academic community, and limited productive feedback into their own universities after their return. All of these were deemed to be important problems. The recruitment of U.S. faculty and administrators for this work abroad was another important need. Also, as universities and colleges in the

Third World attempted to recruit staffs on their own to assist them in the development of their institutions, they needed some facilitating service to aid them in their efforts. O E S was started to perform these services. Its office was within the E W A office in New York and it was under the general authority of the E W A board of trustees. Uniquely, however, O E S had sponsors in addition to E W A: the American Council on Education, the National Academy of Sciences, the American Council of Learned Societies, the Social Science Research Council, and the Institute of International Education. The service was separately funded with an initial grant from the Carnegie Corporation, but was expected to receive most of its program and operating funds in the United States from foundations and agencies of the U.S. government, and abroad from the governments and universities that drew upon its services. Its executive director was the distinguished diplomat and scholar, John Scott Everton, and its Policy Advisory Group was composed of representatives of the sponsoring bodies.

The other operating arm, the Universities Service Center, was established with a grant by the Carnegie Corporation in Hong Kong, operating under the general direction of E W A and its board. With the Communist victory in China in 1949, American scholars had henceforth been excluded from that important country; scholars and students of China had thus been denied access to the country whose people and affairs they were studying. Subsequently, Hong Kong became the center of such studies. The availability of people and current printed materials from mainland China made it the mecca for academic researchers from the United States and other Western countries. However, the scholars arriving in Hong Kong to work for six months or a year faced formidable difficulties, largely logistical in nature but nonetheless real. With a special grant from the Carnegie Corporation to help scholars studying there, E W A established in the fall of 1963 the Universities Service Center in Hong Kong. Its purpose was to help scholars move more quickly into productive research by providing useful contacts and effective access to research resources. Furthermore, it hoped to give advice and guidance on local political situations, to find ways to improve and develop resources, and to offer services and physical facilities for professional scholars carrying on their work in Hong Kong. Although the Universities Service Center was under the general supervision of the E W A board, an advisory board of twelve leading figures in the fields of Chinese studies, higher education, and public affairs in Canada, Great Britain, and the U.S. was created, and this board met from time to time in Hong Kong and gave invaluable assistance to the effort.[3] A distinguished and experienced China scholar, Preston Schoyer, was made director of the center.

To describe the work of the E W A during all these years would require a volume and then the full story would not be told. As what is pertinent to these memoirs is mostly my participation in the enterprise, I shall merely add that I think the accomplishment of E W A in pursuing its purpose was substantial and a record was made of which all connected with the organization can take just pride. Their publications constitute a lasting contribution to the subject of educational world affairs and still furnish valuable guidance and information to those interested in some aspect of the field. During its years of operation nearly every important figure in the field of international studies and education in America had some contact with or participation in the work of E W A. Never before nor since has there been such an enterprise in which the personalities in this field were so universally encompassed. Rather than present a sketchy view of the whole program, I shall mention only two or three special projects in which I had a personal part.[4]

In 1964, at the request of the U.S. State Department, E W A accepted the responsibility of developing a plan for an Indian-American binational educational, cultural, and scientific foundation. It so happened that a large amount of rupees had been accumulating in India to the credit of the U.S. government in payment for food exports from the U.S. These rupees were not transferable and heretofore had only been used for defraying the expense of carrying on our governmental functions in India such as the operation of the embassy, salaries of consulate staff, and so on. As this sum grew it became embarrassingly large and constituted a

3. The board of trustees, chaired by Sir William Hayter, Warden, New College, Oxford, consisted of Frederick H. Burkhardt, President, American Council of Learned Societies; W. A. C. H. Dobson, Chairman, Department of East Asiatic Studies, University of Toronto; John Scott Everton, Executive Director, Overseas Educational Service; Maurice Freedman, Department of Social Anthropology, London School of Economics and Political Science; Robert F. Goheen, President, Princeton University; John M. H. Lindbeck, Associate Director, East Asian Research Center, Harvard University; Lucien W. Pye, Professor of Political Science, Center for International Studies, Massachusetts Institute of Technology; William Marvel of EWA; and Schoyer.

4. My duties as chairman included participating to some degree in all aspects of E W A's work, from money raising to decision making.

difficult fiscal problem for the Indians. Therefore, with the consent of certain congressional leaders, the U.S. State Department decided to propose to India that a foundation along the lines of the Ford Foundation be formed and endowed by a substantial proportion of these PL480 surplus rupee funds. It was proposed that the capital base endowment be in the order of $300 million in rupees (1.5 billion rupees), which, in terms of purchasing power in India, would have made the foundation larger in assets than those that the Ford Foundation had available for its programs in America and world-wide. E W A was asked to undertake the formulation of this project and its presentation to the Indian authorities. I was given principal responsibility for this task and made two trips to India for that purpose. The idea had the enthusiastic backing of Ambassador Chester Bowles and of John Lewis, a former Indiana University economics professor who was then A I D administrator in India. I thought it a capital idea and I assumed the Indians would react to it eagerly. The intent was that the U.S. government would place in the hands of a joint Indian-American board this large rupee endowment to be used for the purpose of supporting unusual men and unusual ideas in India for the social good. We proposed that the Indians have a majority of the members of the board and that the American representation be limited to the number necessary to give guidance from the experience in this kind of organization that America almost alone among countries could furnish. The proposal had enthusiastic backing by Indian educators, but the governmental bureaucracy pointed out that India had a planned society and to inject support for unusual ideas and unusual men would upset the careful planning. Thus the government countered with a proposal that the money simply be turned over to the Indian government as a gift to be used by the government agencies for social and economic development and improvement. Regrettably, in my view, during the Moynihan ambassadorship to India we finally capitulated and turned the funds over to the government. At the time of my mission there, the only high-ranking officers I found in favor of the E W A proposal were the minister of education and Indira Gandhi, who was then minister of communications. She enthusiastically backed the idea saying it was exactly what India needed then to break through the heavy layer of government-planning red tape. The reaction of the Indians was shocking to me because foundations at the time were still viewed with so much favor in America that it did not occur to me that anyone could consider them undesirable. But such was to be the turn of thought even in America in the 1970s. Several voices in Congress and outside decried the power of foundations and asked that they be curbed on the grounds that the power inherent in such large sums of money upset government plans and programs; therefore, it would be preferable to reduce the sums by taxation and let the money be spent by government agencies.

Another activity in which I had a direct part was the study of the international role of the U.S. Office of Education. In mid-1963, E W A was asked by Commissioner Francis Keppel to study the policies, programs, and internal organization of the office with reference to its international educational responsibilities. This report was published in 1964 and the office was reorganized in the early summer of 1965. It used the E W A report on the international dimensions of the office as a guideline for restructuring its handling of international activities.

My involvement in the Office of Education study (I chaired the committee) led logically to another line of E W A's endeavor in which I took an active part, namely, consultation with the Department of State and with the Department of Health, Education and Welfare on the development of a new federal program in international education. A call for increased activity and support in this field was made by President Lyndon Johnson in his Smithsonian speech of September 16, 1965, and legislation was prepared accordingly. This legislation was entrusted to a special task force of the education and labor committee of the House of Representatives, chaired by John Brademas of Indiana.

Congressman Brademas was deeply interested in the subject matter and, as this was the first major piece of legislation of which he had been given full charge, he felt his responsibility very keenly. Accordingly, he asked me as chairman of E W A to assist him during the hearings on this program. I spent most of two months in Washington in almost daily consultation, helping him to marshal the witnesses, prominent educators and scholars, to testify as to the need for the legislation and its benefit to American education. The bill was passed finally, largely due to his adroit generalship. I had already been an admirer of Brademas and this experience deepened my admiration.

By 1965 at Indiana University we began to be increasingly conscious of the fact that a significant milestone in the history of the university, its 150th anniversary, was only five years off and that it would be an excellent time for the Indiana University Foundation to launch a major capital gift campaign. Planning began for this campaign in which, of course, I had to take an active part because of my Foundation duties. However, with the resignation of President Stahr from his post in June, 1968, the trustees were caught unprepared for a change in leadership and as a result asked me to assume the office of university president again while they looked for a successor. Although President Stahr did not formally leave office until the first of August, from about July 1 on most of the problems of the presidency landed on my desk. For the next five months I had little time to give to outside activities until President Sutton was elected to take office December 1. In addition, with the enormous demands upon my time that the major fund campaign was beginning to make, it seemed to me necessary that I phase out of the work of E W A as rapidly as possible.

Meanwhile, because the Vietnam catastrophe and emerging domestic problem areas as well as shrinking resources had caused the foundations to feel that they must retrench, there was little likelihood that E W A could carry on at the level necessary for it to be effective in the role that it had played during most of the 1960s. As a consequence it was agreed that E W A would be merged into the International Council for Educational Development, which James Perkins, who had resigned as president of Cornell University, had launched in New York with modest financing from the Ford Foundation. The reorganization was accomplished on October 1, 1970.

Although I could no longer devote time to E W A, I feel that the decision by the Ford Foundation in effect to liquidate the work of E W A was regrettable. The organization had great promise for future usefulness. Granted a few more years of life, I believe, it would have richly fulfilled early expectations a substantial measure of which was already apparent. Moreover, had E W A been allowed to continue its operation, it might have helped avert the waning interest of American universities in international activities following the Vietnam war. Preoccupied during the 1970s with internal problems, financial stringencies, and the demand for academic programs adapted to the interests of minorities, women, and ethnic groups, universities abandoned or shrank their international curricular and research activities. The loss is regrettable because, as we see now, the necessity of the university's international role has become more evident than ever before. As the nation's international problems mount, many universities are caught ill-prepared to meet the need for scholarly manpower in international studies, languages, and research. Once more we academics learn that we cannot retreat within our own quarters, but must continually interest ourselves in what is occurring beyond our borders.

I stayed on the board of the new organization briefly but soon had to devote full time to the Indiana University 150th Birthday Fund drive, which, happily, by mid-1972 had achieved more than double its goal of $25 million. E W A in its old form had passed out of existence by then.

E W A in its years left a rich legacy in the field of education and world affairs that will be useful for decades to come. I feel privileged to have presided over the deliberations of such a distinguished board of trustees, from each of whom I learned a great deal and for whom I have great admiration and respect. I am proud to have been associated with a talented group of staff members; all of those remaining continue to have a vital role in the field of American intellectual life. I hope that, while records are still available and while the personalities that played a part in this effort are still alive, someone will undertake a full-scale history of E W A and its activities and achievements.

⟨24⟩

○ ○ ○

The Carnegie Foundation for the Advancement of Teaching

ONE OF the most interesting boards on which I have had the privilege of serving during my career was that of the Carnegie Foundation for the Advancement of Teaching. Usually in a community there are a few boards with prestige possibly exceeding the responsibilities that the members of the board discharge. So it is with boards in the professional world and particularly in the world of education. There was a mystique about the Carnegie board that gave it extraordinary prestige. The mystique arose in part, I imagine, from the Carnegie name and from this, America's first major foundation, created by Andrew Carnegie; in part from the central mission of the foundation—furnishing pensions to faculty members—which was of critical significance to the world of higher education; and in no small part from the prominence of the original board members selected by Andrew Carnegie.

In 1941, when I was invited to join the Carnegie board, its membership included some of the most distinguished university presidents in America. Its reputation was unparalleled in the world of academia, making an invitation to serve on its board a prized recognition. My membership on this board automatically opened many doors in the educational world to me. What was possibly more important for me was the impression it made on my faculty colleagues. I was still regarded then with skepticism by some members of the faculty because of my youth and nontraditional academic background. However, they held the Carnegie board in high esteem, if not in awe, and my appointment to it helped reassure many of them that I would be able to represent them properly in the academic world.

The Carnegie Foundation for the Advancement of Teaching was not Andrew Carnegie's first major philanthropy, but years were to prove it to be one of the most significant and best known of his many generous benefactions. Carnegie, as is well known, was a business and financial genius who started as a poor boy in Scotland and emigrated to the United States. Eventually he was able to build a great steel corporation, which he sold to J. P. Morgan and which became the basis of the United States Steel Corporation. He made the sale when he was sixty-five and thereafter devoted himself wholly to his philanthropies. An articulate and energetic man, he wrote and spoke frequently on the subject of the responsible trusteeship of great wealth. He did not create the first philanthropic organization either in America or in the world, but perhaps no other man by precept and example has done so much as he to promote the idea of the importance of private philanthropy and what he called the "gospel of wealth," enunciated in part thus:

> This, then, is held to be the duty of the man of wealth: First to set an example of modest, unostentatious living, shunning display or extravagance; to provide moderately for the legitimate wants of those dependent upon him; and, after doing so, to consider all surplus revenues which come to him simply as trust funds, which he is called upon to administer, and strictly bound as a matter of duty to administer in the manner which, in his judgment, is best calculated to produce the most beneficial results for the community. . . .

Carnegie practiced the gospel he preached. Retiring with a great fortune of $350,000,000, he devoted the remainder of his life to philanthropy and to the intelligent dispensing of his means. He was the benefactor of his native town and of his adopted city; he financed many causes in which he believed; he was the donor of thousands of free public library buildings and church organs, the patron of hundreds of colleges and schools; and there were many other individual benefactions. In addition, he created a number of foundations.

In 1905 he made the first gift to endow the Carnegie Foundation for the Advancement of Teaching. It was the beginning of a philanthropy the principal purpose of which was to provide retirement annuities for the faculty of certain selected universities and colleges. At that time very few institutions had any means of pensioning their retired faculty members, a fact that disturbed Carnegie greatly because he believed the academic profession was underpaid and not only needed but also deserved a pension system. In establishing his original endowment he arrived at the amount after considerable calculation and thought it sufficient to provide pensions in perpetuity for the majority of teachers in the colleges and universities selected. The fact that his calculations were wrong in no way diminishes the significance of his initiative, for that initiative eventually helped solve the pension problem for most teachers in higher education, as I shall explain in a moment.

Advising Carnegie as he studied the feasibility of providing this pension system were Frank Vanderlip, then the famous head of the National City Bank of New York, and especially Henry S. Pritchett, president of the Massachusetts Institute of Technology in Boston, one of the towering figures in education of that era. Carnegie, who had a wide acquaintanceship in the field of education, with the help of Pritchett and Nicholas Murray Butler of Columbia University, picked for his first board of trustees, in addition to Pritchett, Charles W. Eliot of Harvard, Arthur T. Hadley of Yale, William Rainey Harper of the University of Chicago, David Starr Jordan of Stanford, Jacob Gould Schurman of Cornell, Woodrow Wilson of Princeton, and others similarly distinguished although maybe not quite so well known.

Carnegie was able to persuade Pritchett to be the first president of the foundation's board, in which post he served for twenty-five years. With such distinguished leadership, with so important a mission as the provision of pensions for professors, and with a blue-ribbon membership, it is small wonder that the board after a few years was characterized as perhaps the most exclusive educational club in the world, certainly one of the most influential. Henry Pritchett was succeeded by Henry Suzzallo, who died at the end of three years, and then by Walter Jessup, an alumnus of Indiana University, with whom I had counseled when I was acting president.

An additional function of the Carnegie Foundation for the Advancement of Teaching was to conduct studies for the improvement of educational practice, and this purpose was realized brilliantly from almost the beginning. One of the first studies initiated by the foundation was the study of medical education in the United States by a staff associate, Abraham Flexner. The Flexner Report (1910) was destined to revolutionize medical education in the United States within a decade and to have a profound influence upon other types of professional education. Through the years the Carnegie reports have continued to be of a very high order, and many of them have had an important bearing on the direction of higher education in America.

Although, with the growth of higher education, it was soon discovered that Carnegie's original endowment would be inadequate to carry out his great dream of a pension system, the experience gained by the foundation and the studies that it sponsored concerning the pension problem were responsible for bringing into being the Teachers Insurance and Annuity Association, which is now the principal instrument for funding the retirement income of personnel of higher educational and philanthropic institutions.

Carnegie believed in establishing his foundations in perpetuity. Thus, when the responsibility of providing pensions for American higher education was no longer a primary function of the foundation—the foundation has continued to take care of those originally pensioned throughout their lifetimes—the preparation and issuance of reports in higher education became the dominant feature of the foundation. Carnegie left the major part of his fortune to the Carnegie Corporation, which has made grants to the foundation through the years and which uses the foundation as a vehicle for sponsoring studies that continue to be of great significance to higher education, the latest of major importance being a study of the curriculum.

William Lowe Bryan was invited to join the Carnegie Foundation board in 1910 and accepted, considering it a very important assignment. Typically the full board met only once a year. Bryan's trip to New York for this meeting was a major event in his annual schedule and nothing was allowed to interfere with it. He usually was accompanied by Mrs. Bryan. He stayed for some days, not only to attend the meetings of the Carnegie board, but also to meet with leading Indiana University alumni, to transact business on behalf of the university in New York, and to allow the Bryans to avail themselves of the social and cultural opportunities in the city.

I was surprised and delighted to be asked to join the board of the Carnegie Foundation in 1941. I accorded it the same high priority that Dr. Bryan had and found it a source of stimulation, exceptional information, and several new and valuable acquaintances. The membership of the board at that time was still distinguished and studded with vital personalities. Jessup was president. He was a dynamic and provocative individual who gave the board great leadership for ten years until his untimely death. The year I was elected to membership Henry Wriston, then president of Brown University, was chairman, and other notable members who welcomed me to the board were Frank Aydelotte of Swarthmore; Nicholas Murray Butler of Columbia; Samuel Paul Capen of Buffalo, who had earlier been the principal architect of the American Council on Education; Oliver Cromwell Carmichael of Vanderbilt; James Bryant Conant, whose presidential career at Harvard was nearing a decade; the lovable George Hutcheson Denny, president of Alabama, one of the original trustees of the foundation, along with Butler, when Denny was president at Washington and Lee University; Frank Porter Graham, the beloved statesman of higher education in the South, then president of the University of North Carolina at Chapel Hill; William Allan Neilson, a sparkling, witty Scotsman who was the president of Smith; Charles Seymour, the president of Yale; California's one and only Robert Gordon Sproul; the inimitable Casey (Kenneth Charles Morton) Sills of Bowdoin; and others of a similar quality. Two of the most interesting men on the board were not academicians: Thomas William Lamont, member of the banking firm of J. P. Morgan and Company, and Robert Abercrombie Lovett. Lamont was a Harvard graduate, a former Harvard trustee, and a man of wide-ranging intellectual interests who could hold his own with any academician. Lovett, already a noted banker, was to have even greater success in the profession before embarking on a remarkable public career.

At the very beginning Mr. and Mrs. Carnegie had established a pleasant social custom in connection with the annual meeting of the board. On the evening before the meeting, the Carnegies received the members of the board for dinner and, following the meeting the next day, the board members reciprocated with a luncheon in Mr. Carnegie's honor at which they drank a toast of appreciation to him for his benefactions. The luncheons were first held at Delmonico's and then were transferred to the Century, where they continued for most of the years of my membership on the board. After Carnegie's death, Mr. and Mrs. Lamont adopted the custom of entertaining the board at dinner on the night before the meeting and, of course, the luncheons were continued, with a toast offered to Andrew Carnegie's memory.

The Lamonts were a delightful couple. He was a truly cultivated man, the very quintessence of all that is best in the eastern intellectual establishment, including a deep sense of civic responsibility. She was a witty, gracious, lovely lady who was active in academic affairs and, as I remember, was a trustee of Smith. Their dinners were notable affairs that typically included one or two other outstanding people in addition to the members of the board. Frequently the ambassador to the United States from the United Kingdom would make the trip from Washington to join us as a house guest of Mr. and Mrs. Lamont.

At these dinner parties, one guest was invariably Russell Leffingwell, who was also a member of the Morgan firm. He had operated for many years at the very highest level of economic and political decision making, both in this country and abroad. He was the architect of the first Liberty Loan in 1917 and, in the years following the Treaty of Versailles, was a collaborator with Mr. Morgan and Mr. Lamont in negotiating the many reconstruction loans and credits designed to aid the European economy in its recovery from the effect of World War I. He was a founder, member, and long-term chairman of the Council on Foreign Relations. Such a man, naturally, brought to any discussion of international developments—political, economic, or military—rare background and insight. In addition, he was a delightful and sparkling conversationalist. He was, as I remember, also a member of the board of the Carnegie Corporation at that time.

It was a black-tie dinner, and the members of the board, without exception, arrived in New York in time to attend. Mr. and Mrs. Lamont lived in a great New York townhouse that had the usual arrangement of a cloak room and dining room on the ground floor, living room and library on the second floor, and the bedrooms on the floors above. As I recall, we were invited for 7:15 and, after leaving our coats at the ground floor, we were ushered to the second floor, where Mr. and Mrs. Lamont greeted us for cocktails. At 7:45 the gentlemen descended to the dining room and had a delightful dinner served with all the style characteristic of such a house: delicious food, good wine, and impeccable service, with a footman in attendance behind every three or four guests. After dinner we went to the library for brandy and engaged in conversation led by some of the most brilliant practitioners of the art I have ever heard. Someone said it was the best conversation possible on this side of the Atlantic. Customarily, the distinguished, specially invited guest would lead off by giving us some inside view of current international events of significance, and, with that for a start, the members of the board would join in what was a remarkably informative and scintillating conversation lasting an hour or so. The honor guests were normally men of eminence and global perspective. These were stirring times, first the war years and then the period immediately following, and frequently we learned of the possibility of future international initiatives not yet generally anticipated. I began to learn here also that much in the field of diplomacy is rarely reported in the mass media, and when it does appear it is often inaccurate. The meetings also would give insights into as yet not generally discernible intellectual, political, and economic currents abroad in the world. This was very exciting for me. To a small-town lad from Indiana it opened undreamed-of vistas.

Incidentally, it was my custom when I returned to the campus to share with my colleagues some of the insights into the world as seen through the eyes of these distinguished visitors and fellow board members. These reports seemed to interest my colleagues, especially my valued associate, Ross Bartley, who had worked at a top level in government and who was sensitive to international shifts before they became apparent. During the war years in particular we were given perceptions by people such as the British ambassador that we could not have learned otherwise, thereby considerably expanding our understanding of what was happening and what was likely to happen. (In addition, I often brought back some suggestions from the menu for my cook!) It was my first glimpse of that stratum of American society, and I was fortunate to have had that first glimpse in a household of the highest intellectual and social quality rather than in one merely rich and elegant.

The meetings of the board on the following morning were presided over by the president, who first disposed of such routine business of the organization as miscellaneous matters of financial import. Then the major part of the meeting was devoted to the discussion of some educational problem then current; the sense of the discussion was later recorded in the annual report of the president. Sometimes we authorized the making and funding of special studies.

Following the meeting we adjourned to the Century, and there in the fourth-floor private dining room enjoyed an excellent luncheon in the delightful ambience of the club. The luncheon had as its purpose observance of the traditional tribute to Andrew Carnegie. For many years, a senior surviving member of the board appointed by Mr. Carnegie himself, Nicholas Murray Butler, gave the toast at the conclusion of the luncheon, a toast to Mr. Carnegie. By the time I knew him, Mr. Butler had grown blind and was accompanied always by a male secretary, but he was still the active and vigorous head of Columbia University and retained his skill as a remarkable speaker. He would stand at the end of these luncheons and for ten or twelve minutes, maybe fifteen, give an eloquent toast. His toasts were models of well-arranged, beautifully phrased, and effectively delivered thoughts, at the conclusion of which we raised our glasses to the memory of Mr. Carnegie. It was always a moving, nostalgic occasion.

After Mr. Butler's death, it then became the custom to ask the board member who was senior in service and chairing the board to give the toast. In due course, my turn came to perform this function. I must say that I regarded the task with a good deal of trepidation in view of the high standards that had been set by Mr. Butler and by the two or three who had succeeded him. I was still relatively inexperienced in this kind of speaking, since formal toasts were not then offered very often at Indiana gatherings, but I was determined to be worthy of the occasion if at all possible, regardless of the amount of effort and thought that it required to be so.

The spring before I was to deliver the toast at the fall meeting, I had occasion to go to Europe and routed myself so that I could go through Scotland. I had deplaned at Glasgow, gone to Dunfermline, Andrew Carnegie's birthplace, and visited the simple shoemaker's cottage in which he had been born and from which he had migrated to the United States. From Dunfermline I then made a pilgrimage to Skibo Castle at Dornoch Firth in northern Scotland, which Carnegie had built on the foundations of an ancient palace of the bishops of Dornoch and where he generally spent his summers after he became wealthy. The property is owned and still used by the Carnegie heirs. I had made arrangements in advance through the Carnegie office to be received by the estate agent, or manager, at the castle. I drove from Dunfermline up through Inverness and then into the beautiful area where the castle is located, on the northeast coast of Scotland. The Gulf Stream keeps the area verdant in the winter, and in March I found the grass green, the golf course playable, and the flowers in bloom. The estate agent graciously received me and took me through the castle and grounds.

The castle itself was a revelation—a magnificent structure, beautifully furnished, with a huge pipe organ in the central salon where Carnegie used to entertain his friends. One of the traditions of the castle was the awakening of guests each morning to the shrill notes of a bagpiper marching around the castle. I observed the beautiful greenhouses filled with flowers and fruit trees. Fruit could not be grown in the open in that climate, which, although pleasant in the wintertime, was not much warmer in the summertime.

The visual contrast between the simple cottage in which Andrew Carnegie was born and the magnificence of his summer home dramatically illustrated to me the social and economic distance that he had traveled in his lifetime. It helped to bring into perspective the significance of the man who had accomplished so much toward the economic development of America, yet also had become noted for his benefactions: the man who, by his own daring and unselfish philanthropies, had become known as the father of American philanthropy, that is, of the type we associate with foundations and endowments. And with this perspective I prepared my remarks for the toast, which I hoped would prove adequate for the occasion.

Upon the death of Walter Jessup, the foundation presidency passed to Oliver C. Carmichael, Sr., who had a notable record as a college president, particularly in building Vanderbilt University to a position of preeminence. He gave the board continuing vigorous leadership, but, when the likelihood of forced racial integration at the University of Alabama became strong, he resigned to become president of Alabama, his alma mater, thinking that perhaps because of his prestige and wide experience, he might succeed in the peaceful integration of that university, notwithstanding the militant opposition of Governor George Wallace and others of that ilk. He felt that if he were to succeed at Alabama, it would be a major step for integration nationally and thus worth his sacrificial effort. Unfortunately, even with his great tact, wisdom, and skill, the task was beyond him, and he finally gave up the fight and retired. He came to visit me in Bloomington shortly thereafter and told of his disappointment and frustration. I was greatly moved by his story because he had so invested his heart and mind in this effort that he cried as he recounted his failure.

Following Carmichael, John Gardner became the president of the board. He brought an originality, creativity, and vigorous intellect to bear upon our agendas and upon our discussions. Under his aegis the annual report of the president, reflecting the consensus of the discussions of the members of the board, gained even increased prestige and influence in the world of education.

During this period a tradition was sacrificed. The headquarters of both the corporation and the foundation were moved to a new building on Fifth Avenue and thereafter our annual luncheons were held in the board room of the corporation. They were simple business luncheons for the most part, without the delightful ambience of the Century, and the toast to Andrew Carnegie was given with a few words and a glass of sherry at the end of the luncheon. I have often wondered whether the original board members would have approved of such a spartan observance of a once delightful custom.

During my years on the board I served as vice chairman, 1952–53, and as chairman, 1953–54. Then from 1956 until my retirement I was a member of the executive committee, which transacted much of the business of the board and met as required. Since it had become customary for those board members, other than the founding group, who resigned or retired from their university presidencies to retire voluntarily from the Carnegie board to make way for new blood, I honored that tradition in 1962.

My years on the Carnegie Foundation board, especially the early years, were a great opportunity. The experience opened up new intellectual, as well as social and cultural, vistas. It was a rare privilege. All in all, service on this board was an extraordinary advantage for which I shall ever be grateful and from which I gained far more than I was able to contribute. I am confident that these meetings elevated my sights and ambitions for Indiana University.

[25]

○ ○ ○

The American Council on Education and an Introduction to International Associations

I HAVE always been a believer in a cooperative effort by educational institutions in presenting their case to the public and in the study and solution of their problems. For that reason I early began to participate in the work of the American Council on Education (ACE), attending its meetings and interesting myself in its activities. The ACE seemed to me to be of unusual importance because it was the one and only organization so constituted that it could theoretically speak for the whole of American higher education. Its membership was all-inclusive: public and private, land-grant and separated state universities, small and large institutions from every section of the nation—east, west, north, and south. In addition to the participation of many major colleges and universities as institutional members, it had constituent affiliated bodies such as the Association of American Colleges, the Association of Land-Grant Colleges and Universities, the National Association of State Universities, and many others.

The contacts between American higher education and the federal government have been numerous and complicated; they grow increasingly so with the passage of years. But in wartime, these contacts were even more numerous with even more complicated consequences. The impetus for the organization of the ACE came out of the problems that the universities experienced in dealing with the government during World War I. An ad hoc group composed of delegates from eight national organizations concerned with higher education and headed by Samuel P. Capen from the U.S. Bureau of Education was responsible for the formation of the Emergency Council on Education in January, 1918.[1] The stated objective was "to place the resources of the educational institutions of our country more completely at the disposal of the national government and its departments. . . ." In reality, it was organized as an instrumentality to help the institutions deal collectively with the government when it was impossible for them to do so individually. The council's first chairman was Donald J. Cowling, president of Carleton College. When the organization was renamed the American Council on Education in July, Cowling was given the added title of president of the council.

The organizational structure of the A C E consists of a board elected from the membership, a president who is the executive officer, and a chairman of the council and the board, elected annually. When I was active in the A C E, an executive committee of eight members carried on the work for the most part between meetings of the full board and meetings of the membership. Membership meetings were held once a year. The first full-time executive officer of the A C E was Samuel Paul Capen, who gave the organization excellent leadership through its formative years and then resigned to become chancellor of the University of Buffalo. He was succeeded by Charles R. Mann and later, in 1934, by George F. Zook, who had been for a year U.S. Commissioner of Education in the Roosevelt administration. Zook was an experienced man, a man of vigor and imagination, a builder in the best sense of the word. Some called him an "empire builder," but they did so largely in admiration rather than in criticism. He believed in the mission of higher education, and he believed in the ability of the A C E to advance the welfare of institutions of higher education as a matter of national interest. He gave the A C E adroit, effective, and imaginative leadership. He was a man of enormous energy, wholly dedicated to this work, to which he devoted himself unsparingly.

As the United States moved into World War II, the need for the A C E was again highlighted. The federal government and the armed forces had great need for the resources of the universities, and the multiplicity of relationships and problems that arose as a result nearly defied description. The A C E attempted to meet the

1. See Charles C. Dobbins, ed., *American Council on Education: Leadership and Chronology, 1918–1968* (Washington, D.C.: American Council on Education, 1968), p. 3.

challenge with strength and courage. Much of the work of its response and a great deal of the delicate, difficult negotiations with committees and bureaus over policies fell to the lot of the ACE's Committee on the Relationships of Higher Education to the Federal Government. I joined the committee at its formation in 1943 and gave its work high priority on my schedule, attempting always to be present for its meetings and to assist in addition at congressional hearings and in calls made by the committee on federal departments. The committee had an executive officer, Francis "Frank" J. Brown, who was experienced in the Washington scene and knew his way in and out of the intricacies of the halls of Congress and the federal bureaus and departments. He served with this and successor committees until his death in 1959.

The work of the committee took a considerable amount of time because it dealt with a multiplicity of crucial issues such as the draft policies about to be promulgated, the housing of wartime trainees on the campuses, and—at the conclusion of hostilities—the distribution of wartime surplus facilities for the housing of veterans. It dealt also with questions concerning the amount of reimbursement to be paid by the federal government for services to be rendered by a university—the old indirect-cost problem that is still one of the important issues between universities and the federal government —and other issues of paramount importance. Zook frequently attended the meetings of this committee because it dealt with vitally significant policy questions for the ACE, and I became acquainted with him there and in other activities around the office.

In 1943, conscious of the fact that all Americans had to do extra work, I had begun service in the State Department, spending about four days a week in Washington and the remaining days in Bloomington carrying on the work of Indiana University. It was a strenuous schedule, but it did mean that I was in Washington during the effective part of the week and was therefore readily available for meetings, conferences, and other activities of the ACE. The ACE office was located at 744 Jackson Place, less than a half-block from my office in the old State, War, and Navy Building. I suppose it was due to Zook's influence that I was elected chairman of the ACE for the fiscal year of 1944–45. I was surprised and gratified to be selected for this responsibility, representing as it did perhaps the top elective position among the national organizations in American higher education, that is, organizations that consisted of institutional and constituent memberships. I shall speak later of the National Education Association, the other great body, which represented individuals. I also assume that I was elected so early in my career in part because of the shortage of manpower and as I happened to be on the scene. In any event, I served as chairman that year and remained on the executive committee, as was the custom for chairmen, during the following three years until 1948.

The work of the A C E was expanding so rapidly during this period that Zook and others began to feel that it was necessary to find new and larger quarters. I was made chairman of a building committee. We thought that we might try to build a building large enough to rent quarters to the constituent bodies, so that the whole of the organizational structure of American higher education could be in one location. There was no room in the headquarters on Jackson Place for the affiliated bodies. When we investigated the possibility of building, the cost seemed prohibitive at the time. But we discovered we could buy an elegant apartment building that had been occupied by Andrew Mellon as his residence in Washington and by several of his friends. This was a well-designed limestone building at 1785 Massachusetts Avenue, N.W. It was large enough to furnish not only greatly enlarged quarters for the A C E, but also good quarters for most of the principal affiliated organizations such as the Association of Land-Grant Colleges and Universities, the American Association of University Professors, and later the Association of American Colleges. I felt that there would be great advantage in having so much of higher education in one spot, promoting communication between the various bodies and also making it easier for the government to know where to seek educational representatives. The arrangement also made it easier to convene committees consisting of representatives from all the constituent bodies. Experience proved this to be a wise move—financially feasible and useful in furthering the A C E's work. As a result, when, after many years of use, the building became outgrown, it furnished the example and the equity, along with a foundation grant, to build the present large, modern headquarters in Washington.

As I have mentioned, my Latin America trip in 1941 had stimulated my interest in the field of international and intercultural education, which was further whetted by my wartime work in the State Department. It was therefore logical that I accepted the chairmanship of the A C E's Committee on International Education and Cultural Relations when it was organized in 1944. From that time on, to the late 1950s, I chaired a variety of A C E committees concerned with international education such as the Commission on Occupied Areas (1949–51), the Commission on Exchange of Information on International Cultural Relations (1952–53), and the Commission on Education and International Affairs (1952–57). My service to these in a way complemented my own personal activities abroad, which I have related elsewhere.

During the period 1943–45, George Zook began to think about the nature of the structure of international educational activity in the postwar period. Following World War I, the League of Nations had provided for international educational affairs by creating the Committee on Intellectual Cooperation, based in Paris and dominated by the French. This committee dealt not at all with the day-to-day problems of education throughout the world, but rather furnished a gathering point for intellectuals to speak with each other— for Einstein to speak to Einstein, it was sometimes sarcastically said. But the substantive problems of education were ignored: the classroom problems and the problems of teachers and of organizational structures of education throughout the world. Zook was determined to see that this pattern was not repeated, but of course the French were equally determined, for reasons of prestige, to see that it *was* continued in whatever form of international organization succeeded the League of Nations.

Part of Zook's strategy was to make sure that the voice of education would be heard at the conference in San Francisco that would create the post-World War II international machinery that came to be called the United Nations. Some forty-odd voluntary American organizations were invited to have observers at the U N conference at San Francisco. Technically, they were observers from organizations with an interest in the form of the structure for the U N; they were advisory to the United States delegation. The San Francisco Conference ran for two months. I was asked by Zook to represent the A C E for the first month, and he replaced me for the second month, allowing me to return to Bloomington. Fortunately, the National Education Association (N E A) had the same view concerning the form of postwar international education as Zook, and so the two great bodies—the A C E, representing institutions, and the N E A, representing the teachers of the country—could join forces. William G. Carr attended for the N E A, and he and I maintained close working relationships. Fortunately, I got along well with the N E A leadership, but sometimes Zook and the powerful head of the N E A, Willard Givens, an honored Indiana University graduate, had some tensions.

The U N charter made provision for a democratic, broadly based organization in education, the United Nations Educational, Scientific and Cultural Organization (Unesco), and the framework for its organizational structure was created at a London conference by international representatives the following year. It was a thoroughly democratic organization, representative of all nations, and fulfilled a great part of Zook's dream. Another part of his dream was also realized: a democratic, all-encompassing organization of universities throughout the world, devoted to dealing with institutional problems rather than to debating purely intellectual and scholarly problems. The Unesco charter made it possible to create the International Association of Universities (I A U) whose structure was planned at an organizing conference at Nice in 1950. I was expected to be an active member of that conference, but it was impossible for me to get away just at the time that the meeting was held. Instead, Indiana University was represented by Wendell W. Wright, dean of the School of Education, who was an excellent representative. The first regular general assembly of I A U, which I attended, was held in 1955 at Istanbul, and the assemblies have been held quinquennially ever since. I have attended each of them. For ten years I served as a member of the governing board of I A U, five years of that time as its vice chairman. The I A U furnished me one of the most exciting, informative, and useful resources in international education of my lifetime. From it I received an insight into comparative education that I could have obtained in no other way—knowledge of systems and personalities on an international scale. The I A U was able to attract an unsual man, H. M. Roger Keyes, an Oxford don, to be its general secretary. Urbane, adept, and effective, Keyes has been invaluable in furthering the I A U. He is as well a cherished friend.

The San Francisco Conference was exciting and interesting. As Bill Carr and I were friends and had similar interests to represent, we were happy to be assigned a room together in the well-located Hotel Sir Francis Drake. My letters home revealed my impressions at the time:

I missed the opening session yesterday, but it was very brief. Today's session, which I did attend, was longer—Stettinius, Soong, Molotov, and Eden all spoke. The setting in the opera house is impressive, and the surrounding buildings are all handsome. It is easy to see why this site was selected.

It appears that we consultants are to be busy. Moreover, we are being shown every consideration. My seat is on the main floor of the opera house immediately behind the seats of the official delegates. [April 27, 1945]

San Francisco is lovely just now—flowers everywhere. The rhododendrons are especially brilliant. . . . I have never seen such roses.

I have a beautiful view of the ocean. The big bridges and ships are very plain. [May 7, 1945]

The weeks spent in San Francisco were lively and stimulating; there were many meetings to attend, presentations to be made, and personages to be cultivated. Younger leaders from all over the world were present. It gave one a rare opportunity to make foreign acquaintances, which in my case have lasted through the years and have been renewed from time to time in my travels throughout the world or during visits of these foreign friends to the United States. Many of them were connected with educational institutions in one way or another, and for that reason they were of special interest to me. The U.S. delegation was chaired by Secretary of State Edward R. Stettinius, Jr., and consisted of Senators Arthur H. Vandenberg of Michigan and Thomas Connally of Texas; Congressmen Sol Bloom of New York and Charles A. Eaton of New Jersey; Commander Harold E. Stassen, Assistant Chief of Staff of the United States Navy; Dean Virginia C. Gildersleeve of Barnard College; and Cordell Hull, who later received the Nobel Peace Prize for his part in the formation of the United Nations. All of the observers from the forty-two American organizations that had been invited to send representatives to the conference were regularly briefed on national developments by members of the U.S. delgation. Virginia Gildersleeve frequently fulfilled this role for the organizational delegates. Her reports were informative, helpful, and interesting. She was hospitable to the ideas that those of us representing educational institutions had to offer, and these briefing sessions furnished a channel of communication between the consultants and the official American delegates who were representing the ideas of Americans generally in the international sessions.

My own interest was heightened by the fact that an Indiana University colleague, Ed Buehrig, who was on leave to serve in the State Department, and Walter Laves, whom I had come to know in Washington from our various contacts while he was with the Bureau of the Budget and I was on temporary assignment with the State Department, were actively involved with the American delegation. Walter later became a member of the international secretariat of Unesco as deputy director general and still later joined the faculty of Indiana University as chairman of the government department.

San Francisco has a deserved reputation as a colorful city. It was thought to be an ideal setting for such an international conference since it is a cosmopolitan city, a seaport looking out to Asia, and also has deep cultural ties with Europe, especially France. There were many social affairs hosted by citizens of San Francisco who are noted for their social graces. There were gala concerts and other entertainments as well as receptions, cocktail parties, and dinners.

The plenary sessions were held in the then newly constructed civic opera house. It accommodated adequately these plenary sessions in more or less the same kind of arrangement and format that was later provided in the great council chamber of the UN building in New York. As the time approached for George Zook to take my place, I wrote home, "I leave here on the 11th. Should arrive in Bloomington on the following Monday night but may remain hidden until the middle of the week" [May 7, 1945]. I have frequently used this "in hiding" device to catch up on my work after a long absence from the office.

At the final plenary session, the United Nations charter was approved and the United Nations organization was formally launched, subject to adoption by the individual nations. A decade later, in 1955, to commemorate the signing of the document and the creation of the UN, a great celebration, to which I was invited, was held in San Francisco.

Something happened on that occasion that I shall always remember. The group returning for the anniversary met again in the civic opera house to hear speeches by the leading figures in the organization's formation, and the concluding speech was by the president of the United States, Dwight Eisenhower. I was seated near the front of the hall where I could look up directly at the speaker. When President Eisenhower came onto the stage and stepped up to the podium, I was shocked by the appearance of his face. The skin seemed tightly drawn over the cheekbones, and he had a look that I had come to associate with people suffering from extreme hypertension. I had served on committees with Eisenhower when he was president of Columbia University and so had had close-up views of his face, but since he had been in the White House I had seen him only in newspaper photos and on television. The more I looked at him the more I sensed that he was unwell, even on the brink of some kind of disaster. I returned the next day to Bloomington and on the following Tuesday hosted a luncheon for Robert Murphy, then deputy under secretary of state, who had come out from Washington to speak at what was then an annual Indiana University conference on foreign policy. As I had known Murphy well when we were together on Clay's staff and had kept in contact with him through other connections in the meantime, I felt free to mention to him my impression of President Eisenhower's health. "Bob," I went on, "you see the president close up frequently. Is there any basis for my apprehension?" He looked startled for a moment and said, "Why, I don't think so. I see him regularly at the cabinet meetings and I saw him this past week. I haven't observed any change in his appearance. Of course it could be that I see him so frequently I wouldn't notice a change, but I really think he is in fine shape." The fact of the matter is that President Eisenhower in the following September went for a few days to Denver, his wife's old home where he liked to visit and play golf, and there he had his first heart attack, a major one of which I had had the eerie premonition.

The emphasis in my career on international activities was furthered by Indiana University's early entrance into the technical-assistance field, which grew in part out of some of the personal friendships that developed at the San Francisco Conference with educational leaders from the Third World. When it came time for us to begin a massive technical-assistance program, we already had an acquaintanceship with the leading figures in many of the areas in which we were later invited to work. As a result of such experiences, I have had a continuing interest both personal and professional in those areas and have helped the university participate in many technical-assistance projects (see chapter 16).

Following the organization of the United Nations at the San Francisco Conference, there was held some months later in London a preparatory meeting to organize the United Nations Educational, Scientific and Cultural Organization (Unesco) along the lines that

George Zook and others in the A C E had hoped and worked for back in the early 1940s and at San Francisco. Through the A C E I became involved in an early activity of Unesco, and other assignments followed for which some background is necessary. Unesco was created as one of the specialized agencies of the U N; its basic philosophy is expressed in the stirring preamble to its Constitution, which declares in part:

> That since wars begin in the minds of men, it is in the minds of men that the defences of peace must be constructed;
> That ignorance of each other's ways and lives has been a common cause . . . of that suspicion and mistrust between peoples of the world through which their differences have all too often broken into war;

> . . . .

> . . . that the peace must therefore be founded, if it is not to fail, upon the intellectual and moral solidarity of mankind.

> . . . .

> For these reasons, the States Parties to this Constitution are agreed and determined to develop and to increase the means of communication between their peoples and to employ these means for the purposes of mutual understanding and a truer and more perfect knowledge of each other's lives. . . .

Unesco's program was to be carried out under seven broad headings: education, natural sciences, social sciences, cultural activities, exchange of persons, mass communications, and relief services. The constitution made provision for a governing body, called the general conference and composed of representatives of member states appointed by their governments in consultation with national commissions, which were supposed to be established in most of the countries. The United States has a national commission for Unesco on which I served from 1951 to 1955, representing the A C E. Walter Laves was chairman of this commission during two years of my term, and I served as his vice chairman from 1953 to 1954.

For the recently conquered countries there were peculiar problems in establishing national commissions and, as a result, special committees to advise the director general were set up: one for Germany, one for Japan, and perhaps others. I was named a member of the expert committee for Germany and made a number of trips to Paris, the headquarters of Unesco, during 1949–50 as a member of the Unesco Committee on German Questions. The special problems in Germany arose from the fact that Germany was an occupied country and, until the reestablishment of a national government, Unesco had to operate through occupation authorities, who did not agree among themselves. Our committee dealt with many thorny questions, which I will not attempt to describe here, but one concrete result of its work was the establishment of three centers, or institutes, in Germany: the International Institute for Education at Hamburg, the International Institute for Social Sciences at Cologne (Laves was on its board, 1951–60), and the International Institute for Youth at Gauting near Munich. The International Institute for Education had for its purpose to encourage German educators to question the basic concepts and aims of education in Germany, to make them aware of the constructive results of such questioning in other countries, and to serve as a clearing house for information on educational problems. The institute was instructed to study recent educational developments and methods and their possible adaptation to the German situation.

An international board was created to govern each of the institutes. I served as a member of the board of the Institute for Education from 1951 to 1957. Its office was in Hamburg and its director general was Walther Merck, a delightful and distinguished professor of pedagogy at Hamburg University who gave the work of the board excellent direction. He was an extremely well informed man with a broad comprehension of education, not only in Germany, but elsewhere in the world as well—a master of the science of comparative education. We at Indiana University later had the privilege of having him as a visitor on our Bloomington campus.

Service on the board of the Hamburg Institute was a rewarding experience. My membership lasted six years and involved two trips a year to Hamburg to meet with the director and the other board members. It was a widely representative board of imaginative and well-informed men and women. Service with this group gave me an unusual opportunity to keep in touch with what was happening in German education, to trace the evolution of some of the recommendations we had made during the Occupation, and to learn what was being developed through our recommendations. I found it always a delight to be in Hamburg—that old Hanseatic city in its colorful setting—to enjoy its excellent hotels, its superb restaurants and the good fellowship and camaraderie of my fellow board members.

My international interests inevitably caused me to affiliate with and participate in the affairs of many collateral types of organizations dealing with the problems of international relations such as the Foreign Policy Association and the Council on Foreign Relations. Moreover, I have become convinced that, as a result of advances in communication and transportation, our world has indeed grown small and its political and economic survival depends upon a high degree of international, political, cultural, and economic cooperation. I little realized when I became active in the American Council on Education that it would lead indirectly to extending my horizons worldwide.

⟦26⟧

○ ○ ○

The Educational Policies
Commission

S T A Y I N G power in the presidency attracts attention. The longer
I served as president of Indiana University, the greater the number of requests I received to take a guiding role in various groups
concerned with higher education. Some of the invitations came early
in my administration and meant opportunities for me to work with
influential leaders in the educational field while at the same time
shouldering my share of the profession's tasks. From the start I had
felt an obligation to be a good "educational citizen," that is, to be
concerned with policies, problems, and directions that affected not
just Indiana University but also most or all of the higher educational
community. The illustrations I have given in the two preceding
chapters and the two I give in this and the following chapter should
suffice to show the range of service and to suggest its value, in my
experience, to the university. Others I omit not invidiously but as
victims of ruthless space concerns.

For some reason unknown to me, the National Education Association (N E A) decided in 1943 to revive its Department of Higher
Education. I attended the meeting of the N E A in St. Louis that year
and wandered into the meeting room where a group of men in higher
education were discussing the possible leadership of the revived department. Much to my amazement, before the meeting was concluded
I had been elected president of the reestablished organization. The
action was surprising for a variety of reasons, not the least of which
was the fact that I had begun to be active in the work of the American Council on Education (A C E), and the rivalry between George
Zook of the A C E and Willard Givens, president of the N E A, although muted, was nonetheless real and well known. However, it

proved possible for me to be active in both organizations, and I maintained a relationship with the N E A and its leadership—first with Givens, an Indiana University alumnus, and then with his successor, William G. Carr—for a good many years.

One division of the N E A in those years was quite noted, namely, the Educational Policies Commission. I served first as a member of the commission in 1954 and then as its chairman from 1955 to 1958. Among the eighteen members of the commission during that period were Kenneth E. Oberholtzer, my able vice chairman, Carr, Ruth E. Eckert, Finis Engleman, Virgil Hancher, James R. Killian, Jr., and Eugene Youngert. The secretary, a competent and vigorous leader, was Howard E. Wilson.

The pronouncements of the Educational Policies Commission had traditionally commanded considerable respect and influence in educational circles, and, when this group addressed itself to the priorities for education, the project demanded the very best efforts of all its members and staff. One of the obvious problems in trying to envision the future in higher education is the necessity to think in terms of the resources that will be available. As our group began to look toward the future and discuss the question of how much of the gross national product (G N P) could be devoted to education— particularly higher education—without doing damage to other social needs, I was distressed at the timidity with which we seemed to view this matter. For instance, members of the commission were inclined to think in terms of an increase of between 25 percent and 50 percent on the average for faculty salaries. Something had to be done to raise their sights a bit, and, as a consequence, I asked two of my Indiana University colleagues, John Lewis and George Pinnell, to join with me in a study of what increase in expenditures for salaries was socially and economically possible during the next decade.

This study resulted in the preparation of a paper for private circulation in 1956 to members of the commission and to officers of both the N E A and the A C E entitled "Needs, Resources and Priorities in Higher Education Planning." Lewis and Pinnell furnished the facts and most of the work in preparing the article; I furnished the enthusiasm and the excuse for its preparation. In the article we called for a doubling of higher-education salaries in constant dollars by 1970 and through careful analysis argued that a substantial percentage increase in the amount of G N P devoted to higher education was feasible and socially desirable. The report, when received by my colleagues in the Education Policies Commission, was something of a blockbuster. They had not dared to think in any such bold terms, but the report did stiffen their resolution somewhat, and in their own final report (1957) they called for a sizable increase:

> It is imperative, at the very least, that the total amount spent on salaries, reckoned in stable dollars, should be advanced from 75 to 125 percent within the next 15 years—preferably within the next decade. An average annual increase of 5 to 10 percent in terms of stable dollars between now and 1970—with major emphasis on more than average increases during the early years of the period—is a conservative estimate of what is necessary to attract into teaching a reasonable proportion of the available qualified personnel.[1]

At least we increased the ante considerably by our study! The Lewis-Pinnell-Wells study drew heavily upon a study by another Indiana University colleague, Robert Turner. Following the publication of the Educational Policies Commission report in 1957, the Lewis-Pinnell-Wells report was published in the *Bulletin of the American Association of University Professors* in the autumn of 1957. Predictably, it received nationwide attention. I have reason to believe that it did have considerable influence in the thinking of Americans about the need to raise faculty salaries substantially and that the goal we established of doubling faculty salaries in stable dollars by 1970 was accomplished, and more. Actually our projections, instead of being daring, turned out to be rather conservative.

I hope that in my years of association with the N E A, which roughly coincided with my years of even greater activity with the A C E, I helped to smooth the relationship between the two organizations, thereby making them both more effective on behalf of their constituencies.

1. Educational Policies Commission, *Higher Education in a Decade of Decision* (National Education Association of the United States, 1957), p. 131.

{27}

○ ○ ○

The Roots of PBS

M Y EDUCATIONAL activities on a national scale also included participating in the development of educational television. In the early days of television, there was little interest on the part of either the general public or the nation's educators in public or educational television. However, the officers of the American Council on Education (ACE) early believed that television could offer an important educational and cultural resource, and accordingly the Council invited six other national organizations to join with it in forming the National Committee on Educational Television. An executive director was appointed, and the committee began an effort to have channels set aside for noncommercial use. The committee was soon joined in its work by the National Citizens for Educational Television, and the two groups had the support of most of the professional organizations with any conceivable interest in the field, including the National Association of Educational Broadcasters, the National Education Association, and so on. Largely as a result of their efforts, the Federal Communications Commission was induced to reserve in April, 1952, 242 television channels, 80 in the VHF band and 162 in the UHF band, for noncommercial, educational use.

The national effort of these two committees was supported by the Fund for Adult Education, which had been created by the Ford Foundation in 1951. The fund had an effective president, Scott Fletcher, and Robert B. Hudson, an able pioneer in the educational television field, was the professional consultant. It was reasonable for the fund to provide much of the early financial support for the promotion of the movement. The staff of the fund was active in spurring station activations throughout the country, and the fund's vision helped to establish from the beginning the concept that

[388]

American educational television should provide an informational and cultural service for persons of all ages, as well as instructional aid for public school classrooms.

As part of the ongoing movement, in 1954 the Educational Television and Radio Center, later to be known as National Educational Television (N E T), was organized and began weekly cultural and informational service to a small number of fledgling stations throughout the country. Located in Ann Arbor, Michigan, it too was supported in its first years by the Fund for Adult Education. Its prestigious first president was Harry K. Newburn, who had moved from his position as president of the University of Oregon. Since the center had neither a production staff nor equipment of its own, in the very beginning it was conceived basically as an exchange center, with most of its programming to be produced by the member stations or to be borrowed from any source that produced worthwhile programs and with the center acting as a distributing agent.

The organization was still in its formative stage when I was invited to join the board in 1959.[1] The board had strong leadership in the person of Ralph Lowell as chairman, who was the retired chairman of the Boston Safe Deposit and Trust Company of Boston, Massachusetts, and the godfather of the excellent W G B H - T V in Boston, one of the early important public television stations. I found participation in the board useful and stimulating for several reasons. In the first place, I had interest in the field; in the second place, I found the board of exceptional quality, and to meet with them was always an exciting intellectual experience; and in the third place, Indiana University was deeply involved in the distribution of educational films, some of which had originally been programs on the N E T network. The influence and effort of N E T paved the way for the creation and development of P B S.

In the beginning few realized the necessity for a noncommercial broadcasting network. As the quality of its programs and the size of its audience grew with time, almost spectacularly, the public network came to be rightly seen as an irreplaceable national asset. After the board moved to New York, Everett Case, the president of the Sloan Foundation, became its chairman, and Norman Cousins, its vice chairman and later chairman. John White, who succeeded

---

1. The board had a provision in its constitution that its members could not serve longer than two consecutive terms. I served from 1959 to 1964, but, to my surprise, after a year I was again elected and served from 1965 to 1970, when the organization was absorbed into the national P B S.

Harry Newburn as president, gave to the organization dynamic and creative leadership comprising experience, originality, sparkle, and great energy. He now is the president of Cooper Union.

I learned to admire Norman Cousins. He certainly is one of the most interesting and attractive intellectuals in America. I also met on this board for the first time Mortimer Fleishhacker, chairman of the board of Precision Instrument Company in San Francisco, and found him to be a businessman of remarkably broad intellectual and cultural interests. Newton Minow, who had been prominent in Washington circles in the Kennedy administration and who was at the time practicing law in Chicago, was another member of the board whom I found stimulating, as was Peter Peterson, then chairman of the board of Bell and Howell and since that time active in both financial and governmental circles. The board was also graced by the presence of James B. Reston, the well-known Scotty Reston of the New York *Times*, who always added immeasurably to the discussion. In fact, every member of the board was outstanding, and I benefited much from my association with each of them. Their belief in the importance of public television and their unselfish efforts to overcome the public apathy, even antagonism, toward the medium were a decisive factor in the long struggle to establish the fourth network we enjoy today.

From the beginning of N E T there was a debate over its function, whether it was to provide classroom instructional material and public-affairs broadcasting and, if so, in what proportions: how much energy was to be devoted to one and how much to the other? The matter came to a head in 1962. At that time the N E T management was asked by the Ford Foundation to present a ten-year budget projection. Two projections were submitted, one for the general service, that is, the evening service that later became public television; the other, unsolicited by Ford but submitted anyway, a ten-year projection for a second and parallel, school service. The Ford Foundation after reviewing the projections stated that an additional grant for N E T would be made only if N E T would divest itself of the school-service broadcasting and devote its energies solely to public affairs and cultural programming.

This decision on the part of the Ford Foundation, which carried a grant of six million dollars a year, resolved the debate within N E T. N E T proceeded to divest itself of the classroom instructional responsibility. Although events have demonstrated since then the wisdom of the Ford Foundation's requests, N E T's record had been excellent in the production of classroom materials. As a consequence, in 1962 the U.S. Office of Education made a grant to N E T "to demonstrate the educational desirability and economic feasibility of a national agency providing recorded instructional television programs." This experiment was operated by N E T in New York for three years; then in 1965, the demonstration was expanded and relocated here in Bloomington. Edward Cohen, an Indiana University alumnus who had been in charge of the program in New York, came to Bloomington to head the project. With this move, a new entity called National Instructional Television was created, and Dr. Cohen was made its executive director.

At the conclusion of that contract, still more time was needed for development of the idea, and the Indiana University Foundation advanced a substantial amount of money to keep the project going during the years 1968–70, after which it was believed the service could be supported entirely from earnings and over a period of six years could repay the advance made by the Foundation. In fact, the service was able to repay the Foundation ahead of schedule. The crux of N I T's achievement of self-support while continuing to strengthen its product was the recognition that it could not change immediately from entire economic dependence. Rather, a transition stage was necessary in which declining amounts of borrowed capital would complement increased earnings.

In time the chief state school officers of the United States became interested and indicated their willingness to assume sponsorship of the project. As a consequence, in 1973 the entity was renamed the Agency for Instructional Television (A I T) and continues today under the sponsorship of the Council of Chief State School Officers with Edward Cohen as the executive director of the enterprise. The key element in its success has been the leadership of Dr. Cohen, who has given it brilliant and successful direction. The organization, still located in Bloomington, continues to flourish. Thus Indiana University, by providing hospitality and encouragement to this enterprise, saved a program of quality instructional television of national significance.

{28}

○ ○ ○

Trying to Do One's Share

IN OUR type of society, which expects many civic and social
needs to be met by voluntary means rather than by government
action, each able citizen is under some obligation to assume a share
of responsibility for this voluntary work. The responsibility increases
with the prominence of the citizen and his role in society. In America the college or university president is typically a leading figure in
his town, his state, and frequently in the nation. This is certainly true
of the president of Indiana University. The home campus is the dominant factor in both the economic and the social life of the community. As the oldest and largest university in the state, Indiana
University has such eminence that any man who occupies its presidency automatically becomes a prominent figure in higher education and well known generally. If his personal characteristics and
activities further enhance his public recognition, the amount of responsibility placed upon him is very large indeed.

The special nature of the era in which I have lived increased the
number of civic duties to be performed by volunteers. I speak especially of the time during which we were engaged in several wars
that put great strain on the manpower of the nation and that required
that every individual invest himself fully in the work to be done.
Then came the inevitable years of readjustment after the wars. It
has been a period nationally of rapid growth in education and of
expanding international obligations—social, political, and cultural.
I have cited as examples some of the assignments I undertook outside the state and nation. It seems to me important not to neglect
local and state responsibilities that were requested of me.

From the beginning, and continuing to this very day, I have
tried to assume my share of civic responsibilities first in the local
community—to make myself available for committee service, serv-

ice clubs, the Chamber of Commerce, the community hospital, church boards, and other activities as requested. I remember once serving for a number of years with the head of the Chamber of Commerce to promote the economic development of Bloomington. I did this not only because I thought it my duty but also because I felt that development of an industrial sector in the community would make it a more balanced community, a better place for the students to spend four formative years, and would create more employment for the citizens of the community. Not long ago I read a letter to the editor of the local paper in which the writer alleged that Indiana University had always opposed securing industry for Bloomington. Nothing could be further from the truth. Throughout my years with the university I have actively helped in any way I could to secure additional industry for the community, even to the extent of advocating the dedication of a certain amount of university ground for the development of research institutes and light industries.

I have also attempted to serve my church in a variety of capacities, on its boards and committees and especially for a long period as a member of the state board of the Wesley Foundation, which supports the student activities of the church in university communities. The presence of student-oriented churches in a university community is of great value. In addition to providing the means by which students may maintain their traditional church relationships, the resident churches with their student-affiliated foundations and ministers are great sources of counseling assistance for students and even for faculty.

Very early in my career the Indiana General Assembly created a New Harmony Memorial Commission for the purpose of restoring and readying for visitors the pioneer community in southern Indiana that spawned many interesting scientific and social ideas. I served on this commission for many years until it was terminated by the legislature. Now I serve on a reincarnated state New Harmony Memorial Commission as well as on the board of Historic New Harmony, the private organization that is involved in the work of restoration and preservation in that community. Another example of a state-level association in which I have been active for a similar length of time is the James Whitcomb Riley Memorial Association. While this association has university connections, as its principal purpose is to build, support, and develop the James Whitcomb Riley Hospital for Children at the Indiana University Medical

Center, it nevertheless has an independent character and is one of the most prestigious philanthropic organizations in the state. I became a member of its board when I entered the presidency, and my uninterrupted membership from that time to this makes me the senior member in point of service.

Early in my career I was also appointed to membership on the state board of education. This spot, representing the interests of higher education, had been held by the president of Indiana University for some decades. I served on that board for quite a few years until it was reorganized; in the reorganization higher education lost its representation. From 1937 to the present I have served on many other statewide committees, commissions, and boards of state organizations, too many to name here, but for a reader interested in their range a list of them is included in the chronology in the Appendix. That part of my vita represents my belief in and commitment to doing my share of the voluntary activity to be carried on in the city and state.

Another group of organizations in the state to which I committed myself through the years were those that were designed to sustain, encourage, and promote the private sector in higher education. In addition to helping with the organization and promotion of the Associated Colleges of Indiana, I served on occasion as kickoff speaker for fund drives at Wabash College, DePauw University, and Earlham College. For a time I was a member of the Wabash College Development Board; I served on the board of trustees of Earlham College for many years and on the board of the Indiana Institute of Technology; and I also had lengthy service on the board of the Malpas Trust, a charitable trust created by a philanthropic Hoosier for the purpose of providing scholarships for students to attend DePauw. It now is one of the most generous and cherished fellowship programs that that fine institution enjoys.

Through the years I have been afforded an opportunity to continue some practical contact with my early field of banking, as I have related. Also, after my father's death in 1948 I became chairman of the board of the Jamestown State Bank, which he had served as president, and I continued in that position until the bank was sold. This was, of course, a sentimental as well as a family responsibility since I had started to work in that bank when I was thirteen years old. It was a surprise to me to discover that I could still recall and identify many of the customers of the bank as their names appeared in the conduct of the board's business. Since the bank was small and noncompetitive with any other, I could go onto its board without violating a principle that I followed from the beginning of my presidency of Indiana University, namely, that I would not join any commercial board if its business might be competing with the business of other alumni.

This, Too, Was for the University

My outside activities have made visible my belief in voluntarism as an essential American principle. It may seem that my extensive engagement with the work of state, national, and international groups deprived the university of time and effort that could better have been applied directly to the university's needs. Actually, for Indiana University to become what I dreamed for it, its orbit needed to be enlarged and its aspirations elevated. Thus all my external assignments were undertaken with a view to gaining the experience and establishing the contacts that would increase the university's province. While the indirect benefits to the university from my various external associations seem obvious, it may be useful to illustrate this process by citing an instance or two in some detail.

One illustration can be drawn from my international activities. First, my own understanding, knowledge, and perceptions were broadened with each foreign experience; basically I became an informal student of comparative cultures. This gave me empathy with all elements in our faculty concerned with expanding the international dimension of the university and enabled me to offer encouragement, intelligent comment, and occasionally practical suggestion for development. It also gave me a warm relationship with the student organizations that had begun promoting internationalization after World War II. Mother and I regularly attended their meetings and social events, as did many of the faculty. The Cosmopolitan Club staged annual international shows that attracted the interest and attention of the entire campus, faculty and students alike. During this period also the Acacia fraternity inaugurated an annual fall reception honoring foreign faculty and students. My international experiences enabled me to have a closer relationship with the foreign-born members of our faculty, giving me a firsthand understanding of the cultures that they represented and the educational systems that had produced them. This in turn gave them a sense of security and confidence in their work here, I hope, and the feeling that they were appreciated and had a special contribution to make. In addition, we attempted to make sure that our international faculty had widespread social contacts with other faculty members on the campus, thereby breaking down any hesitancies arising from foreignness. We tried as well to suggest indirectly that our having various cultures represented on the campus was an asset to our corporate faculty life, with the result that foreign faculty members enjoyed a position of prominence.

My many academic contacts abroad also gave me an understanding of how foreign faculty visitors should be treated when they came to this campus if we wished them to carry away a favorable impression of our institution. I do believe that one can extend the fame and reputation of a university without leaving the campus simply by the thoughtful, informed hospitality offered to those who visit the campus. In much of the world the academic is more highly respected by society than is his counterpart in America, and we need to bear this in mind when receiving and entertaining visitors from abroad, to be sensitive to their expectations.

We tried to encourage the expansion of the curriculum to encompass new fields, anticipating the onrush of the international role that the country was destined to play as is now more and more evident. Furthermore, the expansion into the various exotic and esoteric languages and into the history and culture of little-known areas of the world represented a push for knowledge for its own sake. It is a purpose of the university to be the repository of knowledge, some of it not usually available from any place other than a center of learning. The wheel of time and circumstance inevitably turns in the direction of the need for this knowledge and lucky is the university that has a reservoir of it.

After I personally had a major experience abroad, I made it a practice to share that experience with my campus colleagues in formal speeches and informal conversations, and invariably incorporated at least some elements of that experience in speeches that I made throughout the state. I made hundreds of speeches of this type, I suppose, in the course of the years, dealing with international experience, international relations, and American foreign policy. We early helped to arrange rather high-level foreign policy conferences annually on the campus, not only for the benefit of our own campus colleagues, but also for the benefit of selected interested citizens throughout the state. In this way we attempted to increase the awareness within the state of the importance of the international dimension in our life—not only its political, social, and military significance, but also its very great economic significance to a manufacturing state such as ours. We may have been a little ahead of our time, but I would hope that the work of that period has stimulated in part the current widespread realization of our interdependence politically, socially, and—above all else—economically. I do not know whether this has been helped in part by the fact that at long last we realize we have to feed the world.

In my professional associations I invariably found myself on the international committees dealing with cultural interchange or with the problems of internationalizing curricula and breaking down nationalistic stereotypes. For an example of this last, I served on a United States–Canadian textbook commission formed to remove from textbooks some of the fallacies and myths about our national histories that had grown up on each side of the border.

Of course, the more interest the administration evidenced in the international dimension, the more pervasive was its influence throughout the university and, to some extent, the state. People have marveled that Indiana University, in a rather conservative, mid-America state, should have become known for its international emphasis. There are those who allege that this happened in part as a result of the university leadership's participation in international activities.

Inevitably, interconnections developed among my state, national, and international activities. My acceptance of responsibilities in the international area, for instance, led to opportunities to accept others in the national arena, until in time I became absorbed in a number of professional educational activities that were demanding of my time and energy but that provided some benefit to the university in its expanding role. A clear example of this interaction, discussed above, was my participation in the United Nations organizing conference in San Francisco as a representative of the American Council on Education (ACE). In a less direct way, my experience in Germany with General Clay and my ACE stint led to my assuming the chairmanship in 1962 of Education and World Affairs.

My participation in national and international organizations had an additional value. Inevitably I had opportunities to suggest the names of my own colleagues as members of various committees, commissions, and the like in process of formation. People get appointed to such committees and commissions simply because someone who knows them happens to be in on the planning and discussion of the personnel for a new group. In this way I could open doors of responsibility and opportunity for many of my valued colleagues in a whole variety of fields. At times colleagues through demonstration of their abilities on national committees or boards had many other opportunities offered to them and were able to bring the strength of all those contacts and connections back to the campus. They were then frequently able to bring conferences here and to have their colleagues from elsewhere see the work of individual departments and gain a firsthand impression of Indiana University.

In short, my activities off campus, undertaken always with some consideration of the university's good, affected the university in many ways, it seems to me in retrospect, and I hope that they were justified from the standpoint of the university's welfare and of the merit of each activity per se.

{29}

○ ○ ○

*With My Hat
on the Back of My Head*

FROM 1928 to the present all my positions have required considerable travel. In the course of the last 50 years I have traveled several million miles by every conceivable conveyance—carriage, train, automobile, airplane, tonga, pedicab, and boats both river-plying and ocean-going. From Easter Island to Capetown, Milford Sound to Helsinki, Bangkok to Vancouver, this travel has taken me to some 115 countries of the world including all the principal countries except mainland China (and that is scheduled for the near future). As I have visited many of these countries several times, I have come to know them rather well. Most of the travel has been for business or, on occasion and with some added days, a combination of business and recreation or cultural exploration. In a few notable instances I have traveled for the sheer sake of enjoyment and the satisfaction of my curiosity and cultural comprehension.

In the course of this journeying I have witnessed a remarkable evolution in travel. I can remember a time when a gravel road in Indiana was considered a good road. The automobiles have changed from the Model-T Ford to the present comfortable and maneuverable cars. I have witnessed the coming and going of electric interurban lines that once upon a time fanned out from Indianapolis like spokes of a giant wheel to reach most of the state. For the most part steam trains were slow and sometimes dirty locals, but there were also the great luxurious trains such as the *Twentieth-Century Limited* from Chicago to New York, the *Southwestern Limited* from St. Louis to New York, the *Capital Limited* from Chicago to Washington, and the *National Limited* from St. Louis to Washington as well as the transcontinental trains from Chicago to the West Coast such as the *Super Chief*, traveling at great speed and affording the passenger not just comfortable but also deluxe accommodations—individual bedrooms, flower-bedecked diners, and club-like observation lounges.

In my undergraduate days the Illinois Central, operating from Indianapolis to Effiingham, Illinois, where it made connection with the important Illinois Central trains from Chicago to New Orleans, carried in addition to its regular passenger cars a combination Pullman and diner, that is, a few Pullman seats and a demidiner that produced excellent food. I remember to this day the bean soup that they served on that diner. I have never had better, including the famous bean soup served in the U.S. Senate dining room in the Capitol. A favorite route of mine was to travel from Lebanon to Indianapolis by interurban and then to take the 6:00 P.M. Illinois Central to Bloomington. The train was comfortable, the scenery beautiful along the way through parts of Brown County, and the nearly two-hour trip from Indianapolis always enjoyable.

Any true Hoosier writing about trains is duty-bound to remember the Monon with gratitude and pride. The Monon was an independent railroad that considered itself the Hoosier line, and so it was in every respect. It inspired poets to sing its praises, politicians to pay tribute in florid phrase, and collegians to amass a whole body of folklore concerning it, some of it unprintable. Its passenger trains between Chicago and Indianapolis were models of speed and comfort with excellent coaches, parlor and observation cars, and a dining service that was nationally famous. The cuisine was proudly all-Hoosier style: the apple pie with glazed crust served with excellent cheddar cheese was an unforgettable delight; the steaks were so tender they could be cut with a fork; and the memory of the chicken pot pie still makes me hungry. The Monon took pride in the fact that its main line served St. Joseph's, Purdue, Wabash, DePauw, and Indiana University. It carried dignified scholars on academic missions and roistering students and alumni to athletic contests with heedless impartiality.

The Monon also provided vital service including all-Pullman specials to the French Lick and West Baden resort hotels. I remember seeing at Kentucky Derby time the railroad sidings between French Lick and West Baden filled with Pullmans and private cars. During such peak seasons, the cloak room at Brown's, the principal casino, was crammed with ermine and sable coats.

The French Lick Springs Hotel under the owner-management of the Taggart family was truly one of the grand hotels of the world. As one entered up the long, canopied stairway, a row of blooming potted plants on either side created a joyful mood in every season of the year. The service was highly personalized and impeccable. Typically the hotel was filled with interesting guests. In season the spacious gardens, all meticulously maintained, were among the most beautiful in the world. The tanbark-covered footpaths through the woodland invited exercise. In those days the food was incomparable for an American-plan hotel. I remember with nostalgia the French lamb chops perfectly broiled that were regularly offered on the breakfast menu.

Before I had my cottage in Brown County, I would use the French Lick Hotel as a weekend retreat or sometimes for a longer period to secure the peace and quiet of the place for uninterrupted work. The hotel had a distinctive personality: all the mystique of the grand hotel yet all the spacious comfort of a resort. And still it managed to be truly a Hoosier institution. I enjoyed every occasion I was there. It was a happy hotel—smart, elegant, good-mannered, and at the same time relaxed. I knew the hotel long before I had experienced the grand, luxe hotels and spas of Europe, but unless my memory deceives me French Lick during that era held its own with the best anywhere.

The 1925 Grand Chapter of my college fraternity was held at West Baden Springs Hotel during the Christmas holidays. I was a member of the committee responsible for the formal dinner and ball. Since we needed beautiful girls as dates for our brother delegates, it was arranged that coeds from numerous campuses who were spending their holidays in Indianapolis would be transported to West Baden via Pullman cars on the Monon. The formal ball was held in the Great Rotunda of the hotel and many believe that it was the most glamorous Grand Chapter ball in the history of the fraternity. The Monon made it possible.

In the heyday of transatlantic ocean travel there was year-round regular service between New York and Europe, the Cunard Line alone running weekly service both ways and, in high season, two or three ships each way weekly. The French, Holland-American, and German lines offered frequent service. There were also many ships from New York plying the southern route to Italy, Greece, and other Mediterranean ports. I have been privileged to experience travel on the great ships during that era, particularly those on the transatlantic run, which were the finest and fastest that man has ever built. Through the years I sailed repeatedly on the *Queen Mary*, the *Queen Elizabeth*, and, more recently, the *QE2*. I have crossed on the *Nieuw Amsterdam* of the Holland-American Line, the *Liberté* and the *Ile de France* of the French Line, as well as the *United States* of the United States Line. The *United States* was the fastest passenger ship ever built and a marvel of advanced engineering, providing a smooth crossing and the ultimate in safety. I crossed only once on the *Independence*, departing from Algeciras after having taken the boat train down from Madrid. It was a slow, leisurely crossing in off-season when passengers receive extra service and attention to their comfort. I had a veranda room at a single-cabin rate, and a severe cold confined me to my private deck most of the time. The doctor, who was a bit of an alcoholic and lonely, spent a great deal of time in his cups recounting to me his sorrows and the problems of the world. I nearly missed a trip on the Italian Line, which sailed between New York and Italy. Fortunately, I was able to go to Algeciras on the *Michelangelo* on one of her last crossings. Having been refurbished, she was in fine condition though losing money and was taken out of service soon thereafter.

I well remember a crossing on the *Nieuw Amsterdam*. Atlantic hurricanes, which usually originate in the Caribbean, sometimes sweep as far as the North Atlantic shipping lanes. On this crossing the *Nieuw Amsterdam* was forced to sail through the upper end of a hurricane, albeit at reduced speed. Mother was confined to her cabin, wretchedly seasick, as were most other passengers. The dining room was largely deserted. Fortunately I am a good sailor, and I remember vividly some hours spent on the top deck near the bridge with one of the officers watching the great waves come crashing up the height of the ship, though the *Nieuw Amsterdam* was huge —eight or nine decks high. It was a beautiful and thrilling sight, furnishing me not just excitement and beauty but also a new understanding of the destructive power of wind and wave.

I have witnessed a change in the pattern of travel. In Indiana fifty years ago hotels were located in nearly every county seat and town with a railroad junction. Business, professional, and commercial travelers needed good hotels every twenty-five to fifty miles to fit their mode of travel. When modes and patterns of travel changed, the result was the demise of most of the country hotels of yesteryear. Once it was unthinkable to go fifty or seventy-five miles for an appointment or a speech and return the same night. One's trip included an overnight stay in a hotel and usually several stops on the way to or from the destination, traveling either by car or train or, as I did in the early days of my travel, by steamboat between Cincinnati and Louisville with stops at certain riverports that were almost isolated because of the poor local roads. The Greene Line maintained daily service between Cincinnati and Louisville with comfortable berths and a good dining salon.

Indiana has been blessed with some excellent hotels. The grand dowager of them all was the Claypool in Indianapolis. It deserved its reputation as one of America's great hotels. It had an elegant lobby and other public parlors, spacious and immaculate bedrooms, superb food in its beautiful dining rooms, and the benefit of an owner-manager who knew what a great hotel should be. The Claypool was the scene of most of the important statewide public dinners. Generally such functions were held in the beautiful Riley Room on the mezzanine floor. In some uncanny fashion the Claypool chef could serve filet mignon to four hundred diners in the Riley Room and each filet would be hot, juicy, and properly pink. Better crusty rolls could not be had even in New York. The waiters were highly proficient. When a well-starched, white napkin slid off a corpulent lap, it was instantly and unobtrusively replaced with a fresh one.

I lived in the Claypool for a couple of years in the late 1920s, when it was in its prime, and experienced the comfort of its suave service and its magnificent cuisine. John L. Lewis, chief of the Indiana and Illinois division of the miner's union and beginning to rise in prominence as a labor leader, lived there at the same time. I remember distinctly that he sat nearly every evening after dinner in a particular chair in front of a big marble column in the huge, three-story-high Claypool lobby. Thus enthroned, he held court— acquaintances, politicians, labor leaders, newspapermen, all stopping by to pay their respects and to chat.

Another notable Hoosier hotel of that era, a close second or perhaps even equal to the Claypool, was the McCurdy in Evansville, owned and operated by one of America's most colorful and flamboyant hotel operators, Harold Van Orman, active not only in hotel circles but also in political and social circles in the state. He served for four years as lieutenant governor, in which capacity he presided over the Indiana Senate. He was a noted raconteur, much sought after as a master of ceremonies and after-dinner speaker. On such occasions he delighted his audiences by asserting that as lieutenant governor he presided over the greatest legislative body that money could buy.

But first and foremost Van Orman was an incomparable hotel operator. He infused into his staff a sense of the importance of the guest. He himself spent long hours in the lobby greeting people. The hotel was beautifully designed and appointed and had a spectacular riverfront location with a huge porch on which one could rock while looking across the garden to the Ohio River. Although a commercial hotel, it had such a delightful location that it could have been a resort hotel as well. Harold Van Orman had a real flair for food, and I remember to this day the magnificent breakfast menus that always included fried, old Tennessee ham with red-eye gravy, grits, and eggs along with soda biscuits—a touch of the South in recognition of Evansville's distinction as the southernmost important city in Indiana.

In that same section of the state along the Ohio River was the William Tell in Tell City, an attractive, white-clapboard country hotel of approximately one hundred rooms, rather simple appointments, but bountiful table. A little north was the Ideal at Huntingburg, also a simple structure—austerely so—but owner-managed and noted for the lavish, American-plan meals served in its dining room. In retrospect I would say the Ideal was more for the gourmand than for the gourmet. When I first visited the Ideal as a brash young man, I said to the clerk that I wished to have a room with bath. He nodded and assigned me a room. It was the policy in all country hotels of that time for guests to remain below and to leave their bags in the lobby until they were ready to go to bed. Bedtime was early, after the guests had dined and visited with each other in front of the hotel in the summertime or, in the wintertime, in the lobby. As I was a newcomer, when it came time for me to go up to bed the clerk condescended to show me my room. As we entered, I looked around for the door to the bathroom and then asked where it was. He said, "Right down the hall, of course." When I explained that I had expected a private bath he said, "Well, young feller, we ain't that fine yet."

Up the Ohio River at Lawrenceburg the Reagan Hotel, even with its primitive plumbing, had such hospitable owner-management and such an excellent country dining room that experienced travelers arranged their itineraries to include it regularly. Farther north was the Sherman House in Batesville, still blessed with the benign ownership of the Hillenbrand family, which is justly famous for the quality of its table. In the far northern part of the state there was an admirable country hotel in Goshen, the Hotel Goshen, with about one hundred rooms, which the experienced traveler sought out for its comfort, the warmth of its owner-management's welcome, and its bountiful table. Then scattered throughout the state were hotels of more modern vintage, erected mostly between the two world wars —the Hotel Elkhart in Elkhart, the Oliver in South Bend, the Keenan in Fort Wayne, the Graham in Bloomington, the Terre Haute House in Terre Haute, the Roberts in Muncie, the Fowler in Lafayette, and the Leland in Richmond. These were all well run and each was a real haven for the weary traveler. More sophisticated in service than their country cousins of which I have spoken, they usually contained a barber shop, a coffee shop as well as a dining room, a newsstand, a beauty parlor, room telephones, and private suites. A somewhat special member of this group was the Hotel Gary, erected I think just after World War I by the United States Steel Corporation as part of its program to make Gary a model city. It was indeed a beautiful hotel, comparable in its physical appointments to any large city hotel, well run and an adornment to the city. It was also a community center where most important community functions were held and where quarters were provided for the principal private club of the city's business and professional men.

Samuel Johnson once pontificated, "There is nothing which has yet been contrived by man by which so much happiness is produced as by a good tavern or inn." I can subscribe to the Johnsonian dictum. I love hotels, I like to explore for new ones while remaining passionately faithful to old friends, and in a sense hotels are one of my collecting interests. I like to collect comparative impressions and experiences in hotels. But what makes a good hotel?

Clearly, what one person regards as a good hotel another may dislike, but there is considerable general agreement. A good hotel must have a combination of superior facilities, a happy location, owner-management or at least management of the highest order, an alert and skilled staff beginning with the front desk and including the bellmen and the chambermaids, an imaginative cuisine, and that elusive quality known as personality. Hotels have distinctive personalities just as individuals do. A hotel without a personality affronts the traveler needing refreshment of spirit and relief from tedium. It has been my privilege to stay in many of the great hotels in the United States and abroad. A few stories from a sampling of them will illustrate the enjoyment they have supplied.

In San Francisco the Palace was once the top hotel; its magnificent garden-court dining room is still beautiful. When I had the privilege of hosting a tour by the International Association of Universities (IAU) Board of Directors to Canadian universities and American west-coast universities, I arranged to have them stay at the Palace, then in its heyday. It is very much in the European "Grand Hotel" tradition, and the members of the IAU board took to it as a kitten takes to cream.

Mother and I wished to do something personal for the group, and knowing that the Palace was noted for its wine cellar and especially for its selection of top-grade California wines, I planned a surprise dinner for the members of the board. Several members, particularly the French and German members of the board, considered themselves great wine connoisseurs, one coming from Dijon in the heart of Burgundy. Earlier in the day while ordering dinner, I described my guests to the maitre d' and asked him to use exclusively California wines of the highest quality but to make sure the guests did not know that it was California wine when it was being served. So there was a superb California white, a good sound red, and then champagne with dessert. All during the meal the connoisseurs kept commenting on the wine and the food. Impressed, they were all trying to guess whether the wine was French, German, or Italian, and the year, the chateau, and so forth. At the end I called the maitre d' and asked him to give them a list of the Californias that he had served, and they were dumbfounded while we enjoyed our moment of chauvinistic triumph for the U.S.A.

I have had the privilege of enjoying many of the fine resort hotels in the United States. Fortunately, most of these accommodate small conferences and therefore I have had an opportunity to enjoy their facilities in connection with attendance at business meetings. On other occasions I have sought them for vacations.

In Honolulu I consider the Kahala-Hilton one of the most comfortable and beautiful hotels I know in the world. Its lobby juts out toward the ocean, giving a guest the sensation of being on an ocean liner; the service is deft and prompt; the rooms are beautiful, spacious, and well maintained—altogether a laudable hotel.

The Ahwahnee in Yosemite National Park is a remarkable hotel, rustic in construction, luxurious in comfort and food, and singular in its setting. A huge window at the end of its lofty dining room affords a spectacular view of the mountains. Until recently it was operated by the Curry family, natives of Bloomington, who went to the West Coast with David Starr Jordan when at the turn of the century he left the Indiana University presidency to found Leland Stanford University.

Nearer home, the Grand Hotel on Mackinac Island is unique in many respects. It is a well-appointed resort hotel dating from the 1880s, situated in flower-filled grounds, beautiful, successful, delightful, with a magnificent view of the Mackinac Straits. It bears the stamp of its inimitable owner-manager, W. Stewart Woodfill, a native Hoosier and truly a "Gentleman from Indiana."[1] While I was chairman of the board of the Federal Home Loan Bank of Indianapolis, one meeting of the board each year was held at the Grand Hotel in conjunction with the annual meeting of the Michigan Savings and Loan Association. It was my custom to remain a few days after the conclusion of the meeting to enjoy the beauty of the island, the clear air, the great swimming pool, and the special courtesies extended me by Stewart Woodfill that typically included drives around the island in his own smart, horse-drawn rig (no automobiles are allowed on the island), and cocktails with him at his lake-front home below the hotel, during which I enjoyed his animated conversation.

The Greenbrier at White Sulphur Springs in West Virginia with its distinctive Dorothy Draper decor of white, green, and splashy red is a distinctive and luxurious hotel. The Williamsburg Inn at Williamsburg, Virginia, furnished entirely in beautiful period furniture with spacious public parlors and luxurious bedrooms deserves its great popularity. Its superb dining room features a justly famous hunt breakfast. But perhaps the top resort hotel in America for my taste is the Homestead at Hot Springs, Virginia, sitting in the midst of a great estate of thousands of acres affording beautiful vistas in every direction. An owner-operated establishment with

1. Mr. Woodfill has just announced the gift of the hotel and other properties to his nephew, R. Daniel Musser.

marvelous food, charm, comfort, relaxed and gracious atmosphere, it is one of the few places in the world where tea is still served every afternoon at four—and that in a flower-filled lobby with a string ensemble playing semiclassical music. Its spa facilities include the natural warm springs used by George Washington and Thomas Jefferson. A half-hour spent in this pool with springs bubbling up around me is pure joy for my arthritic joints.

European hotels in contrast to American hotels depend in part for the distinctive quality of their service upon the concierge. I agree with Joseph Wechsberg's description: "A good concierge has a diplomat's tact, a banker's discretion, a scientist's encyclopedic knowledge, and the ability to forget certain things and never to forget others. . . . He'll advise you what to do, where to go, whom to avoid. He never says, 'I don't know.' If he doesn't know, he'll find out."

In Europe, one of my favorites through the years has been Claridge's in London. It is only one of several top hotels there, but certain things have endeared it to me. I like its quiet, its pure linen sheets, its highly individualized service, its spacious rooms, and its old-fashioned courtesy and methods of operation, including tea in the parlor each day and an out-of-view bar from which drinks are served. A spirited small orchestra entertains during cocktails, and after-dinner coffee and cognac are served in the lounge adjoining the main dining room.

Claridge's is the kind of place about which stories and legends collect. I have a true one. Once, when I arrived in London late at night from New York and was shown to my room, I noticed that there was an interesting double bed in the room and that the room itself was different from the typical room with double bed that I always requested. Claridge's keeps a record of all its regular customers' special wishes and makes a great effort to observe them without being prompted. The next morning I commented to the Irish maid when she came into my room that the bed was the most comfortable in which I had ever slept. In her brogue she replied, "Faith and it should be a good bed." It seems that my reservation came in late, all the rooms with double beds were occupied, so the twin beds in this room were removed and a bed was brought from storage. "This," she said with a flourish, "is the bed we keep for the Queen of Spain when she visits."

On two occasions Mother and I had the opportunity to follow the typical route of an Edwardian grand tour of the Continent. We did not do it all in one trip, but we covered most of it in the course of two trips, and these took us invariably to the great, comfortable, old Victorian piles typically known as the "Grand" or the "Palace" throughout Germany, Italy, Switzerland, and France, as well as in the Low Countries. If I were writing a travel book I would include some of these with fond recollection; here I have confined myself to a few favorites.

The Brenner's Park Hotel in Baden-Baden is certainly on anybody's list of the ten best hotels in the world, and Mother and I have had happy days there in comfortable rooms just over a little stream whose music lulled us to sleep. On our first visit there, in 1963, we flew from Stockholm to Frankfurt and motored to Baden-Baden, arriving late in the afternoon on August 7. We were soon comfortably situated. Upon entering the hotel I had noticed a plaque stating that the famous Russian novelist Turgenev had resided and worked in a house near the Brenner's Park from 1862 to 1870. A few days after we arrived, I received in the mail from my old friend and colleague, Michael Ginsburg, a copy of *The Vintage Turgenev*, volume one, containing *Smoke, Fathers and Sons*, and *First Love*. I casually glanced at *Smoke* and was astonished by its opening sentence: "At four o'clock in the afternoon of August 10, 1862 very many people were assembled outside the famous Konversationshaus in Baden-Baden." The account continues with a description of Baden-Baden as it was in 1862. Here was I, on August 10, 1963, a part of a similar scene being enacted 101 years afterward. Seldom have I received so thoughtfully chosen and opportune a gift as that, and I read it, of course, with great pleasure during my days at Baden-Baden.

On my last visit to Baden-Baden, I found the hotel's standards maintained, its facilities augmented by an indoor swimming pool, and the service and food as great as ever. Baden-Baden hardly seems real. Its spacious, flower-filled parks are an ideal setting for outdoor band concerts. Its truly magnificent spa facilities, its miles of walks cushioned by the needles of Black Forest pines, its chic boutiques and voluptuous pastry shops, its glittering casino patronized by beautiful people in evening dress—all add up to a never-never land. Best of all, at least at the Brenner's Park, the international clientele consists of people who have nothing to prove.

Returning for a moment to my travels with Mother—once when we were in Zurich, Mother expressed a wish to drive to Interlaken to have lunch at the Hotel Victoria-Jungfrau. Believing this to be her last trip to Europe, she hoped to see the Jungfrau once more. On a previous visit, she had had a front room facing toward the mountain and had enjoyed the view. I tried to explain to her that we would probably not be able to see the mountain since its peak is covered by clouds much of the time, but she insisted. Just as we had anticipated, when we arrived the mountain was wholly shrouded by clouds. However, as we were beginning our lunch on the terrace, someone looked up and, miraculously, the clouds had parted. Here was the magnificent Jungfrau's snow-capped peak in all of its grandeur as if displayed for Mother's pleasure. It stayed unveiled for about thirty minutes, long enough for her to feel justified in having insisted on making the trip.

The Grand Hotel in Rome is also one of my favorites: quiet, with superb food and service. It afforded me a memorable dinner, remembered as much because of the circumstances preceding it as for the dinner itself. I had been in the Third World for two or three weeks and was hungry for familiar food, in fact almost counting the hours until I could have a good dinner. But I was fated to have a long wait. On the morning of my scheduled departure from Kabul, I awoke to find a heavy snow falling on an already deep accumulation. Word soon came to the guest house where I was staying that the airport was closed. The members of our Indiana University technical-assistance team concluded that my best chance to reach Rome reasonably soon was to drive to Peshawar and fly from there via Rawalpindi, Lahore, and Karachi to Rome—a roundabout, arduous route. The drive to Peshawar in one of the mission's station wagons was through the picturesque but hazardous Gorge Road, then through the fertile valleys of southern Afghanistan, and across the Khyber Pass. A hard rain and fog had closed the Peshawar airport, however, and my perilous journey continued in a beaten-up taxi with dim lights over a poor road that we shared with occasional flocks of sheep and unlighted carriages. A delay in our air departure from Lahore made it doubtful that I would make my connection in Karachi for Rome, and I sat tensely throughout the flight. At last, however, my fortunes changed: a representative of Qantas Airlines met our plane, escorted me through customs, and onto the already-loaded plane, held for my arrival.

When I arrived in Rome thirty hours after leaving Kabul, I was exhausted. Again I was fortunate: the Grand Hotel, its tradition of hospitality undisturbed by my delayed arrival, had a delightful demi-suite ready—lights on, bed covers turned down, and fresh flowers scenting the air. Soon I went down for dinner and explained to the maitre d' that I wanted a good dinner but that I was so weary I needed to go to bed very soon. What I wished was a light but delicious supper. He immediately understood my requirements and there followed my long-awaited meal. First came an excellent clear consommé, then a marvelous dish of pasta made in the hotel kitchen and served at my table with only hot butter and shredded cheese. This was accompanied by a salad made from fresh dandelion leaves with a delicate, savory dressing. The dessert was fresh pears of just the right ripeness, over which the maitre d' squeezed a generous amount of fresh lemon juice and then added a bit of sugar so that the juice of the fruit, the lemon juice, and the sugar made a sauce. It was so delicious that I have had this dessert served at home from time to time since then. The dishes were accompanied by a lively, white Italian wine. Altogether, this rather simple but skillfully prepared fare was precisely what I needed right then, and the combination served to etch it in my memory.

Among other favorites is the famous old Raffles Hotel in Singapore. It is memorable to me because of several incidents such as a chance meeting I had in the bar with John D. Rockefeller III and his wife, with whom I had a delightful conversation concerning Indiana University's exhibition of Thai art that he had helped finance. The Raffles has rooms built around a garden, and on one of my visits Somerset Maugham was a guest, making another of his farewell trips to Southeast Asia. He made as many farewell trips to various parts of the world as Nellie Melba made farewell concert tours. I remember his majestic progression, trailed by his secretary, across the garden. He had the unique capacity of creating by himself the illusion of a procession. I have a memory also of having tea in that garden, as the petals from frangipani blossoms dropped around me and recalled to me that the frangipani was plucked for a rhyme in Indiana University's Alma Mater—"Gloriana Frangipani."

Still another favorite hotel, similar to Raffles but of much finer quality, is the Peninsula in Hong Kong. Beautifully sited at the waterfront and yet close to fine shops and other attractions, it is incredibly luxurious. Tea is served each afternoon in the open-court lobby by a horde of deft waiters spurred by the surveillance of assistant managers in striped trousers. Not only is the service in the grand style, but tables are filled with characters seemingly right out of a Somerset Maugham novel. Its rooms are spacious though sleekly modern, and each room has its own room attendant, who anticipates the guest's every wish almost before he expresses it. Gaddi's, the hotel's intimate main dining room, illuminated by crystal chandeliers, is world-renowned for the quality of its cuisine. Within the hotel are branches of some of the great luxury shops such as Cartier, Hermès, Gucci, and Ferragamo. The Peninsula in many respects is perhaps the number-one hotel in the world.

The temptation is strong to write about great restaurants of Europe. That I have resisted, but I wish to mention two for illustration. The Horcher family ran a distinguished restaurant in Berlin but emigrated to Madrid to escape Hitler. They were even more successful in their new environment, and they seem to have been able to maintain their traditional standards of excellence even with the pressure of enormous patronage. I last dined there in 1976 with Karen and Peter Fraenkel. It was a delectable dinner: a delicious poached turbot with hollandaise served with an excellent house white wine, tournedos à la bordelaise on an artichoke heart with pureed mushrooms, soufflé potatoes, excellent red wine, and a crepe for dessert—with ice cream, fresh strawberries poached in various liqueurs, and whipped cream—all followed by an excellent brandy. As we concluded a man came from an adjoining table to say that his girl friend thought she might know me. He invited us to join them for a brandy. She turned out to be Jean Hardy Brown, Indiana University class of '63. It was 12:30 before we could break away from the enjoyment of reminiscing. Our dinner had started at 9:30, an early hour for Madrid diners.

Some of the best restaurants are located in the French countryside and one of these, one that some critics consider the finest at the present time, is located in Alsace not far from Strasbourg. It is L'Auberge de l'Ill at Illhaeusern, romantically sited in a country village on the banks of the river Ill. The weeping willows border the stream and the surrounding gardens are fastidiously maintained. The dining room is in light colors, highlighting the polished antique furniture and silverware. In the summertime dinner is served on the terrace and in the garden. I was there in the fall, however, and had the privilege of having a great dinner consisting of a delicate consommé and the restaurant's famous fresh salmon topped with a pike mousse glazed in a white wine cream sauce—a dish for the gods. We finished with the magnificent soufflé citron and the house petits fours, all accompanied by a delicious white wine—an unforgettable meal. The pain of its cost was mitigated by its superb quality.

The mere mention of these places, hotels, and modes of transportation brings to mind the fabulous world of travel: the chateaux of the Loire Valley in the spring with the peach, plum, and pear trees in bloom; Holland ablaze with fields of jonquils, the blossoms being cut as one would mow hay since the flowers were grown only for the bulbs; the grey mist of the North German plain in winter; the sparkling beauty of Stockholm in the summer light when even the medieval buildings seem fresh; the riot of flowers in spring in the English countryside; the grandeur of the snow-capped Swiss Alps; the splendor of the fountains and gardens at Versailles; the blaze of color from the deep red tuberous begonias omnipresent in the vast green parks of Leningrad; the exuberant architecture of Bavarian villages; the tropical beauty of Bali; the awesome monuments of ancient Egypt; the brilliant colors of the desert and of the mountains of Arizona and New Mexico; the way stations along the route across northern Spain, evoking the intensely religious spirit of pilgrims as they traveled to Santiago de Compostela by the millions during the Middle Ages; and the unforgettable splendor of fields of blooming lupin enroute to Milford Sound in the South Island of New Zealand.

I have had the good fortune to travel throughout the world seeing new sights, hearing new sounds, savoring different cultures, meeting a variety of peoples, and, I hope, thereby gaining a perspective to understand better my own land and culture. Notable also in my memory are the visits to the great museums at home and abroad, the National Gallery in Washington, the Chicago Art Institute, the Metropolitan in New York, the National Gallery in London, the Alte Pinakothek gallery in Munich, the Hermitage in Leningrad, the Louvre in Paris, the Prado in Madrid. Each visit to one of these great institutions has been stimulating and mind-stretching. Music and theater in the capitals of Europe as well as in the centers of culture in the United States similarly have brought a refreshment of spirit and inspiration. I have had great pleasure in my travels, and, strange as it may seem, they have not only given me enjoyment but also have provided me with some of my best ideas. When I travel I am freed from the day-by-day routine and stimulated by new sights and sounds and experiences. Generally my mind begins to teem with ideas. And so I come back from every trip with a long list of things to do, opportunities that have been overlooked or ideas that may bear fruit. As Kipling wrote in "The English Flag," "And what should they know of England who only England know?"

There is more than one way to see the world. It can be seen through the eyes of others who write of their travels; it can be seen through the minds of others whose ideas have been stimulated by various cultures; and it can be seen by dint of one's own effort. Travel is not easy. Someone has said, "If you wish to be entirely comfortable, stay at home." But it is rewarding; at least it has been for me. I have always had itchy feet and I hope to keep traveling as long as I live.

Beyond
the Presidency

○   ○   ○   ○   ○

⟦30⟧

○ ○ ○

The Summing Up

W H E N I was elected president of Indiana University, I resolved that, should I be fortunate enough to be allowed to serve for twenty-five years, I would at that time step out of office voluntarily even though it would be prior to my reaching retirement age. To make sure that I would not forget this resolution, I mentioned it from time to time to a number of my colleagues. Therefore, in 1958 and 1959, I began to think of the appropriate time to resign and, conscious of the fact that it takes a while for a university to elect a new president, notified the Board of Trustees on December 12, 1959, that I was approaching the end of my presidency, to take effect on the twenty-fifth anniversary of my entering the office, that is, July 1, 1962.

Fortunately, circumstances made it possible for me to take this step without damaging the university. University affairs were in good order and no major crises or problems confronted us. Had there been major crises as I stepped out, it would have seemed that I was running away from a problem. But the contrary was true. The intervening years had been, in Thomas Clark's phrase, "years of fulfillment." That did not mean they had been without discouragement and setbacks, problems and crises. But, as we came into the latter part of the 1950s, the university was operating smoothly, with students, faculty, staff, and trustees displaying a high degree of cooperation and confidence in each other.

After my first hectic year in office, there followed a time of accelerating activity as the university administration and faculty machinery for decision making took form and worked toward the objective of an ever-improving university. Every major recommendation of the Self-Survey Committee, formed during the first year of my presidency, had been debated, studied and adopted by the faculty and the trustees. In addition, a future program of academic development, supplementing the original recommendation of the Self-Survey Committee, had been projected and adopted by the faculty and the trustees. Then the horrendous problems resulting from our responsibilities in World War II and in the postwar period had been met.

Through the years the university community's determination to retain distinguished faculty if at all possible and to add talented faculty and new areas of strength had continued unabated. Furthermore, from 1945 to 1947 we had met the challenges of the greatest percentage growth in the student body in the history of Indiana University. During this period we were fortunate to have our scholarly resources enriched by the gift of the Lilly rare-book collection, and we made notable strides in developing and strengthening the University Library collections. Meanwhile the university's art collection under the impetus of handsome gifts from James Adams and Henry Hope had increased markedly in size and value and since then has gained a further boost from the princely gifts of Thomas Solley and his family and of the Krannert Charitable Trust, and from Burton Berry's entrusting us with his magnificent classical artifacts.

With the full cooperation of the faculty and the trustees, a vast building program—academic, residential, and recreational—had been planned, its financing projected, and construction started on much of it. The self-liquidating student housing program had been designed to make it possible for every student to have the advantage of some type of group living. The barrier of the Illinois Central Railroad property along the tracks had been surmounted, freeing the university for large-scale building northward. Designed to meet the needs of the university until the 1980s, the building program was perhaps a little conservative in some respects, but it has been followed to a remarkable degree up to the present.

The Indiana Conference on Higher Education had been brought into existence largely under our leadership, and it has served to strengthen greatly our relationship with the private colleges of the state. Parity with Purdue in state allocations had been replaced by a formula for equitable allocation of the state's appropriation among the four state schools, the total to be hammered out in advance of the session and agreed to by each of these institutions. Our legislative and state relationships were cordial and our Alumni Association was flourishing. Our regional centers had been expanded in number and had grown in faculty strength and in plant and enrollment.

Of course, there had been criticisms and accusations in the legislature from time to time. We rarely ever were awarded the full amount of our budget request. My colleagues and I followed a policy of reporting only a few of these criticisms, and only when we found it necessary to do so. We tried to isolate the criticism from the legislature's actions on budget and thus to prevent these criticisms from inhibiting the faculty's sense of freedom in carrying out its work. Moreover, we felt it was the administration's responsibility to try to achieve as creative an internal budget as possible even though additional funds were miniscule, as was true of most appropriations, and we reported to the faculty on what had been awarded in a manner that gave the faculty some hope that continued progress was possible.

The Medical Center had made vast strides and had been able to move from a mainly part-time faculty to a largely full-time clinical faculty, thereby greatly increasing its research contribution to the health sciences. The enrollment and plant had expanded markedly, and the Experimental Program in Medical Education had been started on the Bloomington campus, the success of which gave encouragement to the planning of a statewide medical education program. We laid out a program for acquiring all the ground between the State House and Military Park on the east and White River on the west as the space required for the future growth of our Indianapolis divisions. This was in line with what I called "a vision of congregation," when our various schools and divisions in Indianapolis would be gathered in one main campus. The dental school had similarly flourished and had achieved a very high rating among American dental schools.

Our international activities had grown enormously. We were engaged in technical-assistance programs on behalf of the U. S. government or under the aegis of the Ford Foundation and other great foundations in many parts of the world. At home our international enrollment had increased dramatically, and our area-study offerings and other academic disciplines dealing with international matters had grown in number, strength, and reputation.

The University Press had been formed and was thriving.

By the mid-1950s our faculty and graduate programs were receiving increasing national and international recognition. In fact, our graduate departments were winning high ratings in a gratifying fashion during these years.

During this period we were blessed with a strong Board of Trustees, all of whom were dedicated to the achievement of academic distinction as a first priority.

I had tried to build an administrative team that could use orderly processes of administration to achieve prompt decisions without letting the process become an end in itself; that is, the process was designed first and foremost to serve the needs of the university community. In fact, the success of those years so far as it resulted from administrative actions and leadership was due to the remarkable dedication, wisdom, and intellectual integrity of our general administrative team aided by a succession of effective deans of the academic divisions. I make no mention of personal loyalty. In an academic enterprise an administrative team selected mainly for reasons of loyalty to the president is inappropriate. To reward colleagues solely for demonstrations of personal loyalty is not just unwholesome, it is repulsive. In an intellectual enterprise loyalty to shared ideas and institutional goals is the only worthy basis for a harmonious and effective working relationship.

Although deliberately attempting to flesh out the university structure created during the Bryan administration as our first priority, my colleagues and I had as a secondary goal contributing our share of administrative innovations to the educational scene. For example, we early brought Eunice Roberts as dean for women's affairs to spearhead an effort to make the university curriculum even more responsive to the special needs of women than it had been, a field now expanded enormously throughout all higher education. Another example was the creation of the Junior Division (now, University Division) to provide greater flexibility and guidance for entering students, a division through which all freshmen students would pass on their way to a specialized field. We devised an organizational structure vesting one vice president with responsibility for graduate development and another with responsibility for the whole of undergraduate development. Although the alignment had its weaknesses, some areas were better served by it than they had ever been served before. In a sense, the deliberate creation of several powerful advisory committees—the Medical Advisory Committee, the Science Advisory Committee, and the International Affairs

Committee—was an innovation, useful in marshaling superior talents and interests for creative, productive influence and advance.

Throughout these years I tried to discharge my part in state, national, and international organizations in order to give Indiana University a role in helping to shape public policy for higher education and at the same time to increase Indiana University's visibility in those circles. It was possible for me to do this because of the quality of general administrative officers who unselfishly carried on the work of the university in my absence.

At Bloomington the university's cultural and recreational programs and the development of institutional amenities were beginning to build a reputation for the community as a good place in which to live and learn. By taking a giant leap northward to the Faris farm, we had given our intercollegiate and intramural programs room to develop and thus freed the inner campus for academic expansion. With the exception of the year 1945 when we won a Big Ten championship in football, throughout this period superior standing in football eluded us, and unfortunately football is the standard by which success in athletics is judged by the public. Nevertheless, during the period 1937–62 we did have our share of success in other varsity sports. For example, in basketball we either won or tied for four Big Ten championships and won two national championships.

In the early part of this period, wrestling, indoor and outdoor track, and cross-country were strong. The wrestling teams under Coach Billy Thom and the track teams under Billy Hayes and, later, Gordon Fisher brought us Big Ten championships. Midway through the period our first full-time tennis coach, Dale Lewis, guided his teams to the first Big Ten tennis championships in the university's history. Doc Counsilman came late in the period to build upon the strong foundation laid by Bob Royer, and by 1961 we had won our first of many Big Ten championships in swimming. Hobie Billingsley developed some champion divers as well. With the building of the new golf course, good golf players were attracted to Indiana University, and we won the Big Ten golf championship for the first time in 1962 with Bob Fitch's expert coaching.

In retrospect it can be fairly said, I believe, that during the period 1937–62 we achieved respectability in varsity sports programs through a balance of strength in various fields of competition.

It was a period in which we made great strides also in providing facilities and space for intramural and varsity sports, including the necessary room for future development in athletic programs.

We had started to put in reserve a small sum each year to accumulate a fund for—and soften the shock of—the cost of a major celebration of Indiana University's 150th birthday in 1970. And we had begun to dream of a major capital fund campaign to mark the anniversary.

With affairs generally in fine shape and no crisis apparent on the horizon, I felt free to make good on my resolution of 1937. The trustees were a bit stunned. They argued that since all was going well I should continue, just the opposite of my reasoning. I assured them that I was happy in the position and that, if it were not for my strong belief that it would be well for the university to have new leadership after such a long tenure, I would be delighted to continue. I enjoyed the work of the presidency. I valued my friendships with members of the board, my administrative colleagues, the faculty, the students, and the staff. It would have been easier to have stayed on than to have gone through with my earlier decision. In fact, though, relations had become so harmonious that I was a little frightened by the responsibility that a favorable consensus placed upon me. When I made suggestions, either formally or informally, they were typically accepted by the faculty and the board with very little critical examination. I realize that this was in essence a vote of confidence that freed the university community of a considerable amount of committee work and involvement in the decision-making process, but it placed upon me an awesome responsibility to make sure that my decisions and recommendations were wise.

After a time the board accepted my decision. On April 8, 1960, I wrote to the faculty and staff as follows:

INDIANA UNIVERSITY
Bloomington, Indiana

OFFICE OF THE PRESIDENT   April 8, 1960

To members of the Faculty and Staff:

I am releasing today to the newspapers the attached statement [of resignation]. This announcement is in conformity with what many of you already know from our past conversations.

Our old friend and colleague, Professor Oliver Field, whenever he wrote me on university matters concluded his letters with a single word, "Onward!"

I likewise conclude my communication to you with "Onward!"

Herman B Wells
President

In a subsequent meeting the Board appointed a representative faculty advisory committee to assist them in their job of selecting a new president, and the advisory committee went to work with vigor and imagination, soliciting suggestions from far and wide.

Before I was appointed president there had been a ground swell of university family opinion that the new president should be youthful. Notwithstanding the fact that there were many older men who would have been admirable presidents, I had been chosen, I think, principally because of my youth. Now in 1960 another ground swell of university opinion developed, namely, that, after thirty-five years of leadership by William Lowe Bryan and twenty-five years by me, both of us insiders, the new president should be sought from the outside. As a consequence, several well-qualified insiders who had had experience and were proven administrators were passed over and the judgment of the university community that an outsider would be better was respected.

Because most members of our Board of Trustees had not known a presidential style other than Dr. Bryan's and mine, it seemed to me desirable that they visit a number of the then outstanding presidents, meeting with them in their own offices. The ones selected were all men who would for various reasons not be considered for the Indiana position but who could suggest likely candidates to the board and by their own behavior and record give the board a composite picture of contemporary, successful presidential leaders.

Through the years I found that when I grew complacent about our own development I only needed to visit the campus of another university or college to learn that there were still new frontiers to conquer. Invariably I discovered new programs, new initiatives, new methodologies that would suggest themselves as being desirable for Indiana. In addition to observing other presidents at work I felt that the board could be stimulated if the visits were organized in such a way as to give the trustees an understanding of the institutions they were seeing and of their strengths. With this background they would be in a position to give maximum support to a new president when he began adapting the university to his manner of operation.

Although we had accomplished many of our goals in the past quarter of a century, I was well aware of the fact that growth and development in an educational institution or intellectual enterprise are a never-ending process, that there were still greater opportunities ahead. A new administration would undoubtedly have many new initiatives to propose, and fresh leadership and energy to achieve them, if supported by the faculty and the board. Therefore, I saw these trips to other campuses as a way of dispelling any complacency on the part of the board and of sensitizing them to the need for all-out support for the changes that fresh leadership would bring to the institution.

The trustees were conscious of the need for this kind of experience and consequently pledged themselves to spend the time required to make a rather extensive trip to see other campuses and to meet leading presidents of the day representative of various kinds of institutions. First, a trip to Big Ten institutions was organized. It included a visit to the University of Michigan and President Harlan H. Hatcher and, of course, a tour of the Clements Library and other special facilities; next, to Michigan State University for a visit with President John Hannah and a look at the Kresge Art Center, fine arts then occupying a considerable amount of the board's attention. From there we went to the University of Wisconsin for a visit with President Edwin B. Fred and a cursory view of the scientific research going on there, especially in the biological field; then to the University of Minnesota to see President Meredith Wilson; and, finally, to the University of Illinois and a day with President David Henry. After the trustees had had some time to digest what they had seen, heard, and discussed, we scheduled a trip to the East for the trustees to visit five private universities. We received enthusiastic cooperation from the officers of these institutions, whose interest was piqued by this novel idea. In each instance we were royally entertained, and the president spent substantial time with our board. Wherever appropriate, the board met with other nationally known administrative officers in these institutions. Our itinerary for the eastern trip included the University of Pennsylvania and a meeting with President Gaylord Harnwell; Princeton University and President Robert Goheen; Harvard University and President Nathan Pusey; Columbia University and President Grayson Kirk; New York University and President Carroll Newsom. In addition to visiting the universities in general and looking over their plants, we made a special point of seeing features of each university that would be useful to the board in planning for the future. For example, Isidor Ravdin at that time was the vice president for medical affairs at the University of Pennsylvania—a noted man in medical circles and a loyal Indiana University alumnus; therefore, the trustees spent time with him. They visited the Houghton Rare Book Library at Harvard and the Pierpont Morgan Library in New York because one of our responsibilities was the development of the Lilly Library; the director of Morgan, Frederick B. Adams, was a logical person to advise the board as he was a great friend of the Lilly librarian, David Randall, and had spoken at the Lilly Library dedication. They also visited the undergraduate libraries wherever they were—for example, the Lamont at Harvard. At that time we were debating the question of whether or not we should separate the undergraduate and the graduate libraries, a debate that was resolved by the present felicitous plan, which does indeed separate them but keeps them within the same building. The trustees also enjoyed an evening at the Metropolitan Opera as guests of Director Rudolf Bing. In those days we had a close working relationship with the Metropolitan that enabled us to get advisory assistance from Bing and others for our rapidly developing music school.

Wherever possible the trustees made contact with prominent alumni for private discussions. For example, they had lunch with William Croan Greenough, president of T I A A - C R E F and alumnus of Indiana University. They visited with Charles Cole, vice president of the Rockefeller Foundation; Henry Heald, president of the Ford Foundation; James Perkins of the Carnegie Foundation for the Advancement of Teaching—in each instance asking for names of persons who might be likely candidates for the presidency. The trustees had a very busy schedule in New York; yet, in addition to all of the people they saw, they visited the office of our architects, Eggers and Higgins, to see the substanial amount of architectural work we had in progress there and to pass judgment on it.

Meanwhile the committee's activity and the board's solicitation of the whole alumni body had produced a list of many prospects that the board and the faculty committee winnowed down to a few, eventually deciding to make the offer to Elvis Stahr, then secretary of the army, who was interested in the position but who had alternative opportunities that he wished to consider. He was not sure that he wanted to leave Washington just yet since he enjoyed his position in the Kennedy administration. He hesitated too over returning to academic administrative work, although he had been highly successful in it. While he was wavering, the board asked me to spend some time with him in Washington to answer any questions he might have but had been reluctant to put to the board. We spent a long afternoon together in a suite at the Mayflower Hotel in the course of which I not only answered very frankly his questions about the personalities he had met but also tried to reassure him that, although I would be staying on in Bloomington, I would be as unobtrusive as possible and would support him in every way. I repeated to him what Dr. Bryan had said to me, namely, that he would support me, that he would support me even when I was wrong. I told Dr. Stahr that, after having had the experience of being president on a campus where a predecessor who had served for many years still resided, I knew the problems that were inherent in the situation, but also thought I had learned from the example of Dr. Bryan how to give the new president freedom and at the same time help. Whether or not this was one of the questions in his mind, I do not know, but at least in the years Dr. Stahr served Indiana University with great distinction, our relationship was, I believe, a warm, friendly, and happy one.

Another matter we discussed was the length of time he would serve. The board was conditioned by circumstances to believe a long presidential tenure desirable, and Elvis Stahr had a record of frequent changes in an advancing career—an acceptable type of career pattern but one that the board hoped he would not continue here. They wanted me to ask him whether he would continue until age sixty-five (eighteen years), which seemed to them sufficient time to enable him to make a maximum contribution. He answered that, if he came to Indiana University, he would expect to serve until sixty-five, should it seem wise to do so at that time.

During the two-year period of the search that culminated in President Stahr's election, it was my objective to be as helpful as I possibly could to the board and the faculty in their selection without influencing their judgment in any way. My principal goal, however, was to try to ensure that the university's momentum was maintained during this period. For that reason I hoped that a selection would be made relatively early so that the new president could have a period of free time to become acquainted with the university prior to having to assume the day-to-day duties of the office.

Although Elvis J. Stahr was elected president of Indiana University on April 27, 1962, his term to take effect July 1 when I would officially end my tenure, it developed that Dr. Stahr could not be released from his responsibilities as secretary of the army in time to take up his duties on the campus before September 1. The board asked me whether I would carry on the routine duties of the office until he arrived, a request that I was quite willing to grant.

Little did I imagine then that I would be called upon on two subsequent occasions to resume the duties of the office of the president. The first came when Dr. Stahr suddenly resigned on July 6, 1968, and asked to be relieved by September 1. The board asked me to take over for the time being. I suggested that, instead of their naming me acting president or president without any prefix, the title of interim president be used since this would more properly designate the role I would play. It would help point out that I had no intention of staying in the office indefinitely or of being only a caretaker president for even a short period of time.

This was the beginning of the period of student unrest and thus a caretaker role was inappropriate. I felt, however, that the university's case before the General Assembly would be prejudiced unless by the time the General Assembly convened a permanent president was in office to carry on the negotiations with the Budget Committee and the General Assembly. However, during the fall months I did assume the responsibility, with my colleagues, of putting together our budget request and of making oral presentations to the Budget Committee, the governor, and the power structure of the state.

I decided not to move my office, the office of the university chancellor, but leave it intact while I occupied the president's office. The Board of Trustees, finding it somewhat difficult to agree quickly upon a new president, from time to time urged me to accept a two- or three-year appointment. I refused. I did so not because I was reluctant to carry on the work but because it seemed to me that such a delay would not serve the best interests of the university, as much as I was tempted to accept the excitement and exhilaration of being back again in the president's office. As a result of my refusal and of my urging, the faculty committee and the board did decide to elect a new president, and on November 15, 1968, Joseph Sutton, vice president and dean of the faculties, was elected and took office on December 1, 1968. He was therefore able to represent the university at the next meeting of the General Assembly.

While I did not again occupy the office of president formally, during Indiana University's sesquicentennial celebration, a year of great institutional activity that put heavy demands upon the president's office, I shared some of the representational duties. During much of that year President Sutton was ill, and I stood in for him on a good many formal occasions such as at the Founders Day convocation and the spring Commencement ceremonies at the university's campuses. In fact, with the help of the other administrative officers of the university, I carried on many of the presidential functions.

In looking back over my experience in the presidency with the perspective of time, I am more aware than ever of my great good fortune in having been available and chosen to become the acting president of Indiana University on the first of July, 1937. The period following was an era of tumultuous change, growth, development in American higher education, a period unrivaled in its excitement and achievement perhaps in the whole history of higher education. I was fortunate to have been permitted to play a leadership role in that kind of an era, and it was an extraordinarily exciting and rewarding experience. The presidential role, to be successful, is demanding. It demands all of one's life, energy, thought, enthusiasm, and vision, and still one cannot fully realize its potentials. I think it is the most difficult top leadership post in America other than the presidency of the United States, more difficult than that of being a governor or the head of a large corporation or the presiding bishop of a religious congregation. My good friend David Lilienthal, an erstwhile Hoosier of broad and impressive experience who is a more objective observer of the role, wrote:

> I find fascinating how these university presidents must—to do their job—present a combination of qualities rarely found in a single individual: a respect for learning and a savvy and a toughness with the highly independent people called "professors," with their built-in resistance to innovation as it affects *them* (i.e., their "tenure") in spite of their intellectual and theoretical commitment to thought and, therefore, to change. And these presidents must be *managers*,

too, and be able to dig into a set of figures or leap at once from a beautiful "project" to meet the businessman's demand: "Cost it for us."[1]

I have sometimes said that state universities are so organized that the president, without a grant of final authority from either the faculty or the board of trustees, is nevertheless expected to make all things happen expeditiously and agreeably to all members of the university community and to the larger state community that it serves. In brief, the president has ever-expanding responsibility with limited authority to meet it. So action must be achieved by persuasion. Many frustrations are inevitable. Harassed and exhausted, on a thousand occasions I longed to be released from the torment of the job. But with full knowledge of the trauma, travail, blood, sweat, and tears the office demands, if I were young and given the opportunity, I would eagerly undertake the glorious chore again. For me no other career could have been so satisfying. I have been lucky and happy in my life work.

Catherine Royer, who was my secretary in the president's office and who is still with me, while going through old files not long ago came upon some notes of mine made at the time I was leaving the presidency. I had spent Sunday afternoon cleaning out my desk in preparation for the advent of President Stahr on Monday. Sitting there all alone, I wrote in longhand "Thoughts at the end of the day on Sunday, July 1, 1962 as I leave my office for the last time":

To wish to stay is selfish since a younger man can do more for the university during the next five years than I could.

Nevertheless, this office, which has sometimes seemed like a prison, now seems precious and desirable. Of course, part of it is physical. To have spent most of one's hours for a quarter of a century in this place makes it very precious.

A part of this feeling no doubt is due to a realization that, while I am leaving responsibilities, I am likewise leaving the great opportunities that this office gives to its holders. There is so much to be done and I will have fewer tools with which to work. Perhaps therein lies a challenge that will make my new job all the more interesting.

The years have been long and arduous, yet it seems only yesterday that I began. I remember the flowers that filled this office July 1, 1937.

1. David E. Lilienthal, *The Journals of David E. Lilienthal*, vol. 6, *Creativity and Conflict, 1964–1967* (New York: Harper and Row, 1976), p. 142.

Yet sometimes the burdens have seemed unbearable when many problems came all at once. I hope I have met them with some success.

I think I have assumed too many jobs on behalf of the educational community in recent years, yet this effort has helped I believe to build the university's national standing—so the temptation to accept all important posts has been great. Each seemed to be too desirable to miss for the benefit of the university.

[31]

○ ○ ○

The University Chancellor

AT THE time I left the presidency of Indiana University, I indicated to the Board of Trustees that I had no desire to do anything other than continue to serve the university in some capacity for the rest of my productive life. The trustees responded by creating the office of chancellor, which was then a new title and office for the university. No job description was given; I was told to develop the position, in cooperation with the president, in whatever manner it seemed to the two of us would be in the best interests of the institution. The expectation was, however, that my principal base of operation would be the Indiana University Foundation, of which I was then president, and that I would give that office most of my time. There was an understanding, too, that I would continue to serve on several state and national committees, boards and commissions, at least for the time being and thus provide a liaison for the university with those bodies. Also, it was thought, in the president's absence or illness, I could represent him in the ceremonial duties that would arise from time to time.

In addition, the board and President Stahr thought that, since I had been relieved of line-operating responsibilities, I could undertake ad hoc assignments on projects as they arose. It is a characteristic of a university that such projects do arise frequently and require the time and attention of someone. Since the administrative staff is typically already fully occupied, there is a real need for a person with relatively flexible time to serve in this manner.

This kind of arrangement was generally speaking new to the academic scene but is now a much more common practice. From the very beginning I received numerous inquiries from other presidents about to retire and from boards of trustees, asking for information on our arrangement and its practicality and usefulness. Of course, inevitably the question arose as to the effect of such a position on the president. My relationship with William Lowe Bryan certainly suggested that we could have worked together, and so far as I know my relationships with my successors have been happy ones.

My expectation of spending nearly full time at the Foundation, however, was soon thwarted by the urgent invitation to assume the active chairmanship of the board of Education and World Affairs in New York, of which I have written elsewhere. This position did not divorce me from university work so much as might seem, except geographically, because during this period Indiana University had very active relationships with several of the major foundations located in the New York area. The university was deeply involved in international activities, which were of course the raison d'être of E W A. Moreover, many of the university's important donors and alumni lived in New York, and I could keep in touch with them in an easy and informal manner. During this period it was normal and natural for me to maintain a personal relationship with a substantial number of the top officers of all the major, New York–based foundations. I could constantly relate to the university what I learned about the developing ideas in both government and foundations concerning university activities in the international field at home and abroad and could assist other officers in their foundation contacts. The E W A position enabled me to emphasize two of the functions that had been important during my presidency—fundraising and our international outreach and concern. When I was in that office I frequently referred to the three symbols of my presidency (schoolmaster, beggar, internationalist) as represented by artifacts on my desk: my father's school bell, which he had used as a teacher to summon students in from the playground, the antique begging bowl of a Tibetan monk, and a globe indicating that the world is the university's parish.

I am often asked what a university chancellor does. My answer is likely to be an enumeration of my schedule for that day and the days immediately before and after. With no predecessor in the role and no official line duties, what I do each day and week and year composes the role of the university chancellor as I have conceived it.

With the exception of three or four years, I have been associated with Indiana University in some capacity since 1921. That lengthy association, along with my other experiences, has given me a seasoned perspective—or should have—and seemingly the exercise of this view is considered a major function of the university chancellor. Hence have come a standing invitation to attend trustee and administrative committee meetings, but without obligation to do so except when specially requested by the president because of a particular item of business on the agenda; appointment to the Research Policy Committee; and requests to continue chairing various all-university and campus committees. Among these assignments earlier were the then influential International Affairs Committee and the Research Committee; now they include the committee charged with recommending names for university buildings; the University Heritage Committee with its vital subdivisions—Maintenance of Campus Beauty, Historical Preservation, and Archives; and building committees for university facilities funded largely by donors. The care with which these buildings are planned in their initial stages can be illustrated by the work of the Musical Arts Center Building Committee. At its instigation the architect, Evans Woollen, and Dean Wilfred Bain of the School of Music traveled abroad to study the principal music halls of Europe, gaining from them ideas about what should and should not be included in our building. There were innumerable committee meetings to discuss details as they arose, such as acoustics, mechanical equipment, concert-hall seats, and the like.

The Art Museum Building Committee, formed in 1970 and involved mainly during its early years with selecting an architect to recommend to the Board of Trustees, is now in an increasingly active phase of its service. The Hoosier Heritage Hall Building Committee, trying for some time to modify the planning to fit the funding, is entering a more active stage with the decision to recommend proceeding with construction. For each of these structures I have had as well chief responsibility for the private financing. This kind of responsibility is part and parcel of my second major function as university chancellor: helping persons with philanthropic desires to find suitable and satisfying objects for their benefactions.

The amount of my time devoted to working with private donors and attendant details possibly qualifies this activity as the number-one function of the university chancellor. Now and then other concerns have eaten into that time—for instance, when I was chairman of the board of Education and World Affairs in New York and gave 40 percent of my time to that work, with my salary from it paid to the Foundation; or when I became involved through the urgings of others in writing this account. By contrast, before, during, and immediately after the 150th Birthday Fund drive I was almost wholly absorbed in some aspect of fund raising. I am still in daily contact with the Foundation on matters relating to my several Foundation duties with the Executive Committee, the Investment Committee, Foun-Farm, and so on.

Acting as a representative, official or unofficial, of the university could be characterized as a third function of the university chancellor. Occasionally the representation is as surrogate for the president, but more often it is as an officer of the university. In that capacity I have made trips abroad; served as an official host to visiting scholars, dignitaries, and honorees; participated in university ceremonials; welcomed groups and addressed others (although I do little of that, by choice, now); and tried unobtrusively to make myself available for any such service when needed.

Because, as the years went along, I did not have demanding line responsibilities, it was assumed that I had a great deal of time for public service. As a consequence I was asked to serve on national and international commissions, to devote a good deal of time to the board of the International Association of Universities, and to undertake many local and statewide committee responsibilities. While unofficial representation is more a question of conscience, interest, and judgment than of duty, my presence and participation wheresoever are inescapably associated with the university. Consequently, my service on various external boards, commissions, advisory committees, and the like, whether in New York, Indianapolis, or Bloomington, do constitute an activity of the university chancellor. I describe several types of my latter-day service in subsequent sections of this chapter.

A miscellany of additional matters finds its way to my office, filling my calendar, keeping my mail heavy and my telephone busy. Interpreting the university and its history to students and listening to their problems, greeting alumni and finding answers to their needs or questions as well as keeping an eye out for their children and —yes—grandchildren when they become students here, helping a faculty member find a route to realizing a project or ambition, sharing the joys and sorrows of staff members—these are but samples of what absorbs my attention at my desk.

My hours away from the office are frequently as filled with university-related concerns as my office hours are. Students in their infinite variety are a joy to me, and I accept as many of their invitations as time will allow. Attending the cultural offerings on this campus is, for me, to see the dream I dreamed for Indiana University more than four decades ago. Football and basketball games are a must, not just because I enjoy them, but as a show of support for the coaches and players who compete in the university's name. In the same spirit I attend other university events and make an appearance at activities in which university family or friends are involved. The wealth of interesting lectures can only be sampled, given the other calls upon my time, so I watch the weekly calendar for lectures that can be worked into my schedule. Whatever else may be pending, I also try to visit sick and bereaved members of the university community when I learn of their misfortunes. In recent years, the growing number of bereavements among my friends and acquaintances appalls and saddens me.

Higher Education Surveys

The 1960s were roiling, brawling years on the campuses across the nation. Enrollments grew rapidly—too rapidly to permit the planning and organization needed to accommodate the sudden influx of an increasingly heterogeneous student body. Pressures mounted everywhere—from academic departments, trying to recruit faculty when nationwide there were more positions than faculty to fill them; from physical plants, attempting to stretch available housing and classroom space while overseeing the construction that would ease the situation; and from students, whose growing restlessness became volatile in the last years of the decade. Faced with troubling developments such as these, many boards of trustees and state authorities turned to outside consultants to review their situations and give advice.

I received many requests to participate in studies of this kind but consented to undertake only three, in each case because of some special interest or because of a problem with which I thought I could be helpful: a committee appointed by the Michigan Coordinating Council for Public Higher Education to advise it concerning a possible third medical school in the state of Michigan; a study, commissioned by the New York state legislature, of higher education in the state; and a report on the University of Pittsburgh necessitated by a crisis in its financial affairs. My service as an adviser to the board of trustees of Columbia University while it was in the process of selecting and installing a new president and of coping with the transition problems of the 1960s differed from the three illustrations here because I was not expected to make a formal study of the situation.

The Michigan study, which I chaired, was conducted by a Circuit Court judge, a member of the Michigan State Medical Society, the director of a large medical center, a university president, a foundation president, the board chairman of a major pharmaceutical manufacturing firm located in Michigan, and a representative each from the University of Michigan and Michigan State University. (See Appendix [J] for list of members, consultants, and staff.)

Michigan State wanted its two-year medical program extended to a full degree program. There was a need for more medical school graduates, but the University of Michigan's medical school was underfunded and the question was what would be the best use of state tax dollars for medical education under these circumstances. Our committee was given drafts of various options that we could consider and the material supporting them. We agreed on particular ones we wished to study, discussed them, and decided what to recommend. Our general recommendation was for better accommodation of present students and an increase in first-year places under current programs. We also recommended target dates for specified enrollment increases, suggested the mobilization of private resources to found and operate a medical school, and proposed the establishment of a continuing committee for coordinating the development of health education in Michigan. Except that no private institution ready to undertake medical education could be discovered, most of our recommendations were implemented. Later, circumstances made it possible for Michigan State to develop a full-fledged medical school.

The second survey in which I participated during the 1960s was for the New York state legislature. I was appointed by the state Senate and the Assembly as the legislature's consultant on higher education and given two study associates, John A. Perkins, president of the University of Delaware, and G. Russell Clark, chairman of the board and chief executive officer of the Commercial Bank of North America. The state of New York, which had been slow in providing public higher education, launched a massive multicampus building program with adequate appropriations but with inadequate time to satisfy the expectations aroused by this awesome initiative. So much was going on at the time we entered the picture—the summer of 1963 and during 1964—that it nearly staggered the imagination. With the aid of the talented Sidney Tickton as director of studies and with extensive consultation, we were able to make findings and recommendations that proved constructive. Among our conclusions were these: that the state needed to provide for larger enrollments than projected and a greater variety of programs than planned; that the whole area of graduate education and research needed to be greatly strengthened and three or four centers of excellence developed; that the various campuses should have different emphases and specialties; that there should be cooperation between public and private institutions; that governance should be decentralized to a greater extent; that the business management of the system should be decentralized and made more efficient; and so on. Association with Sidney Tickton of the Ford Foundation, who became vice president of the Academy for Educational Development during the course of the study, was a bonus for me. His knowledge and wisdom were impressive. We worked closely on the final report, agreeing on the content before its drafting and doing the writing on my dining room table at home.

The third survey that I undertook was the Ford Foundation–financed study of the University of Pittsburgh. The Pittsburgh board of trustees had directed its dynamic chancellor, Edward Litchfield, to bring the university to the forefront of American higher education. Litchfield took this challenging directive literally and plunged into a broad plan of change for the university that did revolutionize its program and greatly increase its prestige. In the course of this strong advance, however, grave financial problems were encountered because Litchfield had counted on the availability of a large private fund that did not materialize. The situation was difficult and delicate. Some way had to be found to maintain the gains and continue the progress of the institution, yet prevent financial disaster.

The Pittsburgh board asked the Ford Foundation to have a study made and a course of action recommended. I was asked to head the Study Committee, which consisted of the heads of Case Institute (T. Keith Glennan), the University of California at Berkeley (Roger Heyns), Wayne State University (Clarence Hilberry), and the University of Chicago (Edward Levi). Much of the staff work was carried on by colleagues at Indiana University—Paul Klinge, Joseph

Hartley, John Thompson, and E. Ross Bartley—and the drafting of the report, including the preparation of statistical tables, by Louis D'Amico, Leroy Hull, William Sukel, and Dorothy Collins. Henry Hill, president emeritus of George Peabody College and a former superintendent of schools in Pittsburgh, interviewed leading personalities in that city for us and gave us some essential perspectives. Our recommendations—that the university offer to operate a first-rate undergraduate college on a contractual basis with the commonwealth and that the commonwealth agree to pay the university's cost per student beyond the fee charge (there was ample precedent for partial state support of private institutions in Pennsylvania), that the university coordinate its work with other institutions in the area to reduce duplication, that economies be effected and unnecessary financial drains halted, and that the community increase its private financial support of the university—were for the most part adopted and executed. Today the University of Pittsburgh is a strong, viable, leading institution.

All in all, these experiences were useful in broadening my knowledge of higher educational institutions and certain pitfalls, in extending the network of my acquaintance, and in bringing Indiana University to the attention of many new friends.

White House Committees and Commissions

One of the devices that U.S. presidents have used to explore troublesome public problems or to gain support for their position on particular issues is through the appointment of national commissions or committees, sometimes referred to as White House assignments. Lyndon Johnson used this device often and for a variety of studies. It was my privilege to serve on three of them between 1965 and 1968.

For these groups to be effective, they had to be broadly representative of the nation; that is, considerations of geography, public or private interest, economic loyalties, professions, and political party entered into the selection of appointees. I suppose that my being a Midwesterner, identified with public higher education and moderate in my political views, placed me in a category that fit a need. In addition, it was probably assumed that as an ex-president of a university I must surely have time for public-service assignments. Once cast in this role, I received—and still receive—numerous requests to serve in sundry ways, allowing me to choose ones that may be useful to Indiana University and stimulating to me.

Among these assignments were the Special Committee on U.S. Trade Relations with East European Countries, chaired by J. Irwin Miller of Columbus, Indiana; the National Advisory Commission on Food and Fiber, chaired by Sherwood Berg, dean of the School of Agriculture at the University of Minnesota; and the President's Special Committee on Overseas Voluntary Activities, chaired by Secretary of State Dean Rusk.

The Miller Committee (see Appendix [J] for list of members and staff), as it came to be called in my office, was asked by President Johnson to explore all aspects of expanding peaceful trade with the countries of Eastern Europe and the U.S.S.R. in support of the president's policy of widening constructive relations there. The committee had the advantage of a great amount of material prepared for its meetings by experts from the departments of State, Commerce, and the Treasury. We also had the benefit of testimony presented by some exceptionally able economists in the Central Intelligence Agency (C I A) and from technologists in the Department of Defense. Interestingly enough, the Department of Defense and C I A experts all believed that we should extend our trade with the Soviet bloc and were unanimous in their view that we would lose little and gain much by such increased contact. They informed us that the U.S. had few technological and economic secrets from the Soviets and that trade with the Eastern bloc was certain to be beneficial to us politically as well as economically. The committee recommended peaceful trade in nonstrategic items as an instrument of national policy in our relations with individual Communist nations of Europe. Our report was favorably received in general by the press and by the public, but right-wing opposition succeeded in scaring off congressional support. I have been told, however, that, as bills in favor of expanding trade were presented in succeeding years, our report served as a standard reference point. I found participation in the work of this committee exceptionally stimulating and interesting. It gave me a large store of information concerning a field about which I had known little, and the contact with the members of the committee and the technological staff furnished me useful insights concerning U.S. relationships with the Communist world. I especially valued working with Irwin Miller, one of the most remarkable men I have known in my lifetime: a superb businessman, a devout churchman, dedicated in his attitude toward public service, active in the promotion of arts and education, and supportive of all that is best in American life.

Six months after the Miller Committee had completed its report, I was asked to be a member of another White House commission. The problems of agriculture, which seem to be omnipresent in the American scene, were especially visible in 1965 and as a consequence a rather comprehensive Food and Agriculture Act was passed. To President Johnson, a farmer and a rancher, this was a subject close to the heart. On the occasion of his signing of the act on November 4, 1965, he made a long statement in which he included an announcement that he was establishing the National Advisory Commission on Food and Fiber "to make a penetrating and long-range appraisal of our agricultural and related foreign trade policies." The commission was to undertake the review "in terms of the national interest, the welfare of our rural Americans, and the well-being of our farmers, the needs of our workers, and the interests of our consumers." It was this commission to which I was subsequently appointed.

The commission was composed of thirty men and women of widely differing backgrounds. Some came from organized agriculture, some were dirt farmers, some were from the food-processing industry, and others came from agricultural food-processing and marketing industries as well as from agricultural colleges and their extension services (see Appendix [J] for a list of members).

Given eighteen months to carry on its work and a substantial secretariat to service the study, the commission worked intensely and long from the first to the last of its meetings. Hearings were held in seven major cities, and a number of authorities and experts addressed the commission. I found the subject absorbing because of my own personal interest in agriculture stemming from my small-town, rural background. For instance, that part of the study that dealt with fiber, cotton mainly, was entirely new to me and proved useful to my thinking. In fact, my participation on the commission taught me a great deal, and I hope that in turn I made some small contribution to the final result. But the agriculture problem seems to me ever with us, demanding continuing study, consideration, and the wisest kind of decisions in the formulation of national policies affecting this all-important segment of our economic and social life.

The third of the White House groups upon which I was asked to serve was in many ways one of the most exciting. It was a committee formed to take a look at the subsidies that had been made clandestinely by the C I A to a variety of American nonprofit organizations. Some of these had been created by the C I A specifically for the purpose of dispensing C I A money, but their nature was concealed through a variety of strategies. These so-called specially created agencies, or front agencies, dispensed money abroad in the furtherance of good causes about which there would be no controversy other than the source of the funds for them. Not all had such reputable purposes, however. Furthermore, in time money from certain of the front organizations was channeled into some of the most prestigious American international voluntary organizations without knowledge on the part of their officers and membership of the source of the funds. When this story finally began to break it caused a big uproar in the press, and properly so. As a consequence, a high-level committee consisting in part of Congressional leaders and in part of representatives of the voluntary organizations of the world was formed to make recommendations to the president and to Congress as to what should be done. On the committee were four members of the House of Representatives, four members of the Senate, and eight nongovernmental members (see Appendix [J] for list of members).

Under the chairmanship of Secretary of State Dean Rusk, the committee reached a general consensus that a bipartisan commission of private citizens would have to be created by Congress to funnel money into international voluntary organizations that had legitimate purposes to perform throughout the world and that could be supported only with government money. A mechanism that would ensure that the government money in no way compromised the organizations' impartiality, integrity, or international reputations needed to be devised. Obviously, if their reputations were to be jeopardized, their work would be greatly hampered and perhaps rendered impotent. The committee also recommended an initial annual level of appropriations of about $35 million for the commission, including $10 million transferred from government agencies for American overseas universities, libraries, and book activities.

It suggested more effective use of private voluntary organizations by federal agencies in the carrying out of their programs. And it called for an executive branch study of the current cultural and academic exchange programs and of American cultural relationships abroad.

I should like to believe that the time and effort the men and women spent on these White House commissions and committees contributed to the formulation of sound national policy. I am confident that each of the three with which I was acquainted made some contribution in its field.

An interesting facet of that service was the glimpses it afforded of Lyndon Johnson. In each instance the commission reported personally to the president. In our meetings with him he always evidenced a keen interest in what we were doing and expressed great appreciation for the service we were rendering and assured us that he would attempt to act on our recommendations and secure their passage.

President Johnson took a special interest in the East-West trade committee and in the food and fiber commission. I remember that we made an interim report to him on the East-West trade study one morning when he had been up all night trying to decide what to do about the Nicaraguan situation—whether or not to send in U.S. troops. Finally, after much agonizing of spirit and mindful of the recommendation of the ambassador, he decided that troops had to land to protect the lives of Americans in Nicaragua. The president was bemoaning the fact that he had to take this action—he felt especially beleaguered at that time because of the Vietnam issue—and he added rather wistfully that these were not the kinds of problems with which he had hoped to deal as president. In my judgment, he was much more interested in domestic social and economic problems than in international affairs. It will be interesting to observe what place history affords him, but I will wager that through the perspective of time he will be seen as a president who had a very deep and passionate interest in solving such social ills as poverty, racial injustice, and the problems of ethnic minorities. I doubt that any other president in this century, with the possible exception of Franklin Roosevelt, was as much concerned as he was with these problems. I feel that Johnson had an even greater understanding of the enormity of these problems than did Roosevelt.

Commission on the Humanities

Not long after I became chancellor I was asked to serve on a commission that was national in significance but nonfederal in character. With the launching of Sputnik by the Russians, the federal government had been stimulated to begin massive grants through the National Science Foundation for the development and promotion of scientific study and experimentation in the United States. The very success of this effort in a way threatened an imbalance in American educational and cultural affairs. Considerable discussion, begun in university and other cultural circles about the need for increased support for the humanities, led in the spring of 1963 to the establishment of the Commission on the Humanities, jointly sponsored by the American Council of Learned Societies (ACLS), the Council of Graduate Schools in the United States, and the United Chapters of Phi Beta Kappa. Barnaby C. Keeney, president of Brown University, was made chairman of the commission, and I was made vice chairman in recognition, no doubt, of the lively activity in the humanities on the Indiana University campus.

It was a privilege to work with the distinguished group of men and women appointed to the commission (see Appendix [J] for list of members), which met frequently and produced a well-drafted report that made a persuasive case. It described the state of the humanities in America, America's need for the humanities, the problems of the academic humanist, humanities in the national interest, and the relationships to the federal government. It concluded by recommending that the president and Congress establish a national humanities foundation. The essence of the report was contained in the letter of transmittal dated April 30, 1964:

> We recommend that the three societies take appropriate steps to promote the establishment of a National Humanities Foundation, particularly the enactment of legislation authorizing the appointment of the board of the National Humanities Foundation and the director and staff, and the appropriation of funds for organization and planning. We would hope that the board and the director would then conduct further studies and recommend an appropriation to the Congress.

This report carried the day, and it is now a matter of history that the National Endowment for the Humanities was launched. Barnaby

Keeney was persuaded to leave his post as president of Brown University and become the first director of the foundation. He had been a vigorous and stimulating chairman, and in fact the discussions of the talented members were a joy to hear and participate in. I am sure that the quality of the report, much of which was written by Keeney, was responsible in no small measure for the eventual success of the recommendations. Other beneficial circumstances were that the members of the commission worked closely with certain members of Congress who were interested in the proposal and that the commission was sustained throughout by the steady interest of the A C L S, the Council of Graduate Schools in the United States, and the United Chapters of Phi Beta Kappa. In particular, there was a close relationship between the A C L S and the commission; in fact, there was some overlapping membership.

In a news release issued when we made our report I was quoted as saying that "the realization of our highest national aspirations requires a renewed and vigorous development of the humanities. The steps recommended by the commission are essential to this end. The report, therefore, deserves the sympathetic attention of every citizen." I have participated in many similar types of committees and commissions in the past forty years and rarely have I had the privilege of being a part of one such as this, where the results were so direct and in my judgment so very beneficial for society.

This brief account of public and civic opportunities that have been mine during the years of my chancellorship helps to fill out the picture of how I have spent my time in that office.

Actually, I noticed little change of pace when I moved from Bryan Hall to Owen Hall. Here in an office that had been furnished and decorated at my own expense, by my request, the problems and pressures seemed just as heavy as before—but different. With my new responsibility for research, I had directed a staff that proved efficient and effective in promoting faculty research. My work with E W A, as I have related, absorbed at least half of my time. For a while matters and projects begun while I was in Bryan Hall still occupied some of my attention. Gradually, the transitional period ended and my role as chancellor began to take form, accelerating when President Stahr instituted the reorganization of the university that was not completed until the early years of President Ryan's administration. Throughout the years preceding, during, and immediately following the celebration of the university's sesquicentennial, I was almost wholly preoccupied with the 150th Birthday Fund drive. Recently, after paring some of my responsibilities in order to get on with this book and having been slowed by some sieges with illness, my work has changed in nature but not in intensity. I look forward to the resumption of tasks laid aside while the book was in gestation.

And so I return to the original question, what does a university chancellor do, with a sense of great good luck that for seventeen years Indiana University has had a position, and allowed me to fill it, that offered a potpourri of challenges and pleasures, opportunities and satisfactions, obligations and usefulness. I shall ever be grateful to the administration and to the trustees that they have permitted me to retain an active title and have granted me the resources to carry on my office and to work effectively, even after I reached the age of seventy and became an unsalaried laborer in the vineyard.

[32]

○ ○ ○

Epilogue

WITH THE "summing up" and the description of my present duties, it seems a proper time to bring this volume to a close. Other topics could have been treated and perhaps should have been—for example, the Hoosier political personalities I have known, the Ristine-Wells Committee to study the reorganization of the State Department of Public Instruction, the New Harmony Memorial Commission, the boards of the James Whitcomb Riley Association and of Lilly Endowment, the boards of various colleges and universities (Earlham, American University in Cairo, Howard, Tulane, and others), the High Council of Sigma Nu and the board of its Education Foundation, the TIAA-CREF board, the Council on Library Resources board, the board of the International Association of Universities, and many others.

For my readers who search here in vain for a topic in which they are interested, I offer the assurance that those topics were not omitted because I felt them unimportant. In a long life so many things seem important that the task of selecting among them is extremely difficult. But I have had to choose in order to keep this volume to a manageable size and also because, as I thought about the past, invariably the present intruded and my mind teemed with new opportunities that seemed available if my years allowed. I am reluctant to delay undertaking them longer while I write about the past.

Some day perhaps the most attractive opportunities that I now see ahead can be realized. I hope that at that time the spirit will move me to write about the topics untreated here, Providence being willing. Until then I beg the compassionate understanding of my friends who find themselves and their enterprises omitted from this modest volume.

APPENDIX

A. CHRONOLOGY

Compiled by Dorothy Collins and David Warriner

June 7, 1902 Birth in Jamestown, Indiana
1920–1921 Freshman, University of Illinois
1921–1924 Undergraduate student, Indiana University
1924–1926 Assistant Cashier, First National Bank of Lebanon, Indiana
1926–1927 Graduate student, Indiana University
1927–1928 Assistant and graduate student, Department of Economics, University of Wisconsin
1928–1931 Field Secretary, Indiana Bankers Association
1930–1933 Instructor, Department of Economics, Indiana University
1931–1933 Secretary and Research Director, Study Commission for Indiana Financial Institutions
  (study of country bank failures in Indiana and how to prevent them)
1933–1935 Assistant Professor, Department of Economics, Indiana University (on leave)
1933–1935 Supervisor, Division of Banks and Trust Companies, and Division of Research and Statistics, Department of Financial Institutions, State of Indiana
1933–1936 Secretary, Commission for Financial Institutions, State of Indiana
1934–? Member, Official Board, First Methodist Church of Bloomington, Indiana
1934–1935 President, Indiana Society of Economists and Sociologists
  (later renamed Indiana Academy of Social Sciences)
1935–1937 Dean, School of Business Administration, Indiana University
  (Professor of Business Administration, 1935–1972)
1935–1936 Chairman of the Conference and Member of the Committee on the Standardization of Call Report Forms
  (tried to standardize and coordinate national and state forms used by the banking regulatory agencies that were sent to banks and had to be published from time to time)
1936–1971 Public Interest Director, Board of Directors, Federal Home Loan Bank of Indianapolis (Chairman, 1940–1971)
1937–1962 Chairman of the Board, Indiana University Foundation
  1962–1969 President

[447]

> *1969–1972   Chairman of the Board*
> *1969–present   Chairman, Executive Committee*
> *1975–present   Vice Chairman*

July 1, 1937–
 March 22, 1938   Acting President, Indiana University

1937–1960   Advisory Member, Research Council, American Bankers Association

1938–1962   President, Indiana University

1938–1962   Member, Committee of Thirteen (Became Council of Ten in 1951; Chairman, 1947–1962)
> *(presidents of Big Ten institutions)*

1938–1939   Member, Joint Committee on Accrediting, Association of Land Grant Colleges and Universities/National Association of State Universities
> *(reviewed programs of colleges and universities for accreditation)*

1939–1955   Member, New Harmony Memorial Commission
> *(state committee to advise on preservation and restoration of historic buildings and homes of New Harmony, Indiana)*

1940–1941   Secretary-Treasurer, State University Association (Member, Executive Committee, 1940–1945; President, 1941–1942, 1952–1953)
> *(professional association for administrators of non-land–grant state universities)*

1941–
 present   Member and Vice-President, Board of Governors, James Whitcomb Riley Memorial Association
> *(raises and administers funds for Riley Memorial Hospital for Children, Indianapolis, and for research on childhood diseases and disabilities)*

1941–1962   Member, Board of Trustees, Carnegie Foundation for the Advancement of Teaching (Vice Chairman, 1952–1953; Chairman, 1953–1954)
> *(administers teacher pension fund and sponsors higher education studies)*

1942   Vice President, National Association of State Universities (President, 1943)
> *(professional association for administrators of state universities)*
>
> *1939–1945   Member, Executive Committee*
> *1944–1949   Member, Committee on Military Affairs*
> *1945   Member, Special Committee on Distribution of War Surplus Commodities*
> *1953–?   Member (representing NASU), National Commission on Accrediting*

1942–1943   Member, Interim Committee on the Reestablishment of a Department of Higher Education, National Education Association

1943–1957 Chairman, Indiana War History Commission
(concerned with preservation of fugitive materials dealing with war effort and with a suitable history of the war)

1943–1944 President, Department of Higher Education, National Education Association

1943–1944 Deputy Director/Special Advisor on Liberated Areas, Office of Foreign Economic Coordination, U.S. Department of State
(concerned with preparation for rehabilitation of devastated areas)

1944–1945 Chairman, American Council on Education
(effective professional organization for higher education)

    1943–1947 Member, Committee on the Relationships of Higher Education to the Federal Government (Member, Advisory Committee, 1948) (monitored bills, regulations, etc., affecting higher education)

    1944–1949 Member, Executive Committee

    1944–1945 Member, Canada-United States Committee on Education (to correct textbook inaccuracies about each other)

    1944–1945 Member (representing ACE), Liaison Committee for International Education

    1944–1949 Chairman, Committee on International Education and Cultural Relations (interested in exchanges and free flow of scholarly information among nations)

    1945 Chairman, Building Committee (found new quarters for ACE and had them remodeled)

    1945 Consultant on Education (from ACE) to U.S. Delegation at San Francisco Conference (organizing conference for the United Nations)

    1946 Chairman, Regional Housing Advisory Committee

    1949–1951 Chairman, Commission on the Occupied Areas

    1951–1955 Member (representing ACE), U.S. National Commission for Unesco (Member, Executive Committee, 1952–1955; Vice-Chairman, 1953–1954)

    1952–1957 Chairman, Commission on Education and International Affairs

    1952–1953 Chairman, Committee on Exchange of Information on International Cultural Relations

1945–1953 Member, Indiana State Board of Education
(dealt with vast problems of State Office of Public Instruction)

1945–?	Member, Board of Trustees, Council for Inter-American Cooperation *(title of seminar group that toured South America in 1941)*
1946– present	Member and Director, Sigma Nu Educational Foundation *(concerned with obtaining funds for Sigma Nu scholarships)*
1946	Member, Allied Missions for Observation of the Greek Elections with Rank of Minister *(first overseas assignment)*
1946–?	Member, Committee on Public Debt Policy, Brookings Institution *(reviewed policy studies and reports)*
1947–1951	Member, Academic Advisory Board, U.S. Merchant Marine Academy *(reviewed educational policies of the Academy)*
1947	Member, Advisory Committee for Planning a Cooperative Midwestern Deposit Library *(Indiana University was a participant in this project to plan a central depository for little-used documents)*
Nov. 1947– May, 1948	Adviser on Cultural Affairs to Military Governor and Acting Chief, Educational and Cultural Affairs, U.S. Occupied Zone, Germany *(concerned mainly with postwar education in American sector of Germany)*
1948–1969	Member and Chairman, Board of Directors, Citizens State Bank, Jamestown, Indiana
1949–1977	Member, College of Electors, Hall of Fame, New York University *(elected members of Hall of Fame)*
1949–1951	Member, Ad Hoc Committee to U.S. Surgeon General to Study the Public Health Service Programs of Research and Educational Grants and Fellowships and the Costs of Medical Education, U.S. Public Health Service
1949–1950	Member, Unesco Committee of Experts on German Questions *(advisory committee to the director-general)*
1950–?	Consultant on German Educational Affairs, U.S. Department of State
1951–1972	Member, Board of Directors, Indiana Bell Telephone Company
1951–1957	American Member, Governing Board, Unesco Institute for Education, Hamburg, Germany *(two trips abroad annually and paperwork in between)*
1952–?	Member, Indiana Selection Committee for the Rhodes Scholarships
1952–1972	Member, Board of Trustees, College Retirement Equities Fund *(teachers' retirement mutual fund)*

1953–1956	Member, Board of Directors, Showers Brothers Company *(Bloomington furniture-manufacturing firm)*
1954–1958	Member, Educational Policies Commission, National Education Association (Chairman, 1955–1958; Adviser, 1958–1961) *(made study of faculty salaries, etc.)*
1955–1956	Member, Educational Advisory Committee, International Cooperation Administration *(federal technical-assistance agency)*
1955–1965	Member, Governing Board, International Association of Universities (Vice President, 1955–1960)
1956– present	Trustee, American Universities Field Staff *(organization to provide member universities with firsthand information about political and socioeconomic conditions in various countries)*
1956– present	Member, Board of Directors, Council on Library Resources *(deals with general policy problems in the research library field)*
1956–1975	Member, Board of Trustees, Howard University
1957	U.S. Delegate to the 12th General Assembly of the United Nations
1957–?	Member, Advisory Committee on the College Housing Program Chaired by Community Facilities Commissioner
1957–1959	Member, Board of Directors, Educational Television and Radio Center (merged into National Educational Television, 1959; Member, NET Board of Directors, 1959–1964, 1965–1970) *(precursor of AIT and PBS)*
1956–1961	Member, Board of Trustees, Committee for Economic Development *(influential group sponsors studies of aspects of the economy)*
1958	Member, Group of American Educators Who Surveyed Higher Education in the Soviet Union
1959–1965	Member, Board of Directors, Learning Resources Institute
1959	Adviser to the Ministry of Education of Pakistan *(recommended changes in the development of higher education)*
1960–?	Director, Inter-University Committee on Travel Grants *(selected grantees for travel abroad to study, do research, attend meetings, etc.)*
1960	Head of U.S. Delegation in Bangkok of South-East Asia Treaty Organization Preparatory Commission on University Problems
1960–1961	Member, Board of Directors, United Nations Committee of Experts to Review Activities and Organization of the United Nations Secretariat

1962–	
present	University Chancellor, Indiana University
1962–1972	Chairman, Board of Directors, Aerospace Research Applications Center, Indiana University
	(made space research information available to industry)
1962–1971	Member, Board of Trustees, Earlham College
1962–1971	Member, Board of Trustees, Indiana Institute of Technology
1962–1970	Member, Wabash College Development Board
1962–1969	Member, National Board of Directors, Goodwill Industries of America
1962–1963	Adviser to the Chicago Public School System
1963–1977	Trustee, Malpas Trust
	(fund provides full scholarships, DePauw-related)
1963–1970	Chairman of Board and Trustee (to 1971), Education and World Affairs
	(broad spectrum of international projects)
1963	Member, Committee of the Michigan Coordinating Council for Public Higher Education to Consider Expansion of Medical Education in the State of Michigan
1963	Advisory Committee, U.S. Educational and Cultural Programs, Brookings Institution
1963–1964	Legislature's Consultant on Higher Education, State of New York
1964–1972	Chairman, Indiana Advisory Commission on Academic Facilities
	(vehicle for distribution of federal funds for academic buildings)
1964–1965	Member and Vice Chairman, National Commission on Humanities
	(recommended federal support)
1965–	
present	Member, Board of Visitors, Tulane University
1965–1970	Member, Board of Trustees, Center for Applied Linguistics
1965–1968	Director, Indiana Judicial Study Commission
1965–1966	Chairman, Ford Foundation Committee to Survey the University of Pittsburgh
	(survey prompted by financial difficulties)
1965	Member, President's Committee on U.S.-Soviet Trade Relations
	(recommended increased trade)
1965–	Member, Committee on AID-University Relations
	(important in relation to technical-assistance programs)
1965	Member, National Citizens' Commission on International Cooperation
	(prepared paper for White House Conference on International Cooperation Year)
1966–1976	Member, Board of Trustees, American University in Cairo

1966–1974	Member, Review Committee on Higher Education to Haile Selassie I, Addis Ababa, Ethiopia
	(advised the emperor about Haile Selassie I University)
1966–1967	Member, President's National Advisory Commission on Food and Fiber
	(large group made recommendations for agriculture and processing)
1967	Member, President's Special Committee on Overseas Voluntary Activities
	(recommended safeguards against CIA's funneling of funds anonymously to American voluntary organizations overseas)
1968–present	Member, Board of Trustees, Indiana Historical Society
1968–1970	Regent and Chairman of Board of Trustees, Sigma Nu National Fraternity
Sept. 1–Nov. 30, 1968	Interim President, Indiana University
1970–present	Member, Board of Directors, Chemed Corporation
1970–1974	Member, Board of Directors, the Indiana Forum
	(carries on study projects relative to public policies in Indiana)
1970–1972	Member, Board of Directors, National Interfraternity Conference
1971–1974	Chairman, Public Finance Task Force, the Indiana Forum
1971	Co-Chairman, Committee on Reorganization, Indiana State Department of Public Instruction
1972–present	Professor Emeritus, School of Business, Indiana University
1972–	Member, Board of Directors, Environmental Quality Control
	(state project)
1973–present	Member, Board of Directors, Lilly Endowment
1973–1978	Member, Technical Advisory Board, Milbank Memorial Fund
1974–1975	Member, Board of Directors, Lincoln Open University
1974	Consultant to the Ford Foundation's Office for the Middle East and Africa to advise the Public Service Review Commission, the National Universities Commission and the National Manpower Board of Lagos
	(personal survey of higher education in Nigeria)
1976–present	Chairman, Advisory Committee, Academy in the Public Service
1976–present	Member and Chairman (to 1978) of the Board, American Research Institute for the Arts
	(conducts research projects in the arts)
1978–1979	Chairperson, Indiana Public Television Review Committee
	(to advise legislature and public)

1979–
   present   Chairman, White Star Endowment
              (fund raising for scholarships)

ACTIVITIES OF RELATIVELY BRIEF
OR UNDEMANDING NATURE

1936–?   Member, Indiana Advisory Committee, National Youth Admin-
           istration
           (advisory to state director; had NYA program on campus)
1937–?   Member, Board of Trustees, Hoosier Salon Patrons Association
           (to promote creative arts in Indiana)
1937–1939 Member, Permanent Endowment Fund Committee, Sigma Nu
           National Fraternity
1939–?   Director and Chairman of Wesley Foundation (Bloomington)
           (youth foundation of Methodist Church)
1939–1940 Chairman, Indiana Committee to Raise Funds for the Franklin
           D. Roosevelt Library
1942–1943 Mediator, U.S. National War Labor Board
           (one meeting for a week in Washington, D.C.)
1942–1943 Member, Advisory Board, Consumer Education Study, National
           Association of Secondary School Principals, National Education
           Association
1943–1944 Member, Navy College Training Program Selection Committee,
           U.S. Navy
1944–?   Member, Federal Savings and Loan Advisory Council, Federal
           Home Loan Bank
           *(met in Washington with members from their districts to re-
           view national policy of Federal Home Loan Bank Board)*
1944–?   Trustee, National Board of Education, Methodist Church
1945–1948 Member, Commission on the Arts, Association of American
           Colleges
1945–1946 Member, Board of Directors, Conference of American Small
           Business Organizations
1947   Member, Board of Directors, Citizen Conference on Interna-
           tional Economic Union
1947   Chairman for Indiana, Greek War Relief Association
           (fund raising)
1947   Trustee, Film Council of America
1947   Member, Indiana Committee, Great Books Foundation
1948–1949 Member, Seal Sale Sponsoring Committee, Indiana Society for
           Crippled Children
           (fund raising)
1949–1960 Member (Chairman, 1949–1960), Board of Directors, National
           Thrift Committee
           (sponsored by Savings and Loan League to promote thrift)
1949–?   Member, National Advisory Council, Junior Achievement
1949–?   Member, Board of Directors, Freedom Films

1950–?	Member, Sponsoring Committee, Japan International Christian University Fund *(fund raising)*
1950–?	Member, Indiana Committee, Crusade for Freedom
1951	Member, National Advisory Committee on Civil Defense Training and Education, U.S. Federal Civil Defense Administration
1952–?	Member, Board of Trustees, Lincoln Free Press Memorial Association
1952–?	Sponsoring member, Special Committee of Educators, Aid Refugee Chinese Intellectuals
1954	Member, Board of Directors, Lafayette Bicentennial Association
1955–present	Member, Board of Directors, Foundation for Economic and Business Studies *(publication vehicle for scholarly papers and periodicals)*
1955–1977	Member of Board, Davis Medical Foundation *(raised funds for scholarships, etc.)*
1956–1962	Member, First Board of Regents, American Savings and Loan Institute, Graduate School of Savings and Loan *(conducts the Graduate School of Savings and Loan)*
1956–1959	Member, Board of Trustees, Jefferson National Expansion Memorial Association
1956–?	Member, Board of Sponsors, World University Service
1956	Member, International Humanitarian Award Committee, Variety Clubs International
1957–present	Chairman, Board of Directors, Foundation for the School of Business *(Indiana University)*
1957	Member, American Committee for the Observance of the 10th Anniversary of the Founding of the State of Israel
1957	Member, Board of Trustees, Bi-Partisan Council on American Foreign Policy
1957	Member, Committee to Protect Our Children's Teeth *(pro-fluoridation; chaired by Dr. Benjamin Spock)*
1957	Member, National Advisory Panel, Institute of Research on Overseas Programs
1958	Member, Advisory Council, National Society of Arts and Letters *(patronage group)*
1959–1961	Member, Board of Directors, Foreign Policy Association
1959–?	Member, Advisory Committee, National Arts Foundation
1959–?	Member, National Committee for the Florence Agreement *(to ease importation of foreign educational materials)*
1959	Member, Committee of Educators, Recording for the Blind
1961–?	Trustee and Voting Member, National Fund for Medical Education; Chairman for Indiana, 1962–?

1962–1974	Member, Board of Directors, People-to-People
1962–?	Member, Board of Directors, National Association on Standard Medical Vocabulary
1972–?	Member, Management Division Policy Panel, Academy for Educational Development
1974–present	Member, Board of Directors, Historic Landmarks Foundation of Indiana
1974–?	Member, Board of Directors, American Friends of Ethiopia

HONORS

Of the numerous honors that Dr. Wells has received, the following are a sampling:

Twenty-six honorary degrees
Foreign decorations awarded by the Federal Republic of Germany and the Emperor of Thailand
Benjamin Franklin Fellow, Royal Society of Arts (London)
Fellow, American Academy of Arts and Sciences
Member, American Philosophical Society, Phi Beta Kappa, Beta Gamma Sigma
Gold Medal Award, International Benjamin Franklin Society
Brotherhood Award Winner and Member of National Honor Corps of the National Conference of Christians and Jews
Honorary Fellow, International College of Dentists
National Interfraternity Conference Award
The Robins Award of America
Distinguished Service in School Administration Award, American Association of School Administrators
Caleb B. Smith Award, Indiana Grand Lodge, F. & A. M.
Lifetime Honorary Chairman, Federal Home Loan Bank of Indianapolis
Charter Member, Indiana Academy
First Annual Award, New York Alumni Chapter of Beta Gamma Sigma
Honorary Fellow, American College of Dentists
Honorary Member, DeMolay Legion of Honor
Honorary Member, United Steelworkers of America, District 30
Liberty Bell Award, Young Lawyers Section of Indiana Bar Association
One of "America's Ten Outstanding Young Men of 1939," United States Junior Chamber of Commerce
Indiana Arts Award, Indiana Arts Commission
Hoosier of the Year Award, Sons of Indiana in New York
Distinguished Service Award, Indiana Junior Chamber of Commerce
Man of the Year Award, Indianapolis *Times*
Medal of Honor, University of Evansville
Distinguished Alumni Service Award, Indiana University Alumni Association

B. TRADITIONAL RITE AT FRESHMAN CONVOCATION

THE SPIRIT OF INDIANA: Of all the pleasures and responsibilities which come to a university, one of the greatest is that of welcoming its new members to the collegiate body, to unite into one family the individual members of its academic group.

The spirit that is Indiana knows no limitations of age, color, creed, doctrine, social, political, or economic bounds. The Indiana that welcomes you here includes in its membership all parts of the collegiate body from the youngest freshman to the oldest member of the faculty and of its administrative staff. It includes all those who have come for the purpose of seeking truth and intellectual freedom. Of such, it requests that they partake of its spirit and feel themselves shareholders in its privileges and in its responsibilities.

The spirit that greets you here is the rich heritage of a glorious past made possible by students, who, like yourselves upon entering the university, felt strangely far from home and intimate friends, but who soon adapted themselves to their new environment. The university covets for each of you a like experience. The traditions of the institution must be carried on by the entering classes who take up and carry on where the graduating classes leave off. As rich as is the heritage which you find here, it should be and must be made richer and better because of your having been here.

Soon, even to those of you who stay longest, will be given the commencement farewell. The credit which you eventually reflect upon the university will depend to a great extent upon how you conduct yourselves in the interval between this induction and your graduation. Make the most of the opportunities while here, acquaint yourself with the best traditions of the university, leave here richer in tradition than when you entered. Such is the Law of Progress. All that has been and all that is of the spirit of Indiana University welcomes you unreservedly.

PRESIDENT'S CHARGE

I am for those who see our University as it is, with all its strengths and yet all its needs, and who therefore know it at its best—its resolute integrity, its allegiance to the whole truth, its long service in bringing the young people of this State toward the fullness of the life of the mind, its passion for a clean and just democracy. I am for those who see through the superficialities to the University's basic purpose: The intellectual development of her sons and daughters. It is in their growth that she exults, for by their excellence will the world judge her. Across the earth these sons and daughters join you in the pledge of the Psalmist of old:

> If I forget thee, let my right hand
>   forget her cunning.
> Let my tongue cleave to the roof of my mouth,
>   if I remember thee not.

A PLEDGE FOR THE UNIVERSITY

At the age of eighteen every free-born Athenian youth (ephebus) took an oath of consecration to civic, military, and religious duty. This oath I now administer is in a form freely adapted to meet modern occasions and the case of an educational institution:

I will not disgrace the University from which I have received my education, nor will I abandon the comrade who stands by my side.

I will fight for its best interests, whether I stand alone or have the support of others.

I will revere and preserve its ideals and traditions, and will incite like reverence in others.

I will strive always to quicken among my fellows the sense of social and civic duty.

I will cherish the sacred institutions of my country. In all these ways I will strive to transmit this our heritage not less but greater and better than it was transmitted unto us.

C. *TIME* ON WELLS

GOURMET & PRESIDENT

Indiana University waited a year for Paul Vories McNutt to decide whether he wanted to be its president. Once dean of its law school, later Governor of Indiana, now High Commissioner to the Philippines, but still Indiana's political boss, Paul McNutt is looking for the best road to the U. S. Presidency. Last fortnight, after he had talked to the university trustees (his appointees) and President Roosevelt, he made his decision. Back he flew to the Philippines to keep in active touch with politics. Last week Indiana University appointed as president Paul McNutt's jovial friend, Herman B (for nothing, and without a period) Wells, 35, youngest president of a State university.

Rolypoly "Hermie" Wells (5 ft. 7 in. and 228 lb.) had been holding the chair for Paul McNutt since old Dr. William Lowe Bryan retired last year. On the serious side, he is an economist who has made studies of Indiana's financial institutions, has written a new State banking law, was dean for two years of the university's business school. He is a good friend of Utilityman Wendell Lewis Willkie. But the campus knows him best as a jolly, convivial gourmet, and a Rabelaisian storyteller. His chief crony is Sam Gabriel, who runs a haberdashery shop across the street from the president's office. They roar about Bloomington in a bright blue touring car with the top down, in summer repair to a cabin in Brown County for merrymaking. For exercise Hermie Wells wields a paddle on initiates in the Sphinx Club, waddles around the campus, rides horseback, takes sunbaths.

Indiana, one of the oldest state universities (118 years), calls itself the "mother of college presidents" because it has produced some 70 of them, including Swarthmore's famed Frank Aydelotte. Hermie Wells is the latest to be added to the list.

HEAVYWEIGHT CHAMPION

When he took over Indiana University in 1937, fun-loving Herman B (for nothing, and please no period) Wells alarmed hidebound Hoosiers with his penchant for dressing up in a coonskin coat and roaring around Bloomington in a bright blue touring car with the top down. For all his bulk (228 lbs. at 5 ft. 7 in.), the nation's youngest (then 35) president of a state university looked like a lightweight. Happily, the pessimists were dead wrong. When he stepped down last week at 60—to be replaced by Army Secretary Elvis Stahr Jr.—"Hermie" Wells was known throughout U.S. campuses not only as the man who remade Indiana University but also as just about the best old-pro prexy in the business.

Son of two schoolteachers in Jamestown, Ind., and dean of Indiana's School of Business Administration before he moved up to the presidency, Economist Wells proved to be a master at charming cash out of state legislators, and he used it to buy academic quality. Up surged the English department, the music and medical schools. The faculty blossomed with top scholars: Heart Surgeon Harris B. Shumacker Jr., Nobel-Prizewinning Geneticist Hermann J. Muller and the late Sexologist Alfred C. Kinsey, whose scholarship Wells stoutly defended when Kinsey first began to publicize his findings.

Indiana's plant has quadrupled under Wells, enrollment has quintupled to 25,000, the university's vast research program spans everything from nuclear cloud chambers to training teachers in Thailand. Wells broke down racial barriers at Indiana, quietly opened dormitories and the swimming pool to Negroes (in 1959, Miss Indiana University was a Negro). Not least, Wells in 1956 snagged Drug Manufacturer Josiah Kirby Lilly's collection of 20,000 first editions and thousands of manuscripts, which made Indiana one of the nation's leading rare-book centers. Bachelor Wells, lover of antiques and fine food, has gained not only 50 lbs. or so in his 25-year regime but also heavy respect as an academic statesman.

Wells now takes over the Indiana University Foundation, which finances research and handles private gifts. He leaves a rich heritage to Kentucky-born President Stahr, 46, lawyer and Rhodes scholar, who had the highest academic average in the history of the University of Kentucky, later taught law at Kentucky, became vice chancellor of the University of Pittsburgh and the youngest president (1959–61) in the history of the University of West Virginia.

Less successful were Stahr's 15 months at the Pentagon, where his academic personality failed to mesh with hardware-oriented Defense Secretary Robert S. McNamara. Stahr once admitted that he did not know a battle group from a battalion, and blame for foul-ups in last year's call-up of Army reservists landed on his desk. He should be happier at Indiana, where his talents are more suitable.

D. TAKING THE ARTS TO THE PEOPLE

THIS COLLEGE CAMPUS IS THE WHOLE STATE / KARL DETZER

Into the office of the president of Indiana University there recently breezed an athletic youth. "You're too fat, Hermie," he remarked. "Give me two evenings a week and I'll train 70 pounds off you."

If this is an unusual way for an undergraduate to address his college president, the explanation is that Herman Wells is an unusual president. At 36, he is the youngest state university head in America, and he has held the job two years. At a time when most colleges require even an assistant professor to be a Ph.D., Wells has no doctor's degree; he hasn't had time to get one. He knows thousands of Indiana citizens by their first names, and more than half his 6000 students call him by his. Fat, energetic, good-humored, he combines the earthy background of Midwest small-town upbringing with the politician's capacity to make and keep friends.

But the *most* unusual thing about him is his belief that a modern state university should not be a stay-at-home; that it should go out and aggressively carry its message to *all* the people. Through forums, music, drama, movies, radio, he is pushing the influence of Indiana University to the farthest corners of his state. As a result, housewives, steel workers, farmers, with no thought of diplomas, are getting a cultural education at home. "I'll not be satisfied," Wells says, "till we have a symphony orchestra in every county, singing societies and art classes for all who want them, a little theater group in every town hall."

In part he is carrying on, with a crusader's zeal, the program that was under way before he became president. When mill-workers in industrial Gary asked the state university for help in forming an orchestra, they got it. The Calumet Symphony was the result. When the amateur singers of the district sought aid, the university formed three large choruses, built around existing societies which had been struggling to keep music alive amid industrialdin. Members range in age from 18 to 60, speak 20 languages, include stenographers, teachers, laborers, chemists, engineers, housewives. The university provides sheet music and directors, public schools furnish practice rooms.

Meanwhile, groups in the same region were asking for a place where they could draw, design, paint, model in clay. Like orchestra and choruses, it sprang from the creative yearning of common citizens. Wells immediately furnished a director, arranged with public schools for studios. Drawn by a 15-week course which cost but $8, 50 men and women from smoky Hammond, Whiting, and East Chicago were soon going into Gary three evenings a week to study art.

To help these beginners, as well as teachers and clubwomen, miners and farmers all over the state, the university recently finished a feature-length film called *Water Color*. Captions explain each move, as Eliot O'Hara, a leading American water-colorist, creates a painting. Any interested group may borrow the film at a small rental, run it and re-run it while they study technique. Twenty Indiana communities asked for it in the first month, and high schools in Cleveland, Toledo, New York and Baltimore are on the waiting list. Rental fees will pay its cost in one year. A second such film is in production.

The university has also launched a traveling art collection which, like two others to follow it, consists of 12 small canvases. "Most exhibitions,"

Wells explains, "are the privilege of the few." This exhibit often hangs in schoolrooms in dingy neighborhoods, in country churches, in labor union halls.

But thousands of people are interested in other subjects than music and art. "What about drama?" citizens wanted to know, "and economics? Why can't we take up nature study?"

"Why not?" Wells repeated, and told his extension divisions to make the new services self-supporting. This winter, taxpayers in 12 scattered counties are taking part in social and economic forums. Chambers of Commerce, women's clubs, farm granges are sponsoring the groups. As leaders, President Wells sends advanced students from his campus; from the university library, free of charge, goes literature needed for the discussions.

But Wells' program does not stop at taking the university out to the people. Just as vigorously, it brings the people to the university. This winter, for example, 250 Indiana bankers accepted Wells' invitation to a three-day conference on the Bloomington campus, with professors, Federal Reserve officers and banking experts as instructors in credit analysis, investment policies, taxation and personnel. Hardly had the bankers gone when a hundred newspaper editors came to brush up on history, government, economics, physics and law.

Perhaps Wells' educational philosophy is best stated in his invitation to these editors: "The University fulfills its true purpose," he wrote, "not only in the classroom, but also by affording facilities and trained personnel to coöperate with all citizens in the solution of their particular problems. It is in this spirit Indiana University invites you."

Mortgage lenders, retail merchants, prosecuting attorneys, high school principals, and leaders of women's clubs have accepted similar invitations. To catch up with the latest developments in their special fields, doctors, dentists, policemen, safety supervisors and radio announcers will gather on the campus before spring. There will be short courses devoted to education, school bands, state planning and business.

Specialization, however, never entirely overshadows the broader cultural values which can—and which Wells insists must—come out of such conferences. To the surprise of the bankers, for example, Wells introduced an eminent biologist from Johns Hopkins University to lecture on "The Biological Basis of Sociality." Every man or woman who attends these conferences will return home with at least a taste of scholarship in some field unrelated to his own.

It is in this welding of business and erudition, art and economics, that Indiana University is believed to be pioneering. Where other schools reach out cautiously in a few directions, Wells is seeking to widen the cultural front until every taxpayer gets some intellectual return from his state university.

Indiana is very likely to go along with him. Hoosier-born, product of the public schools, he graduated in 1924 from the university he now heads. After two years as cashier of a country bank, he returned to the university to teach economics. The governor then drafted him for a commission to rewrite the banking laws. That done, he went back to the lecture hall and in less than two years was appointed dean of the business school. Enrollment in that school doubled in the two years he headed it. When the university president retired, it was he who suggested young Wells as his successor. Students cheered the choice. They knew that every one of the 1500 graduates of the business school, under Wells, had a job waiting for him as soon as his diploma was dry!

When the enthusiastic state legislature appropriated $2500 for his inaugural ceremony, Wells sent the money to the research departments. "No need for pageantry," he said, and ordered a brief program which cost the state nothing. Then he traveled 33,000 miles to pick the dozen men who would replace elderly faculty members retired under a new state law.

Once back on the campus, he launched his whirlwind campaign to make this state university the people's own. It developed on many unexpected fronts. To pave the way for a broadcasting station, the university radio workshop participated in a state-wide survey to determine Indiana's radio tastes and coverage. University workers undertook a school-to-school study of the speech and hearing difficulties of children. Financed jointly by a $10,000 grant from women's clubs and the university, this study will reach every child in the state. Parents will be told how to guard against increased deafness, how to improve the speech of lispers and stutterers.

Again, Wells imported designers from New York and made plans for a great center of the arts on the Indiana campus, with theaters, radio studios, workshops and recital halls. "Before long," he says, "I hope we'll have district contests in drama, with plays written, directed and acted by Hoosiers, and each year a great drama festival right here on the campus."

Thus functions the dynamo of Indiana culture, the man who is striving to bring culture to the crossroads. When writers like Tarkington, Ade and Riley, statesmen like Beveridge and Marshall, lived and labored on the banks of the Wabash, Hoosiers called their state the Athens of America. The giants died or moved away; the torch of Hoosier culture dimmed. Coal, corn, steel and gasoline took precedence, and for years no cultural leader emerged to guide Indiana to a renaissance. Today many Hoosiers think they have found one. His name is Herman Wells.

E. TELEGRAMS FROM GENERAL LUCIUS CLAY

My dear Governor Gates: Recently at my request, Dr. Wells, president of Indiana University, visited Germany to examine the problems which we face in the reeducation of the German people. At the conclusion of his visit, I urged him to return for a year as my personal adviser in this field and to supervise our activities not only in the field of direct education through the school system but also in the re-establishment of sound cultural relations with Germany and in disseminating to the German people information pertaining to democracy as we know it.

Our major objective in Germany is in the development of a democratic government in which the people will have confidence, and such a government is essential if we are to successfully prevent the penetration of Communist influence into western Germany. We can succeed if we have the highest type of American leadership.

I am convinced that Dr. Wells will provide this type of leadership. I do not know of any more important service which could be rendered to our country and I would be grateful indeed if Dr. Wells could be given a leave of absence for a year to undertake this program. I would be even more grateful for your support to this end.

My dear Judge Wildermuth: As you know, military government is striving earnestly to establish democratic procedures in Germany which will serve to resist the penetration of communism and to permit the entry of Germany at some future date into the family of democratic nations. In accomplishing these objectives, there is no more important assignment than the reeducation of the German people, not only in their schools but in every walk of life. If this is to be accomplished, the highest type of American leadership is essential. For this reason I have urgent need for a personal adviser in the field of education who will supervise and direct our efforts in this field, to include the reestablishment of cultural relations between America and Germany and in the dissemination of information pertaining to democracy.

I have met Dr. [Herman] Wells, president of Indiana University, and I know that he would give us the type of leadership which we need if he could come to us for a year. I do not believe that America has any more important task, and I would be grateful indeed to you for any support you can give to making him available to us for a year.

F. CURRENT DIRECTORS
INDIANA UNIVERSITY FOUNDATION

William S. Armstrong
President
Indiana University Foundation

Glenn L. Banks
President
Banks Lumber Company, Inc.

James W. Cozad
Executive Vice President
Standard Oil Co. (Indiana)

Donald C. Danielson
Senior Vice President
City Securities Corp.

Oscar L. Dunn
Chairman and Chief Executive
New York Chamber of Commerce
and Industry

Don B. Earnhart
Administrative Trustee
Krannert Charitable Trust

Byron K. Elliott
Retired Chairman and President
John Hancock Mutual Life
Insurance Co.

Jean Edward Smith, ed., *The Papers of Lucius D. Clay: Germany, 1945–1949*, vol. I (Bloomington: Indiana University Press, 1975), pp. 424–25. Messages sent through Major General Daniel Noce, Director, Civil Affairs Division, U.S. War Department, September 11, 1947.

G. INDIANA UNIVERSITY
150TH BIRTHDAY FUND SUBSCRIPTIONS

TRANSMITTAL 309, JULY 28, 1972 (FINAL)

Project Designated by Donor

Unrestricted—gifts not designated for a particular use		$ 2,000,821.79
Assembly Hall	$ 422,223.58	
Astro Turf	171,300.45	593,524.03
Fine Arts Pavilion[1]		5,133,511.50
Hoosier Heritage Hall[2]		3,719,683.49
Indianapolis Center for Advanced Research[3]		2,953,577.20
Library Acquisitions		2,729,593.35
Musical Arts Center		4,312,194.30
Professorships		1,877,197.55
Regional Campuses:		
IU at Ft. Wayne[4]	$ 476,774.86	
IU at Kokomo	6,202.00	
IU-Northwest	76,434.34	
IU at South Bend	17,215.20	
IU-Southeast	586,461.30	
Regional Campuses-General	2,971.86	
IU-Indianapolis	10,390,236.49	11,556,296.05
Scholarships[5]	$ 4,278,367.81	
Scholarships for Athletes	349,212.80	4,627,580.61
Miscellaneous		
Carillon		490,746.00
Chi Omega Projects		16,454.50
Golf House Project		120,642.36
Showboat MAJESTIC II		350,361.00
Annual Giving Contributions 2/68-6/72		4,859,680.24
Other—gifts designated for a use other than one of the		5,876,181.28
campaign goals		$51,218,045.25

1. Includes $2,555,612.50 designated by donors for purposes other than construction.
2. Includes $1,635,000.00 designated specifically for Glenn A. Black Laboratory.
3. Includes ½ of IU-PU Advanced Research total which is credited to 150th.
4. Includes ½ of IU-PU Ft. Wayne total which is credited to 150th.
5. Does not include scholarships designated for Regional Campuses which total $285,784.42 and included in Regional Campuses total.

H. MESSAGE TO THE UNIVERSITY COMMUNITY, November 1, 1968

When I agreed to talk to interested students on the subjects of recruiting in our recreational facilities, "learning how to kill in our classrooms," and performing military research in our laboratories, I felt that the University community had a right to know my views and my information on these topics.

Six days after that agreement, I was presented a list of points described as demands, supported by the Young Socialist Alliance but mentioning repeatedly and prominently "S.D.S.," the initials of an organization known as Students for a Democratic Society. Spokesmen requesting the original meeting were members of the delegation presenting the demands. Through a letter to "Mr. King et al.," I explained that the original invitation tendered to me to speak to these issues had been qualified by conditions which made it apparent that my views and information were of minimal interest to those students who had requested a meeting. Therefore, I would present my statement instead to the *Indiana Daily Student* and would have copies available for anyone interested.

The questions raised by the S.D.S., I wish to emphasize, do not concern extracurricular activities or regulations affecting student life as have issues raised earlier by students. The S.D.S. demands invade the area of academic programs and the scholar's freedom to pursue his research interests.

The impropriety of "demands" as a form of questioning policy and practice in an academic community should be evident to every member of the community. Nevertheless, I shall respond to them specifically in giving my views and the information I have, in order to keep the record as clear as possible.

I believe that any community of scholars would agree that *no* special interest group, internal or external, should be allowed to impose its particular point of view upon the university. This does not imply any restriction on questioning, making suggestions, seeking information or peaceful and orderly advocacy—although usually there are more direct sources of information than the President of the University. It does mean that the policy of an open campus in which freedom of inquiry is protected is of highest importance to the university community. Indiana University has an unblemished tradition of preserving an open campus.

In times of national stress, when public opinion is divided, pressures are invariably brought to bear upon the University to support the views of one or the other side by excluding controversial speakers, activities or programs. The sharp cleavage of opinion about the national involvement in Vietnam has produced such pressures. This background of the open campus and the pressures to restrict it should be kept in mind throughout my discussion of the nine points raised by the S.D.S.

The S.D.S. document delivered to me through my assistant began: "SDS rejects Indiana University's role as a subserviant, uncritical flunky of the military establishment and of the agencies formulating American policy. We reject this university's commitment to the objectives of American foreign policy and its commitment to train armies and police forces and their spies. Consequently SDS demands that President Wells immediately sever Indiana

University's ties to all military and paramilitary organizations and specifically that:

"1. All R O T C programs be eliminated. In other words, that Indiana cease supplying academic credit for R O T C courses, academic personnel to teach these courses, and classroom and office space for R O T C programs. And that Indiana University cease to have any direct or indirect military presence on campus."

My response: Indiana University offered military training sporadically from 1841 to 1874. Its R.O.T.C. program was established in 1917 and military training has been part of the undergraduate curricula ever since then. The program was compulsory for most male undergraduates until September, 1965, when, by action of the Board of Trustees, it was made voluntary. The inclusion of military training in the curricula was instituted on each occasion at the urgent request of students.

Land-grant institutions such as Purdue University are required to provide military training by the Morrill Act of 1862 which established them. Students desiring to come to I.U. but who are intent upon taking R.O.T.C. should not be limited in their choice to land-grant institutions. Furthermore, as a result of R.O.T.C. programs at civilian institutions, the large majority of the men in officer ranks are R.O.T.C.-trained college men and partly because of this, the United States fortunately has not developed a narrow professional group with a stake in militarism.

R.O.T.C. continues to be offered at I.U. because many of our students desire officer training in conjunction with their college education to prepare either for military careers or for a period of military service. The presence of an R.O.T.C. unit on campus in no way interferes with conscientious objectors any more than, for example, the existence of our School of Medicine interferes with students who are Christian Scientists. R.O.T.C. is included as an integral part of the accepted academic program at the Ivy League universities and at all the major state universities.

The University's R.O.T.C. program has been reviewed many times and at least three times in the last seven years by the Curriculum Committee of the College of Arts and Sciences. These reexaminations and one now in progress reflect the fact that the faculty of the College, like the faculties of the other Schools with undergraduate divisions, establishes the number of credit hours in military science applicable to the satisfaction of its degree requirements. Originally, military training at I.U. was associated with a program in civil engineering. Its availability now as an option for students in each of the undergraduate schools is indicative of the variety of duty assignments in the armed services.

The University's agreement with the Department of Defense with respect to the R.O.T.C. program commits the University to granting appropriate academic credit applicable toward graduation for successful completion of courses offered in military science. The University provides classroom and office space as it does for other programs in which courses are taught for credit; the Department of Defense furnishes instructors, equipment, clothing and student retainer pay.

In recent years there has been some experimentation with the R.O.T.C. curriculum. At I.U., students in Army R.O.T.C. may satisfy one of its requirements by taking a course in American History which is open to all interested students and a course in Government is offered under similar conditions to students in Air Force R.O.T.C. and others. The possibility of including additional University courses as part of the R.O.T.C. program can be further explored. This, of course, is not a question of supplying academic personnel to teach R.O.T.C. courses, but rather of permitting course work in various departments to be counted toward satisfaction of R.O.T.C. program requirements.

As a credit program, R.O.T.C. grades are figured in the overall accumulative average of a student in any of the undergraduate colleges except the College of Arts and Sciences, which includes grades of advanced R.O.T.C. work only.

The chairman of the Committee to End the War in Vietnam [C E W V], Grant Williams, has asked me to respond to several questions about R.O.T.C. which I am including in this discussion. He asked whether such nonacademic factors as appearance, obedience and political beliefs count in R.O.T.C. grades. Factors which contribute to such grades vary as they would in any professional-type training program. For example, appearance, uniforms and obedience are essential factors in the I.U. Marching Hundred and other factors are crucial to H P E R courses. Political beliefs, in the sense of a choice among alternatives available to any citizen of a democracy, provide criteria for neither exclusion from nor inclusion in R.O.T.C. If such beliefs as conscientious objection to war are meant by the question, the fact that R.O.T.C. is voluntary makes such a point irrelevant.

Mr. Williams also asked whether admission to advanced R.O.T.C. was limited by such factors as sex and physical qualifications, and if so, was this policy consistent with academic requirements. As a matter of fact, female students may enroll for credit in Army and Air Force R.O.T.C. with the approval of appropriate military authorities. Driver Training, Physical Education for Men, Dentistry, and numerous other areas of study have limiting factors for enrollment, including sex or physical qualifications.

Credentials of officers nominated for positions in the Department of Military Science and Air Science are transmitted through the Dean for Undergraduate Development to the University President for appointment. The President need not approve an appointment and he can request relief of an officer for cause.

The C E W V chairman has suggested that R.O.T.C. could be made a voluntary student group, such as the Chess Club. In 1861 military training was provided through an organization called the University Cadets. However, such an approach would not only be in violation of our agreements with the Department of Defense but would place professional preparation for military service at an unwarranted disadvantage in relation to other professional programs.

Mr. Williams further suggested the establishment of a Department of Peace with an equal status to the R.O.T.C. program. Peace, given its broadest meaning, undoubtedly embraces a large number of courses already offered. The rationale for instituting a Department of Peace apparently is that this would be a positive approach to achieving peace. It should be remembered that many people have long held that an important way to achieve peace is through the deterrent of adequate military preparation. Moreover, all who now decry defense should recognize that the nation faces many problems in this area in addition to Vietnam.

I might point out that in 1918, when students became enlisted soldiers while in residence, classes in War Aims were instituted which dealt with the immediate causes of the war and the underlying conflicts of points of view as expressed in the governments, philosophies and literatures of the warring countries on each side of the struggle.

Before concluding my discussion of R.O.T.C., I wish to make two points. If in this time of war hysteria we should be persuaded to cancel out the R.O.T.C. program for political reasons, we would in effect be yielding to precisely the same kind of pressures which from time to time have demanded that we cease teaching anything about Karl Marx, Russian history, and Slavic languages and literature. There is little practical difference to the University whether those demands come from inside or outside the University community. Secondly, while it is understandable that many people who bear the terrible brunt of war should be opposed to war, our national involvement in Vietnam is nonetheless a fact, as is the draft. The likelihood that many of your fellow students will be called upon for military service still remains unfortunately strong. In your zeal to end the war and promote peace, consider the effect of your attack upon R.O.T.C. Its existence is less essential to the war effort than to fellow students who wish to have the advantage of preparation in the skills that will equip them for a better chance of survival in the performance of their mandatory military service. Opposing R.O.T.C. may satisfy your hunger for action but its crucial effect will be to remove the option of valued training for many of your classmates.

S.D.S. demand: "2. Cease actively channeling students into military and military-related agencies (*i.e.,* the Defense Department, State Department, CIA, FBI, Army, etc.) by allowing their recruiters to use University facilities."

My response: The University is not engaged in "actively channeling" students into anything other than its instructional programs. (I mean by this that students are assisted through the University's counseling program to be aware of fields of study for which their scholastic aptitudes and interests fit them.) But, as all students know, they are completely free to choose their courses of study, their fields of concentration and their careers, within the limitations of their capabilities. No one is pressured into accepting any job. Everyone is a free agent, free to accept, reject or ignore recruitment efforts.

Historically, the University began to furnish placement services as a convenience and aid to graduating students in their search for jobs. In recent years, as more jobs became available than graduates to fill them, employer representatives have come to the campus for interviews, a development which again was to the advantage of students.

After a group of students objected to the presence on campus of employer representatives associated with Dow Chemical Company, the Faculty Council elected a Steering Committee to Study Policies Governing Picketing and Demonstrations and added student representatives. One of the first recommendations of that committee was as follows:

> The Faculty Council reaffirms the present policy of providing student placement services and allowing any employer to interview any student for the purpose of lawful employment, subject to the nondiscrimination policy established by the Board of Trustees, July, 1967.

This recommendation, in the form of a motion, was passed unanimously at the Faculty Council meeting of February 20, 1968.

At the Faculty Council's meeting on March 12, 1968, the committee submitted a more comprehensive resolution on this subject which was passed after lengthy discussion.

The resolution reads:

> The Faculty Council hereby resolves:
> 1) THAT IT IS THE SENSE OF THE COUNCIL:
> THAT PUBLICIZING EMPLOYMENT AND CAREER OPPORTUNITIES AND RECRUITING FOR SUCH OPPORTUNITIES SHALL BE GOVERNED BY RULES AND REGULATIONS THAT ACCORD NO PREFERENTIAL TREATMENT FOR ANY TYPE OF EMPLOYMENT OR SERVICE;
> THAT ANY ORGANIZATION, PUBLIC OR PRIVATE, BE PROVIDED UNIVERSITY FACILITIES FOR RECRUITMENT ONLY WHEN ONE OR MORE STUDENTS HAVE INDICATED AN INTEREST IN BEING INTERVIEWED BY THAT AGENCY;
> THAT RECRUITMENT INTERVIEWS OR THE PUBLICIZING OF EMPLOYMENT OPPORTUNITIES, PUBLIC OR PRIVATE, SHALL BE CONDUCTED IN PRIVATE, EXCEPT THAT CAREER INFORMATION MEETINGS, AS DISTINGUISHED FROM RECRUITMENT INTERVIEWS, MAY BE HELD IN DESIGNATED ROOMS, AND THAT REASONABLE PUBLICITY BY NOTICES PLACED ON BULLETIN BOARDS OR BY LITERATURE DEPOSITED FOR PICK-UP AT DESIGNATED LOCATIONS, MAY BE PERMITTED;
> 2) THE OFFICE OF THE PRESIDENT, THE BOARD OF DIRECTORS OF THE INDIANA MEMORIAL UNION, AND THE DIRECTORS OF UNIVERSITY PLACEMENT SERVICES ARE REQUESTED TO TAKE ANY NECESSARY STEPS TO BRING CAMPUS RECRUITING PRACTICES INTO CONFORMITY WITH THIS RESOLUTION.

It should be pointed out that the Indiana Memorial Union is a student building, financed by student fees. Every student officially enrolled on the Bloomington campus of I.U. is an active member of the Indiana Memorial Union. The legal title to all funds and property of the Indiana Memorial Union is vested in and subject to the control of the Trustees of Indiana University. However, The Board of Directors of I M U, comprised of twelve students and five representatives of the faculty and administration, is "empowered to promulgate and administer such bylaws and house rules as may be needed to govern the activities and conduct of members, guests, visitors and organizations in, on, or about the premises of the Union Building."

By long-standing policy, the Union Board's regulations permit representatives of the armed services as well as of other organizations to reserve tables in the Commons Lobby for three days in a five-week period as an informational service to students.

At present, the policy committee of the Union Board is conducting interviews to ascertain the opinions of key people on the campus concerning this policy. The Board will hold an open hearing on this subject Monday afternoon, November 4.

Although the Faculty Council and the Union Board differ in respect to the locations in which recruiters may provide information and conduct interviews, both support the "open campus" policy I discussed in my opening comments.

The argument has been advanced from time to time that to allow recruitment is to approve of the agency doing recruitment. The reverse is more cogent: refusal to permit recruitment by a particular agency means condemnation of that agency.

Now, placement services and recruitment are admittedly adjuncts to the educational process. They need not take place on the campus except as a matter of convenience for students. But for the University to select from among the agencies of government, business, industry, etc., which ones should be permitted to recruit would place it in the untenable position of passing judgment on an agency.

Those who wish to ban military recruitment on campus either because of their pacifist views or as a means of protesting governmental policy have an obligation to consider the full and long-term effect of using the University for promotion of their own position on war generally or the Vietnam War in particular. Pressure to use the University for promotion of any group's particular position on an issue constitutes an assault upon the integrity of the University. Yielding to that pressure would make the University vulnerable to any and every special plea. The plain fact is that those who are objecting to military recruitment simply wish to use the University as a means of protesting or even coercing governmental policy. This is an ineffective and even reprehensible use of the University.

S.D.S. demand: "3. All military-financed research be immediately terminated and the University cease to accept contracts and grants from any military or military-related agency."

My response: The University has no contracts or grants which provide for faculty members to engage in military research, if by "military research" one means research directed toward the production and use of military weapons such as tanks, guns or bombs, or to engage in research on chemical or bacterial warfare methods.

Indiana University received $1,281,145 from the Department of Defense agencies last year to support basic scientific research. This represented about 4.4% of our total research support from outside sources. It should be emphasized that these projects are *basic* research, and *in every case the project was initiated by the faculty member himself*. Each project represented a research interest of the faculty member, frequently pursued for a long period of time prior to the submission of a proposal. There are no restrictions on publication of the results; that is, *none of the research is classified*.

The history of the discussion leading to the decision of the government to support basic scientific research through DOD (Department of Defense) agencies is pertinent. After World War II with its disruption of fundamental research, the scientific community urged the Federal Government to support basic research. Since there was neither a National Science Foundation (established 1950) nor an Atomic Energy Commission (established 1946) the government turned to the Office of Naval Research and similar DOD agencies and granted them funds specifically to support scientific research. These agencies have continued to administer funds of this nature. DOD agencies have *not* asked our faculty to do specific research for the government. To the contrary, our faculty have made their own proposals in their own fields of interest. They seek support wherever available. The DOD agencies use panels of distinguished, non-agency scientists to evaluate the scientific merit of these proposals and to select those to be funded with the monies available. May I repeat, *no* restrictions are placed on publication of results.

In order to avoid too much overlapping of effort, each agency has established certain areas of specialization but these are not necessarily exclusive. It is desirable to have more than one source of possible support, should one agency not have funds available or should some review panels or administrators become biased against a particular area of science.

A special word about the Themis project, which is funded by the Air Force. Our faculty proposed three projects which they wanted to pursue under this program and which they felt were within the areas outlined for support with the original funds available to the DOD. One of these was selected by the agency for support and was funded. This project, directed by Dr. Bullard of our Department of Anatomy and Physiology, is entitled "Environmental Hazards to Biologic Systems" and continues work he and others in his department have been engaged in for a lengthy period. The project has to do with physiological adjustments of men to heat, cold, work and altitude, in relation to the effects of aging, physical condition and status of physiological adaptation. It also is concerned with X-irradiation effects, oxygen, sound and light on the nervous system, biological rhythms in amphibians and the regulation of sweating. These are obviously of interest to athletes and space travelers among others. It is good, basic, fundamental research; such research has in the past [saved] and will continue in the future to save lives of persons whose conditions of stress do not relate to military activities in any regard, as well as the lives of some who are in military service. It has been prominent among the special areas of research of our Department of Anatomy and Physiology.

Let me reaffirm in the strongest terms our intention to defend the right of every faculty member to carry on without fear of censure or disruption the research in which he is interested. We will seek support for him from any and all legal sources. I need only mention the Kinsey research to illustrate that the University has braved heavy criticism to prevent the subjects of research and of classroom instruction from proscription by external or internal pressure groups.

S.D.S. demand: "4. All special training programs for police forces, foreign or domestic, be ended."

My response: I confess to some bafflement here, having understood that widespread agreement exists on the desirability of the best possible training for police forces everywhere. Consistent with *that* understanding, we have a Department of Police Administration in the College of Arts and Sciences. The University has recognized police administration as a profession since the establishment of the Institute of Criminology in June, 1935. The department exists for students who wish to pursue professional careers in this field. Its faculty perform research to increase knowledge of the field and to improve methods of professional practice. Instruction and research are appropriate university functions. Determination of the curricula is, by statute, a faculty responsibility. Over the nearly century and a half of Indiana University's existence, a narrow classical curriculum has evolved into diverse curricula with many specializations. In general, the developments have represented a response to student interest and needs of our state and society. Within this framework, the existence of a Department of Police Administration asserts the social desirability of University-trained individuals in positions of responsibility for community and state police forces, and evidences a continuing choice by I.U. students to pursue careers in this field. Foreign students enrolled at I.U. naturally have that same option.

Also, as a service to the State of Indiana we have entered into annual contracts with the State for the use of classroom and housing facilities by the Indiana State Police Department in its training program. This is, of course, always subject to the availability of the facilities.

Indiana University, as an agency of the State, is sensitive to the areas of cooperation and service which it can provide when requested to do so. The use of its facilities for another State agency's training program is not inconsistent with the purposes of the University.

S.D.S. demand: "5. The University cease all special training programs for military and intelligence of any kind."

My response: Since I cannot find that we have a single program of this kind, we can hardly *cease* having what we do not have.

S.D.S. demand: "6.a. The University cease intimidation of student political activity by: removing all plainclothes and secret police from the campus;"

My response: I do not accept the premise that the University intimidates student political activity. This "when did you stop beating your wife" type of trap need not confuse the discussion.

I want to remind you also that the abandonment of registration procedures for student organizations makes identification of a student with any political organization impossible, except as the student himself establishes that identity. But I do not condone intimidation of students, faculty or administrators who are engaging in lawful pursuits by police *or* by student groups, for that matter.

Now, to the question of plainclothes and secret police. I know of no secret police on the campus. The University quite naturally cooperates with law enforcement agencies, except when a request conflicts with a University policy such as the confidentiality of personal records.

We will not protect illegal activity on the campus and will cooperate with the efforts of law enforcement officers to detect violations and enforce the law in the legitimate performance of their duties.

We do have three investigators on the Safety Department staff at Bloomington in addition to Director Spannuth who customarily do not wear uniforms. There is nothing either sinister or secret about their presence. They are here to protect the University community, its property and the University's property.

S.D.S. demand: "6.b. The University cease intimidation of student political activity by: sending only clearly labeled administrative observers to political events;"

My response: I do not know what useful purpose labeling of individuals would serve, but if that is generally desired, I suggest that everyone be labeled—students and faculty members as well as administrators. Faculty observers and administrative observers are present at demonstrations and for the same purpose: to obtain first-hand information about the event. In earlier incidents, claims and counter-claims by the parties involved produced a confusing picture of the actual sequence of events and of the conduct of the participants. The presence of observers helps guarantee as accurate a report as possible, which is certainly in the interest of students participating. The University is concerned that no wrongful complaints be made against any of its students.

S.D.S. demand: "6.c. The University cease intimidation of student political activity by: ending intimidation of students through the use of cameras and recording devices at such events;"

My response: Again, the University is interested in accurate reports of events. It is not apparent to me why the recording of what is actually said or done could be anything but helpful to students who are not guilty of any violation. Students themselves bring these "devices" to "such events."

S.D.S. demand: "6.d. The University cease intimidation of student political activity by: removing from the campus all implements of political repression such as tear gas, chemical mace and riot clubs, whose only use could be against students."

My response: There is a sly appeal in the picture of the campus as a tranquil place which has no need for a safety division. By implication, the existence of such a division with its supply of deterrent tools must surely be for some questionable purpose. The S.D.S. would have students believe that the division exists to intimidate student political activity. What are the facts?

During the month of September, 1968, the Bloomington campus Safety Division was called upon to investigate 134 reports of incidents, *viz.*:

> 92 larcenies
> 20 acts of vandalism
> 5 assaults
> 5 vehicle thefts
> 3 breaking and entering
> 3 minor sex offenses
> 2 trespasses
> 1 suicide
> 1 attempted suicide
> 1 attempted rape
> 1 impersonation of a police officer

The monetary losses reported amounted to $8,872.80.

Clearly the campus is not a crime-free environment and the campus residents need protection. A majority of the suspects involved are outsiders, rings of thieves, etc., who operate out of large cities. It is patently absurd to charge that provisions for protection are disguises for intimidation of student political activity. Campus elections, Dunn Meadow political gatherings, marches around Showalter Fountain, discussions in the area south of Woodburn Hall have always been carried on without Safety Department interference with legitimate activity. The presence of Safety Department personnel at large assemblages, whether for an Auditorium Series event, an athletic contest or a student political rally signifies primarily a recognition of the accident potential in crowds. Quite honestly, there is an additional factor of concern, however, when an emotionally charged issue is to have partisan presentation before a student gathering, namely, that representatives of the opposing side will lose their constraint.

In either event, the presence of Safety Department personnel is for protection in cases of emergencies and loss of equanimity. Moderate subduers for crowd control have prevented accidents resulting from hysteria and have permitted the resolution of diffierences to occur in a less emotionally charged atmosphere.

However, the entire question of Safety is under study by a faculty committee and its report will undoubtedly deal with some of these matters.

Finally, I wish to exercise the prerogative of speaking to one subject of my own choosing. That is our foreign contracts. I do this to correct the impressions left by various assertions made in publications circulated on campus that the University is engaged in supporting reactionary governments abroad.

The facts are:

1) I.U.'s relationships in every case are with universities, not governments;

2) All of the contracts are connected with development—that is, with advising universities on their training programs in order to assist in the development of progressive professional leadership; and

3) Only two of the projects, in Afghanistan and Chile, are funded by an agency other than the Ford Foundation; these two are AID-supported.

Our present contracts are with universities in Afghanistan, Chili [sic], Indonesia, Pakistan, Peru, the Philippines, Thailand and Yugoslavia. Through this aid we hope not only to further the educational progress of newly developing nations but also to discharge our debt to the world of scholarship which we and other American universities incurred when older universities in Europe gave us invaluable assistance during our early years. Happily, the repayment of our intellectual and scholarly debt is financed by the Ford Foundation and AID, without cost to the Hoosier taxpayer. Dean Merritt or I will be pleased to discuss the nature and details of these projects with any of you who are really interested in the facts about our overseas projects.

I thank you for your interest in my views and information on these several topics. May I add that, while I am sensitive to the strong pacifist sentiment among some of our students and faculty members and the depth of their convictions about the United States' involvement in the Vietnam War, I am even more sensitive to the vital necessity of preserving the principle of the open campus. I strongly oppose the exclusion of recruiters and the banning of R.O.T.C., just as I have successfully opposed efforts to have the University oust individuals active in anti-military and other controversial causes. I fully support the discussion and study of issues involved in the Vietnam War, in war itself, and in the presence of the military on campus. I would support as well thorough, objective, unbiased research into the history, development and nature of the military arm of government and its role in enabling American citizens to live according to their Constitutionally determined choices.

Each of us has a crucial stake in seeing to it that Indiana University enters the post-war period, which will come, still invulnerable to the pressures that would erode its strength and violate its cherished principles: freedom to teach, to learn, to seek new knowledge and to serve society.

I. INDIANA UNIVERSITY TECHNICAL-ASSISTANCE PROJECTS

Teacher Education	Minas Gerias, Brazil	1956–64
Trade Union Training Program	Cyprus	1962–64
Public Administration Program	Djakarta, Indonesia	1959–63
Office Administration Program	" "	1963–64
Program for Development Statistics	" "	1964–66

Nursing Education	Korea	1959–61
Communication Media Project	Nigeria	1959–66
Basic Medical Science Training	Pakistan	1957–65
Business Administration Program	Dacca, Pakistan	1965–74
Teacher Education Program	Lahore, Pakistan	1959–66
Modernization of University Procedures	San Marcos, Peru	1964–67
Mindanao State University Basic Science Program	Philippines	1966–71
English Instruction for Saudi Arabia Educational Mission	Saudi Arabia	1964–
Communications Media Project	Freetown, Sierra Leone	1961–64
Peace Corps Representative	" "	1964–65
Teacher Education Program	Bangkok, Thailand	1954–64
Public Administration Program	" "	1955–64
NIDA	" "	1965–73
Peace Corps Volunteer Training	Thailand, Tunisia, Sierra Leone	1962–65
Mechanical and Electronic Engineering Education Program	Universidad del Trabajo, Uruguay	1963–66
Economics Teaching and Curricular Assistance	Catholic University, Caracas, Venezuela	1964–67
Graduate Program in Business Administration	Ljubljana University, Yugoslavia	1965–79

J. SPECIAL COMMISSIONS AND COMMITTEES

MEMBERS, CONSULTANTS, STAFF OF COMMITTEE APPOINTED BY MICHIGAN COORDINATING COUNCIL FOR PUBLIC HIGHER EDUCATION TO ADVISE ON NEED FOR THIRD MEDICAL SCHOOL

MEMBERS

Herman B Wells (Chairman), Chancellor, Indiana University
Judge George E. Bowles, Circuit Court of the Third District
Bradley M. Harris, M.D., Chairman, Medical School Liaison Committee, Michigan State Medical Society
Joseph C. Hinsey, M.D., Director, New York Hospital, Cornell Medical Center
Herbert E. Longenecker, President, Tulane University
Emory W. Morris, President, W. K. Kellogg Foundation
E. Gifford Upjohn, Chairman of the Board, Upjohn Co.

REPRESENTATIVES

Warren M. Huff, Member, Board of Trustees, Michigan State University
Eugene B. Power, Regent, University of Michigan

CONSULTANTS AND STAFF

William N. Hubbard, Jr., M.D. (Secretary), Dean, University of Michigan Medical School

Gordon H. Scott, M.D., Dean, Wayne State University Medical School

Charles J. Tupper, M.D. (Recording Secretary), Associate Dean, University of Michigan Medical School

MEMBERS AND STAFF OF THE SPECIAL COMMITTEE ON U.S. TRADE RELATIONS WITH EAST EUROPEAN COUNTRIES AND THE SOVIET UNION

MEMBERS

J. Irwin Miller (Chairman), Chairman of the Board, Cummins Engine Co., Inc.; Member, Executive Committee, World Council of Churches

Eugene R. Black, Chairman, Brookings Institution; Past President, International Bank for Reconstruction and Development

William Blackie, President, Caterpillar Tractor Co.; Director and Chairman of the Foreign Commerce Committee, U.S. Chamber of Commerce

George R. Brown, Chairman of the Board, Brown and Root, Inc.; Chairman, Board of Trustees, Rice University

Charles W. Engelhard, Jr., Chairman, Engelhard Industries; Director, Foreign Policy Association

James B. Fisk, President, Bell Telephone Laboratories; Past Member, President's Science Advisory Committee

Nathaniel Goldfinger, Director of Research, A F L-C I O; Trustee, Joint Council on Economic Education

Crawford H. Greenewalt, Chairman of the Board, E. I. du Pont de Nemours and Co.; Chairman, Radio Free Europe Fund

William A. Hewitt, Chairman of the Board, Deere and Co.; Trustee, U.S. Council of the International Chamber of Commerce

Max F. Millikan, Professor of Economics and Director, Center for International Studies, Massachusetts Institute of Technology; President, World Peace Foundation

Charles G. Mortimer, Chairman, General Foods Corp.; Trustee, Stevens Institute of Technology

Herman B Wells, Chancellor, Indiana University; Former U.S. Delegate to the United Nations General Assembly

STAFF

Edward R. Fried, Secretary to the Committee

James A. Henderson, Deputy Executive Secretary to the Committee

MEMBERS OF THE NATIONAL ADVISORY COMMISSION ON FOOD AND FIBER

Sherwood O. Berg (Chairman), Dean, Institute of Agriculture, University of Minnesota

Harry B. Caldwell, Executive Vice President, Farmers Cooperative Council of North Carolina

Willard W. Cochrane, Dean, International Program and Professor of Agricultural Economics, University of Minnesota

C. W. Cook, Chairman, General Foods Corp.

George C. Cortright, Chairman of the Board, National Cotton Council

Woodrow W. Diehl, Farmer, Iowa

Edmund H. Fallon, Executive Vice President, Agway, Inc.

Carl C. Farrington, Vice President for Development, Agricultural Group, Archer Daniels Midland Co.

Frank Fernbach, Assistant to the President, Special Projects, United Steelworkers of America

Roscoe G. Haynie, President, Wilson and Company, Inc.

Fred V. Heinkel, President, Missouri Farmers Association

Roy Hendrickson, Executive Secretary, National Federation of Grain Cooperatives

William A. Hewitt, Chairman, Deere and Co.

George K. Hislop, President, National Wool Growers Association

J. G. Horsfall, Director, the Agricultural Experiment Station, New Haven, Connecticut

Herbert J. Hughes, Farmer, Nebraska

D. Gale Johnson, Dean, Division of Social Sciences and Professor of Economics, University of Chicago

Herman S. Kohlmeyer, Broker, New Orleans, Louisiana

Robert Magowan, Chairman, Safeway Stores, Inc.

L. L. Males, Farmer and Conservationist, Oklahoma

Edward F. Mauldin, Farmer; Partner, Preuit and Mauldin (implement dealership); Chairman, First Colbert Bank of Leighton, Alabama

Paul Miller,[1] President, West Virginia University

W. B. Murphy, President, Campbell Soup Co.

Ernest J. Nesius,[2] Vice President, West Virginia Center for Appalachian Studies and Development; Director, Cooperative Extension Service, West Virginia University

Leon Schachter, Vice President, Amalgamated Meat Cutters and Butcher Workmen of North America, A F L-C I O

Janice M. Smith, Head, Department of Home Economics, University of Illinois

Lauren Soth, Editor, Editorial Pages, Des Moines *Register*

Jesse Tapp,[3] Retired Chairman of the Board, Bank of America

Jay Taylor, President, Texas Livestock Marketing Association

Herman B Wells, Chancellor, Indiana University

John Wheeler, President, Mechanics and Farmers Bank of Durham, North Carolina

1. Resigned from the Commission, July 29, 1966.
2. Replaced Paul Miller, November 1, 1966.
3. Died, January 19, 1967.

MEMBERS OF THE PRESIDENT'S SPECIAL COMMITTEE ON OVERSEAS VOLUNTARY ACTIVITIES

U.S. Secretary of State Dean Rusk (Chairman)
Attorney General Ramsey Clark
Budget Director Charles Schultze
Senator Carl Hayden (Ariz.), Chairman, Appropriations Committee
Senator Richard B. Russell (Ga.), Chairman, Armed Services Committee
Senator J. W. Fulbright (Ark.), Chairman, Foreign Relations Committee
Senator Milton R. Young (N.D.), member, Appropriations and Agriculture Committees
Congressman George Mahon (Tex.), Chairman, House Appropriations Committee
Congressman L. Mendel Rivers (S.C.), Chairman, Armed Services Committee
Congressman Thomas Morgan (Pa.), Chairman, Foreign Affairs Committee
Congressman Frank Bow (Ohio), member, Appropriations Committee
Milton S. Eisenhower, President, Johns Hopkins University
Thomas S. Gates, Jr., President, Morgan Guaranty Trust Co. of New York (formerly Secretary of Defense)
James H. McCrocklin, President, Southwest Texas State College
Paul R. Porter, Washington attorney
Frank A. Rose, President, University of Alabama
Henry S. Rowen, President, Rand Corporation
Robert M. Travis, President-elect of the student body, University of North Carolina
Herman B Wells, Chairman of the Board, Education and World Affairs; Chancellor, Indiana University

MEMBERS OF THE COMMISSION ON THE HUMANITIES

Barnaby C. Keeney (Chairman), President, Brown University
Herman B Wells (Vice Chairman), Chancellor, Indiana University
Kingman Brewster, Jr., President, Yale University
Carl Bridenbaugh, Professor of History, Brown University
Paul H. Buck, Director, Harvard University Library
Edgar M. Carlson, President, Gustavus Adolphus College
Arthur H. Dean, Senior Partner, Sullivan and Cromwell
William K. Frankena, Professor of Philosophy, University of Michigan
Pendleton Herring, President, Social Science Research Council
Rev. Theodore M. Hesburgh, President, University of Notre Dame
Harold Howe II, Superintendent of Schools, Scarsdale, New York
Devereux C. Josephs, Former Chairman, New York Life Insurance Company
Clark Kerr, President, University of California
Robert M. Lumiansky, Professor of English, Duke University
Whitney J. Oates, Professor of Classics, Princeton University
Henri M. Peyre, Professor of French, Yale University
Mina Rees, Dean of Graduate Studies, City University of New York

Andrew C. Ritchie, Director, Yale University Art Gallery
Glenn T. Seaborg, Chairman, United States Atomic Energy Commission
Thomas J. Watson, Jr., Chairman, International Business Machines Corp.

K. "ALL'S WELLS THAT ENDS WELL"

Early in my presidency, Eleanor and Newell Long presented one of their inimitable musical shows entitled "The Inauguration of the Boy President" as a greeting to me in that office. With a sense of the fitting, they wrote "All's Wells That Ends Well," performed on March 16, 1962, under the auspices of the University Club. More than 125 members of the club—unaccustomed thespians among the faculty, staff, administration, and their spouses—trod the boards that night. The *Daily Student*, in a special edition for the occasion, carried a rave review:

> The University Club acted like students for a couple of hours and produced a combination boress-tribute Friday evening at 8 P.M. in Alumni Hall. The show—"All's Wells That Ends Well"—hit almost every phase of campus life and closed with a grand tribute to President Herman B (no period) Wells.
> And the audience loved every minute of it!
> The orchestra, undoubtedly the best unpaid group in the world, colored the production with all types of music. The cast was talented, too. . . .
> Nearly a hundred University Club members humored the full house in Alumni Hall with such routines as "Student Squares," " 'How-to-succeed-in-business-without' Professors," "Bachelor Bait," and "Merry Medicos." . . .

Light, comically amateur, delightful, it represented a generous investment of time and energy on the part of my colleagues that was as heartwarming as the show itself and as memorable for me.

INDEX